WITHDRAWN

Southern Masculinity

D1075702

Southern Masculinity

Perspectives on Manhood
in the South since Reconstruction

EDITED BY *Craig Thompson Friend*

The University of Georgia Press   *Athens and London*

© 2009 by the University of Georgia Press
Athens, Georgia 30602
www.ugapress.org
All rights reserved
Set in Ehrhardt by Newgen Imaging

Printed digitally in the United States of America

Library of Congress Cataloging-in-Publication Data

Southern masculinity : perspectives on manhood
in the South since Reconstruction /
edited by Craig Thompson Friend.
      p. cm.
  Includes bibliographical references.
  ISBN-13: 978-0-8203-2950-5 (hardcover : alk. paper)
  ISBN-10: 0-8203-2950-9 (hardcover : alk. paper)
  ISBN-13: 978-0-8203-3232-1 (pbk. : alk. paper)
  ISBN-10: 0-8203-3232-1 (pbk. : alk. paper)
  1. Masculinity—Southern States.
2. Men—Southern States—Social conditions.
I. Friend, Craig Thompson.
  HQ1090.5.s68s68   2009
  305.310975—dc22   2008024054

British Library Cataloging-in-Publication Data available

ACC LIBRARY SERVICES AUSTIN, TX

CONTENTS

From Southern Manhood to Southern Masculinities: An Introduction

Craig Thompson Friend

In 1990, political columnist George F. Will assessed Georgia Senator Sam Nunn's skepticism about President George H. W. Bush's militaristic response to the Gulf crisis: "Nunn is a Southerner with that region's regard for military values. Is he not a hawk? . . . The pedigree of Nunn's statecraft runs back to [Georgia Senator Richard] Russell, and hence back, in a sense, 125 years. For most Americans today, the Civil War is a television series. For many Southerners, . . . the 'lost cause' is a lesson of perennial relevance: Things often do not work out well." Between 1953 and 1971, Russell had argued against American involvement in Vietnam. In 1990, Nunn unceasingly questioned presidential war powers and the quick decision to wage war against Iraq. Both men embodied the contradiction between traditional southern martial violence and a less well-understood southern wariness about war, a circumspection that Will tracked to their peculiarly "southern" perspective on defeat, humiliation, and the pain of Reconstruction.[1]

The long shadow of the Civil War stretches across the South, shaping southern men and masculinity. The predecessor to this volume, *Southern Manhood*, concluded in the midst of that national conflict, exploring the opportunities that it offered to emancipated men in creating new definitions of black manliness. The collapse of slavery freed African American men from the emasculation that whites had attached to enslavement. Freed peoples redefined manhood, particularly in light of their new freedoms to vote, hold office, and strengthen families and communities. The war simultaneously destabilized white southern manliness, creating a "crisis in gender," as historian LeAnn Whites labeled it. Former Confederates had to find new ways to frame white manhood without the mastery that slavery had offered or the honor that victory would have provided. The war's outcome did not eradicate mastery and honor as the primary axes about which white manhood formed, but it did force a reconfiguration of how those ideals could be met.[2]

British Prime Minister Winston Churchill once proclaimed that "History is written by the victors." When considering manhood in America, this is unavoidably true. The fall of the Confederacy was quickly and persistently interpreted as the collapse of a weakened and degenerate civilization, and historians have consequently paid overwhelming attention to the victorious northern manliness of the late nineteenth and twentieth centuries at the expense of grasping its manifestations in the South. E. Anthony Rotundo's *American Manhood* and Michael Kimmel's *Manhood in America* are excellent studies of masculinities, but neither is as encompassing as its title implies. Rotundo did not even feign interest in the South, readily admitting his focus on the northern middle class, "a small proportion of the American population who used their vast economic and cultural power to imprint their values on the nation." Kimmel touched occasionally on southern men, but he typically cast them as looking backward and consequently rubbing against the modernizing grain of American self-made manhood: for example, the Ku Klux Klan sought "reclamation of southern manhood," the Populists worked for the "restoration of the cooperative commonwealth with its noble vision of manhood," and early twentieth-century southerners who drank and brawled and hunted wanted "a tonic to restore lost manhood and provide manly solace." Gail Bederman's *Manliness and Civilization* similarly situates southern manhood, especially with its extraviolent and overtly racial overtones, as a counter to northern (read: American) manliness. Indeed, Bederman and others' relegation of southern manhood to, at best, a secondary consideration exposes their own reservations about southern contributions to the development of American gender ways.[3]

This collection of essays contextualizes and complicates the narrative of American manhood by drawing attention southward to explore masculinity in the South since the Civil War and the many ways it has reflected and framed "southernness." Collectively these original works of scholarship demonstrate that race, class, age, sexuality, and locale allowed and sometimes forced communities and individuals to alter their perceptions of and requirements for manliness. Honor and mastery had been the dominant idealized masculine traits among antebellum southern whites, but gone with the wind was the world of plantations, slaves, and the exclusivity of the gentlemanly class. As the works of our contributors demonstrate, honor and mastery transformed into new structures of masculinity, evidenced by the diverse men who populated the South between Reconstruction and the turn of the twenty-first century.[4]

Still, it is important to question how and why southern manhood differed from that in the North, and Rotundo, Kimmel, and Bederman offer useful analytical structures to understand the differences. If we consolidate their individual narratives into one framework, we have an elaborate chronology of northern manhood. The early nineteenth century was dominated by a "communal manhood" that Rotundo associates with the Colonial and Revolutionary eras, and which Kimmel distinguishes as "Genteel Patriarchs" tied to the land and "Heroic Artisans" bound to their handiwork. Rotundo demonstrated, however, that as the century progressed, middle-class "self-made manhood" became more respectable and increasingly hegemonic in the North, leaving the rough-and-tumble communal manliness of preindustrial America to the working class. Kimmel finds that many of these self-made men partook of "masculine domesticity," basically involving themselves more in home life, specifically to ensure that they raised manly sons. For that reason, as the physical demands of frontier life and farming became less accessible to men in the late nineteenth century, leisure and sports became more important as arenas of manly display. Rotundo agrees, although he finds this digression away from self-made manhood significant enough to categorize it separately as "passionate manhood," the essence of which was celebration of male emotions through acts of competition, aggression, force, sexuality, self-fulfillment, and a new attention to the male body. Older versions of manliness did not fade away, but passionate manhood redefined the qualities to be associated with proper manliness. Bederman concludes that passionate manhood brought with it a "primitive masculinity"—a primal virility that drew men into nature and into "savage" activities—that clashed with the "civilized manliness" of earlier models of manhood.[5]

The competitive, aggressive drives of passionate manhood carried well into the twentieth century, competing with lingering expressions of "civilized" masculinity. Those contestations of manliness, what Bryce Traister identifies as crises of American masculinity, recurred throughout the century. The 1910s were marked by "fears of national and masculine enfeeblement." The 1920s and 1930s "put a severe stress on . . . those who idealized the masculine past" and its emphasis on aggression and domination. World War II and its aftermath transformed men from their "attachment to the all-male world" of the military to roles as "heterosexual domestic and corporate man." After the 1950s (a decade usually associated with stable manliness), American masculinity confronted new threats in feminism, the civil rights movement, and "greater uncertainty of authority born of the Vietnam War." Throughout these trials, primitive masculinity and the expression of male passions increasingly muted civilized manhood, evolving and manifesting in several forms: the team player, the existential hero, the pleasure seeker, and the spiritual warrior. Each drew from passions that had long been identified as masculine: competitiveness, assertion of authority, sexual and physical indulgence, and a return to sheer primitivism, respectively. Kimmel attributes the popularity of primitive masculinity in the twentieth century to a reaction against the power of the late nineteenth century's Christian model of manliness, resulting first in "muscular Christianity," then "suburban playboys" and "weekend warriors"—all variations on the self-made man. Of course, significantly, this narrative pertains to hegemonic white heterosexual masculinities. African American men, Native American men, and homosexuals serve to help frame the primary narrative, leaving their own models of masculinity only vaguely defined.[6]

So, how are we to place southern men—white, black, Native American, straight, gay—in this metanarrative? In many regards, all postbellum southerners had remained committed to the communal manhood of an earlier era, in which their identities were inseparable from their familial and communal responsibilities and from their public worth. For a variety of economic, political, and social reasons, few southerners turned to self-made manhood, although it tempted many. Instead, they viewed themselves in opposition to what they described as urban, industrial, liberal, corrupt, effeminate men of the North. Even as the nineteenth century drew to a close, they remained entangled in codes of honor and virility that characterized communal manhood.[7]

Beginning with Reconstruction, a new purposefulness characterized definitions of manliness. One of the lessons of *Southern Manhood* is that antebellum southern men (and women) thought about their gendered images and calculated their actions accordingly. While not all men had subscribed to the ideals of honor and mastery, all shared a sense of the very public nature of their private characters. Unlike femininity, which occupied the domestic realm, antebellum masculinity had required regular public performance. For enslaved men, of course, any attempts to demonstrate public masculinity had been met with physical and psychic violence meant to emasculate them; still, they had been aware, as had white southerners, of the need to publicly demonstrate manliness.

The Civil War changed all of this. Freed from emasculating enslavement, blacks found in Reconstruction a moment, however slim, to develop a "race-neutral language" of manhood, as historian Stephen Kantrowitz phrased it. African American men not only could imagine their manliness defined by the same public roles and private responsibilities as those of white manhood, but they could act upon those expectations. And unlike black masculinity in the antebellum South, the postbellum years empowered African American men to publicly challenge white attempts to emasculate them. When, in 1868, the Georgia legislature barred black members from the chamber, Bishop Henry McNeal Turner calculated it as an affront to his manliness: "I am here to demand my rights, and to hurl thunderbolts at the men who would dare to cross the threshold of my manhood."[8]

Opportunity for new forms of black manliness coincided with the transformation of white manliness. Out of the war emerged two distinctive forms of manhood, both drawing upon the old codes of honor and mastery. First evolved the Christian gentleman, modeled largely upon the example of Robert E. Lee and in reaction to the emasculation of being conquered. Northerners took special joy in mocking Confederate president Jefferson Davis (and by extension, the manliness of former Confederate men) who had dressed as a woman to flee capture, even composing a fairly popular song, "Jeff in Petticoats," with the chorus:

> Oh! Jeffy D.! You "flow'r of chivalree,"
> Oh royal Jeffy D.!
> Your empire's but a tin-clad skirt,
> Oh, charming Jeffy D.

But "chivalree" was not dead: Lee and thousands of former Confederates demonstrated it through self-esteem, self-control, and a respect for the dictums of war. Lee, in particular, was beyond reproach in a political atmosphere in which emasculation was actively employed to belittle southern men and reduce southern influence. He embodied the intractability of southern civilization even with the defeat of the Confederacy. In contrast to what they perceived as the effeminate nature of northern Christian men, particularly those who came southward as missionaries and reformers, white southerners made Lee a model for their own form of the Christian gentleman—honorable, master of his household, humble, self-restrained, and above all, pious and faithful. Additionally, as the church became the more crucial center for black life during Reconstruction, and racial barriers to black civic participation became relaxed, African American men also appropriated the Christian gentleman as a model for manliness. The Christian gentleman, then, provided a "race-neutral language" for masculinity, situating manliness in terms of religious and civic presentations that were available to black men as well as white.[9]

The second white manhood to emerge during Reconstruction was the masculine martial ideal. White southerners exalted Confederate veterans and their sacrifices, demonstrating that while the Confederacy had fallen, southern civilization had not. Overlooking the causes and consequences of the war, celebrants found in their military heroes—with Lee again the prototype—models for a warriorlike and heroic manliness. Like the Christian gentleman, martial manliness built upon the ideals of honor and mastery. Unlike the Christian gentleman, however, it filtered those ideals through the war experience. The rough-and-tumble violence of earlier decades became insufficient evidence of manliness.

Rather, violence had to contain a broader and more ideological purpose, specifically to demonstrate honor in and protection of one's self, family, and region.[10]

Lee as the model for both types of manhood alludes to how closely connected the two actually were. Just as honor and mastery were bound to each other before the war, Christian gentlemanliness and the masculine martial ideal buttressed each other, as explored in the first two contributions to this collection. In her study of four men in Reconstruction-era Savannah, Georgia, Karen Taylor finds that the four Christian gentleman at the center of her narrative often adopted martial behavior to advance their causes. Additionally, Taylor's essay demonstrates that, while masculinity may have momentarily appropriated a "race-neutral language," race continued to play a prominent role in defining manhood. Joe Creech argues that not only were the two brands of masculinity related, but in its emphasis on independence, the more evangelical strain of Christian gentlemanliness *had* to employ violent, martial tactics to protect dependents and demonstrate manliness. From conversion to theology to salvation, evangelicals' heavy investment in individualism culminated in Thomas Dixon's notion of independent Christian mastery over others, and a right to violently protect those others from external threats. Of course, Dixon's *The Clansman* (1905) became the inspiration for *Birth of a Nation* (1915), both reinforcing the notion that even the more pious men should not hesitate to safeguard their families and communities, violently if necessary.

By the late 1870s, such arguments contributed to the rise of the Redeemers—white southerners like Ben Tillman of South Carolina who opposed political domination of the South by the Radical Republican coalition of freedman, carpetbaggers, and scalawags. As they "redeemed" southern states, culminating in the Compromise of 1877, a reinstated white political leadership disfranchised black men through Jim Crow laws, undermining their shared citizenship and potentially common masculinity. By trying to force black men back into emasculation, the Redeemers and other southern white men returned to lingering remnants of prewar definitions of white manhood, specifically as historian Bertram Wyatt-Brown categorized them: "honor and virility, righteous adherence to biblical inerrancy in the forms of belligerent racism and an assertion of manhood over effeminacy and even women in general." Kris DuRocher's essay explores the resurgence of this specifically white masculinity as it was taught to children, particularly sons, through lynching rituals. Not surprisingly, the catalysts for lynching were so often black men's public actions (in the arena where manhood was to be proven) which were then interpreted as threatening to white womanhood and hence white manhood. Overt black masculinity had to be punished publicly by what DuRocher termed "a version of white male masculinity that was able to counter all threats"—or at least wanted to present that appearance. Thomas Dixon's vision of southern manhood had come into its own.[11]

Even as they counteracted black male claims to manhood through violent intimidation and by restricting the most public of performance spaces—citizenship—white southern men also worked to counteract allegedly effete characteristics that they associated with northern men. Antebellum contempt for northern dandies and reformers evolved into postbellum disdain for carpetbaggers and missionaries who had come to reconstruct the South and southern men. Foppishness, passivity, gentleness, interest in home life, even finding friendship with one's wife rather than the guys—such characteristics signaled effeminacy and a threat to southern manhood. Georgia Senator Thomas Norwood denounced the carpetbagger as "at best, but Cinderella at the Ball"; defining the Yankee interloper as woman was, of course, purposeful. White southern men were particularly aggrieved that the war had essentially eviscerated their prewar ideals of manliness and emboldened northern manhood. This retreat to Old South manhood irritated northerners who wearied of resurrected southern appeals to honor and mastery. Oliver Wendell Holmes, who had donned a Union uniform, chastised a historian and southern sympathizer: "I hope that time will explode the humbug of the Southern Gentleman in your mind. . . . The Southern gentlemen generally were an arrogant crew who knew nothing of the ideas that make the life of the few thousands that may be called civilized."[12]

Locating southern men in opposition to, and indeed in ignorance of, "civilized" men was not just rhetorical on Holmes's part. As Gail Bederman explained, Darwinism, Anglo-Saxonism, and Protestant millennialism created late nineteenth-century expectations about cultivating the white race and its definitions of manliness and womanliness. "This millennial vision of perfected racial evolution and gender specialization," she wrote, "was what people mean when they referred to 'the advancement of civilization.'" Holmes and other white northern men viewed white southerners as having diverged from the trajectory of American civilization and manhood, and much in need of "civilized" reform.[13]

It was a similar logic to that which they applied to "primitive" darker-skinned peoples—American Indians, African Americans, Asians, Africans, and South Americans—whom they claimed lacked the "racial genius to exercise 'manhood rights'" and self-government. Michael Kimmel argues that, faced with emasculation, Native Americans turned to increased alcoholism, the peyote cult, and the Ghost Dance and Sun Dance religions. Yet, as Rose Stremlau's essay on Cherokee masculinity demonstrates, some American Indians joined in the critique of northern manliness, counterattacking with more hopeful and empowering constructions of manhood based in part upon their critiques of Anglo-Americanism. Two generations after their ancestors' removal from their southeastern lands, the Cherokees lived on the periphery of the old Confederacy, in the Indian Territory that would soon become Oklahoma. During the Civil War, the Cherokee nation had been rift by the same forces that split the white nation around them. By the 1890s, Cherokees found some national healing as they collectively faced pressures to allot tribal lands as individual plots. They responded by articulating a masculinity framed by republican government, communal land ownership, and self-sufficiency, all attributes of a manhood "superior" to that of the Americans who sought to reform them. Still, Cherokee manliness reflected many of the same ideals that shaped northern white masculinity, especially "domestic masculinity" and greater attention to physically training the body. They also joined in white southern manhood's proclivity to define manliness through race. Indeed, in the same decades that Cherokees argued for the superiority of their civilized manhood, they also wrestled with the racial consequences of the Civil War. Before the war, many Cherokees had held black slaves. The Reconstruction Treaty of 1866 had guaranteed those former slaves living in Indian Territory the rights and privileges of full-blooded Cherokee citizenship. But the Cherokee Council did not interpret this as extending to communal landownership, creating decades of legal battles that were eventually resolved by the very "degenerate" white civilization that the Cherokees denounced.[14]

Since Native American and white southerners conceptualized manhood racially, we should not be surprised that blacks too configured masculinity, at least partially, through racial constructions. Missourian James Milton Turner, the lawyer who spearheaded blacks' equal rights efforts in Cherokee Territory, declared in 1883 that "While the Indian goes down showing no longevity to withstand civilization, the Negro . . . shows a desire for the text books and takes to the ways of civilized life. . . . the Negro is in no sense advanced or improved by contact with the Indians." In his study on recent African American masculinity, Philip Brian Harper claimed that "subscription to black identity itself bespeaks a masculine status because the courage thus to attain social autonomy is precisely what constitutes conventional manhood." One need not look at the late twentieth century for evidence: in the late nineteenth century, black men's association of their own race with civilized advancement and social autonomy contributed to their formulations of manhood.[15]

Importantly, coincidental to these racial contests over manliness, the American lexicon found a new noun: "masculinity." The adjective "masculine" had been around for a while, referring to the collective characteristics of a man or men, whether those qualities were physical or psychological, good or bad. When people wished to discuss a man's character, however, they had used "manhood" and "manliness." Take, for example, Mark Twain's comment that "The government is not best which secures mere life and property—there is a more valuable thing—manhood." If one replaced "manhood" with "masculinity" in 1873 when Twain wrote this line, it made little sense that government is best when it differentiates between men and women. Rather, government is best when it empowers men to be more than just their biology. "Manhood," then, meant courage, valor, virility, honor, and every other noun and adjective that characterized Robert E. Lee and could be applied to any man to indicate that he was morally or physically equal to all and superior to most other men. "Masculinity" was more a category than a characteristic, and the emergence of Darwinian evolutionary theory, Freudian psychoanalysis, and Nietzsche's *Übermensh* reinforced that purpose.[16]

"Manhood" as a term for manly attributes was deeply embedded in Victorian gender ideals, however, and as Victorianism began to loosen its cultural grip with the arrival of the twentieth century, Americans began to reconceptualize their gender categories. By the Great Depression, "masculinity" became the more common term for middle-class white male aggressiveness, sexuality, and physical force. "Manhood," in contrast, became increasingly associated with a rougher and less "civilized" manliness, as found among immigrants, African Americans, the working classes, and southerners.[17]

Redefining masculinity, then, became a crucial feature of the rhetoric of the New South—a movement led by would-be industrialists and capitalists who hoped to restore the South's economic vitality. In *Race and Reunion*, David Blight concluded that, in the late nineteenth century, the South "needed a new religion of nationhood," but southerners sought as well a new theology of manliness. Beginning in the 1880s, men like Henry Grady and Daniel Tompkins used the North as their model to bring industry and agricultural diversification southward, and with it the rewards of a more robust economy, including uplifting the poor by providing manufacturing jobs, empowering a new southern aristocracy, and giving rise to a white middle class. While they never articulated how their brand of economic development would affect southern masculinity, New South spokesmen represented the arrival of self-made manhood. Of course, self-made men had existed in the South throughout the nineteenth century, but the New South represented a dramatic attempt to make self-made manhood the hegemonic form of masculinity in the South, as it had become in the North. The desolation and poverty of the South evidenced the incredible failure of the old communal manhood that had pulled the region into civil war. In promoting industrial growth and agricultural diversification, New South advocates specifically pushed southern masculinity away from its past.[18]

New South self-made manhood also promised a new direction in race relations. Whites' masculine martial ideals had dissolved any possibility of a "race-neutral language" of masculinity and had elevated violence as the best means by which to preserve the racial status quo. Grady and others—including Booker T. Washington, who promoted his own version of New South industrial education for black students—believed that economic development needed racial peace. It was a challenging task. As part of the packaging of primitive masculinity, whites had created myths of African American male sexuality as uncontrolled, ravenous, and the primary threat to white womanhood and, therefore, whiteness. This was the fiction that underlay white Christian manhood and energized the white masculine martial ideal. It was also the fiction to which black Christian gentlemen and black martial men felt obliged to respond.[19]

By World War I, then, at least three models of manhood—the Christian gentleman, the masculine martial, and the self-made man—coexisted uneasily in the South and across racial boundaries. For men like William Raoul, none of these models were acceptable or avoidable. As Steve Blankenship's exploration of Raoul concludes, the young socialist could not escape the New South creed that his father had chased, even though he overtly rejected the bourgeois values that characterized the business leaders of Atlanta. Still, while Raoul rejected one masculinity and embraced a more marginal and radical form, his unpublished autobiography, "The Proletarian Aristocrat," was attuned to a key masculine trait: honor. His aristocratic origins emphasized business acumen and mastery of one's self and others; his proletarian persona embraced the older, rougher, and more libertine communal manhood of the working classes.

Raoul's story highlights an upper-class man who sought commonality with regional lower classes. He shaped his manliness within the context of an emerging southern liberalism that argued for social responsibility even as it maintained racial and gendered structures of regional life. Working men, African Americans—stabilizing marginalized groups became the causes that early twentieth-century southern liberals faced with the strains of New South development. Exacerbated class and racial tensions, as well, forced men to consider how their masculine personae would be interpreted by individuals beyond their immediate social circles.

Raoul's story also relates how very disenchanted some southern men had become with the South. As Blight noted, faced with the dynamic and often disconcerting changes that accompanied New South development, most southerners sought out "another world to live in." Like Raoul, some sought redemption through less popular causes. Most, however, "yearned for a more pleasing past in which to find slavery, the war, and Reconstruction." The flowering of southern literature in the 1920s and 1930s testified to this search for another South, and it brought with it a different approach to southern masculinity, surprisingly resurrecting the old paradigm of honor and mastery. As Wyatt-Brown explains, the "ethic of the Old Order was reexamined in order to provide an angle of moral vision never before attempted in the South." Among the leaders of that literary reevaluation were William Faulkner and William Alexander Percy, both of whom warrant attention in this collection.[20]

In his examination of *The Sound and the Fury* (1929), Christopher Breu describes how Faulkner purposefully situated twentieth-century southern masculinity in reaction to the nineteenth-century version of southern manhood founded on honor and mastery. The three brothers at the center of the novel represent not only three different masculinities, but three different ways in which southerners of the era sought other worlds in which to live. Quentin Compson, the eldest, embraces the mythic southern past and the aristocratic model of southern gentlemanliness that it bred. The next brother, Jason, attaches himself to the present and the emerging southern liberalism that framed the rise of the New South and Raoul's life within it. The youngest brother, Benjy, is beyond time, however, "stripped of history, memory, and authority" as well as conceptualizations of race and southern approaches to gender. Faulkner's works exposed the complexity and, in his opinion, unnecessary exaggeration of twentieth-century southern masculinity. As historian Joel Williamson explained of Faulkner's perspective, "Society required men to be much too masculine, and women too feminine." While not a "crisis of gender" on the level of that following the Civil War, the atmosphere in which Faulkner's male characters live (and in which Faulkner lived) is one of hesitation and often gendered confusion. Faulkner purposefully confused ideals of masculinity, attributing to self-made men skills and attitudes that more appropriately characterized nineteenth-century domestic masculinity or martial masculinity. For Faulkner, society made manhood more complicated than it need be, leading to frustration in love and marriage.[21]

Faulkner was not alone in representing this ambivalence, and in many ways, William Percy not only wrote about it but lived it as well. In his contribution to this collection, Benjamin Wise demonstrates how Percy, in both *Lanterns on the Levee* (1941) and his lifestyle, provided a portrait of southern masculinity rooted in communal, patriarchal, and familial contexts. In his autobiography, he assailed those who threatened the purity of traditional white southern manhood and the traditional South—blacks, poor whites, and even himself. As a homosexual, Percy knew he could not explore the fullness of his masculinity in the American South, and that any demonstration of his sexuality was an affront to southern manliness. In his cosmopolitanism, Percy escaped the South that he so emphatically loved. Greece, France, Switzerland, New York City, Boston—Percy's travels, as Wise concludes, "helped him manage life in the South by giving him access to a freer life in the larger world."[22]

Both Percy and Faulkner offer representations of masculinity in their writings and their lives, but the most famous images of southern masculinity to emerge from the era were Rhett Butler and Ashley Wilkes, the two main male characters in Margaret Mitchell's *Gone with the Wind* (published in 1936, made into movie in 1939). From the Christian gentlemanliness of Ashley Wilkes to the self-made manhood of Charles Hamilton to the martial masculinity of Frank Kennedy, Mitchell found all of Scarlett's initial love interests and husbands lacking in manliness—an interesting critique of the masculinities that had dominated southern society since Reconstruction. Wilkes is white, the purest white, and willing to marry into his own bloodline to preserve the race. He is equally effeminate, to the point that Mitchell described him at one point as "queer, it's not crazy I'm meaning. . . . But he's queer in other ways, and there's no understanding him at all." Butler, in contrast, is powerful, viral, erotic, unmistakably heterosexual, and "dark of face, swarthy as a pirate, and his eyes were as bold and black as any pirate's appraising a galleon to be scuttled or a maiden to be ravished." Even though Butler was not black, his character embodies the image of black masculinity as primitive and sexually potent that framed much of white southerners' ideas about black southern men. Importantly, according to scholar Elizabeth Young, the strongest character in the novel is Scarlett O'Hara, who portrays femininity while "simulating as well a stimulating masculinity." As Young concluded, Mitchell designed her male characters out of her belief that "white Southern masculinity is so exhausted that it requires rebuilding from an outside source." Mitchell, Faulkner, and Percy all grasped that the "crisis of gender" of the postbellum South had not been resolved. Instead of coalescing around the powerful themes of honor and mastery that had characterized the hegemonic masculinities of the Old South, southern masculinity seemed unanchored and susceptible to multiple interpretations and critiques.[23]

But honor and mastery were not dead. Rhett Butler became the masculine ideal for many white southern men because he represented a new form of individualized honor, one that revered drinking, hunting, swearing, cunning, physical pleasure with women, and even fighting as a powerful remedy for weakened southern masculinity. Aggressive and even combative, this attitude arose in the South alongside the masculine culture of sport and fitness. Competition became the means by which honor and power were demonstrated. Historian Ted Ownby has described how hunting became a "participant sport" and southern "cultural institution" by the turn of the twentieth century. While less a participant sport, college football had also become a cultural institution among southerners, leading to the organization of the Southern Intercollegiate Athletic Conference in 1895 and the creations of the Southeastern Conference in 1932 and the Atlantic Coast Conference in 1953. Another cultural institution emerged during the Depression as bootleggers in the Appalachians modified their cars for speed, handling, and enlarged cargo capacity. With the repeal of Prohibition, they began organizing unofficial races, leading to the birth of NASCAR in 1948.[24]

Racing, competing in football, making a big kill—such activities were the early twentieth century's equivalent of proving manhood in antebellum dueling or sharpshooting. The rules of the hunt or the sport were designed to ensure fair play and, therefore, honorable victory. And as in the Old South, public demonstration of honor and success in competition enabled white men to claim rewards. As an example, between 1915 and 1973, the tradition among Texas A&M football players was to visit the notorious Chicken Ranch brothel after victories over their rivals at the University of Texas, symbolically making sexual pleasure the reward for successful demonstrations of manly power.[25]

Yet this new form of honorable masculinity directly conflicted with the region's increasingly evangelical religious culture. "Southern men often found themselves wondering how far they could go," explained Ownby, "in satisfying the demands and enjoying the pleasures of male culture without violating the standards of evangelical morality." While honor had been resurrected in sports and hunting, mastery had found a new home in religious visions of masculinity. Evangelicals promoted a physically powerful and hypermasculine image of Jesus, adopting muscular Christianity's iconography of Jesus to emphasize the militant and aggressive nature of faith and equate their religion to a "holy crusade"—an idea early appropriated by the Ku Klux Klan to justify its activities. They also critiqued the homosociality of male culture as a threat to domestic stability and possibly even contributing to homosexuality. Only through faithful mastery of one's self—the animal, the sinner within—could white southern men become worthy masters of their families and communities. Across the twentieth century, this tension between the primitive masculinity of honor and evangelical demands for mastery of the animal within increasingly became the primary paradigm of white southern masculinity.[26]

Black southern men, too, wrestled with the contradictions between evangelical religion and more secular masculine ideals. As historian Martin Summers describes, at least through the 1920s, black men subscribed to male identities quite similar to those in the white community. But white and black evangelicalism were two very different institutions. The white church had to account for white men's imagined obligations to vigilantly oppress blacks and protect white womanhood. That demand did not exist in the black church, thereby offering greater latitude to black southern men in conceptualizing masculinity. In other words, by World War II, southern whites had limited themselves to two acceptable models of manliness that were in constant tension. Southern blacks, however, had greater options in formulating manhood.[27]

One of the more important phenomena in black masculinity was the appearance and evolution of the black Christ as a symbol of masculinity. In his contribution to this collection, Edward J. Blum explores how the imagery of Jesus was employed by evangelical and nonevangelical black southerners to substantiate their visions of racial and manly advancement. From Booker T. Washington, whose "race-less" version of Christ promoted blacks' economic and social development in line with the vision of white New South promoters, to the black subversive radical Jesus found in W. E. B. Du Bois's writings (the "southernness" of which Blum claims has been grossly ignored), Blum traces the ways in which southern blacks understood themselves through imagery of Jesus. Some scholars have described the differences between Washington's and Du Bois's ideas of African American masculinity as a choice between emasculation and rage. Blum, however, finds that black depictions of Jesus suggest more continuity within black ideas of masculinity and offer a way to explore the roots of the liberation theology of the 1960s, the ideas and themes of which may have spoken to northern African Americans but "were rooted in Southern black experiences and efforts to assert black manhood."[28]

While the black church created possibilities for masculine imagery and formulation similar to that of white evangelicalism, Jim Crow and segregation severely limited black southern men's opportunities to engage in the sports-oriented primitive masculinity that white southern men enjoyed. Very few African Americans were hunters; the racial barrier in college football remained until 1955; and despite Willy T. Ribbs's success in 1986, NASCAR is still a good ol' white boys club (although some white women are revving their engines). When sports became a venue for black manhood, then, the opportunity proved symbolically important not just for black masculinity but for conceptualizations of race and gender across the South.

Throughout southern history, as we have seen, masculinity was performed publicly, but African American men were restricted from public venues in which they could compete against and join with white masculinity. Steve Estes' argument in *I Am a Man* that manhood was a basic concept in the civil rights movement makes a great deal of sense, then. Radical groups like the Black Panthers and the Nation of Islam successfully recruited young black men by offering a revisionist masculinity that emphasized protection of family and self-defense. Then again, even milder strains of the civil rights movement offered empowerment to men for whom public validation of masculinity had largely been withheld.[29]

Arthur Ashe's life drew upon two major themes of twentieth-century southern masculinity: its increasingly sports-oriented display, and this transformation of black masculinity promoted by the civil rights movement. Matthew Mace

Barbee traces how Ashe's controlled and dignified manner upon winning the 1968 U.S. Tennis Open contrasted sharply with the violence and unrest that contemporaneously characterized the civil rights movement. Ashe explicitly rejected the type of manliness that more radical groups championed. The complexity of Ashe's life, including his struggle as a heterosexual man with a disease largely associated with homosexuality, produced a more pragmatic, patient form of manliness—one that did not fit neatly with the political urgency of the civil rights movement. When his hometown of Richmond, Virginia, decided to erect a posthumous monument to Ashe alongside the many memorials to the state's Confederate sons on Monument Avenue, residents had to deal with "Ashe's status as a new model for southern masculinity."

While the civil rights movement may have been at least partially about redefining manhood, the gay rights movement has mostly been about the right to reformulate or even reject gender identity. As William Percy's life demonstrated, there was little public space for homosexuality in the rural South of the early twentieth century. By the 1970s, however, with the rise of the Sunbelt, gay men could find safer spaces in the urban South. The Sunbelt phenomenon brought dramatic population growth, creating metropolises out of previously small cities like Orlando, Charlotte, San Antonio, and Houston, and energizing older cities like Atlanta and New Orleans, yet demographic and urban growth did not translate into a more liberal social and political atmosphere. As John Howard explores in his contribution, within the contexts of the Sunbelt South, gay men seeking to live and love confronted the conservative sexual standards maintained by southern states. Two landmark Supreme Court cases—*Bowers v. Hardwick* (1986) and *Lawrence v. Texas* (2003)—originated in Atlanta and Houston, respectively. Howard argues that as these local cases became issues on the national stage, they allowed for the continued interpretation of a backward South, a theme that we saw enunciated during Reconstruction and maintained throughout twentieth-century American history. Howard also demonstrates, however, that "victory" in the final case "delineated a narrow band of acceptable lesbian and gay comportment, in line with dominant notions of white middle-class respectability." In other words, in seeking legal and social acceptance, southern gay men have also abandoned, at least partially, their challenge to traditional gender constructions.

In the conservative South, homosexuality has always rubbed against the grain of masculinity. Viewing gay physicality as emasculating, white and black southerners are very cautious about insinuations of homosocial activities taken too far. There is a reason that so many Americans, particularly southerners, remember the sodomy scene from the movie *Deliverance* (1972) in which a "primitive" hillbilly rapes a suburban weekend warrior: it reinforces far too explicitly the fears attached to male culture throughout the century. When men go hunting or camping, when they are showering together after a football game, or when they participate in a Womanless Wedding, what are the possibilities for homosexual activities and, therefore, emasculation of the participants and consequential weakening of the family and community?

Oh, unfamiliar with Womanless Weddings? Dating back to the late nineteenth century, they are community events usually performed for charities in which men play all the roles in a wedding ceremony. The men who donned the gowns were typically community leaders like mayors, firemen, teachers, and others who, because they wielded local power, could mock community standards without fear of retribution. Such shows were, and continue to be, found throughout the country, although they proved most popular in the upper Midwest and throughout the South. As Craig Friend's study of Womanless Weddings explains, although foremost silly and fun events meant to entertain, performances were also moments of social inversion and satire that could challenge moral values. Use of blackface, blurred gender boundaries, and opportunities for insinuations of homosexuality inspired increasingly conservative criticisms of such performances in the South and, by the turn of the twenty-first century, contributed to more limited ideas about masculinity.

The Christian gentleman, the martial masculine, primitive masculinity, passionate manhood, muscular evangelicalism, radical civil rights masculinity, sports-oriented manliness, the good ol' boy, weekend warriors—southern masculinity has been anything but static. Of course, these are all ideals. In actuality, southern men like Raoul, Percy, and Ashe have acted on characteristics appropriated from multiple categories, shaping individual personae that either blended with or reacted to more hegemonic ideals. Interestingly, what is missing in these essays is the way in which men defined themselves in opposition to women. Most of the contributors touch upon it, but only briefly. For example, DuRocher contrasts girls' and boys' participation in lynching rituals, and Friend's essay notes how, in performing Womanless Weddings, men acted out stereotyped ideals of southern womanhood. The final essay in the collection, however, makes it a central analytical theme.

Seth Dowland's study of the Southern Baptist Convention elaborates on the South's largest religious denomination's reaction to second-wave feminism's perceived threat to manhood. Observing ecclesiastical debates over women ministers, homosexuality, and the breakdown of the traditional family in other denominations, the SBC exemplified the conservative resurgence in the Sunbelt South. Not only did the SBC embrace biblical inerrancy to argue for a return to and strengthening of patriarchy within the family and community, but it was so reactionary in its stance that it denied any role for women.

Michael Kimmel once explained that American masculine identity shifted when men could no longer produce their manhood—on the frontier, on farms, in the hunt—and instead had to consume it through sports, gyms, and cars. They could no longer act out of "manhood [which] was synonymous with the term adulthood, the opposite of childhood"; they turned to "masculinity," which was best demonstrated in opposition to "femininity." However, the articles in this collection also demonstrate that masculinity, at least in the South, is not so simply defined as dichotomous to femininity. Race, class, and sexuality are vital and equally influential factors as well, creating multiple masculinities reacting to multiple influences. Southern "crises of masculinity" have occurred when society could not locate a hegemonic masculinity among the challenges raised by femininity, race, class, and sexuality. Dowland's findings, as well as Howard's and those in the latter half of Friend's essay, can be contextualized within a contemporary "crisis of masculinity" in the South (and throughout the United States). Deindustrialization, second-wave feminism, the end of the Cold War, the Gay Rights movement, downsizing in corporations and the military, the rise of a significant new Latino minority—men faced, and continue to do so, dramatic changes to the cultural underpinnings of southern masculinity, even as traditional southern expectations remain. How these factors will challenge southern masculinities and give rise to new forms of manhood lies before us in the twenty-first century.[30]

NOTES

1. George F. Will, "Georgia on Our Minds," *Newsweek*, 17 December 1990, 72; Caroline Ziemke, "Richard B. Russell and the 'Lost Cause' in Vietnam, 1953–1971," *Georgia Historical Quarterly* 72 (1988): 30–71.

2. LeeAnn Whites, "The Civil War as a Crisis in Gender," in *Divided Houses: Gender and the Civil War*, ed. Catherine Clinton and Nina Silber (New York: Oxford University Press, 1992), 3–21; Gail Bederman, *Manliness and Civilization: A Cultural History of Gender and Race in the United States, 1880–1917* (Chicago: University of Chicago Press, 1995), 16–20. For a discussion of honor, mastery, and their historiographical developments, see Craig Thompson Friend and Lorri Glover, "Rethinking Southern Masculinity: An Introduction," in *Southern Manhood: Perspective on Masculinity in the Old South*, ed. Craig Thompson Friend and Lorri Glover (Athens: University of Georgia Press, 2004), vii–xvii.

3. E. Anthony Rotundo, *American Manhood: Transformations in Masculinity from the Revolution to the Modern Era* (New York: Basic Books, 1993), 2; Michael Kimmel, *Manhood in America: A Cultural History* (New York: Free Press, 1996), 95, 108, 124–25; Gail Bederman, *Manliness and Civilization: A Cultural History of Gender and Race in the United States, 1880–1917* (Chicago: University of Chicago Press, 1995); Paula Baker, "The Domestication of Politics: Women and American Political

Society, 1780–1920," *American Historical Review* 89 (1984): 620–47; Baker, *The Moral Framework of Public Life: Gender Politics, and the State in Rural New York, 1870–1930* (New York: Oxford University Press, 1991).

4. Bertram Wyatt-Brown, *The Shaping of Southern Culture: Honor, Grace, and War, 1760s–1880s* (Chapel Hill: University of North Carolina Press, 2001), 280.

5. Rotundo, *American Manhood*, 2–6; Bederman, *Manliness and Civilization*, 22–23; Kimmel, *Manhood in America*, 9–10. For the relationship between self-made manhood and passionate manhood, see Elizabeth and Joseph Pleck, eds., *The American Man* (Englewood Cliffs, N.J.: Prentice-Hall, 1980), 21–28.

6. Bryce Traister, "Academic Viagra: The Rise of American Masculinity Studies," *American Quarterly* 52 (2000): 288; Rotundo, *American Manhood*, 286–88; Bederman, *Manliness and Civilization*, 232–39; Kimmel, *Manhood in America*, 155.

7. Kimmel, *Manhood in America*, 74–77; Wyatt-Brown, *Shaping of Southern Culture;* Wyatt-Brown, *Southern Honor: Ethics and Behavior in the Old South* (New York: Oxford University Press, 1982); Eugene Genovese, *The World the Slaveholders Made* (New York: Vintage, 1969), 158; Elliott J. Gorn, "'Gouge and Bite, Pull Hair and Scratch': The Social Significance of Fighting in the Southern Backcountry," *American Historical Review* 90 (1985): 18–43. For examples of the inability of self-made manhood to take root in the South, see L. Diane Barnes, "Fraternity and Masculine Identity: The Search for Respectability among White and Black Artisans in Petersburg, Virginia," in Friend and Glover, eds., *Southern Manhood*, 71–91; Craig Thompson Friend, "Belles, Benefactors, and the Blacksmith's Son: Cyrus Stuart and the Enigma of Southern Gentlemanliness," in Friend and Glover, eds., *Southern Manhood*, 92–112; John Mayfield, "Being Shifty in a New Country: Southern Humor and the Masculine Ideal," in Friend and Glover, eds., *Southern Manhood*, 113–35; Stephen Berry, ed., *Princes of Cotton: Four Diaries of Young Men in the South, 1848–1860* (Athens: University of Georgia Press, 2007).

8. Henry McNeal Turner, "I Claim the Rights of Man," in *Lift Every Voice: African American Oratory, 1787–1900*, ed. Philip S. Foner and Robert James Branham (Tuscaloosa: University of Alabama Press, 1998), 475–76; Stephen Kantrowitz, "Ben Tillman and Hendrix McLane, Agrarian Rebels: White Manhood, 'The Farmers,' and the Limits of Southern Populism," *Journal of Southern History* 66 (2000): 497–524.

9. "Jeff in Petticoats," in *Songs of the Civil War*, ed. Irwin Silber and Jerry Silverman (New York: Bonanza Books, 1960), 345; James C. Klotter, *Kentucky Justice, Southern Honor, and American Manhood: Understanding the Life and Death of Richard Reid* (Baton Rouge: Louisiana State University Press, 2003), 55; Charles Rosenberg, "Sexuality, Class, and Role in Nineteenth-Century America," in Pleck and Pleck, eds., *American Man*, 219–54.

10. David W. Blight, *Race and Reunion: The Civil War in American Memory* (Cambridge, Mass.: Harvard University Press, 2001), 95; Klotter, *Kentucky Justice, Southern Honor, and American Manhood*, 55–56; Amy Greenberg, *Manifest Manhood and the Antebellum American Empire* (New York: Cambridge University Press, 2005).

11. Kantrowitz, "Ben Tillman and Hendrix McLane, Agrarian Rebels," 497–524; Wyatt-

Brown, *Shaping of Southern Culture*, 293; Bederman, *Manliness and Civilization*, 71–75; Jane Dailey, "Deference and Violence in the Postbellum Urban South: Manners and Massacres in Danville, Virginia," *Journal of Southern History* 63 (1997): 553–90.

12. Wyatt-Brown, *Shaping of Southern Culture*, 178–79; Rotundo, *American Manhood*, 263–65; "The Carpet-Bagger as Described by Senator Norwood," *Savannah Morning News*, 6 November 1874; Oliver Wendell Holmes to Albert J. Beveridge, n.d., in *The Unwritten War: American Writers and the Civil War*, ed. Daniel Aaron (New York: Alfred A. Knopf, 1973), 166–67; Nina Silber, "Intemperate Men, Spiteful Women, and Jefferson Davis: Northern Views of the Defeated South," *American Quarterly* 41 (1989): 614–35.

13. Bederman, *Manliness and Civilization*, 22, 26.

14. Gary R. Kremer, "For Justice and a Fee: James Milton Turner and the Cherokee Freedmen," in *A Question of Manhood: A Reader in U.S. Black Men's History and Masculinity*, vol. 2: *The Nineteenth Century: From Emancipation to Jim Crow*, ed. Earnestine Jenkins and Darlene Clark Hine (Bloomington: Indiana University Press, 2001), 71–82; Kimmel, *Manhood in America*, 94.

15. James Milton Turner to James H. McLean, 2 June 1883, in Kremer, "For Justice and a Fee," 74; Philip Brian Harper, *Are We Not Men? Masculine Anxiety and the Problem of African American Identity* (New York: Oxford University Press, 1996), 69.

16. Albert Bigelow Paine, ed., *Mark Twain's Notebook* (New York: Harper & Bros., 1935), 357; Bederman, *Manliness and Civilization*, 16–20.

17. Bederman, *Manliness and Civilization*, 16–20; Elliot J. Gorn, *The Manly Art: Bare-Knuckle Prizefighting in America* (Ithaca, N.Y.: Cornell University Press, 1986), 179–206.

18. David W. Blight, *Race and Reunion: The Civil War in American Memory* (Cambridge, Mass.: Harvard University Press, 2001), 221; Edward L. Ayers, *The Promise of the New South: Life after Reconstruction* (New York: Oxford University Press, 1992); Paul M. Gaston, *The New South Creed: A Study in Southern Mythmaking* (New York: Alfred A. Knopf, 1970).

19. Ayers, *Promise of the New South*, 322–23; Martha Hodes, "The Sexualization of Reconstruction Politics: White Woman and Black Men in the South after the Civil War," *Journal of the History of Sexuality* 3 (1993): 403; Laura F. Edwards, *Gendered Strife and Confusion: The Political Culture of Reconstruction* (Urbana: University of Illinois Press, 1997).

20. Bertram Wyatt-Brown, "The Evolution of Heroes' Honor in the Southern Literary Tradition," in *The Evolution of Southern Culture*, ed. Numan V. Bartley (Athens: University of Georgia Press, 1988), 116; Blight, *Race and Reunion*, 221–22.

21. Joel Williamson, *William Faulkner and Southern History* (New York: Oxford University Press, 1993), 375, 381.

22. On the emergence of queer masculinity, see George Chauncey, *Gay New York: Gender, Urban Culture, and the Making of the Gay Male World, 1890–1940* (New York: Basic Books, 1994), 12–23.

23. Margaret Mitchell, *Gone with the Wind* (1938; reprint, New York: Avon Books, 1973), 37, 99; Elizabeth Young, *Disarming the Nation: Women's Writing and the Civil War* (Chicago: University of Chicago Press, 1999), 233–86; Joel Williamson, "How Black Was Rhett Butler?" in Bartley, ed., *Evolution of Southern Culture*, 87–107.

24. Ted Ownby, *Subduing Satan: Religion, Recreation, and Manhood in the Rural South, 1865–1920* (Chapel Hill: University of North Carolina Press, 1990), 12; Stuart A. Marks, *Southern Hunting in Black and White: Nature, History, and Ritual in a Carolina Community* (Princeton, N.J.: Princeton University Press, 1991), 161; Ben A. Shackelford, "Going National While Staying Southern: Stock Car Racing in America, 1949–1979" (Ph.D. diss., Georgia Institute of Technology, 2004), 117, 198. For a different interpretation of white southern manhood in the early twentieth century, see Trent Watts, "Introduction: Telling White Men's Stories," in *White Masculinity in the Recent South*, ed. Trent Watts (Baton Rouge: Louisiana State University Press, 2008).

25. Jan Hutson, *The Chicken Ranch: The True Story of the Best Little Whorehouse in Texas* (New York: Barnes, 1980).

26. Ownby, *Subduing Satan*, 17; Kimmel, *Manhood in America*, 125, 288. On muscular Christianity, see Donald E. Hall and Gillian Beer, eds., *Muscular Christianity: Embodying the Victorian Age* (New York: Cambridge University Press, 1994); Clifford Putney, *Muscular Christianity: Manhood and Sports in Protestant America, 1880–1920* (Cambridge, Mass.: Harvard University Press, 2001).

27. Ownby, *Subduing Satan*, 17; Martin Summers, *Manliness and Its Discontents: The Black Middle Class and the Transformation of Masculinity, 1900–1930* (Chapel Hill: University of North Carolina Press, 2004), 269.

28. Andrea G. Hunter and James Earl Davis, "Constructing Gender: An Exploration of Afro-American Men's Conceptualization of Manhood," *Gender and Society* 6 (1992): 464–79; William J. Grier and Price M. Cobbs, *Black Rage* (New York: Basic Books, 1968); William H. Turner, "Myths and Stereotypes: The African Man in America," in *The Black Male in America*, ed. Doris Wilkinson and Ronald Taylor (Chicago: Nelson-Hall, 1977).

29. Steve Estes, *I am a Man! Race, Manhood, and the Civil Rights Movement* (Chapel Hill: University of North Carolina Press, 2005).

30. Michael S. Kimmel, "Consuming Manhood: The Feminization of American Culture and the Recreation of the American Male Body, 1832–1920," *Michigan Quarterly Review* 33 (1994): 21.

Reconstructing Men in Savannah, Georgia, 1865–1876

Karen Taylor

I f Tunis G. Campbell looked for friends and supporters among the people who witnessed his progress along the streets of Savannah, Georgia, or glared into the faces of enemies, he left no record of it. It was 12 January 1876, and Savannah's populace was as divided over issues of race as it was about most everything else. Even many African American Savannahns found men like Campbell embarrassing, if not frightening. Although he attracted as many people as he frightened, there Campbell was, at age sixty-three, on his way to Colonel Jack Smith's Washington County plantation, where men were measured by their abilities to "keep up or die."[1] His crimes were the arrest of white men and the arrogance to think that black people deserved equal rights. Campbell's "progress"—in chains—personified the defeat of that democratic ideal and screamed warning to other "uppity" black men.

This is the story of Campbell and three other men—Richard D. Arnold, Henry M. Turner, and John E. Bryant—whose experiences in Savannah between 1865 and 1876 suggest that southern Reconstruction merged two competing masculine ideals, resulting in a bifurcated masculinity that required all men to espouse self-restraint and democratic equality but to act with aggressive self-interest. That confluence had profound consequences for American domestic and foreign policy—and for masculinity itself.

The stories of these four men also represent the intersection of two historiographies: that of Reconstruction and that of nineteenth-century masculinity. Most historians agree that Reconstruction was a failure, or in Eric Foner's words, an "unfinished revolution." There are two prominent interpretations of that failure. One is that racism so saturated American culture that white people were unable to relinquish their racist understandings of African Americans and treat them as equals. The other is that big business interests and white planters' desires to retain property and control black labor (what W. E. B. Du Bois called a "dictatorship of property") coincided to the extent that they shaped political outcomes, including interference with the military occupation of the South and underfunding of the Freedman's Bureau.[2]

Historians also agree that nineteenth-century men wrestled with what being a man meant. Over two centuries, European colonization of the Americas, the American Revolution, industrial capitalism, and nineteenth-century reform triggered questions about autonomy and self-interest as aspects of masculinity. Those questions generated a contradictory set of values: one embracing a democracy in which all men were created equal; the other committed to a republic in which white men pursued a manifest destiny of conquest and domination over women and "inferior" men. The result was a continuum of male role models ranging from "communal" to "self-made" that, by the mid-nineteenth century, had resolved into two conflicting ideals: the Christian gentleman, who was sober, industrious, and self-restrained; and the martial man, who was aggressive, honorable, self-interested, and if necessary, violent. Few men fit either ideal perfectly, their behavior mediated by race, class, age, and the exigencies of the moment, but most men knew their status depended on their abilities to match appropriate behaviors to varying circumstances, a challenge complicated by the fact that women workers, reformers, and feminists were challenging men's monopoly on the public sphere.[3]

Examining Reconstruction from a gendered perspective allows us to illuminate the deployment of racism and self-interest—the two causes of its failure—by revealing the mechanisms that prompted men to act in racist or antiracist ways, or to pursue economic interests at the cost of humane or human interests. From a gendered perspective, the Civil War was the most visible manifestation of the conflict between men whose status came from behaving like Christian gentlemen and men whose status required them to act like martial men. The Civil War—and the debates that preceded it—reified those two understandings of manhood, and Reconstruction provided the stage upon which they auditioned for the definition of American masculinity.[4]

In the postwar South, victors and vanquished faced one another daily in the struggle to restore social order, a situation made urgent by the fact that, in the expanded political realm that resulted from the emancipation of slaves, whiteness was no longer a legal signifier of superiority in hierarchies of masculinity. Neither white Christian gentlemen nor white martial men could be defined as prone to embracing nonwhite men as equals: prominent martial men were generally vociferous in deprecating the nonwhite men with whom they engaged in disputes over territory or over whom they had been masters. Christian gentlemen, in contrast, were often reformers and inclined to see nonwhite men as educable and therefore potentially redeemable, certainly in a religious sense and, at least theoretically, in a political one.

Tunis Campbell, Richard Arnold, John Bryant, and Henry Turner were reformers who occupied very different race and class hierarchies, but embodied the Christian gentleman version of manhood. Campbell was an African Methodist Episcopalian minister, reformer (he once shared the stage with Frederick Douglass), hotelier, and author of *The Hotel Keepers', Head Waiters', and Housekeepers' Guide* ("the first manual by an American about the supervision and management of first-class hotels"). He was born in 1812 in Middlebrook, New Jersey, to a free African American blacksmith and educated to be a colonizationist at an Episcopal school in Babylon, New York. He came to Savannah as a Freedman's Bureau agent with the first wave of carpetbaggers in 1865, and General Rufus Saxton made him governor of Brunside, Ausaba, Saint Catherines, Sapelo, and Colonels islands off the coast of Savannah. Of the same generation as Campbell, Richard M. Arnold was a white, wealthy, renowned physician and slave owner as well as mayor of Savannah at the moment of its surrender.[5]

John E. Bryant and Henry M. Turner, the other two men in this quartet, were in their thirties. Bryant, a thirty-five-year-old white schoolteacher, reformer, and avid temperance man from Maine (he took pride in his claim that he had taken the oath of temperance when he was six months old—administered by his father—and had never broken it), had a brand-new wife and a reputation for controversy when he arrived in Augusta, Georgia, in 1865 as an agent of the Freedman's Bureau. There, he no doubt ran into Henry McNeal Turner, also an agent of the bureau, as well as an African Methodist Episcopal (AME) pastor and a highly educated man (he studied at Trinity College). Turner was born free in 1834 in Newberry, South Carolina, to Sarah Turner, and he signaled his character early by running away from an apprenticeship in a cotton field to become a janitor and eventual protégé to young white law clerks at an Abbeville law firm. He was thirty-one when he arrived in Macon in 1865.[6]

These men shared the dream of establishing a more democratic society. Arnold wanted African Americans to be treated like people: he spent much of his time prior to the war either tending to them medically (often for free) or acting on their behalf as "guardian," a legal role that enabled free African Americans to own property and conduct business—rights technically unavailable to them. While he considered slaves naïve and uneducated, he still recognized their human dignity. On one occasion in 1862, for example, he instructed his manager and son-in-law to "sell Master Owen . . . for he would only worry and disgrace his family." He was also appalled by the "extortion" perpetrated by white producers of the "necessities of life"—a "more selfish unpatriotic lot never cursed a country."[7]

Turner, Bryant, and Campbell had similarly egalitarian goals. Bryant appealed to workers, white and black. As he wrote, "The laborer should be as independent as the capitalist." He said of white southern men's attempts to keep freedmen tied to their former masters, "If cheap negro labor is secured, . . . the white man who makes the cotton by his own labor will be forced to compete with cheap negro labor." Turner, who championed literacy as a reward for African American men's military service during the war, became a lobbyist for the Georgia Equal Rights Association, the goal of which was "to aid in securing for all, without regard to race or color, equal political rights" and the recognition of "black men's 'full dignity of manhood.'" Campbell wanted to do something about the inequities inherent in a capitalist system that exploited people by race and class, and therefore made true democracy impossible: "I ask the laboring men and women of this nation, How long will it be before you have no rights that the capitalist or property-holder is bound to respect?"[8]

As in most everything else, however, race made a difference. Paradoxically, as high-status, free African Americans, Turner and Campbell had something of an edge on Bryant and Arnold because they were accustomed to having to fight for what they wanted. Ministers were of the highest rank in African American male hierarchies and, like black abolitionists, represented not only material success but also education, freedom, and the courage to stand up for their rights. As respectable white men, Bryant and Arnold were in an entirely different position: their status depended on a willingness to conform to the expectations of more powerful white men and the peers they wanted as advocates. That was true for Bryant, whose parsimonious childhood left him ambitious to study law and accumulate wealth, but also of Arnold, whose position as a town father rested on his ability to satisfy the economic and political interests of his constituents and to maintain his reputation as a gracious host and a convivial speaker.

In order to garner support for their visions of a democratic South, these four men had to negotiate race and class within the treacherous territory of victor and vanquished *and,* at the same time, confront and try to resolve the underlying conflict between Christian gentlemen and martial men. In the immediate aftermath of the Civil War, Christian gentlemen in the South had an advantage over martial men because slave-owning Rebels had lost the Civil War, an implicit (and sometimes explicit) victory of the democratic virtue embodied by abolitionists over the racially based hierarchy promoted by slaveholders. Christian gentlemen were at a disadvantage in the larger scheme of manliness, however, for three reasons: their victory was based on the Union's conquest and military occupation of the Confederacy; white businessmen, former slaveholders, and politicians had multiple connections that predated and mostly survived the war; and martial men shared a lack of respect for white reformers and African American men. Campbell, Turner, Bryant, and Arnold had to cultivate their common interests with the martial men who surrounded and empowered them, while at the same time persuading those men that the values of Christian gentlemanliness exemplified true manhood.

In the minefield of barely suppressed hostilities that was Reconstruction-era Georgia, the necessity to restore social order required men to tread softly. Men in general attempted to reestablish order through public discourse—in speech, writing, and behavior—that differentiated "good" men from "bad" men. In Savannah, that differentiation evolved through three phases that roughly corresponded to phases of Reconstruction. During presidential Reconstruction, Christian gentlemen and martial men proceeded cautiously, defining "good" manhood as a mishmash of combined traits and "bad" as any man who disturbed the peace. By the time Congressional Reconstruction descended on Georgia in 1867, both had become frustrated with their inability to assert their values, and they recommenced defining each other as "good" or "bad" according to which side they chose in the fight for African American rights. In the final phase, which began when Democrat "Redeemers" gained control of the governor's office and the state legislature in 1871, "good" Savannah men had become democratic and aggressive in their self-interests, and "bad" men were paradoxically either afraid to stand up for their rights or violent in pursuit of them.[9]

The newspapers were a critical arena for that evolution because, as one editor declared, newspapers made "men aware of their position in society . . . [and made] every individual nature self-dependent and thoroughly conscious of his manhood."[10] Because their behavior and status frequently placed Arnold, Turner, Bryant, and Campbell on stage in the newspapers, they were local symbols of either "good" or "bad" manhood (depending upon the perspective of the commentator), which mediated both their own behavior and the actions of men around them. By the end of their Reconstruction experience, these Christian gentlemen had become more martial in their behavior, while the martial men around them had adopted the language of democratic equality—in both cases as the means to their own ends. Tunis Campbell's appearance in chains in Savannah's newspapers, therefore, like his appearance in chains on the streets, had multiple meanings, and to understand them we need to start with a moment almost exactly ten years earlier.

It was 22 December 1865, and fifty-five-year-old Savannah mayor Richard Arnold was leading a contingent of "notable citizens" (white men of business and standing) and the inevitable and ever-present rabble of "lesser" Savannahns, mostly poor white and African American women and men, down Bay Street to meet their conquerors, William T. Sherman and his troops. About Sherman and his armies, the people of Savannah knew too much to feel comfortable in their surrender. As the man to whom the role of surrenderer fell, Arnold's words to Sherman were "Peace, peace, for God's sake, peace." Confronted with the responsibility of defining conquered manhood, Arnold tried to behave in ways that were simultaneously conciliatory, dignified, and honorable. He believed it would require the "heart of a Philanthropist and the head of a Statesman to work out this problem.[11]

The newspapers gave Arnold a variety of scripts from which he could read his performance. Some editors thought Savannahns had betrayed the Confederacy, as did the editor of the *Charleston Mercury* (whose words were reported in the *Savannah Daily Herald*): "If conquered, he [the Confederacy] falls not by the force of the enemy in front, but by the unlooked for blows from behind. . . . Had he expected this foul play, . . . [he could] by one effort have felled this puny creature in his rear." Cast implicitly as a puny creature, Arnold could "feel gratified" when other writers took a view that reinforced his manly wisdom in giving up. J. E. Hayes of the *Savannah Republican,* for example, told a parable of "a young Roman . . . [who] voluntarily held his right arm in the fire until it was entirely consumed" and continued until the fire consumed his whole body, all the while claiming that "'I can endure more.' . . . Such conduct might have challenged the admiration of a heathen people, but all enlightened men would have cried 'fool!'"[12]

Arnold was probably too busy to notice Tunis Campbell, John Bryant, or Henry Turner when they arrived in Georgia, but the newspapers also provided scripts to them. Despite the goodwill of the Freedmen's Bureau, which promised "to please master as well as slave, and reconcile good men of all classes to the existing condition of things," the newspapers interspersed advertisements for minstrel shows with stories about African Americans being shot for being "altogether too unruly" and others about Sherman expounding on the fact that "he expected to own two thousand slaves himself one of these days." Although Hayes advised his readers that Savannahns should "all get bravely over our sectional prejudices," he thought the ruin that had come to the South was "far more tolerable than association with the hated Yankees."[13]

The loudest discourse articulated in news reports concerned "manliness," defined as strength, "pluck," integrity, honesty, intelligence, honor, courage, and respectability. Soldiers—especially those who had died for their cause—were the ideal "good" men, "having . . . a perfect manhood." "Repentant rebels," and even Sherman and his officers, became models of masculinity. One *Savannah Republican* writer, "Leferve," was "apprehensive that some pointed [verbal] arrow might fall from the victor's bow" as he passed among them, but he was pleased by Sherman's officers' "refinement, urbanity and manliness," and thanked "God that if a *captive,* [he] was in the hands of gallant and noble victors."[14]

Articles praising African American men were few, and only African American men who agreed with martial men's gradualist agendas for equality were laudable. "Good" black men knew their place: it was to labor in white men's fields or, at the very least, to admit that black men did not know how to govern themselves. As General Rufus Saxton said at a freedmen's meeting in February 1865, "Freedom does not mean laziness, idleness, [or] liberty to steal," but to "be industrious . . . and live like enlightened, civilized people." Saxton's Chaplain, Rev. Mansfield French, urged them to "be patient and forgiving under insults—never returning railing."[15]

Black men's labor was the thread that unraveled the fragile peace of presidential Reconstruction. Arnold had little control over the day-to-day decisions that structured Savannah life, and reduced to a figurehead, he worried that "unless labor, the source of all well-being in this world, shall be re-organized in some practical form, a dreary future awaits the South." Campbell successfully organized those African Americans who had gathered on the islands into hardworking farmers, but when President Andrew Johnson fired Saxton, who disagreed with his policy of returning land to white owners and forcing former slaves to work for them, Davis Tillson, Saxton's replacement, harassed Campbell at every opportunity. Tillson finally fired Campbell in 1866 for the alleged misconduct of pocketing bureau funds and paying freed labor with liquor, forbidding him even to visit the islands. Barely daunted, Campbell purchased 1,250 acres of land on the coast from "a Northern sympathizer" and founded the BelleVille Farmers Association with the freedmen who chose to follow him there.[16]

Bryant ran into equally depressing resistance despite his enthusiastic report to his wife that he wished she could see "these people as they step from slavery into freedom . . . They almost consider Mr. French and myself their deliverers." He developed a reputation as "the impersonation of depravity" by attempting to force whites to pay fair wages to African American workers. In 1866, Tillson dismissed him, too, from the bureau, claiming that it would furthermore employ civilians only as clerks. Bryant responded by working with Turner to establish the Georgia Equal Rights Association: Bryant became its first president, and Turner its vice president and representative in Washington. Bryant used the *Loyal Georgian,* the association's newspaper, to air complaints about the bureau's increasing support of white planters and eventually pricked Tillson's honor so effectively that they spent most of 1866 in open conflict, at one point resulting in a "most cowardly and brutal" attack with a club on Bryant by an unknown assailant, and investigations of both Bryant and the bureau. From Washington, Turner assured him that he had "friends in this state by hundreds" whom he could turn to if he needed help or money.[17]

By 1867, after Congress refused to seat Georgia's senators because they were former Rebels and Congressional Reconstruction imposed more egalitarian criteria for Georgia's reentry into the Union, men had become, like Bryant and Tillson, much less cautious in articulating their positions. Southern martial men who hoped to reclaim their status constructed a world in which "carpetbaggers," "scalawags," and their African American "dupes" aligned in absolute opposition to "loyal white southerners" and "intelligent colored" men. White and black men who wanted democratic equality depicted their opponents as dishonest abusers of African Americans, and themselves as "men of justice and vision." To win other men to their cause—or defend themselves against their accusers—all men had to articulate and defend their own values. In doing so, they invoked gender—masculinity—as the ultimate validity for their arguments, and thus directly entangled themselves in the contradictions between the values of Christian gentlemen and martial men.

"Loyal white southerners" stated their values in terms of African Americans' incapacity for political participation and defended those values by calling their opponents colorful names. Ready to accept their status "as a conquered people," they wanted to elect delegates who were "pure-minded, high toned, honorable, and last, though not least, discreet" to a constitutional convention so they could rid themselves of people like Campbell, Bryant, and Turner, "the corps of unscrupulous political buzzards who are already in eager expectation of gaining power . . . over wounded and bleeding Georgia." Newspaper editors worried that the "almost universal disfranchisement" would prevent "the intelligent and honorable white men of Georgia from voting or participating in the Convention," and result in a "black man's Convention," though they declared themselves to be "against a white man's party."[18]

Newspapers' characterizations forced white men to choose sides. How closely they aligned themselves with "Negro Rights," and how they defined those rights, decided their public status. Martial men engaged in "bold and manly discussion" when the issue arose, and exhibited "moderation and self-control" to "save the lives of . . . deluded colored people," but they did not cross the line between helping black "inferiors" and treating black men as equals. The "worst" white men were those who supported full rights for black men. Savannah newspapers reported that Georgia's government was in the hands of such white "military chieftains" and "white wire-pulling and office hunting" northern men who plotted with a "half deranged . . . class of colored men" and thereby threatened the future of Georgia.[19] Despite those aspersions, Turner, Bryant, and Campbell were elected delegates to the constitutional convention and, in 1868, to the Georgia legislature.

Many newspapers both nationally and locally began a campaign to reinforce white supremacy. They enlarged the definition of "white" to include people whom nativist Americans had previously excluded, and cultivated the notion that northern and southern white men had much in common. The *Savannah Weekly Republican* of 19 October 1867, for example, reported that former president Franklin Pierce exulted in the fact that the "white race, the German, Italian, French, Irish, and Anglo-Saxon people, are still to be the controlling power on this continent." Editor Hayes reinforced the point with an adjacent story in which a white man, "growling anathemas at the party he himself had helped to place into power," fled a sleeping car when he found himself sharing it with "a huge male negro."[20]

Discourse about solidarity among white men was accompanied by an increase in stories about the "depredations" of "savage" Native Americans, and comparing Chinese and Japanese "heathen" behavior and rights to those of African Americans. One of the litmus tests for the appropriateness of the Civil Rights Bill was California's stance on the Chinese.[21] The Conservative (Democratic) Party quickly became the mouthpiece for those sentiments in Georgia, dragging Arnold, an active member, with it.

Arnold struggled to articulate his own beliefs about African Americans' humanity against the pressure to conform to the party line, but he was worn down by the newspapers' depictions of a vindictive North and the political conflict around him. At an 1868 Conservative meeting in Savannah, he told delegates that "the Chinese are a people older in the history of the world than we are, and yet the people of California will not give them suffrage. . . . If the negro can educate himself, then we can see what can be done. . . . If [a white man] has not learned to read and write, I say he ought not to vote. If this qualification was made there would be but few negroes who could vote." Reassuring his audience—and perhaps himself—that this was a manly stance, he urged them not to "submit quietly to whatever may come. If we must die then let us . . . vindicate our character as men."[22]

White men whose status depended on racial hierarchy saw the issue of black suffrage clearly as a matter of manhood. As Hayes wrote, "When the Southern people willingly surrender to the cruel and humiliating terms of Universal Suffrage, . . . they barter all their manhood." For Turner, Campbell, and Bryant ("the person to whom the whole colored race is bound to look as their greatest champion," according to the *Atlanta Daily Intelligencer*), white men's protests against black male suffrage were evidence of white men's insecurity. As Turner put it, "If we are inferior by nature, . . . why bleat over the county so much about negro rule, War of races[?]"[23]

Savannah's version of the "deranged" black dupe was "the notorious brawler," Aaron Alpeoria Bradley, "one of the sharp-edged tools pliantly used by the blackest kind of white adventurers." Bradley, a free, Georgia-born African American who had spent much of his adult life in the North practicing law, had the "arrogant presumption, ignorance, bullyism and impertinence" to advocate "equal rights to colored voters and poor white persons." Men who would consort with Bradley were like white Republican legislator W. L. Clift, "a sour little fellow, with weak, wicked eyes." Worse yet, they were cowards. The *Weekly Republican* reported that "none of the white clique that were the prime movers and instigators" behind Bradley "had sufficient moral courage to show their hypocritical faces" at a Radical rally.[24]

Fear of being labeled black dupes forced black men to take sides. The members of the Colored Union League of Savannah, for example, offered a "manly protest" in which they repudiated "the sentiments of the wiseacre" Bradley, an action widely applauded, even by the *New York Times.* Their chief complaint was that he had "transcended the bounds of propriety, and brought reproach upon . . . the respectable colored men of this city." Sometimes those divisions had graver consequences, as when Aaron Hurt, a "poor demented and inoffensive negro" was tarred and feathered by six African American men after he "urged his colored hearers" at a public rally "to stick to work, and not listen to the teachings of demagogues."[25]

Even Turner and Bryant tried to distance themselves from Bradley. Turner reminded his colleagues, "It is well known . . . that Mr. Bradley and myself are hostile opponents, that we seldom agree on any point, and no persons on this floor have ridiculed each other more." Bryant gained status when he objected to Bradley's behavior, arguing that Bradley had, "on various occasions, insulted the House," to which a reporter added with implicit approval that the delegates "displayed a certain degree of uncertainty in [Bryant's] appearance, as if they were afraid to act as become men."[26]

Frequently, newspapers tweaked white men's imperiled dominance by linking African American men's enfranchisement to women's suffrage—the latter already threatening to dilute the power that defined white masculinity. "The Arkansas Constitution," reported the *Weekly Republican,* "enfranchises females and negroes, and makes them competent as jurors." White women's betrayal of white men was also a popular topic. In an article about a model (designed by Harriet Hosmer) for the Lincoln Monument, the *Weekly Republican* noted that Lincoln was "surrounded by four negroes ('insatiate sculpist!' would not one suffice?)—and four female figures, the latter in the act of investing the colored population with liberty."[27]

Republican Radicals were, in fact, in favor of some rights for women. As the editor of the *Savannah Daily Republican* put it, "The latest Radical judicial decision . . . is that the word 'male' in a legal document means *female.*" At the Republican Convention in 1868, Radicals proposed that "all the property of the wife in her possession at the time of her marriage, and all property given to, inherited or acquired by her, shall remain her separate property and not liable for the debts of the husband." Most incendiary was the threat of miscegenation, a problem the *Weekly Republican* pointed out in February 1868, accusing Bradley of "bargaining" to support white delegates' amendments in exchange for their vote on the "marriage bill."[28]

As "men of justice and vision," Bryant, Turner, and Campbell appealed to reason and integrity more often than character assassination. Despite their reluctance to associate themselves with Bradley, when white delegates tried to expel him from the convention for having served a prison term in New York for the crime of seduction (all evidence suggests he was guilty of sex with a white woman), Campbell, Turner, and Bryant (among many others) spoke in his defense. Turner warned his colleagues—many of whom were former slaveholders—that seduction was "a dangerous subject . . . I fear there may be gentlemen . . . [present who] have treated their accidentals as my father treated me. . . . If Mr. Bradley is expelled, I give notice that several more will be called upon to prove their right to seats on this floor. . . . Let each one retrospect his own life, . . . [to see] if the crime of seduction taints our memory in any form."[29]

At no point were their values more clearly defined than when white congressmen ousted African American men from the Georgia legislature in July 1868. Bryant appealed to Christian values, raging that this was "the age of progress," and "all persons are equal, socially, politically, and otherwise, the Bible sustains the proposition." Turner was equally incensed and more combative. "I am here to demand my rights and to hurl thunderbolts at the men who would dare to cross the threshold of my manhood," he informed them at the beginning of a lengthy speech that might be summarized as "Having Rights While Black": "Never before was man arraigned before a legislative body for an offense committed by God himself [the offense of being black]." Campbell responded to the ouster of African American representatives by citing the law: "[T]he constitution and the laws of Georgia strictly provide that no law shall be made or enforced which shall abridge the privileges or immunities of citizens of the United States, or of this state, or deny to any person within its jurisdiction, the equal protection of its laws. Therefore . . . we do enter our solemn protest against the illegal, unconstitutional, unjust, and oppressive action of this body."[30]

In terms of rational argument—one of the characteristics nineteenth-century men thought set them apart from women—the Christian gentlemanliness exhibited by men like Bryant, Turner, Campbell, and even Arnold clearly revealed the paucity of reason articulated by the martial men who surrounded them. Christian Gentlemen's vindication was the revocation of Georgia's admission to the Union, the return of military occupation by December 1869, the reinstatement of African American legislators in 1870, and the ratification of the Fifteenth Amendment. But victory based on military might was tenuous at best, and these men knew that real success, and possibly their lives, depended on their ability to win martial men over to their values, especially as Democrat Redeemers, using every means from bribery to violence, reclaimed control of Georgia. Pinched between military threat on one side and violent intimidation on the other, martial men adopted the rhetoric of equality and Christian gentlemen conceded to the necessity for aggression. Three factors facilitated that shift: self-interest, corruption, and violence.

"The politics of livelihood" made self-interest a crucial aspect of masculinity.[31] As the most insecure men in Savannah, African American men were most vulnerable to the pressures of self-interest. Turner tried to balance his desire to serve his people against the fact that he needed white toleration and African American approval to maintain his livelihood as a minister. When he moved to Savannah in February 1872 to become pastor of St. Philips Church, the editor of the *Savannah Morning News* heralded him as "the notorious negro preacher and Radical bummer," asserting that "the Macon negroes couldn't stand his morals." But the newspapers quickly began to cultivate his cooperation, suggesting that Turner was "probably one of the best leaders the colored people have, . . . [though] some of his statements . . . in reference to the oppression of the colored people were notoriously without foundation." One of the ways editors appealed to Turner was to compare his behavior to Bryant's and judge Turner superior. In an 1872 article about Bryant nearly causing a riot at the polls, for example, the *News* reported that Turner "saunter[ed] around . . . [and] took no active part in the contest." Turner was well aware of such meager scraps of approval (or lapses in disapproval), stating in a letter to the editor in June 1874 that "your columns have been kind both to me individually and to my church since I have been the pastor."[32]

Turner's greatest controversy in Savannah was his advocacy of colonization, a position he reluctantly adopted when it seemed that white men would never accept black men as equals. His vision conformed to general colonization ideology: slavery was part of God's plan for uplifting Africans and spreading democracy. He argued that colonization would produce "a negro nationality . . . [in] Africa that will be an everlasting monument of honor to the whites of this country." He was dismayed by the fact that most African American men did not support him. "I am startled at times," he said in a letter to the editor of the *Colored Tribune*, Savannah's only African American newspaper, "at the ignorance displayed by many of our prominent colored men, upon the real condition of our race in this country." Only if African American men built their own nation would "the nations of earth . . . admire our manhood and genius."[33]

The *Tribune*, which began publication in December 1875, demonstrated clearly the conflicted position of African American men: "We believe it to be our duty to say to our people cultivate honest manhood, be courageous, accumulate wealth and education." While they advocated cooperation with whites and recommended that "angry passions cool down," they also demanded "that the negro shall be allowed the free exercise of every public right, exactly as white people are," and repudiated white men who "trample[d] upon the Constitution of Georgia" or African American men who would "bow and scrape to white men and obey their bidding like slaves." Steadfastly Republican, their loyalties were still anchored in race, and they devoted as much print to condemning "dirty, worthless negro men" because they "reflect[ed] very much upon their people," as they did praising upstanding African American men.[34]

White men also scrutinized their associates' behavior for its impact on their own reputations. Arnold became increasingly concerned about corruption, in reformers' parlance an endemic and "unmanly" male characteristic that could only be controlled by self-restraint. He recognized that many of the men with whom he was forced to ally were personally reprehensible, as was Georgia Senator Ben Hill, "a self-acting gas-bag, always inflating himself for his own grandeur," and he feared that "the maneuvering Politicians have sold the Democratic Party." He saw the Fifteenth Amendment as leverage against such men, noting at a meeting in September 1872 that since the redistricting of the state had given them "a large preponderance . . . of those extraordinarily intelligent Fifteenth Amendment citizens, who are held in the shackles of Radicalism, . . . it behoove[s] us to select good men to represent the county." Unfortunately for men like Bryant, Campbell, and Turner, corruption plagued the Republican Party. Governor Rufus Bullock, accused of crimes ranging from pillaging Georgia's coffers to taking "three champagne baths at seventy-five dollars each," was the epitome of local corruption.[35]

Bullock's behavior split the Republican Party in 1869 and left Bryant (who helped lead the campaign against him) vulnerable and, like Turner, dependent on the kindness of supporters. Bryant tried newspaper publishing and law, but when neither proved successful, he took a position as deputy collector of the Customs House (a political appointment) in Savannah in 1872.[36] His haphazard employment undermined his ability to support his wife, Emma, and their daughter, and frequently separated them, which plagued him because, as her 1873 visit to a doctor in Cleveland with whom she subsequently went riding alone reminded him, "in domestic affairs the freedom of the wife leads to free love."[37] Bryant's sensitivity to Emma's behavior was probably enhanced by the fact that the same papers that called him a "vile carpet-bagger" and deemed carpetbaggers "at best, but Cinderella at the Ball" openly mocked women's rights. Newspaper castigation and his opposition to Bullock convinced many African American men, including Campbell, that it was in their self-interest to spurn Bryant and his ilk. But Bryant won approbation by publicly breaking from Bullock. The Augusta *Chronicle* marveled that "a 'Union soldier,' a 'carpet-bagger,' a Radical—is seen standing in the breach, baring his breast to a storm of abuse and bludgeons, maintaining 'the honor of Georgia.'"[38]

Bryant's desire to live up to that image often involved him in violence. In January 1870, for example, fellow legislator Tweedy and other "Bullockites" attacked him with sticks, "sending him to the doctor with a head injury" after he called Tweedy "a miserable liar" during a debate.[39] On election day in October 1872, in his capacity as one of the "gentlemen challengers" who were meant to see that no "irregularities" occurred, Bryant was clubbed by a deputy and arrested for "attempting to draw his pistol" after he tried to stop a white man from voting who had not paid his poll tax. Perhaps because Bryant's values aligned closely with his own, Arnold and another Democrat bailed Bryant out of jail.[40]

Campbell was also driven to endorse violence in the face of conspicuous intimidation. He later recalled how he "could see Democratic members, with their hands on the butts of their pistols, with their teeth shut hard together, and using threatening gestures" at him, even in legislative meetings. One of his first acts as superintendent of the islands in 1865 was to organize an African American militia to ward off white men. On the numerous occasions when he was arrested for "falsely imprisoning" white men who abused their power, in his capacity as justice of the peace of McIntosh County (a position he won after his banishment from the islands), his militia intervened, leading to violence on more than one occasion and prompting judges to incarcerate him in the Savannah jail rather than in Darien. Confronted with an "iniquitous, unjust, and diabolical" law that would place McIntosh County under the control of a state-appointed, seven-member board of commissioners (usurping even his authority as justice of the peace) in 1872, Campbell foreshadowed Malcolm X's "any means necessary" by declaring that if need be "freemen" would use their "one resource left": "the musket and Bayonet."[41] Backed by his militia, Campbell was a force that most white men were afraid to reckon with—at least directly.

With men like Campbell threatening armed resistance, newspapers increasingly decried violence or assigned it to "inferior" men. "Gentlemen" now settled their differences peacefully. Editors portrayed violence as a behavior perpetrated by men looking for trouble, the Ku Klux Klan, or Native Americans "who murder, scalp, pillage and burn." "Negroes" were always "brandishing pistols" to achieve their ends, but were ultimately controlled by white men who "manfully executed" their official duties.[42] In that milieu, Campbell—and violence—became the definition of "bad" manhood.

That redefinition of violence forced martial men around Campbell to confront his power like Christian gentlemen—with the law. White attorney and Democrat politician William Gignilliate decided that "[i]f [Campbell] could be . . . dismissed for malpractice as a Justice of the Peace . . . he would then be obliged to quit the County or starve," urging state Senator Rufus E. Lester of Savannah to present the legislature with a petition from McIntosh citizens. Many citizens who testified against Campbell were African American officeholders from McIntosh County who felt disinclined to let Campbell's continued recalcitrance endanger their status, though numerous McIntosh citizens—both black and white—testified to Campbell's integrity, and circulated their own petition supporting him.[43]

After that campaign failed, Campbell's opponents resurrected lapsed indictments against him. Two in particular, the false imprisonment cases of Isaac Rafe and John Fisher, both white men, were the means by which they finally removed him.[44] By 1875, Campbell's life was constantly disrupted by those cases, and he languished in jail while his lawyers attempted to force Judge Henry B. Thompkins to accept bail, challenged the McIntosh County Superior Court for rigging juries, and tried to get changes of venue, situations so fraught with duplicity that they eventually involved the federal courts and Campbell's numerous friends, including two U.S. attorneys. The public debate that surrounded his trials forced his persecutors to articulate the justness in their behavior. The *News* devoted multiple stories to the Rafe case when Thompkins refused habeas corpus in November, and pages to the contestation of venue, citing lengthy sections of the judicial code to prove that "having such a vile and unscrupulous agitator as Tunis at liberty" was not a matter over which the federal court had jurisdiction.[45] Campbell's legal struggles exemplified both Christian gentlemen's failure to create a democracy that recognized African American men as equals and martial men's acknowledgment that brute force could no longer secure their position at the top of male hierarchies.

Arnold's death, as it was presented in the *News,* is a metaphor for these four men's Reconstruction experiences. The announcement of his death on 11 July 1876, was bookended by violence and the calumny of Reconstruction. On the front page, the *News* commemorated "The Sacrifice of Custer" for his "heroism . . . at the Little [Big] Horn." They devoted page 3, as always the site of Arnold's importance, almost entirely to announcements of Arnold's death. After a story in which the mayor eulogized Arnold as the man "compelled to ask the protection of General Sherman," there was an article about a horrific assault on the daughter of a white Baptist minister by "three negro . . . wretches" who "had been idling about, which under the Radical laws, is no crime." The reporter concluded that "the Sioux Indians can scarce excel in [the] barbarity [of] these negro thieves and villains. . . . Here is a good chance for . . . tender-hearted Radicals . . . to save a negro murderer's neck."[46]

Though these men had different understandings of their place in the masculine world, Reconstruction pressed them to reconstruct themselves in uncomfortable ways in order to survive. The gentle Arnold, hardened by his efforts to preserve his status and sickened "by the rascality of the world," never lost his desire to judge African Americans by their own merits. Even in 1875, he described one of the teachers at the African American school as "a capable one too, [and] coal Black."[47] The last sight of Bryant in the *News* was paradoxically appropriate to a man torn between self-righteous zeal and self-discipline: in a letter to the editor in November 1876, he had explained that he had not "assaulted" Collector of Customs Atkins, but only defended himself when Atkins attacked him with a chair. "I did not go to the custom house to fight, but to report for duty," he told Savannahns; "I desire to gain no glory by engaging in personal encounters 'a la Hee-man.'"[48] The anguish and absurdity of Turner's position as a colonizationist who hoped to bring democracy to Africa rang clear in a sermon at Union Church in Philadelphia in 1876: "The acts of blood and carnage which have disgraced this nation for the last half-dozen years . . . are so revolting to the very instincts of a savage that I should not be surprised to see Hottentots coming as missionaries to this country."[49] Campbell, the most martially behaving of the four, continued to cling to the ideals of the Christian gentleman, believing that his innocence would vindicate him. When he was finally convicted of false imprisonment in the Rafe case, a male reader's letter to the editor reflected the tragedy of his "heavily ironed" departure: "I would say more on this subject if I could write for weeping."[50]

Reconstruction may have failed, but men like Campbell, Turner, Bryant, and Arnold—because they forced a public debate over the nature of democracy that was at heart a debate about how democratic men behaved and believed—did not. Campbell's performance of slavery at a moment when slavery was legally dead had multiple meanings. On the surface it was clearly an articulation of white power: white men could still (and implicitly forever) subjugate a powerful, free black man. But within that message was a subtler text. Like the contemporaneous first-wave feminists who fought for women's rights (with whom these men may or may not have agreed), Campbell, Arnold, Turner, and Bryant—and men like them—sought to redefine politics in ways that made manhood less oppressive. In doing so, they helped develop a vocabulary of resistance that reverberated in the language that other and later generations of men used to deconstruct the rigid gender roles that inhibited equality.

NOTES

The author thanks Stephanie Contway for her initial research, colleagues in the College of Wooster's Feminist Research Roundtable for their feedback, and James Wiley and April Contway for their patience as sounding boards.

1. Tunis G. Campbell, *Sufferings of the Rev. T. G. Campbell and His Family in Georgia* (Washington, D.C.: Enterprise, 1877), 25–26.

2. For interpretations that focus on racism, see C. Vann Woodward, *The Strange Career of Jim Crow*, 3rd ed. (New York: Oxford University Press, 1974); Eric Foner, *Reconstruction: America's Unfinished Revolution, 1863–1877* (New York: Harper and Row, 1988). For interpretations that focus on economic self-interest, see W. E. B. Du Bois, *Black Reconstruction in America* (New York: Russell and Russell, 1935); James M. McPherson, *Ordeal by Fire: The Civil War and Reconstruction* (New York: Knopf, 1982).

3. Charles Rosenberg first used the term "Christian Gentleman" in "Sexuality, Class, and Role in Nineteenth-Century America," in *The American Man*, ed. Elizabeth Pleck and Joseph Pleck (Englewood Cliffs: Prentice-Hall, 1980), 219–54. "Martial men" comes from Amy Greenburg's spectacular study of Manifest Destiny. She uses "martial manhood" to describe men who "believed that the masculine qualities of strength, aggression, and even violence, better defined a true man than did the firm and upright manliness of restrained men [Christian gentlemen]." Although Greenberg does "not think it is correct to identify restrained manhood entirely with what other historians have labeled 'evangelical manhood'" because U.S. culture at that time was "partially defined in opposition to religious conviction," I have stuck with the phrase "Christian gentlemen" because the four men who are the focus of this study were deeply religious. See Amy S. Greenberg, *Manifest Manhood and the Antebellum American Empire* (New York: Cambridge University Press, 2005), 11–12; E. Anthony Rotundo, *American Manhood: Transformations in Masculinity from the Revolution to the Modern Era* (New York: Basic Books, 1993); Michael Kimmel, *Manhood in America: A Cultural History* (New York: Free Press, 1996); Darlene Clark and Earnestine Jenkins, eds., *A Question of Manhood: A Reader in U.S. Black Men's History and Masculinity*, vol. 2: *The Nineteenth Century: From Emancipation to Jim Crow* (Bloomington: Indiana University Press, 2001). For discussions of women's increasing power, see Ann Douglas, *The Feminization of American Culture* (New York: Knopf, 1977); Catherine Clinton, *The Other Civil War: American Women in the Nineteenth Century* (New York: Hill and Wang, 1984); Dorothy Sterling, *We Are Your Sisters: Black Women in the Nineteenth Century* (New York: W. W. Norton and Co., 1984).

4. For theoretical explanations of my approach to the study of masculinity, see Caryl

Emerson, "The Outer World and Inner Speech: Bakhtin, Vygotsky and the Internationalization of Language," in *Bakhtin: Essays and Dialogues on His Work*, ed. Gary Saul Morson (Chicago: Chicago University Press, 1986); Andrew J. Weigert, "'To Be or Not': Self and Authenticity, Identity and Ambivalence," in *Self, Ego, and Identity: Integrative Approaches*, ed. Daniel K. Lapsley and F. Clark Power (New York: Springer-Verlag New York, 1988); Louise Lamphere, Helena Ragone, and Patricia Zavella, "Introduction," in *Situated Lives: Gender and Culture in Everyday Life*, ed. Louise Lamphere, Helena Ragone, and Patricia Zavella (New York: Routledge, 1997).

5. Russell Duncan, *Freedom's Shore: Tunis Campbell and the Georgia Freedmen* (Athens: University of Georgia Press, 1986), 15. See also E. Merton Coulter, "Tunis G. Campbell, Negro Reconstructionist in Georgia," *Georgia Historical Quarterly* 51 (1967): 401–24, and 52 (1968): 16–52; Edmund L. Drago, *Black Politicians and Reconstruction in Georgia: A Splendid Failure* (Baton Rouge: Louisiana State University Press, 1982). Details about Arnold's life can be found in Richard H. Shyrock, ed., *Letters of Richard D. Arnold, M.D., 1808–1876* (Durham, N.C.: Seeman Press, 1929).

6. For Bryant, see Ruth Currie-McDaniel, *Carpetbagger of Conscience: A Biography of John Emory Bryant* (Athens: University of Georgia Press, 1987); Ruth Douglass Currie, ed., *Emma Spaulding Bryant: Civil War Bride, Carpetbagger's Wife, Ardent Feminist. Letters and Diaries, 1869–1900* (New York: Fordham University Press, 2004). For Turner, see M. M. Ponton, *Life and Times of Henry M. Turner*, 2nd ed. (New York: Negro University Press, 1970); Stephen Ward Angell, *Bishop Henry McNeal Turner and African-American Religion in the South* (Knoxville: University of Tennessee Press, 1992).

7. Richard Arnold to William C. Cosens, 31 March 1862; Arnold to J. H. Waldburg, 14 August 1863; Arnold to Dr. J. G. Robertson, 14 April 1864, all in "The Arnold Letters," *Historical Papers*, ser. 16 (Durham, N.C.: Duke University Press, 1926), 105, 110, 111. See also Whittington B. Johnson, *Black Savannah, 1788–1864* (Fayetteville: University of Arkansas Press, 1966).

8. Bryant and Turner, quoted in Currie-McDaniel, *Carpetbagger of Conscience*, 59, 60, 131; Campbell, *Sufferings*, Preface.

9. In *Manifest Manhood*, Greenberg argued that the Civil War "led to a near total acceptance of restrained masculine practices in the post-bellum era," but like Rotundo and most other historians she agreed that "aggressive expansionism and martial manhood ("primitive" or "passionate manhood" in Rotundo's terms) had a rebirth at the end of the century" (see Greenberg, *Manifest Manhood*, 17). While I agree with the latter assessment, it seems to me that a merger of Christian and martial manhood (rather than "near total acceptance of restrained" manhood) more convincingly explains the emergence of "primitive" masculinity.

10. "An American Characteristic," *Savannah Republican*, 27 April 1865. The newspapers in effect "staged" masculinity in the same way that public occasions and organizations did, thereby (to borrow Diane Barnes's words from her excellent study

of fraternalism) constructing "power relations that made masculinity the most important framework for organizing social life." See Barnes, "Fraternity and Masculine Identity: The Search for Respectability among White and Black Artisans in Petersburg, Virginia," in Friend and Glover, eds., *Southern Manhood*, 71. In *Their Words Were Bullets: The Southern Press in War, Reconstruction, and Peace* (Athens: University of Georgia Press, 1969), Hodding Carter argued that the newspapers fought a virtual war that exacerbated the hostilities between North and South.

11. As quoted in Johnson, *Black Savannah*, 172; Richard D. Arnold to Harrison O. Briggs, Esq., 17 March 1865, in "The Arnold Letters," *Historical Papers*, 11.

12. "Late Rebel Papers: A Variety of Interesting Extracts: Two Gladiators," *Savannah Daily Herald*, 17 January 1865; Arnold to Harrison O. Briggs, Esq., in "The Arnold Letters," *Historical Papers*, 126–27; "Resources of the South," *Savannah Republican*, 4 January 1865. Arnold believed that "[w]here resistance is hopeless, it is criminal to make it," and that his "course, officially and personally, was taken with due deliberation"; Arnold to Briggs and Henry D. Hyde, 13 April 1865, in "The Arnold Letters," *Historical Papers*, 119.

13. "Meeting of the Freedmen," *Savannah Republican*, 5 February 1865; "The Result of Insolence," *Savannah Republican*, 16 January 1865; *Savannah Republican*, 9 January 1865; "A Grand Gala Night!" *Savannah Republican*, 14 January 1865; "Metropolitan Minstrels! . . . A Select Troupe of Original Burlesque Nigger Delineators," *Savannah Republican*, 15 January 1865; "Sherman on the Slavery Question," *Savannah Republican*, 16 January 1865; "Salutory," *Savannah Republican*, 29 December 1864; "What the War Has Done," *Savannah Republican*, 4 January 1865.

14. Fenian, "The Patriot Dead," *Savannah Republican*, 3 January 1865; "Reconstruction and Unionism in Georgia," *Savannah Daily Herald*, 12 January 1865; Leferve, "General Sherman's Levee," *Savannah Republican*, 9 January 1865.

15. "The Freedman's Meeting in Savannah," *Savannah Republican*, 5 February 1865.

16. Arnold to W. H. Baldwin, Esq., 8 February 1865, in "The Arnold Letters," *Historical Papers*, 113; Duncan, *Freedom's Shore*, 36. Campbell ran the community he established like a city, complete with constitution and a variety of democratically elected public offices.

17. Currie-McDaniel, *Carpetbagger of Conscience*, 50, 67, 71. In *White Land, Black Labor: Caste and Class in Late Nineteenth-Century Georgia* (Baton Rouge: Louisiana State University Press, 1983), Charles L. Flynn thought that black men's labor remained the crucial problem for Georgia because white planters were more concerned with maintaining the caste system than with prosperity. For a slightly different interpretation, see Joseph P. Reidy, *From Slavery to Agrarian Capitalism in the Cotton Plantation South: Central Georgia, 1800–1880* (Chapel Hill: University of North Carolina Press, 1992).

18. "The Election for Convention," *Savannah Weekly Republican*, 28 September 1867; "A Conservative Meeting in Raleigh," *Savannah Republican*, 5 October 1867. Although Hodding Carter judged the *Savannah Republican* one of the two "reputable, unselfish, and honest" newspapers of the period, it was like many newspapers in the

South: while its editors claimed to be "Republican" they were in fact violently anti-Republican and steadfastly Democrat (Carter, *Their Words Were Bullets,* 45).

19. "The Freedom of Colored Soldiers' Families," *Savannah Daily Herald,* 16 January 1865; "Credible and Gratifying," *Savannah Weekly Republican,* 5 October 1867; "The Election for Convention," *Savannah Weekly Republican,* 28 September 1867; "A Sobering Effect," *Savannah Weekly Republican,* 26 October 1867. In *The Tragic Era* (Cambridge, Mass.: Houghton Mifflin, 1929), Claude G. Bowers referred to Bryant as "a glib, subtle Uriah Heep" (302).

20. "From Washington" and "Trying to Force Negroes into Sleeping Cars with White Men," *Savannah Weekly Republican,* 19 October 1867. Newspapers also devoted a good deal of space to closing ranks between workers and the men who employed them. See "Manufacturers and Workmen in Massachusetts" and "The Working People," *Savannah Weekly Republican,* 11 January 1868.

21. See, for example, "Letter from Bishop Remy," "The Crow Indians," or "From Kansas," *Savannah Weekly Republican,* 21 September 1867; "From Washington" and "From the West," *Savannah Weekly Republican,* 28 September 1867. When it could be used as evidence of how corrupt the national (Radical) government was, the plight of Native Americans became a sympathetic cause. See, for example, "Winter in the Indian Country," *Savannah Weekly Republican,* 14 March 1868; "Suffering Among Indians," *Savannah Weekly Republican,* 28 March 1868.

22. "Conservative Meeting at Firemen's Hall," *Savannah Weekly Republican,* 11 January 1868. For his feelings about the newspapers' constructions of northern attitudes, see Arnold to Briggs, 6 September 1865; Arnold to Dr. George T. Elliot Jr., 28 September 1865; Arnold to Dr. Henry M. Fuller, 28 March 1868, in "The Arnold Letters," *Historical Papers,* 126–29, 138. He also personally confronted prejudice; see Arnold to Dr. J. G. Robertson, 29 July 1865, in "The Arnold Letters," *Historical Papers,* 123. Arnold's struggle is more easily understood by comparison to a more prominent Democrat of the period, Joseph E. Brown, whose switch from Democrat to Republican (and back again) made him the target of Republican and Democrat vitriol (Derrell C. Roberts, *Joseph E. Brown and the Politics of Reconstruction* [Tuscaloosa: University of Alabama Press, 1973]).

23. "Alabama's Probable Redemption," *Savannah Weekly Republican;* "The Georgia Radical Convention," *Savannah Weekly Republican,* both 15 February 1868.

24. "More Misery and Mischief," *Savannah Weekly Republican,* 21 September 1867; "We Find to Our Great Astonishment . . . ," *Savannah Weekly Republican,* 11 January 1868; "Speech of Hon. Henry S. Fitch," *Savannah Weekly Republican,* 28 March 1868; "A Confiscation-Homestead Pow-Wow!" *Savannah Weekly Republican,* 5 October 1867. Du Bois claimed that Bradley, along with Campbell and Turner, were "among the most capable colored members" of the constitutional convention; *Black Reconstruction,* 498. There is little historical evidence of who Bradley was. The *Savannah Weekly Republican* called him a "shoemaker by trade . . . [who] also practiced law"; "The Georgia Radical Convention," *Savannah Weekly Republican,* 15 February 1868.

25. "An Emphatic Veto of the Clift and Bradley Programme," *Savannah Weekly Republican*, 21 September 1867; "A Most Infamous Outrage," *Savannah Weekly Republican*, 19 October 1867. The *New York Times* article was reported in "Demagogues at the South," *Savannah Weekly Republican*, 26 October 1867. The separation of "respectable" African Americans from Radicals was underscored by a longstanding black racial hierarchy in which "mulattos" were perceived by both African Americans and whites as superior. Eric Foner noted that free African Americans were frequently reluctant to involve themselves with freedmen (a circumstance that Turner found alarming) (*Reconstruction*, 100–101). The newspapers reinforced the idea that giving African American men political power indiscriminately was a recipe for calamity by focusing on black men who raped, murdered, robbed, burgled, set fires, and refused to work.

26. "The Georgia Radical Convention," *Savannah Weekly Republican*, 15 February 1868.

27. "Washington," *Savannah Weekly Republican*, 15 February 1868; "The Lincoln Monument," *Savannah Weekly Republican*, 15 February 1868. The proposed Lincoln Monument sparked a vigorous public debate that was in essence a debate about African American masculinity; see Kirk Savage, "'Freedom's Memorial': Manumission and Black Masculinity in a Monument to Lincoln," in *Race and the Reproduction of Modern American Nationalism*, ed. Reynolds J. Scott-Childress (New York: Garland, 1999), 21–42.

28. *Savannah Daily Republican*, 3 February 1870; "The Georgia Radical Convention," *Savannah Weekly Republican*, 29 February 1868; "Reconstruction and Miscegenation at Atlanta," *Savannah Weekly Republican*, 1 February 1868. James Roark quoted one southern woman who thought that "Southern women would have their revenge when Northern soldiers took the 'bitter cup' of miscegenation back home"; *Masters without Slaves*, 97.

29. "Georgia Radical Convention," *Savannah Weekly Republican*, 15 February 1868. White men's rape, sexual assault, and sexual coercion of enslaved and later freed African American women were as explosive issues for African American men as miscegenation was for white men. When the *Colored Tribune*, Savannah's only black newspaper, began publication in 1876, its editors were merciless in that regard; see *Colored Tribune* (Savannah, Ga.), 15 January 1876; "Rather Be a Negro Than a Poor White (Wo)Man," *Colored Tribune*, 19 January 1876.

30. Currie-McDaniel, *Carpetbagger of Conscience*, 94; Henry Turner, "I Claim the Rights of Man," in *Lift Every Voice*, 475–83; Duncan, *Freedom's Shore*, 54.

31. Quote from Currie-McDaniel, *Carpetbagger of Conscience*, 122. Although Craig Friend's article on Cyrus Stuart is about one particular young man in the antebellum South, it describes perfectly the uncomfortable position most men were in with regard to their status because "genteel stratifications" in the hierarchies of manhood were all but insurmountable; see Friend, "Belles, Benefactors, and the Blacksmith's Son: Cyrus Stuart and the Enigma of Southern Gentlemanliness," in Friend and Glover, eds., *Southern Manhood*, 92–112. "Self-made" men increasingly made even

men who had inherited wealth and status insecure in their ranking at the top because the competition for high(est) status never stopped.

32. "A Politico-Religionist," *Savannah Morning News*, 23 February 1872; "The Battle of the Grand Faction," *Savannah Morning News*, 17 July 1872; "The State Election," *Savannah Morning News*, 3 October 1872; "Completion of St. Philip's (colored) Church—Religious Jubilee," *Savannah Morning News*, 11 June 1874. The fact that the article directly below his letter ("Off for the Penitentiary") was about convicts "(all negro)" who were being sent off to the penitentiary for crimes ranging from rape to attempted murder to burglary can scarcely have escaped Turner's notice, and was no doubt a reminder that the *News* was more likely to figuratively slap him down than they were to be "kind."

33. "The Proposed Negro Exodus," *Savannah Morning News*, 16 October 1875; "The American Colonization Society—Letter from Dr. H. M. Turner," *Colored Tribune*, 19 February 1876; "Letter from Dr. Turner," *Colored Tribune*, 18 March 1876. The *Tribune* was in fact critical of his colonization plan. For examples of colonizationist ideology, see Leonard Sweet, *Black Images of America, 1784–1870* (New York: Norton, 1976).

34. "The American Colonization Society Again," *Colored Tribune*, 26 February 1876; Robert E. Perdue, *The Negro in Savannah, 1865–1900* (New York: Exposition Press, 1973), 93; "Hard Times," *Savannah Tribune* (the editors changed the name from *Colored Tribune* to *Savannah Tribune* "for reasons that are perfectly satisfactory to ourselves but unnecessary to be now stated" on July 29), 2 September 1876; "Equal Rights at the South," *Savannah Times*, 11 November 1876; "The Legislature," *Colored Tribune*, 15 January 1876; "Our Position, and Our Duty," *Colored Tribune*, 1 January 1876; "Editor Tribune," *Colored Tribune*, 29 April 1876; "Briefs," *Colored Tribune*, 15 January 1876. They also spent significant space on how women should behave and were not in favor of women's suffrage; see, for example, "A Wife's Power," *Colored Tribune*, 15 January 1876; "Brooklyn Tabernacle," *Colored Tribune*, 18 March 1876.

35. Arnold to the Editor of the World, 25 June 1872, in "The Arnold Letters," *Historical Papers*, 156; "Democratic Meeting," *Savannah Morning News*, 3 September 1872; "Champagne Baths," *Savannah Daily Republican*, 30 January 1870. President Andrew Johnson's impeachment and the presidential campaign of 1868 provided numerous opportunities for editors and reporters to expound on Republicans' lack of manliness; see "Sustaining the President" and "Impeachment," *Savannah Weekly Republican*, 7 March 1868. Anthony Rotundo argued that by the mid-nineteenth century, "aggression, deceit, competition, and a spirit of self-interest . . . were vital elements in the quest for the manly goal of power"; see *American Manhood*, 170. Kimmel has a particularly interesting discussion of corruption in the development of Jacksonian politics in "The Birth of the Self-Made Man," in *Manhood in America*, 13–42.

36. After Bryant's falling out with the Bullock faction in 1869, he was appointed postmaster in Augusta (where "half of his appointments went to blacks") but Bullock,

still governor, had him removed. He then started the *Georgia Republican* in Augusta as well as a YMCA for African Americans and the Mechanics and Laborers Association, and established a law practice (Currie-McDaniel, *Carpetbagger of Conscience,* 106). Foner argued that "for Republicans losing an office meant economic disaster" because they were so unpopular and, if northerners, distant from family and other networks of support (*Reconstruction,* 350).

37. Fragments of letter from August 1873, in Currie, ed., *Emma Spaulding Bryant,* 167. See also Shan Holt, "The Anatomy of a Marriage: Letters of Emma Spaulding Bryant, 1873," *Signs: Journal of Women in Culture and Society* 17 (autumn 1991): 187–204. Arnold's wife died prior to this period, and he never remarried. Turner's wife and children remained in Atlanta, and Campbell's wife and family were in Darien for most of this period. What the state of their relationships was and how it affected them remains to be discovered, though in his *Sufferings,* Campbell praised his wife for braving physical danger to come to his aid several times when he was in jail.

38. "Bryant's Waterloo" and "The Carpet-Bagger as Described by Senator Norwood," *Savannah Morning News,* 6 November 1874; *Savannah Daily Republican,* 9 February 1870. See also "Georgia at Washington," *Savannah Daily Republican,* 11 February 1870. The *News* peppered its pages with evidence of what could happen if a man did not control his wife and daughters, and was fervently against women's suffrage.

39. "Georgia Legislature," *Savannah Daily Republican,* 30 January 1870. In 1868, one of Bryant's close friends and law partner, Colonel C. C. Richardson—another white man from Maine and, like Bryant, a carpetbagger—was murdered by Captain E. M. Timony, secretary of the Georgia Union League; see "Georgia and Florida News," *Savannah Weekly Republican,* 15 February 1868. See also "The Georgia Radical Convention," *Savannah Weekly Republican,* 15 February 1868; Currie-McDaniel, *Carpetbagger of Conscience,* 86–87, 108.

40. "The Radical Glorification," *Savannah Morning News,* 3 October 1872. Because they were all living in Savannah by 1872 (Turner, Arnold, and Bryant resided within a five-block radius), politics frequently threw them—and Campbell—together. In 1874, when Campbell and Bryant were on opposite sides of the split in the Republican Party, they clashed several times at political rallies in Darien. At one such meeting, when Bryant "slandered Campbell, the crowd 'made a rush for the stand and smashed it to a hundred pieces. Bryant escaped the county with a mob [of Campbell's supporters] at his heels'" (Duncan, *Freedom's Shore,* 98).

41. Campbell, *Sufferings of the Rev. T. G. Campbell,* 9; Duncan, *Freedom's Shore,* 89, 104.

42. "Shall We Have a New Conflict with the Mormons?" *Savannah Daily Republican,* 3 February 1870; "Outrage by a Negro Register," *Savannah Weekly Republican,* 12 October 1867. The Savannah newspapers often claimed that the Ku Klux Klan was an African American and Radical organization.

Although dueling appeared prominently in papers early in Reconstruction, and editors were inclined to praise participants for being "plucky," by 1870 they emphasized "gentlemen's" self-restraint and inferred disapproval for men who could not restrain themselves; see "Duel Near Augusta," *Savannah Weekly Republican*, 21 March 1868; "Hunting a Fight and Finding It," *Savannah Daily Republican*, 2 February 1870.

43. Duncan, *Freedom's Shore*, 84, 85–86. When the Georgia Senate Committee on Privileges found Campbell (a state senator at the time) "guilty of using disrespectful and slanderous language towards the Senate . . . [and] trying to excite an insurrectionary spirit among the people of his district," in August 1872, senators refrained from taking any action at all to discipline Campbell, possibly, as Duncan argued in *Freedom's Shore*, because they feared he would draw federal troops down on Georgia yet again (Duncan, *Freedom's Shore*, 93).

44. Duncan, *Freedom's Shore*, 90–91, 95, 100–107.

45. "Superior Court," *Savannah Morning News*, 15 November 1875; "The State and Federal Courts," *Savannah Morning News*, 29 November 1875; "The Conflict between Federal and State Authorities," *Savannah Morning News*, 12 January 1876. Thompkins was openly hostile to African Americans and bent on getting rid of Campbell, who had just won a seat in the Georgia House. For full details see Duncan, *Freedom's Shore*, 99–107.

46. "The Sacrifice of Custer," "Death of Hon. Richard D. Arnold," "Special Report of the City Council," and "A Villainous Outrage," all in *Savannah Morning News*, 11 July 1876.

47. Arnold to Dr. Meredith Clymer, New York, 11 October 1871; Arnold to Miss Mattie K. Tracy, Boston, Mass., 16 July 1875, both in "The Arnold Letters," *Historical Papers*, 156, 164.

48. "Trouble in the Buzzard Roost," *Savannah Morning News*, 24 November 1876. After the competition for congressional nomination in 1876, Atkins tried to have Bryant removed from his position as deputy collector of the Customs House (Bryant "reciprocated by asking President Grant to remove Atkins"), and withheld his pay (Currie-McDaniel, *Carpetbagger of Conscience*, 141–42).

49. Turner, "How Long?" in *Lift Every Voice*, 579–80. Turner's use of the term "Hottentots," like much of his language, was deliberately provocative. When eighteenth-century Dutch explorers first encountered the Khoikhoi people in South Africa, they called them Hottentots, and the term came to represent to Europeans the lowest form of human development.

50. "Shocking," *Colored Tribune*, 22 January 1876. Campbell became a model prisoner and head of the "wheelwright and blacksmith's shops" for Colonel Smith; was released in 1877; and moved to Washington, D.C, where, calling Georgia "the Empire of Rascality," he tried to persuade people to aid African Americans in Georgia.

The Price of Eternal Honor: Independent White Christian Manhood in the Late Nineteenth-Century South

Joe Creech

It is easy to imagine American evangelical Christianity and the ideals of southern manhood in opposition. Nineteenth-century evangelicalism, in the North and the South, has typically been portrayed as women's domain: women were more in attendance at congregational activities, and pastors bent over backward to accommodate theological ideals to feminine sentimentality even as the culture at large considered women more naturally inclined to spiritual and moral matters than men. Men, in contrast, and especially in the South, were beholden to a code of honor that, among other things, encouraged violence—martial, retributive, or vigilant—gambling, blood sports, sowing wild oats, hunting, and, especially by the early twentieth century, organized sports. When it came to church and men in the nineteenth century, we might imagine that never the two did meet.

But meet they did, and late nineteenth-century southern evangelicals—or most southern religious folk—understood manhood and evangelical piety to be tightly connected, especially in articulating the relationship of men to God, to families or other dependents, and to society at large. In connecting piety, violence, and family, nineteenth-century southerners frequently emphasized the way true men were divinely appointed protectors of property, life, society, religion, morality, and, perhaps most importantly, independence, and they emphasized as well that such a role often involved vigilance or even violence.

For example, to justify the resort to arms in 1861, one minister cast martial violence as a proper response to the northern aggression that threatened southern house and home. "In this unhappy war," he wrote, "we find on our side no compromise of Christian principle." He continued:

The South has accepted it as a last necessity—an alternative in which there was no choice but submission to a dynasty considered oppressive, and in its very principles antagonistic to her rights and subversive of her existence. Hence, her sons, who are true Christians, have no compunctions of conscience when they go forth in her armies. They find, on the contrary, an approbation of conscience in their decision to fight for homes and altars. "In the name of our God we set up our banners." We go to meet the invaders "in the name of the Lord of hosts."[1]

Even when such violence was metaphorical, southerners again often connected God—or more precisely God's providence, plans, commands, or moral governance—to martial imagery and manhood. A member of the Farmers' Alliance in the 1880s and 1890s (a farmers' union and precursor of the Populist movement) feared that economic and political forces threatened, like the armies of McClellan or Grant, the sanctity of his rural livelihood. Casting his struggles as part of a sacred drama, he wrote that the

> very men who have since the dawn of history, defended manfully and bravely their country . . . are incited to action in order to save their country from eternal damnation and destruction of the money lord and money devil. They are being stripped of all their God-given liberties and unless resistance is offered we fear the triumph of the plutocrat and money-monger. Let all be men and stand up for their rights. Be manly; be brave; be honest, and fight to overthrow the powers that now harass and oppress the great multitude of people in this country.[2]

The quotation suggests a critical connection between manly piety and violence. Although numerous scholars have identified important components of southern masculinity or manhood that no doubt connect to vigilance—honor, paternalism, mastery—there seems also to be a discourse of independence connecting piety and this metaphorical call to arms. Drawing on cultural resources including evangelical theology, republican political thought, and memories (manufactured or real) of southern resistance during the Civil War, nineteenth-century southerners believed that men were true or manly only if they were wholly free to *think* and *act* independently and that preserving or protecting such independence, which extended from self to family and society, required vigilance. Reflecting on his memories of the Civil War, another Confederate minister expressed such a discourse on independence like this:

> The attempt to coerce the South into submission, after the right of self-government had been asserted in the most solemn and authoritative forms, was felt to be a war of invasion, and the determination to resist was deep and almost universal. The strong feelings of religion and patriotism were evoked at the same moment, and by the same act, and men entered the ranks under the conviction that

in doing so they were faithful alike to God and their country. This we must bear in mind, or we shall not be prepared for that pervasive spiritual influence which so eminently marked the Southern armies.[3]

The idea of masculine independence was on some level religious because southerners, most of whom were in some way religious if not evangelical, adhered to a moral philosophy rooted in the idea that humans were free moral and spiritual agents who, having discerned the good that conformed to God's will and plan, had to act freely in accord with the good to be themselves upright instruments in creating and sustaining a good and just society. Because piety or ethics therefore involved moral freedom, humans could also act *against* the good; they could make bad decisions, the consequences of which damned not only the man in question but his familial, social, economic, and political realms of influence.

On a personal level, then, being good meant being vigilant. It involved moral and intellectual development so that as one matured one gained "backbone"—a conscience so well tooled in spiritual, intellectual, and moral truth that it could guide one to make right decisions. Similarly, in the white southern Christian family, the male, along with the true Christian woman, had to protect the family against any encroachments, be they spiritual, intellectual, economic, or physical. At the public level, moral governance connected to economic and political governance, requiring free moral agency in the form of white male participants who could act in accord with God's truth to provide laws and executive or judicial decisions that extended the rule of God and, therefore, ensured economic and political progress and stability. Hence, men in public roles had first to attain individual backbone through moral, spiritual, and intellectual independence in order to act as agents or representatives in human governance or in human economic structures. In this way, God could govern the political and economic realm through God's male moral agents.

Just as individual moral agency involved vigilance, so did the expression of truth, morality, or the way things were to be in the public sphere. The Alliance farmer's insistence that men in public be "manly" meant that they "be brave; be honest, and fight to overthrow the powers that now harass and oppress the great multitude of people in this country." Insistence on both free moral agency and God's governance, both of which are religious in essence, provided a critical connection between vigilance (and in extreme cases, violence) and what southerners meant by true *Christian* manhood. Connecting independence and manhood became a significant cultural logic (in Geertzian terms) in the nineteenth-century South that still reverberates in the region.

Historians such as Gail Bederman, Glenda Gilmore, Bertram Wyatt-Brown,

Kristen Hoganson, and Stephen Kantrowitz have shown how southern men in this period valued honor, martial qualities, and chivalry—conceptions evident in martial references like those quoted above. These historians have related how true southern men, besides enjoying hunting, gambling, or carousing, protected dependents by exercising "mastery" over women, children, and African Americans, consequently reinforcing oppressive paternalistic relationships of power and undergirding white supremacy.[4] Nevertheless, these interpretations, while certainly helpful, come up a bit short considering the ways southern evangelicals thought about manhood. While enjoying a good day of squirrel hunting and certainly valuing courage and honor, many southerners—especially evangelical ones—were also skeptical about southern codes of martial prowess, and many of them derided blood sports, gambling, football, boxing, and general carousing. In fact, many southerners considered church leadership, theological prowess, and an active prayer life the grounding for true manhood.[5]

Though there has been surprisingly little scholarship on manliness before the nineteenth century, at least two models of American manhood were present nationwide at the eve of the Civil War. The first, drawing on Puritan and Enlightenment ideas, stressed the degree to which manhood was marked by self-control—that is, control over one's passions such that reason or conscience, rather than the lower primitive or animal drives, moved one to action. In other words, a true man practiced genteel restraint. A variant might be called "republican manhood," or the idea that men who govern the nation must promote laws that benefit the entire nation, not the interests of a single person or group.[6]

The second model of true manhood, linked to the market revolution that was in full swing by the 1840s and 1850s, was the "self-made man." Like the genteel man, the self-made man practiced Franklinesque discipline—long hours at work, scrupulous saving, and so on, though, in contrast to the man of genteel restraint, the self-made man did not so much stifle but rather harnessed and utilized self-interest in order to create and attain wealth. Moreover, the self-made man was in step with the egalitarian ideals of the period: anyone with the proper gumption and discipline could attain manhood. A variant of the "self-made man" was the farmer and artisan notion that true men were those who produced wealth by their own labor as opposed to dandy nonproducers who merely manipulated nontangible markets or processes.[7]

After the Civil War, there emerged a third model of manhood that took shape around the 1890s—the ideal of "masculinity" or rugged, primitive manliness. As opposed to older models of manhood that in one way or another stressed restraint of the nonrational elements of the human psyche, champions of masculinity such as Teddy Roosevelt and G. Stanley Hall worried that the soft life of cities, white-collar labor, and a feminized literary and religious culture—not to mention the challenges of the "new woman"—were emasculating men. As a result, men were weak, flabby, given to effeminacy, and subject to neurasthenia. Fighting these feminizing influences required the development of body and mind: the body should be exercised to exhibit maximum physical prowess; the mind and soul should channel the more "primitive" components of the psyche through hunting, sports, and other forms of male dominance. Scholars such as Kristin Hoganson have also linked the new emphasis on masculinity to the martial, imperialist, and even jingoist spirit that characterized America between the late 1890s and the First World War. Others, too, have linked it to the propagation of fraternal groups, the Boy Scouts, organized—especially college—sports, and an artistic fascination with men's bodies.[8]

Traveling back south of the Mason-Dixon Line, in connecting masculinity and southern identity, scholars have gravitated toward two rather loosely connected paradigms of white southern manhood—one connected to honor, another connected to mastery, and both of which were tied to southern paternalism. Bertram Wyatt-Brown has identified and explained the way southern men adhered to a code of honor, meaning, in brief, an almost primal urge for revenge connected to a deep sense that one's own merit and personal integrity were tied to the way one was perceived in the public (meaning both public in the broad sense and in one's immediate family). Wyatt-Brown and other scholars have noted how this code of honor became entrenched in the South largely because white southerners retained an older, agrarian mode of life in contrast to the market revolution expanding in the higher latitudes of the United States. Honor manifested itself in the antebellum South in a variety of ways: duels, sporting contests, and rituals of public humiliation or celebration, along with southern legal conventions, political ideals, and ultimately Confederate nationalism (the idea that the election of Lincoln and later "northern aggression" were affronts to southern honor). This ideal connected also to the southern martial ideal as well as to southern paternalism as men were only manly if they protected, with violence if necessary, not only their reputations from reproach but the safety, reputation, and security of their household dependents—an outlook often referred to by scholars and southerners at the time as "chivalry."[9]

While a number of scholars and even Wyatt-Brown himself have, over the years, modified certain aspects of southern honor (noting, for example, that it was most strong in the coastal/plantation regions and manifested itself quite differently, if even at all, in the piedmont and mountain South), it certainly was a feature of southern white male identity. Yet Christian men not only attempted to maintain honor before their peers but also stressed the need to maintain honor before God—a deity, of course, as real to them as their flesh-and-blood neighbors. Honoring God, it turns out, involved a number of pietistic characteristics, such as having a passionate life of prayer and devotion, having a commitment to attaining intellectual and especially theological or doctrinal prowess, defending one's inner life and by extension one's family from threats both spiritual and physical, and spreading the gospel with the aim of converting others. Christian southern men thought of these last factors in martial terms as a form of "spiritual warfare."[10]

Mastery, which like honor has been tied to paternalism, corresponded to the idea that, as white male identity developed in the slave South, manhood more diabolically involved not just care of but mastery over women, children, and especially slaves and African Americans. As one scholar succinctly notes, "The denial of black manhood was central to white manhood." While mastery during the antebellum period certainly involved managing wife and children, this racially charged image of mastery manifested in the planter class most viscerally through the sexual and violent subjugation of slaves. After the war, it found expression in public suppression of African Americans through segregation, disfranchisement, and violence. Like honor, the ideal of mastery, as expressed through the idea of Herrenvolk democracy, helped forge Confederate nationalism and later southern identity as white men, great and small, saw themselves as masters of their own domains, and this mastery involved the "denial of black manhood." As historian Donald Mathews has written of late, mastery was perhaps most frighteningly exemplified in the blood rituals of lynching.[11]

Almost all of the aforementioned authors have assumed that, by the 1850s, the predominant religious paradigm of nineteenth-century American evangelical Protestantism was a female domain. Drawing on the long-popular but problematic ideas of Ann Douglas, most figured that the evangelicalism of the eighteenth century, with its Calvinist stress on damnation, sin, and the need for complete regeneration, gave way to an evangelicalism that stressed a feminized belief in Christian nurture. As canonized in the theology of Horace Bushnell, Catherine Beecher, and others, evangelicals by the 1850s (in Douglas's telling) envisioned the church not as a fire purging the damned from sin but as a nursery. The reason for this shift might, as Douglas suggested, have been tied to the predominance of women church members who possibly pressed their pastors to mitigate some of the harsher doctrines of evangelical Protestantism. Regardless of how it came about or even whether it came about, scholars have typically positioned the ideals of the "self-made man," southern honor, and especially late nineteenth-century masculinity in opposition to such feminized religion. To be manly, in other words, meant eschewing or modifying the predominant strains of American evangelicalism.[12]

If we accept this narrative of feminization, then one attempt to modify American Protestantism was the emergence of "muscular Christianity." Even though its most important propagators—social gospelers like Washington Gladden, Josiah Strong, and Lyman Abbot—preached the virtues of muscular Christianity in the late nineteenth and early twentieth centuries, the roots of the idea go back before the Civil War. Responding to the perception that religion was becoming a female domain, New England elites began channeling the writings of Thomas Hughes and Charles Kingsley in England (who were fighting the "effeminizing" influences of the Oxford Movement in the Anglican church) who argued that true Christian men should exercise their bodies as well as their souls in order to advance the kingdom of God overseas or against Catholics and other heretics at home. This idea was an affront to the older notion that participating in leisure activities was mundane and even a sinful use of one's valuable time. In proclaiming such a "muscular Christian" ideal, then, by the late nineteenth-century groups like the YMCA and the Men and Religion Forward Movement urged men to develop themselves through exercise and sport. In staving off the feminine influences over themselves and the church, they would be aggressive and effective ambassadors for Christianity throughout the nation and world.[13]

In connecting religion and manliness in the South, most scholars have combined the aforementioned stresses on mastery and honor with the idea that the church was the domain of women. Historian Ted Ownby, for example, argued that southern evangelical men's obsession with blood sport, revelry, and hunting were escapes from the drudgery of feminized piety. But was evangelical piety in the South actually and always opposed to white conceptions of true manhood? While there is little doubt, especially among the elites, that the ideals of honor and especially mastery weighed heavily on the way white southern evangelical men understood themselves as men, there existed another model of true Christian manhood that stressed moral, spiritual, economic, and political independence. While often touching on honor and more often on ideas of mastery, the ideal did not envision evangelical religion as inherently hostile to manhood. In fact, it drew deeply on certain evangelical theological ideals to assert that the only men worthy of the appellation "true" were deeply religious, and this ideal in turn provided a cultural logic or connection between intense piety and violence.[14]

So, then, how did evangelical southerners connect manhood to intellectual, religious, and moral independence, and how did those ideals connect further to metaphorical and actual violence? Although not all southerners, or even southern Christians, would have considered themselves evangelicals, this brand of Protestantism held deep cultural and intellectual sway in the South. Evangelicals are best differentiated from other Protestants by their stress on an individual and experientially assured conversion or spiritual "rebirth." Although southern evangelicals often supported a conservative social outlook and reinforced boundaries of class, race, and gender, their emphasis on individual rebirth led southern evangelicals to also stress the role of individual consent in conversion and the right of individuals to hold their own theological views, to read the Bible for themselves, and to come to their own conclusions on particular ethical dilemmas. In 1889, Rev. Thomas Dixon Jr. stated, for example, that "I believe in religious liberty—the right of every man to worship God according to the dictates of his conscience." Another Baptist noted that "Baptist faith leads to 'Independence.' . . . The Baptist reads the Bible for himself and teaches his children to do likewise."[15]

Politically speaking, evangelical emphasis on individual choice also undergirded many southerners' belief in the verity of participatory democracy. Such evangelicals considered the "voice of the people" to have been "the voice of God." In other words, they believed that people like themselves were the conduits through which God governed the affairs of humans through set and immutable principles or laws. Looking again at the Populists, one evangelical Alliance leader, in justifying his departure from the Democratic Party, which he considered an affront to his individual liberty, referred to his fellow Populists as "the same men who were chosen by Christ to give to the world the grand truths of Christianity; the same men that stood by Luther in the Reformatory," and the same who "stood by Washington from Bunker Hill to Yorktown" and "who followed Lee and Grant, Jackson and Hancock and so often bore their burdens to victory." He added, "Yes these are the men, the common people. . . . They have crossed the Rubicon, the die is cast and with the great cry of all freemen 'vox populi; vox Dei.'"[16]

As the evangelical Alliance man would have seen it, human beings, like his fellow farmers, were a part of God's moral governance—which implied economic and political governance—only insofar as they embodied God's eternal principles. For human beings, the embodiment of these ideals began at conversion and grew as one reached true Christian manhood (and womanhood). An individual conscience, freed from spiritual, intellectual, or physical coercion, enabled such principles to be embodied; as Christians obeyed their consciences, they embodied and thus participated in God's governance, or agency. To be a true Christian or to experience Christian manhood thus meant exhibiting a fully integrated belief system rooted in an independent conscience—in other words, having the "backbone" or "courage" to act in accordance with one's conscience, one's internalized, eternal principles.[17]

For true southern white evangelical men, acting upon independent conscience meant honoring God and protecting one's own soul, family, and society from spiritual threat (which could and did manifest in physical forms ranging from Billy Yank to "black male brutes"). More precisely, Christian men honored God, family, and society by being brave enough to stand for the truth of the gospel in a world of infidelity and sin, to face the arrows of Satan in the form of vice and temptation, and knowledgeable enough in the things of God to evangelize, to lead prayer meetings, church services, and family devotions, to exhibit egalitarian love for fellow humans, and, as one Baptist put it, "above all and in all, [to] show his religion boldly." Methodists expressed their conception of true manhood in this obituary of one Rev. Joseph Wheeler, a North Carolina Methodist minister:

> As a man he was the highest type of a Christian gentleman. . . . He had a mind superior to fear, selfish interest and corruption, which no outward circumstances could conquer, no vacillating multitude turn from its purpose of right, which no promise of ease or gain could cause for a moment to prove false to its deepest convictions of duty, and which no pleasure could melt into effeminacy, nor distraction sink into dejection. This is the mind which forms the distinction and eminence of men. We can conceive of no circumstances under which he would have been either afraid or ashamed to act his path with firmness and constancy. He was true to the God whom he worshiped, true to the faith in which he professed to believe. He was full of affection to his brethren, faithful to his friends, and warm, with compassion, to the unfortunate.[18]

Honoring God through such devotion and piety also meant developing theological and intellectual abilities more generally, as these were marks that a man's conscience had been freed from the coercive influences of ignorance and heresy. Given that the development of intellectual independence and theological precision also involved martial images of spiritual warfare—that the word of God or adherence to the right theological constructions were the swords with which one battled the enemies of God—it is perhaps not surprising then that when southerners elevated men for their spiritual and intellectual acumen, they often thought first of figures from the Civil War (especially Lee, Jackson, and Leonidas Polk).

For example, in his much-read memoir, *Christ in the Camp,* J. W. Jones lionized one soldier who, in confronting an officer who was deriding religion, "modestly asked permission to say something in defense of Christianity." Noting how he "began in a low, conversational tone to answer all that had been said," Jones wrote that, "as he progressed he became more and more interested in the subject, until his whole soul was aroused, and quite a crowd had gathered around and were eagerly listening. The result was that the [offensive] officer was astonished and silenced, and they who had not previously known the speaker were inquiring who the little fellow was that had made such a defense of Christianity." According to Jones, this "incident illustrates not only his moral and religious character, but also that of his mind . . . In him the mental and the moral were happily blended. The quick and retentive memory, the correct judgment, the delicate taste, susceptible of the highest degree of refinement, all characteristic of his vigorous and grasping mind, were sweetly harmonized by the spirit of fervid but unpretentious piety of this Christian soldier—a 'champion of the Christian religious' who 'went bravely forth to the defense of his country' and 'fell in the forefront of the battle' . . . and this solider still 'rests in a land hallowed by his efforts in the cause of liberty.'"[19]

Likewise, prayer involving the passions—even to the point of tears—and compassionate kindness were also regarded as ways to honor God; in fact, Confederate officers such as Lee and Jackson were heralded for their passionate, tearful prayers and warm concern for their men. Passionate prayer and kindness marked the way such a man had not only gained mastery over his emotions (another enemy of an independent conscience) but could further channel those emotions—master them, if you will—so as to honor God. Regarding the death of the "gallant" Colonel W. S. H. Baylor, one southern soldier remembered that Baylor was "mourned not only by the company that had followed him so long, but by every soldier who knew him . . . as a Christian gentleman." He remarked further that "as a soldier and officer he was a model; to his company he was exceedingly kind," and yet even with such kindness, "in action he was perfectly fearless, yet his courage was controlled by a sound discretion. On such occasions he was possessed with a peculiar enthusiasm—an unconquerable zeal and determination to meet the foe—and consequently he was always seen among those gallant spirits who go farthest in the direction of the foe." He added that "such earnestness of disposition—such humility—such devotion to Christ's cause; not inducing noisy demonstrations, but those quiet, irresistible movements, which are like the silent flow of deep streams. How rare are such characters! I have never known one as young as he so faultless. His piety was active—a real living principle, whose movements and influences were seen and felt, not only by his fellow-Christians, but also by all who came in contact with him." Drawing on another mark of true Christian manhood, the writer noted that Colonel Baylor also strove "to secure the salvation of his company . . . and to compass this end he was much in prayer, and abounded in good works. As often as circumstances permitted, he distributed religious reading—tracts, newspapers, memoirs, etc.—among his company and sometimes in the regiment. It was also his custom, as occasion offered, to assemble his company nightly before the door of his tent for religious services."[20]

In addition to drawing on evangelical patterns of thought, southern men also tapped into Jeffersonian and producerist notions of manly independence as they asserted, for example, that farm life was the optimal place to develop such manly independence. This is a critical point, because freedom or independence of conscience implied economic independence. Before the war, this ideal helped knit ideas of independence to the slave economy both for planters and yeomen. But for non–slave holders or for southerners after the Civil War, economic independence continued to be wed to prewar producerist notions and Jeffersonian ideals to manly independence.

One southern farmer wrote: "There is one thing of which the farmer may possess which every man in any other avocation may well envy him, and that is his absolute independence." In typical southern rural fashion, the writer then mentioned how town living could stunt the growth of independence; merchants, for example, "were subject to the whims of consumers who may boycott; hence they are not free to be true to themselves." The "farmer, however," had "nothing of this kind of fear. He is absolutely his own master, and neither his religion, moral, political or social beliefs or misbeliefs may in any way be used to the injury of his prospects. He wears no man's collar." Thomas Dixon Jr. noted similarly the ways in which town life corrupted true manhood and womanhood: "The city of today is destroying the character and manhood of the nation. The modern city as at present constituted does not produce men and women capable of really fighting the battles of life." So-called city first churches similarly threatened Christian manhood, for in towns, paid pastors rather than local lay leaders preached on a weekly basis, led prayer and Bible study meetings, and generally took on the Christian responsibilities that should have been handled by other Christian men; such "hireling" ministers thus robbed city Christians of the means to develop Christian manhood.[21]

The problem with hireling ministers and dependent commercial types was that their freedom to think and act according to principle was limited by the "collars" of economic need. Along with such hirelings, other foils to southern white Christian gentlemen were, on the one hand, those who lacked the anchors of an integrated belief system and who were thus blown about by popular opinion or self-interest, and on the other hand, children, weak women, and African Americans who had yet to develop an independent conscience. This first category, which included Dixon's "hirelings" along with other "invertebrates," "effeminates," and "dandies," lacked, among other things, an inner moral compass that enabled them to follow God's principles. On the other side, children, weak-minded women, and African Americans required conversion and Christian education to induce such manhood and womanhood, but until they realized states of maturity, their mastery by manly men was required. Many evangelicals were confident, however, that with conversion and proper education, such folks could certainly come to constitute independent agents in God's governance (even though that independence would be practiced in different arenas).

One conservative white southern Presbyterian insisted that black ministers be educated so they would gain "independence" and thus be "both politically and ecclesiastically free as all others to serve God according to the dictates of their own consciences."[22]

Scholars have been correct, then, in connecting manhood—and by extension independent Christian manhood—to the care of dependents: the women, children, and servants of their immediate families. For white Christians, personal male independence bore with it the responsibility to care for those still dependent, such as the poor and African Americans in their midst, and for missionaries and evangelists, to care for the unsaved and heathen. Service to dependents usually meant providing economic sustenance, emotional support and care, physical protection, and spiritual guidance; serving the heathen meant dispensing the gospel. Tied to vigilance, it also meant protecting these dependents from spiritual or physical threat.

In "Truth and Freedom," Rev. Thomas Dixon Jr. explored this complex relationship between independence, Christianity, and "mastery" over others. To connect the two, Dixon reiterated his long-standing claim that human liberty, or freedom of conscience, is the heart of Christianity, noting that since "man only attains freedom as he attains it within," and since "man is free only as he knows the truth" and "cannot be bound either by institutions, kings or priests," that "the Christian is the only man who is really free," having the "liberty to do what he pleases" since "he always pleases to do what is right when he works within the circle of his Christian life" as he "partakes of God's own nature, becoming a law unto himself, the law of love having swallowed all the technicalities within this universal domain."[23]

Moving toward his main point—that such independence dovetailed with the responsibility to care for those who were in the sphere of one's dependents—Dixon linked independence to this law of love, asserting that "faith . . . embodies itself in a life of love—love to God, and love to God through love to man." By the end of the sermon, Dixon linked this love and independence to a code of behavior we could call mastery, but in doing so revealed some of the deep complexities of southern evangelicals' thinking about individual autonomy as it connected to dependents. For because personal independence was intricately tied to dependency, hierarchy, and relationships of power (including oppressive ones), independent manhood entailed caring for dependents as a form of mutual obligation, reciprocity, or even one step in a long chain of dependency running from God to animals, plants, and on down the great chain of being. For Dixon, to be spiritually "free" or independent therefore meant having to act independently within one's own place, which, for white males, meant on the one hand being dependent on God or Christ but on the other exercising care or responsibility over women, children, and on down the line. White men like Dixon certainly included African Americans in their sphere of dependents. Dixon ended his sermon as follows:

Love does bind, but with such chains: Golden chains! Lives are bound by the chains of love. I am a slave to my loved ones. I work for them. I account it gain to be able to be a slave. . . . Love does bind. Stanley lecturing to the world, making his fortune, receives a message from beyond the seas telling him of weakness and helplessness in the heart of darkest Africa. And his heart is so bound in love to the race that he drops his work and crosses the seas and goes into three long years of privation and want, and coming out of Africa's dark forest sends flashing around the world his message of faith and love. The priest who enters the colony of lepers and lays down his life for his fellow man is a slave, if love be slavery. The woman who lays her life upon the alter [sic] of love, unworthy of so much a sacrifice, may be called a slave.[24]

As Dixon suggested, protection of family extended outward to include protection of society politically, spiritually, and probably imperially. Southern men extended their responsibilities toward their family outward to society in managing its political and economic affairs. We can see how such patterns of deference and independence in the home served as a model for civil society in the mind of one southern evangelical, who argued that a democratic society should exhibit brotherly love or egalitarianism within an equal male electorate. This citizenry, however, was united in its common subjection to King Jesus, since each individual received instructions from and submitted to his Lord. The writer further condemned political or ecclesiastical coercion since it broke this ideal system down by replacing submission to Jesus with submission to a human lord. "The authority of Christ as the one Master in the midst of an equal brotherhood must extend," he wrote, "in its final radius, to every province of life, whether in Church or State. Christ is the great emancipator and the great equalizer; and he will continue the liberation of peoples and the overthrow of tyrannies until all the nations of the earth and all the churches of the kingdom of God have acknowledged his supremacy, and have entered into a world-wide fellowship of mutual service one to another, and of unquestioning loyalty to Christ."[25]

When tying these ideals to political action, southern evangelicals again drew on ideas of independence as they argued that only true Christian men who embodied the voice of God and had the independence of mind not to be swayed by party rhetoric or emotional whim were fit to vote, hold political office, and be proper conduits of God's governance. One Baptist put it like this: "A man's religion and politics should be of such a type and so well founded on principle and truths until they become a part of the man, he can practice and preach the same things." In other words, for southern evangelical men who entered the rough-and-tumble political world of the late nineteenth century, only white men who would not be compromised by bossism or bribery needed to apply (hence the general exclusion of women and, by force or other forms of coercion, African Americans).[26]

Rev. James I. Vance of Baltimore captured well this sentiment. In comparing Joseph of the Old Testament to Theodore Roosevelt (who was in Vance's view a true Christian man), he argued that Joseph introduced "an administration of affairs which would be economic, efficient and honest; to give to every laborer decent wages, and to every slave a message of hope." He argued that in elevating Joseph to a position of political power, God "inaugurated the reign of manhood . . . that saved the day. It always does. The lesson is especially pertinent to America, where every citizen is a part of the throne." Then Vance took to preaching the importance of independent manhood for the survival of American democracy in the face of the centralizing tendencies in government and economics:

> We need men more than new laws. We need honest manhood at the polls more than we do commercial prosperity. . . . [God] is concerned for good government. Christ came to establish a kingdom and his teachers powerfully affect social conditions. The ills of vicious and corrupt government are not all ancient history. They exist to-day and here in America. There are political abuses that need to be cured . . . the rights of the individual stolen. . . . Bad political conditions can be cured . . . by the reign of manhood, by paying the "price of eternal good citizenship." . . . The reign of manhood is not the reign of machine. We have had enough of political bosses. It is not the reign of intimidation where the honest convictions of the individual are strangled by powerful corporate interests. Nor is it the reign of money or any of the things for which money stands. . . . Independence and intelligence are the qualities which invest a man with the right to reign. . . . It is a good sign of the times that independence of opinion on political matters is on the increase. . . . We need to vote as we pray, to pray "God give us men," and then to help God answer our prayers. . . . When God's indignation against iniquity begins to flame in the public mind and conscience takes fire against sin, the good citizenship of any community will arise, and when it does it can always sweep into oblivion those who have dared defy the eternal forces of right and righteousness.[27]

While such calls to progressive activism drew on the cultural and religious constructions of manhood, Gilmore, Kantrowitz, Mathews, and others have shown that conceptions of males had other, darker political and social manifestations as well. Rubrics of honor or, perhaps more importantly, mastery, shaped whites' perceptions of African Americans as threats and also shaped the responses of segregation, disfranchisement, and racial violence.

Despite the multiple ways in which gender could manifest itself in southern society, basic models of male honor or mastery were not, as is often suggested or implied, in opposition to mainstream evangelical theological or social thought. Rather, evangelical thought supported, legitimated, and shaped the southern discourse on manhood and family as well as the social and political manifestations of that discourse. Moreover, the central connection between evangelical religion and gender discourse—one that undergirded the conceptions of honor and mastery—was the idea of independence. Men honored God by developing independent, educated, and righteous consciences and by actively engaging in spiritual warfare, and they further honored God by protecting their dependents from spiritual and physical threats to economic, political, and spiritual independence. Of course, this argument is hardly novel; Edmund Morgan argued years ago in *American Slavery, American Freedom* that independence and, for colonial southerners, African slavery were mutually dependent.

As improbable as it may seem, then, evangelicalism's theology and intellectual emphases provide a basic cultural logic that can and has, at times, connected piety and violence in the form of vigilance. Manhood was not easily obtained but had to be acquired through developing moral and intellectual independence. This development entailed battling against the enemies of independence, both metaphorical (sloth, ignorance, heresy, immorality) and physical (those who might attempt to place a collar around one's neck). But as we saw with Dixon, independence also implied protection or mastery, which demanded vigilance against metaphorical and physical threats to family, home, or, in the case of the Civil War, state. Dixon himself, after he became a white supremacist novelist with *The Leopard's Spots* (1902) and *The Clansman* (1905), wove these ideas together time and time again, as individuals and groups (the Ku Klux Klan) violently defended the Christian South and their families against the twin diabolical assaults of socialism and "black rapists." This is nowhere better seen than in *The Leopard's Spots*, when the main character urges his friends to fire their guns into a group of African American males who have abducted his daughter, knowing that the shots will, and did, kill his own daughter.[28]

Of course, not every pious exemplar of white Christian manhood would carry this violence as far as soldiers, lynch mobs, or Dixon. The cluster of psychological factors that prompt physical acts of violence certainly could not be "caused" solely by this or any other cultural logic. Nevertheless, the components of this outlook still inform evangelical or right-wing rhetoric about gun control, criminal law, national defense, and so on, just as it provided a framework for seeing one's Christian duty to enact violence against Yankees or other threats in the nineteenth century. At its core, this discourse suggests that there is not a fundamental contradiction between evangelical piety and true manhood, even male violence. For the independent Christian man, there has often been little contradiction among a call to fervent prayer, spiritual warfare, protecting one's own against the darts of Satan, and firing a handgun at an intruder in one's nation or home. In his mind, both are critical elements of his identity as a Christian man and echoed in this eulogy of Leonidas Polk, the Episcopal bishop of Louisiana and a Confederate general who fell in battle on 14 June 1864:

> Full of heroic purposes as he leaped into the arena of life . . . he has been made, by the overruling hand of God, to display that heroism in the fields which Christ his Master illustrated, teaching the ignorant, enlightening the blind, gathering together the lost sheep of Israel, comforting the bedside of sickness and affliction, watching long days and nights by the suffering slave. . . . He has always been a hero; and the bloody fields which have made him conspicuous are but the outburst of the spirit which has always distinguished him. Battles which he fought long since with himself and his kind; which he waged against the pomps and vanities of the world and the pride of life; which he contested with the pestilence that walketh in darkness and the destruction that wasteth at noonday—were far more terrific than Belmont, or Shiloh, or Perryville.[29]

NOTES

The author thanks Beth Schweiger, Donald Mathews, David D. Hall, Tracy Leavelle, and the members of the Young Scholars in American Religion, 2005–6, who read and commented on drafts of this paper. The responsibility for how he has used and interpreted their criticism, advice, and help is his alone.

1. William W. Bennett, *A Narrative of the Great Revival* (Philadelphia: Claxton, Remsen, and Haffelfinger, 1877), 92.
2. *Farmers' Advocate* (Tarboro, N.C.), 14 September 1892. Such references to masculinity in Alliance and Populist literature are numerous; see, for example, "Select True Men," in *Progressive Farmer* (Raleigh, N.C.), 29 July 1890.
3. Bennett, *Narrative of the Great Revival*, 87.
4. Stephen Kantrowitz, "Ben Tillman and Hendrix McLane, Agrarian Rebels: White Manhood, 'The Farmers,' and the Limits of Southern Populism," *Journal of Southern History* 46 (August 2000): 497–524; Kantrowitz, *Ben Tillman and the Reconstruction of White Supremacy* (Chapel Hill: University of North Carolina Press, 2000), 1–2; Glenda Gilmore, *Gender and Jim Crow* (Chapel Hill: University of North Carolina Press, 1996), especially chaps. 3–4; Gail Bederman, *Manliness and Civilization* (Chicago: University of Chicago Press, 1995); Kristin L. Hoganson, *Fighting for American Manhood* (New Haven, Conn.: Yale University Press, 1998); Bertram Wyatt-Brown, *Southern Honor* (New York: Oxford University Press, 1983); Wyatt-Brown, *Honor and Violence in the Old South* (New York: Oxford University Press, 1986); Wyatt-Brown, *The Shaping of Southern Culture* (Chapel Hill: University of North Carolina Press, 2001).

5. Certainly many of the ideas that characterized white manhood carried over to black conceptions of Christian manhood in the South as well, though with different power and hierarchical dynamics. See, for example, Edward E. Baptist, "The Absent Subject: African American Masculinity and Forced Migration to the Antebellum Plantation Frontier," in *Southern Manhood: Perspectives on Masculinity in the Old South*, ed. Craig Thompson Friend and Lorri Glover (Athens: University of Georgia Press, 2004), 136–73; Monica Najar, "Evangelizing the South: Gender, Race, and Politics in the Early Evangelical South, 1765–1815" (PhD diss., University of Wisconsin, 2000); Michele Mitchell, *Righteous Propagation: African Americans and the Politics of Racial Destiny after Reconstruction* (Chapel Hill: University of North Carolina Press, 2004); Martin Summers, *Manliness and Its Discontents: The Black Middle Class and the Transformation of Masculinity, 1900–1930* (Chapel Hill: University of North Carolina Press, 2004); Gilmore, *Gender and Jim Crow*, 80–83, 119–75; Hoganson, *Fighting for American Manhood*, 107–32; Eric Anderson, *Race and Politics in North Carolina, 1872–1901* (Baton Rouge: Louisiana State University Press, 1981), 296.

6. Bederman, *Manliness and Civilization;* Gilmore, *Gender and Jim Crow*, 61; Michael S. Kimmel, *Manhood in America* (New York: Free Press, 1996); Anthony Rotundo, *American Manhood: Transformations in Masculinity from the Revolution to the Modern Era* (New York: Basic Books, 1993). See also George L. Mosse, *The Image of Man: The Creation of Modern Masculinity* (New York: Oxford University Press, 1996); and the essays in *Meanings for Manhood: Constructions of Masculinity in Victorian America*, ed. Marc C. Carnes and Clyde Griffen (Chicago: University of Chicago Press, 1990).

7. Kimmel, *Manhood in America*, esp. 28–19; Rotundo, *American Manhood*, esp. 15–16.

8. Bederman, *Manliness and Civilization*, esp. 16–17; Hoganson, *Fighting for American Manhood*, esp. 10–11, 39, 200–208; Kimmel, *Manhood in America*, 83, 107–109, and chap. 4; Rotundo, *American Manhood;* John Kasson, *Houdini, Tarzan, and the Perfect Man: The White Male Body and the Challenge of Modernity in America* (New York: Hill and Wang, 2001); Clifford Putney, *Muscular Christianity: Manhood and Sports in Protestant America, 1880–1920* (Cambridge: Harvard University Press, 2001).

9. Wyatt-Brown, *Southern Honor;* Wyatt-Brown, *Honor and Violence in the Old South;* Wyatt-Brown, *Shaping of Southern Culture*. For a good overview of the two primary trajectories of honor and mastery, see Craig Thompson Friend and Lorri Glover, "Introduction," in Friend and Glover, eds., *Southern Manhood*, vii–xvii.

10. On honor, see Wyatt-Brown, *Southern Honor;* Wyatt-Brown, *Honor and Violence in the Old South;* Wyatt-Brown, *The Shaping of Southern Culture;* Kantrowitz, *Ben Tillman*, 120–22; Hoganson, *Fighting for American Manhood*, 16–37, 70; Friend and Glover, "Introduction," viii; Ted Ownby, *Subduing Satan* (Chapel Hill: University of North Carolina Press, 1990). For scholars who mitigate the prevalence of honor as the predominant paradigm for understanding southern manhood, see Gilmore, *Gender and Jim Crow*, 64–65, 255–56; Lorri Glover, "Let Us Manufacture Men," in Friend and Glover, eds., *Southern Manhood*, 42; Kurt O. Berends, "'Wholesome

Reading Purifies and Elevates the Man': The Religious and Military Press in the Confederacy," in *Religion and the American Civil War*, ed. Randall M. Miller, Harry S. Stout, and Charles Reagan Wilson (New York: Oxford University Press, 1998), 136, 158n14. On honoring God, see Bennett, *Narrative of the Great Revival*, 16.

11. Quotation from Baptist, "Absent Subject," 137. Also see Donald G. Mathews, "Lynching Is Part of the Religion of Our People: Faith in the Christian South," in *Religion in the American South: Protestants and Others in History and Culture*, ed. Beth Barton Schweiger and Donald Mathews (Chapel Hill: University of North Carolina Press, 2004), 153–94; Mathews, "The Southern Rite of Human Sacrifice," *Journal of Southern Religion* 3 (2000), http://jsr.fsu.edu/jsrlink3.htm. On mastery and paternalism, see especially Kantrowitz, "Ben Tillman and Hendrix McLane," 497–524; Kantrowitz, *Ben Tillman*, 1–9; Hoganson, *Fighting for American Manhood*, 3, 45, 156–79; Wyatt-Brown, *Honor and Violence in the Old South*, 59, 85–115; Friend and Glover, "Introduction," vii, xi; Bederman, *Manliness and Civilization*, 4, 5, 20; Gilmore, *Gender and Jim Crow;* Charles H. Lippy, *Do Real Men Pray? Images of the Christian Man and Male Spirituality in America* (Knoxville: University of Tennessee Press, 2005); Laura F. Edwards, *Gendered Strife and Confusion* (Urbana: University of Illinois Press, 1997); Stephanie McCurry, *Masters of Small World* (New York: Oxford University Press, 1995).

12. Ann Douglas, *The Feminization of American Culture* (New York: Doubleday, 1977). On Douglas, see Lippy, *Do Real Men Pray?* 9–12; Berends, "Wholesome Reading Purifies and Elevates the Man," 141; Putney, *Muscular Christianity*.

13. On muscular Christianity, see Tony Ladd and James A. Mathisen, *Muscular Christianity* (Grand Rapids: Baker, 1999); Gail Bederman, "'The Women Have Had Charge of the Church Work Long Enough': The Men and Religion Forward Movement of 1911–1912 and the Masculinization of Middle-Class Protestantism," *American Quarterly* 41 (1989): 432–65; Putney, *Muscular Christianity;* Lippy, *Do Real Men Pray?* 82–112; the essays in Donald E. Hall and Gillian Beer, eds., *Muscular Christianity: Embodying the Victorian Age* (New York: Cambridge University Press, 1994). For whatever reason, however, the muscular Christianity of the late nineteenth century had little to no impact in the South, perhaps because southerners did not face the pressures of urbanization and immigration that drove northern angst about masculinity; see, Ladd and Mathisen, *Muscular Christianity*, 23–24.

14. Ownby, *Subduing Satan*, 1–12. Also, Wyatt-Brown, *Honor and Violence in the Old South*, 24, 51–55, 83, who follows Douglas's assumptions.

15. Thomas Dixon Jr., *Living Problems in Religion and Social Science* (New York: Charles T. Dillingham, 1889), 189; *The North Carolina Baptist* (Fayetteville, N.C.), 17 February 1892.

16. *Farmers' Advocate*, 30 March 1892. On *Vox Populi, Vox Dei*, see *Hickory Mercury* (Hickory, N.C.), 2 December 1891; *Biblical Recorder* (Raleigh, N.C.), 17 February 1892; Anne C. Loveland, *Southern Evangelicalism and the Social Order* (Baton Rouge: Louisiana State University Press, 1980), 31–32, 69–71, 109–11; Mark Noll, *America's God* (New York: Oxford University Press, 2002); Nathan Hatch, *The Democratiza-*

tion of American Christianity, 9–12, 76–81, 162–89; and sermons by Thomas Dixon Jr. in *Progressive Farmer*, 2 June 1891 and 9 June 1891; *Caucasian* (Goldsboro, N.C.), 3 March 1892; and *Living Problems in Religion and Social Science*, 50–69. For a general discussion of the merger of republican ideals with evangelical theology in the late eighteenth and early nineteenth centuries, see Nathan O. Hatch, *The Democratization of Christianity* (Cambridge, Mass.: Yale University Press, 1991); Robert M. Calhoon, *Evangelicals and Conservatives in the Early South, 1740–1861* (Columbia: University of South Carolina Press, 1988), 67–130; Joe Creech, *Righteous Indignation: Religion and the Populist Movement* (Urbana: University of Illinois Press, 2006), chap. 2.

17. On Scottish Common Sense Realism and simple Baconianism in American evangelical thought, see George M. Marsden, *Fundamentalism and American Culture* (New York: Oxford University Press, 1980), 11–22, 55–62. On its connection to moral governance and on the importance of moral governance to evangelical thinking, see E. Brooks Holifield, *The Gentleman Theologians* (Durham, N.C.: Duke University Press, 1978), ix, 4, 72–154; James Turner, *Without God, without Creed: The Origins of Unbelief in America* (Baltimore: Johns Hopkins University Press, 1985); Bruce Kuklick, *Churchmen and Philosophers: From Jonathan Edwards to John Dewey* (New Haven, Conn.: Yale University Press, 1985); Calhoon, *Evangelicals and Conservatives in the Early South;* Loveland, *Southern Evangelicalism and the Social Order*. By the late nineteenth century, few rural or well-educated evangelicals adhered strictly to formal Common Sense Realism; nevertheless, its basic assumptions were pervasive.

18. "Manly Men Defined," *North Carolina Baptist*, 8 April 1891; *Journal of Proceedings*, North Carolina Annual Conference of the United Methodist Church, South, 1890, n.p., 31, Divinity School Library, Duke University, Durham, N.C. For similar calls for men to be spiritual leaders, see Minutes of the Presbyterian Synod of North Carolina, 1895, 360, Divinity School Library; Proceedings of the Classis of North Carolina of the Reformed Church in the United States, 1886, 23–26, Divinity School Library. For a few examples of such views of "manhood," see *North Carolina Baptist*, 25 November 1891; *Farmers' Advocate*, 10 June 1891 and 2 November 1892; *Caucasian*, 4 March 1897; Dewitt Talmage, sermon in *Caucasian*, 26 March 1891; President Crowell of Trinity College, sermon in *Caucasian*, 10 October 1889; Thomas Dixon Jr., sermon in *Farmers' Advocate*, 2 June 1891; *Caucasian*, 11 February 1892 and 20 April 1893; Bennett, *Narrative of the Great Revival*, 24, 31; J. W. Jones, *Christ in the Camp* (Richmond, Va.: B. F. Johnson and Co., 1887), 146–47; Dixon, *Living Problems in Religion and Social Science*, 65–76. Christine Heyrman argued that these expressions of pious manhood in the antebellum period reflected the attempt by evangelical ministers to unite secular conceptions of manhood with Christian piety in order to win over male planters; see *Southern Cross* (Chapel Hill: University of North Carolina Press, 1998), 205–52.

19. Jones, *Christ in the Camp*, 427. I am aware, as noted by Reid Mitchell in "Christian Soldiers? Perfecting the Confederacy," in Miller, Stout, and Reagan, eds., *Religion and the American Civil War*, 297–309, that books like Jones's *Christ in the Camp*, Bennett's *Narrative of the Great Revival*, and Southern hagiographies of Lee, Jackson, and Polk

present a case that the *actual* spirituality of generals, soldiers, and the Confederacy was to some extent created after the war. But what interests me here is not whether these generals or officers did what was written of them (though my citations come from wartime letters reprinted in these books), but how the memory of the Civil War and Confederate soldiers and officers was constructed in the 1880s and 1890s. For similar reflections on the idea that true men exercised intellectual and theological acumen, see J. B. Shearer, *A Discussion of Higher Education* (Charleston, S.C.: Walker, Evans, and Cogswell Co., 1890); William Mecklenburg Polk, *Leonidas Polk, Bishop and General*, 2 vols. (New York: Longmans, Green, and Co., 1915), 1:226–27, 2:369–70, 392–53; Berends, "Wholesome Reading Purifies and Elevates the Man," 137–66; Beth Barton Schweiger, *The Gospel Working Up: Progress and the Pulpit in Nineteenth-Century Virginia* (New York: Oxford University Press, 2000), 3–9, 11–33, 55–75; Bennett, *Narrative of the Great Revival*, 22–24, 47–48, 121. For more examples of using martial metaphors to describe Christian manhood as involving "spiritual warfare," see Phillip Shaw Paludan, "Religion and the American Civil War," in Miller, Stout, and Reagan, eds., *Religion and the American Civil War*, 24; Jones, *Christ in the Camp*, 15–16, 35.

20. Jones, *Christ in the Camp*, 142–43. On the ideals of expressing passionate prayer, humility, and tearful devotion, see Polk, *Leonidas Polk*, 1:313, 2:352–53; Jones, *Christ in the Camp*, 57, 77, 81–87, 102–33, 398–99, 427, 445, 450; Bennett, *Narrative of the Great Revival*, 20–21, 72. On true manhood's tie to converting others, see Polk, *Leonidas Polk*, 2:353–55; Bennett, *Narrative of the Great Revival*, 98.

21. "Men Who Own Themselves," *Windsor* (N.C.) *Public Ledger*, 19 October 1887; *Caucasian*, 20 April 1893. On Jeffersonian manliness, see *Progressive Farmer*, 25 August 1887; Dixon, *Living Problems*, 35, 39; *Biblical Recorder*, 25 May 1888, 13 November 1893, and 17 August 1892; *North Carolina Baptist*, 18 April 1894; Hoganson, *Fighting for American Manhood*, 188–24, 201; Putney, *Muscular Christianity*, 28–31, 43; Bennett, *Narrative of the Great Revival*, 24, 31; Jones, *Christ in the Camp*, 146–47; Kimmel, *Manhood in America*, 28–29. For women, such independence was confined to a proper, "private" sphere. Even though women were to exhibit mastery in their own sphere, they were also to observe proper deference to men's leadership in the home since, for men, independence carried overtones of mastery over one's household as well as one's passions. Thus, even though women were independent to a certain degree, they largely genuflected to the husband's leadership and thus exhibited patterns of deference and dependency.

22. T. C. Johnson, *A History of the Presbyterian Church, South* (New York: Christian Literature Co., 1894), 380. My point here is to modify the idea presented by Kantrowitz and others that appeals to independence were mere rhetorical devices designed to mask power relationships between southern whites and especially over blacks. Perhaps for Ben Tillman this was the case, but I find contrary evidence that masculine independence was a deeply held cultural value that in the best of times was applied, with qualification, to all people. That appeals to independence could function in other ways is, of course, certainly the case. See Kantrowitz, "Ben Tillman and Hendrix McLane," 497, 501, 511, 522; Kantrowitz, *Ben Tillman*, 1–9.

23. Thomas Dixon Jr., "Truth and Freedom," *Caucasian*, 3 March 1892.

24. Ibid. This sermon was an attack on Colonel Ingersoll's assertion that Christianity retarded social progress. For other examples of the way southern evangelicals connected manhood to care for dependents, see Harry S. Stout, Randall Miller, and Charles Reagan Wilson, "Introduction," in Miller, Stout, and Reagan, eds., *Religion and the American Civil War*, 3–18, esp. 7; Bennett, *Narrative of the Great Revival*, 89–91, 98; Burton and McArthur "*Gentleman and an Officer*," 162–65; Polk, *Leonidas Polk*, 1:226–27; D. W. Herring, *A Manly Boy* (n.p.: n.d.), D. W. Herring Papers, North Carolina Baptist Historical Collection, Wake Forest University, Winston-Salem.

25. Lyman Edwin Davis, *Democratic Methodism in America* (New York: Fleming H. Revell Co., 1921), 12.

26. J. F. Click, *Hickory Mercury*, 6 October 1897. Also *Corinthian* (Hickory, N.C.), August 1896 and September 1896; *Christian Sun* (Elon College, N.C.), 12 April 1891; *North Carolina Baptist*, 9 December 1891, 25 May 1892, 6 July 1892, 19 October 1892, 8 March 1893, 6 June 1894, 17 October 1894, and 31 October 1894; *Asheville* (N.C.) *Baptist*, 2 July 1889, 24 September 1889; *Biblical Recorder*, 14 February 1894, 29 April 1896, 10 February 1897, sermons by Thomas Dixon Jr., *Caucasian*, 18 February 1892, 28 April 1892, 7 July 1892; Hoganson, *Fighting for American Manhood*, 3–11, 24–25.

27. Rev. James I. Vance, "The Reign of Manhood," *Reformed Church Standard*, 1 July 1908.

28. For a detailed discussion of Dixon's ideas about family, violence, and religion in his novels, see Laura J. Veltman, "(Re)Producing White Supremacy: Race, the Protestant Church, and the American Family in the Works of Thomas Dixon, Jr.," in *Vale of Tears: New Essays on Religion and Reconstruction*, ed. Edward J. Blum and W. Scott Poole (Macon, Ga.: Mercer University Press, 2005), 235–56.

29. Polk, *Leonidas Polk*, 1:394. Of course, other scholars have similarly linked honor and manhood to defiance and vigilance, but again, I connect this to religious sentiment as well as to independence. See, for example, Kantrowitz, *Ben Tillman*, 148–50; Hoganson, *Fighting for American Manhood*, 45–87; Wyatt-Brown, *Honor and Violence in the Old South*, 166–88; Wyatt-Brown, "Church, Honor, and Secession," in Miller, Stout, and Reagan, eds., *Religion and the American Civil War*, 89–109. Certainly, the force of this argument rests on my reading of Clifford Geertz's understanding of the way religion works as a set of symbols that reflect and motivate human action—symbols that constitute "webs of meaning" for a culture's activities. See Geertz, "Religion as a Cultural System," in *Interpretation of Cultures* (New York: Basic Books, 1973).

Violent Masculinity: Learning Ritual and
Performance in Southern Lynchings

Kris DuRocher

At the 1916 lynching of Jesse Washington in Waco, Texas, one father, when questioned about the propriety of holding his young son on his shoulder so he could get a good view of the mob that kicked, stabbed, castrated, and incinerated Washington, replied: "My son can't learn too young the proper way to treat a nigger."[1] Between 1877 and 1939, similar events occurred repeatedly across the South, and, as this example—a white man with his son— suggests, the social hierarchy of the New South rested upon a foundation of race and gender. Concerns about the future of white supremacy prompted white male southerners to show the next generation the need to maintain white superiority through ritualized aggression against African Americans. Claude McKay, in his 1922 poem "The Lynching," further articulated these social expectations:

> Day dawned, and soon the mixed crowds came to view
> The ghastly body swaying in the sun
> The women thronged to look, but never a one
> Showed sorrow in her eyes of steely blue
> And little lads, lynchers that were to be
> Danced around the dreadful thing in fiendish glee.[2]

In the antebellum South, white men's ability to control those within their households and below them in the social hierarchy, primarily slaves and women, reflected their race and masculinity.[3] Without the system of slavery, white male southerners struggled to uphold their supremacy in the face of postbellum challenges, including economic depression and political movements such as Populism and women's suffrage. As the New South modernized, it became imperative

46

that white males find alternative ways to demonstrate an effective manhood. The lynching ritual offered a public space for white male southerners to reassert idealized roles of being, as anthropologist David Gilmore termed it, "Man-the-Impregnator-Protector-Provider."[4] As spectators, young children, girls, and women confirmed their dependence on white adult males and justified their actions.

Ritualized lynchings allowed the white community to model, produce, and reinforce a distinct class, racial, and gendered identity while also sending a message to the black community as well as white women and children to obey boundaries set up by white males. Public rituals such as parades, pledges, and holidays are culturally constructed spaces that communicate social realities by defining and setting a common cultural agenda. Participation in a public performance reinforces an idea that allows participants to assert a conception of identity to themselves and to those around them in the larger social context. In the post-Reconstruction South, the lynching ceremony, a public ritual of physical brutality, functioned as a space in which white southerners defined and defended white male supremacy.[5]

Although mass mob violence created and exhibited masculinity, the racial and gendered socialization necessary for the maintenance of white supremacy began much earlier. Young boys and girls learned from an early age the consequences if they failed to uphold their adult gender positions. Southern, white, self-proclaimed "social reformers" often struggled to understand how they adopted their distinctly "southern" identity. As these southerners recalled their childhoods in their autobiographies and writings, they recognized their own socialization into the mores of segregation. Whites all across the South, regardless of gender or economic status, understood that whiteness resided in their bodies and that they must protect this whiteness at all costs, for their race granted them power.

Although the lessons transcended class and geography, the ways adults taught their children reflected gender distinctions. Men remembered boyhood lessons from the public sphere, through observing white men, while women reformers tend to recall their socialization happening in the private sphere from their mothers. White southerner Katherine Du Pre Lumpkin's autobiography, *The Making of a Southerner* (1947), recounts her childhood lessons. In her early years, she heard the "words and phrases at all times intimately familiar to southern ears and in those years of harsh excitement carrying a special urgency: white supremacy, Negro domination, intermarriage, social equality, impudence, inferiority, uppitiness, good darkey, bad darkey, keep them in their place." Failure to act appropriately, Lumpkin remembered, would lead to the unthinkable: "To be ruled by Negroes! The slave ruling over the master!" Only white supremacy could counter this "disaster, injustice, and outrage." As the daughter of an upper-class planter family, Lumpkin learned to fear not only losing her racial advantage, but her economic one as well. She had a personal stake in this privilege, as her elite white position would continue only as long as she enforced the rules of segregation.[6]

Anne McCarty Braden recalled similar lessons in her youth. Born in 1924 in Louisville, Kentucky, Braden spent most of her childhood in Anniston, Alabama. In her autobiography *The Wall Between,* Braden recalled accepting at an early age that "I was one of the 'better' human beings, more privileged because my people came of a 'superior stock.'" The class connotation became more explicit as Braden noted that such lessons "were impressed on the mind of the white child of the South's privileged class almost before he could talk by the actions that speak louder than words." Because of her elite position, Braden's mother took pains to teach her daughter the appropriate language and behavior for an aristocratic young woman, exemplified in her memory of the day her daughter mentioned a "colored lady." "You never call colored people 'ladies,' her mother lectured. 'You say colored women and white lady—never colored lady."[7] As Braden discerned, the word "lady" conferred a status of privilege and respectability reserved only for whites. The privilege of being a "lady" even extended to lower-class white women, but never to African American women, regardless of economic status.

In contrast to females, male reformers learned childhood lessons through observing the public behavior of others, and their stories often contain elements of racial brutality. Will D. Campbell grew up poor in rural Amite County, Mississippi, and during his childhood in the 1930s recalled an incident of racial violence. In the midst of playing, Will and his brother saw a group of African American women running toward the schoolhouse. They followed and saw on the ground the dead body of a young black man. Campbell and his brother Joe, excited to see a crime scene, stayed to watch the sheriff collect evidence. "By circulating through the group which had gathered at the old schoolhouse, Joe and I had learned the story. . . . We were little boys and the black men who had been present did not hesitate to talk to one another in our presence. The crime had actually been an execution." Noon Well, the dead man, had apparently enjoyed the favors of two women until John White, a jealous white man, had shot him through the heart. The black men discussed how "White had steadied his pistol against a tree, and with careful aim, shot him through the heart. He [Noon] fell backward into the door opening and his own knife had been taken from his pocket and placed beside him." This version of events, however, differed from the one reported at the preliminary hearing the next day. "The sheriff testified that Noon Wells has obviously approached John White with a knife in a gambling dispute and that John White had no recourse but to kill him." After observing this drama, which Campbell remembered with disappointment since his uncle cancelled a planned fishing trip in order to attend the preliminary hearing, he understood that "crimes of black against black were not as serious as white against white. And certainly not as serious as black against white."[8] What is most important in this example is what Campbell failed to mention: white crimes against blacks. As a young white boy, he did not even consider white men's attacks upon African Americans as crime. By watching the actions of the whites around him, Campbell internalized the racial code of Jim Crow, recognizing that white men could kill African Americans, and the white community would protect them.

White southerner Junius Irving Scales also internalized the racial order from those around him. As a five-year-old, Scales shouted at Aunt Lou, his black nanny, "Take your old black, nigger hand off me!" when she tried to brush his hair.[9] Scales modeled his actions on another white boy's treatment of an African American, and while Scales learned a disparaging term for his nanny from a peer, his slapping of her hand also shows a recognition of his own power, even as a white boy, over an adult black female. Both Campbell and Scales, despite their class differences, observed and mimicked their future roles as white males.

In order to protect their whiteness, adults taught white children to keep themselves separate from blackness at all cost, and that the exchange of bodily fluids, even saliva, represented not only an intolerable closeness and familiarity between the races, but also the contamination of whiteness. Melton McLaurin's autobiography, *Separate Pasts: Growing Up White in the Segregated South,* recounts his youth in rural Wade, North Carolina. At thirteen, McLaurin's childhood lessons culminated when he and his childhood black friend, Bobo, prepared to play a game of basketball. Finding the ball flat, Bobo began to reinflate it. After a while, McLaurin took his turn, placing the inflation needle, to which Bobo had applied a "lavish amount of saliva," into his mouth. To his horror, McLaurin comprehends what he has done: mixing blackness with his whiteness. This blackness, this spit, defiled him, and he imagined black germs infiltrating his body and jeopardizing his racial purity. McLaurin felt that this contamination threatened his existence "as a superior being, the true soul of all Southern whites"; his revulsion resulted from his understanding that blackness had degraded him and made him, like Bobo, "less than human." McLaurin angrily threw the ball at Bobo, and then tried to reclaim his purity by repeatedly rinsing out his mouth. This event helped him realize that he and Bobo "belonged to two fundamentally different worlds" as uncompromising "as life and death."[10]

White adults and community members taught boys and girls to keep whiteness pure of blackness, focusing primarily on females due to the consequences for white supremacy if young women failed to keep their bodies free from all contact, especially sexual, with blackness. If white women had sex with black men, the resulting children would destroy the racial binaries that underpinned the system of white supremacy. In an effort to control white women's intimate relations and prevent interracial sex, white southerners taught young girls to fear their bodies and sexual desires. One of the first lessons that white southerner Lillian Smith remembered learning from her mother was "that the body was a 'Thing of Shame.'" As a white woman, she never was to show her naked body to anyone except the doctor and "never desecrate it by pleasures." Despite learning to be shameful and secretive of her body, Smith also recognized that her white skin offered a "source of strength and pride which proved one better than all other people on earth."[11] Thus, Smith discovered during her childhood, as many southern white girls likely did, the contradictory nature of the white female body.

Unlike females, taught to take defensive measures in upholding segregation, the charge of physically upholding supremacy fell most heavily on males. In the Old South, male children had been "under special obligation to prove early virility," and attitudes toward male children emphasized the protection of white women, their families, and their honor. If such guardianship required violence, society justified it as a necessary action. The development of physically strong and aggressive men mirrored the developmental goals for boys in the era of segregation as well. In Raleigh, North Carolina, in 1906, eleven-year-old Jack McClay, a white boy, and his white friend played "lynching." McClay tied a rope around the neck of his playmate, secured it to a nail in the wall, and left him hanging with just his toes touching the floor, severely hurting the boy. His playmate's parents brought the case to court. Jack's mother, however, proudly refused to reprimand her son for his rough yet masculine play.[12]

The appropriate age at which the community considered boys ready to take on adult male roles remains undefined and variable. Generally, however, as boys entered adolescence, they began to enforce segregation between the races. Marion Wright, born in 1894 in Trenton, South Carolina, played with African American boys, which "was more or less the custom in the South at that time." This interracial play, however, shifted as he entered adolescence; Wright's family informed him that he had outgrown his African American playmates. He needed to begin fulfilling his role as a white man, which demanded he begin to control those below him in the social hierarchy, especially African American males. Wright noted that, once he entered his teenage years, his relationship with African Americans was "much less informal than it had been up to that time . . . You lapsed more or less compulsively into a masterful and subservient relationship."[13]

Rhetoric about the necessity of violence to uphold white supremacy led many white boys to accept their often-violent male roles. Rollin Chambliss learned by the age of ten that "the Negro had to be kept in his place, and I was resigned to my part in that general responsibility." Chambliss took these duties so seriously that as an adolescent, he almost murdered an African American man. One afternoon, as he and some white friends lounged by a roadside, a black girl passed them. The group began to make suggestive remarks to her, and Chambliss felt that "she might have been flattered" as "she was a bad sort." An African American man approached from the road and attempted to defend her. Since a black man had never spoken back to any of the white boys, they ran to Chambliss's house to get a gun, but once armed could not find the man. Chambliss did not doubt, however, that he would have used the gun "if necessary, to keep a Negro in his place." Chambliss's unapologetic story is ironic due to its place in the introduction of his 1933 master's thesis from the University of Georgia entitled "What Negro Newspapers of Georgia Say about Some Social Problems."[14] This example not only shows the effectiveness of these lessons on how to uphold the supremacy of whiteness, but how white boys, by their teenaged years, understood the need to enforce their roles with violence.

Popular culture, photographic evidence, and white accounts, as well as the pamphlets and proceedings of antilynching and African American protest movements, testify to the constant presence of boys and girls of all ages at lynchings. There is, unfortunately, no statistical evidence that attests to the number of children who attended or participated in racial violence. There is, however, evidence that white adults went to great lengths to secure youth's participation. At a lynching in Bailey, North Carolina, a minister, Dr. E. C. Manness, brought several children with him to view the dead man. "'That's enough,' he said, when they had one good look, awed."[15] If the community announced a lynching in advance, parents excused their children from school in order to attend. In 1915, schools in Fayette County, Tennessee, delayed their school schedule "until boy and girl pupils could get back from viewing the lynched man." Other times the town declared the event a local holiday. On 1 February 1893, after a manhunt from Arkansas to Michigan, a train carrying Henry Smith, the African American accused of murdering white four-year-old Myrtle Vance, returned to the town of Paris, Texas. In celebration of his return, the mayor granted the town's children the day off from school, and they joined their families to watch male members of Vance's family, including her father, brother, and two uncles, place Smith upon a scaffold and torture him with hot pokers. For almost an hour, these men burned Smith's feet, legs, stomach, back, and arms; they burned out his eyes, and thrust the hot pokers down his throat. The crowd, including the white schoolchildren, shouted with approval. Ultimately, the crowd doused both the scaffold and Smith with oil and set him on fire.[16]

As the "favorite" day for such violence, the Sunday lynching not only held a religious connotation but also allowed participants time to perform and view the violence. One photograph from 1935 shows a white family, along with several other whites, on a Sunday outing in Fort Lauderdale, Florida. In the center of the photograph is the corpse of Rubin Stacy, hanging from a noose attached to a tree. The mob lynched the homeless black tenant farmer after he frightened a white woman, Mrs. Jones, when he approached her to ask for food. The photograph shows white girls posing around the corpse, their whiteness framing his blackness.[17] Such brutal images are far from rare.[18] An 1891 postcard pictured a group of nine- and ten-year-old white boys standing beneath the corpse of a lynched black man. Scrawled across the back the caption, "this fucking nigger as hung in Clanton, Alabama Friday, August 21, 1891" and signed below "the lynching committee." During his visit to England, the Reverend C. F. Aked, one of Ida B. Wells's supporters, widely circulated this postcard. Such vulgarity and violence, both symbolically and literally, led the English to assume the photograph a fake. They "refused to believe that a group of children would pose this way or that such an image could be authentic." Outsiders had difficulty understanding the carnival-like atmosphere of mass mob violence or that it was "considered family entertainment."[19]

Members of the white community, in addition to encouraging children's attendance, also protected children, especially boys' participation in mobs. As antilynching efforts increased and popular sentiment began to condemn such barbaric displays in the 1920s and 1930s, white communities often hid evidence of lynchings to avoid outside criticism. Fredrick Van Nuys of Indiana presided over the 1934 Senate Judiciary Subcommittee on "A Bill to Assure to Persons within the Jurisdiction of Every State the Equal Protection of the Laws and to Punish the Crime of Lynching," which explored the possibility of an antilynching law. In questioning George W. Colburn, called as a witness regarding a lynching in Princess Anne, Maryland, Senator Van Nuys became increasingly frustrated that the community not only condoned boys' behavior at lynchings, but also protected them from legal punishment.

SENATOR VAN NUYS: Was your community depopulated that night or was the usual number of people on the streets?

MR. COLBURN: I would say it was depopulated from a certain class; yes sir.

SENATOR VAN NUYS: What class?

MR. COLBURN: Youngsters.

SENATOR VAN NUYS: Boys of what age, would you say?

MR. COLBURN: Twelve to twenty-five years.

SENATOR VAN NUYS: Nearly all the youngsters were out of town that evening?

MR. COLBURN: They were not visible in our place of business; no, sir.

SENATOR VAN NUYS: Did any of them pretend to have any first-hand knowledge about the mob and who led it or anything along that line?

MR. COLBURN: Not that I could identify by name; no sir.

SENATOR VAN NUYS: Were they boys of your town?

MR. COLBURN: Yes, sir.

During the exchange, it is interesting that Senator Van Nuys assumed the male gender of the participants. The senator then attempted to discern the boys' activities. Colburn continued to deny knowledge of the boys by name or that they had been active in the mob. Van Nuys did not believe Colburn and continued his questioning: "Did some of them pretend to know who were leaders of the mob? Did some of them say that they were present at the mob?" Colburn responded, "I have heard some of them say they were present in Princess Anne, but I could not give any names now because it did not impress itself on my mind at the time."[20] Colburn confirmed the presence of boys from his town, yet his unwillingness to recall their names or their actions suggests that his and the community's best interests lay in safeguarding the boys' identities.

Inquiries into the violent deaths of African Americans, even those where prominent men and women of the community attended, usually resulted in the declaration that death occurred at "the hands of persons unknown." While Colburn may have been protecting the boys, they themselves often lacked discretion. At the same hearing, Arthur Garfield Hays, a representative of the American Civil Liberties Union, noted that one boy "was unavoidably identified with the lynching through his own boastful statements made on the occasion to the newspapers under his own signature." After his identification as a participant, however, communal sentiment resulted in the release of the boy after only a fleeting attempt to punish him. Although boys' presence always played a socially important role within the community, by the 1930s, boys' actions gained a new significance as their attendance began to protect adult mob members from legal recourse. A court would not charge or sentence a child, an antic to circumvent punishment noted by antilynching advocates. The NAACP report on the 1916 lynching of Jesse Washington in Waco, Texas, noted how "they got a little boy to light the fire (Legally you could not arrest a little boy)."[21]

Children's attendance at lynchings reflected parental and communal desire for them to attend, and while not all youths witnessed or partook in lynchings, they likely heard or read accounts of them. Elizabeth S. Harrington of the National Student Council remarked that "lynching is something that the Southern student knows about; something that they have heard discussed since their childhood. There are few students in the South who have not lived in the vicinity where lynching has not been, and perhaps still is, a part of the town. Some of the members of our student movement have actually seen lynchings." In 1895, the *Charleston News and Courier* noted that white adolescents had "learned only too well" the lessons taught in the "lynching school in which all boys of the state are being educated." This comment was in response to an account of four white youths who broke into a sixty-year-old black fisherman's house and shot him. African Americans also noticed white children's, especially boys', knowledge of lynchings. An Alabama African American woman who worked for a white family observed in 1902, "I have seen very small white children hang their black dolls. It is not the child's fault; he is simply an apt pupil."[22]

The lynching ritual offered several ways for young males to participate. A boy could function in the mob as a helper, assisting adult men but not participating directly. Boys commonly supported the disorder of the lynch mob: shattering windows and helping men seize victims, emulating the violence rather than taking independent action themselves. In 1930, the *Atlanta Constitution* informed its readers that a mob of men and boys overpowered the National Guard in its attempt to seize a victim. At a lynching in Omaha on 28 September 1919, boys in the mob broke lanterns, took the oil out of them, and ignited it on the street, probably in imitation of the fire started by adult men to burn the victim. In Memphis, Tennessee, boys cursed, spat on, and slashed with knives at Lee Walker, the mob's victim. In Texarkana, Arkansas, an unknown number of boys, alongside men, in 1891 "amused themselves for some time sticking knives into [Ed] Coy's body and slicing off pieces of flesh." They then poured oil over him, and the women lit the fire.[23] In roles such as these, boys supported the functions of men, joining, helping, and observing the roles that they would someday fulfill.

Although the lynching ritual focused on teaching and reinforcing masculinity, this celebration of white male domination would not have worked without an audience of women, girls, and young children. Occasionally, women and girls participated by lighting the pyre or scavenging for souvenirs, which, although less passive, did not infringe on the male right of directly attacking the victim during the ritual. In 1919, girls in a mob in Omaha distributed rocks from tin buckets for men to throw. The young women, however, did not take on the violent action of throwing the rocks. Although most females refrained from direct aggression against the victim, exceptions exist. In Atlanta, Georgia, in 1920, four young women pushed their way to Philip Gathers with guns, which they had somehow obtained, and shot him. These women, however, quickly stood back and allowed the men to mutilate the body.[24] Despite this example, the need to observe proper female behavior as dictated by southern society more often limited young women's roles.

As an audience, girls and young women served several purposes; primarily, white males needed spectators to approve their exhibition of masculinity. White male patriarchy required that white women possess feminine virtue and maintain the communal hierarchy by being subordinate to and dependent on white males. This rhetoric represented an idealized conception of womanhood, but one that the ritual needed, for it excused the actions of males and justified the idea that African Americans had an insatiable desire for raping innocent white women without provocation. This "rape-lynch" complex further strengthened the ideal of female passivity and the need for white womanhood's protection from black men.[25] In making the primary justification of lynching the protection of white womanhood, females' presence created a cycle of dependency, for their attendance proved their reliance on white males for protection.

The rape-lynch complex hid fears that white men could not maintain sexual control over white women, who might willingly seek out black sexual partners. The validity of this justification required that white women never desire to engage in sexual relationships with black men, so this discourse not only portrayed southern females as victims in need of protection, but also reinforced white men's exclusive sexual access to white women. Alice Spearman Wright, born in Marion, South Carolina, in 1902, recognized that white patriarchy required white males to control white and black sexuality: "It was some kind of worship that I guess men have of women when they kick them upstairs while they are kicking the blacks downstairs, and keep them both under control."[26] This rhetoric, as Wright noted, created a double standard. White women's sexual intercourse with black men offered the possibility of a biracial child who would blur the black and white dichotomy of segregation. White male sex with black women, however, did not threaten future white generations, for southern society considered black any child born to African American women. In claiming to kill in defense of white women and their purity, white men not only exhibited their masculinity but also reinforced their social, political, economic, and sexual prerogative over black men and white and black women.

The invocation of the rhetoric of protection of white womanhood to initiate action often came from young men and boys. On 9 May 1930, while the judge considered the verdict for alleged rapist George Hughes in Sherman, Texas, a mob of boys gathered. One boy, impatient for the judgment, threw a can of gasoline through a courthouse window. Another threw in a match. When the gasoline did not catch on fire, the second boy climbed in the window, struck another match, and remarked, "Now the damned courthouse is on fire." One of Sherman's older residents who witnessed the scene stated, "The rosters of the Sherman public schools would show the name of every boy in that group." The schoolboys' actions helped incite a mob, which attempted to seize Hughes from the courtroom. The boys continued to provoke action as they tore an American flag from the walls of the courthouse while yelling for men to assault the "nigger who had raped a white woman," compelling white men to take action.[27]

Ironically, women and children's vulnerability not only supported mob actions, but also at times functioned to protect male mob members. James Cameron's account of his attempted lynching in 1930 included a description of how several white men entered his cellblock, one with a gun, followed by "a young white girl, very pretty still in her teens . . . her eyes were wide, like a frightened and startled doe."[28] She justified the white mob's actions, which they cited as necessary for the protection of white womanhood. She also, however, acted as a shield, protecting the men from trigger-happy law enforcement officers. Mobs often placed girls in the front of lynch mobs when storming jails or courthouses to make the police or militia "less inclined to use their firearms." Although many authorities willingly surrendered African American prisoners, by the 1930s, fear of legal retribution and the increasingly violent behaviors of mobs led some authorities to defend themselves. Having women and children in a mob, however, did not always ensure that the authorities would not retaliate. In the extreme case of Sherman, Texas, the crowd became so large and uncontrollable that after the destruction of the courthouse, the governor called in the National Guard, which used tear gas against the inciting men, women, and children.[29]

Although the ritual required a supportive and dependent audience, the mob's intended victim played a crucial role within the ritual. Mobs overwhelmingly selected young African American males who, like their white counterparts, had not experienced the social system of slavery. With their ability to taint whiteness through sexual relations with white women, African American men offered the greatest threat to white supremacy.[30] In torturing black bodies, white men attacked black sexuality, which threatened, legitimately or not, white males' exclusive sexual access to white women. The ritualized castration of the victim by white males became a central aspect of mob lynchings. By castrating the victim, men and boys showed their willingness to protect white womanhood by physically taking black manhood. *The Chicago Defender*'s headline of 13 October 1917 read, "Boy Unsexes Negro before Mob Lynches Him." When an argument got out of hand between Bert Smith, an African American, and a white man in Houston, Texas, several oil drillers observing the argument attacked Smith. They "then forced a 10-year-old white lad who carried water around the camp to take a large butcher knife and unsex him."[31] The wording makes it difficult to discern whether the men actually forced the boy to participate or if the barbarity of the deed made it necessary for northern readers to believe that such an act required force. The boy might have participated freely in order to prove his masculinity, or the men may have required him to do so as a test of manliness. Regardless, they denied Smith his masculinity by having a ten-year-old boy sexually mutilate him.

Another way that white southern men asserted power over blacks occurred after the lynching. Boys and young men figured predominantly in the aftermath of lynching by gathering "relics [such] as the teeth, nails, and bits of charred skin" from the victim. On 23 May 1936, the *Journal and Guide* of Norfolk, Virginia, ran the front-page headline "Souvenir Hunters Loot Ruins of Slain Pair's Home," which included a picture of several boys digging through the ruins. The next day, the headline proclaimed "Ominous Calm Pervades Gordonsville on Sabbath, Guide Reporter Discovers." The correspondent noted the many people who drove to view the scene, including a "school bus of children" who journeyed to examine the spot where a mob of two thousand lynched sixty-five-year-old William Wale.[32]

In collecting souvenirs, whites symbolically consumed the sacrificed body, which reinforced communal values. Devouring the victim and the nearby scene may have been a type of communion, an embracing of the dominant values of the society, and a way to savor the perceived righteousness of such violent actions. Collecting souvenirs offered communities a way to remember rituals and (temporarily) restore order following such events. At the lynching of Sam Hose in Atlanta, Georgia, the crowd fought over pieces of his heart, liver, and crushed bones. Hose's knuckles became a display in the front window of a grocery store for all to see, proudly reminding the community of its actions. At times, boys sought to profit from these grisly mementos by selling them to those who witnessed the violence and those who wished they had.[33] The *Chicago Record Herald* reported on 27 February 1901 that after burning George Ward's body for several hours, his feet remained intact. Someone in the crowd "called an offer of a dollar for one of the toes, and a boy quickly took out his knife and cut off a toe." Other offers followed and "the horrible traffic continued, youths holding up toes and asking for bids." These acts of castration, both the physical and literal carving up of African American bodies for white consumption, demonstrate white male sexual fears regarding their own masculinity against the threat of black sexuality.[34]

At times, young men tested their masculine roles outside of the lynching ritual. In June 1934, a group of white youths interrupted a picnic of several African American teenagers where they "made some improper advances to some of the colored girls. Of course, that was resented by the colored boys." When the black boys objected and sought to defend themselves and their girlfriends, a fight ensued. The white gang went for reinforcements, returned, and lynched Dick Blue, one of the African American youths who had stood up to them. On Sunday, others came to view the body, reinforcing pride in the youths' actions and creating a sense of white unity through the spectator aspect of viewing the black body.[35] Boys old enough to commit violence knew that while white female sexuality required aggressive protection, segregation offered black women no such protection.

As white youths assumed for themselves white male roles, they often attacked those who committed a minor violation of segregation's mores or those who made easy, yet allowable targets, such as older male African Americans. Some white youths tested the boundaries of Jim Crow by instigating fights with African American boys, knowing that if the boys responded by fighting back, they violated Jim Crow and justified vigilante punishment. In Laurens, South Carolina, African American George Robertson observed several white boys attacking a black boy, whom he rushed to aid. For defending the boys' victim, the town accused Roberson of assault, and a mob subsequently removed him from jail. The town interpreted Robertson's response as an attack on the larger white male community and responded by hanging him from a railroad bridge outside the city. Similar acts by white boys showed their readiness for adult roles and, perhaps, violent entertainment. Boyd Cypert, the district attorney of Little Rock, Arkansas, told NAACP investigators looking into the lynching of John Carter that "two white boys went out one night with the definite and expressed intention of killing a Negro, for a lark." They shot an elderly black man and "left him beside the road." Cypert admitted that the community "felt that this was going too far." Still, many in the town felt jail too harsh a punishment for the boys, and when the case went to trial the "jury brought a verdict of not guilty, and afterwards expressed the opinion that the scare and expense of the trial were punishment enough."[36]

Teenagers at times used such tacit approval to take matters into their own hands. Henry Bedford, an African American, and Mr. Cawthorne, a white, argued over some land that Bedford had mortgaged to Cawthorne. During the argument, Cawthorne felt that Bedford's attitude was "rather 'sassy' for a 'nigger' to a white man" and ordered him off his land. His son told a friend of the argument, and young Cawthorne "got two of his young friends to go after Bedford." When they found him, they put him in a car, drove him outside of town, and proceeded to beat Bedford to death. The sheriff detained the boys, but was "criticised [sic] severely for arresting them and putting them in jail and holding them there for several days for 'just killing a nigger.'"[37] The community defended the youths, suggesting that at least some saw their actions as commendable.

There existed a difference between ritualized violence justified and performed by older boys and men and uncontrolled violence or inexcusable actions. The socialization of white males offered a steady progression from boyhood to manhood. Adult men determined the appropriate actions for boys and young men to undertake, and on a few occasions, adult males attempted to rein in white boys' violent actions if they overstepped their roles. *The Richmond Daily Enquirer* on 30 March 1900 reported "the boys of the East End of Richmond who had been having trouble with the Negroes of the section, became so enraged last Tuesday they decided to take the matter at once in hand and lynch the offenders." A gang of white boys, less than thirteen years old, chased a twelve-year-old black boy, throwing stones at him until the boy, fearing for his life, ran into the house of a white woman. The white boys yelled outside the house "they would get him if they had to die." The white woman sent for the police, who arrested four of the boys, fined them, and warned them against more violence.[38] Adult males disciplined the boys, who had infringed on white men's social prerogatives.

Southern whites sought to teach and exhibit proper white male behavior to the next generation through lessons in racial violence. Boys mimicked adult males under the watchful eyes of their parents and community members, supporting and observing the roles that they would someday fill. Unlike older adolescents, white adults might reprimand boys who took matters into their own hands without an adult's legitimizing presence, for within patriarchy white adult males maintained the responsibility of policing racial violence. For white male adolescents, the lynching ritual offered a public venue in which to prove their readiness for manhood. Male adolescents understood that white female sexuality required aggressive protection, and their direct participation in the violent ritual proved their masculinity. Public displays of masculinity at lynching rituals offered white men a space in which to demonstrate their ability to uphold the tenets of white southern masculinity, as well as perpetuate white supremacy to the next generation. Their actions reveal how white southerners conceived, taught, and perpetuated white male masculinity in an attempt to preserve racial segregation and patriarchy. Outside of lynchings, young men practiced their masculine roles, carrying out gang violence against African Americans whom the teenagers considered easy targets. Communities viewed such acts as young men attempting to perform their conceptualized honorable and masculine role of defending white supremacy.

For the white community, racial violence restored order and publicly reasserted its commitment to white patriarchy, yet eventually a person or event would contest segregation, and white supremacy would again become unstable. Public violence offered an opportunity to celebrate, if only for a short time, a version of white male masculinity that could counter all threats. White men maintained control of the ritualized violence in order to have their supremacy acknowledged by those below them in the social hierarchy. Interestingly, every aspect of ritualistic lynching focused on displaying a strong white male masculinity, from the cheering women and children, to the mutilation of a black male body and the collection of souvenirs. The overwhelming desire to display a capable white manhood hints that perhaps this ritual was required because white males were indeed losing their ability to control white women and African Americans.

NOTES

1. Elizabeth Freeman, report, 1916, 24, File: Lynching: Waco, Texas, 1916, Group I, Series C, Box 370, National Association for the Advancement of Colored People Collection, Library of Congress, Manuscript Division, Washington, D.C. (hereafter NAACP Collection); Grace Hale, *Making Whiteness: The Culture of Segregation in the South 1890–1940* (New York: Pantheon Books, 1998), 218. Freeman's report was circulated to raise money for the antilynching cause.

2. Claude McKay, "The Lynching," in *Black on White: Black Writers on What It Means to Be White*, ed. David Roediger (New York: Schocken Books, 1998), 335. Ida B. Wells was among the first to investigate the motivations behind lynchings. In 1892, she argued that the rhetoric of a bestial black rapist, who violated pure white females and deserved torture and death, cloaked acts of social terrorism whose primary purpose was to maintain white social power and supremacy (Jacqueline Jones Royster, ed., *Southern Horrors and Other Writings: The Anti-Lynching Campaign of Ida B. Wells, 1892–1900* [Boston: Bedford Books, 1997], 3); Pamela Newkirk, "Ida B. Wells-Barnett; Journalism as a Weapon against Racial Bigotry," *Media Studies Journal* 14 (2000): 31–36. Other early studies argued that lynching was the work of lower-class whites; see James Cutler, *Lynch-Law: An Investigation into the History of Lynching in the United States* (New York: Negro Universities Press, 1969); Arthur Franklin Raper, *The Tragedy of Lynching* (Baltimore: Black Classic Press, 1933). Recent scholarship has complicated these views, noting that lynching united whites and oppressed blacks psychologically, economically, socially, and politically. See Jacquelyn Dowd Hall, *Revolt against Chivalry: Jessie Daniel Ames and the Women's Campaign against Lynching* (New York: Columbia University Press, 1993); William Fitzhugh Brundage, *Lynching in the New South: Georgia and Virginia, 1880–1930* (Urbana: University of Illinois Press, 1993).

3. As social constructions, race and gender are mutually reinforcing, contextually variable, and inseparable. Joan Scott, "Gender: A Useful Category of Historical Analysis," *American Historical Review* 91 (1986): 1053–75.

4. David D. Gilmore, *Manhood in the Making: Cultural Concepts of Masculinity* (New Haven, Conn.: Yale University Press, 1990), 222–23. Southern historians have debated segregation's beginnings and stability for decades. See W. J. Cash, *The Mind of the South* (New York: Houghton Mifflin Company, 1941); C. Vann Woodward, *Origins of the New South, 1877–1913* (Baton Rouge: Louisiana State University Press, 1951); Woodward, *The Strange Career of Jim Crow* (New York: Oxford University Press, 1955); John W. Cell, *The Highest Stage of White Supremacy: The Origins of Segregation in South Africa and the American South* (New York: Cambridge University Press, 1982); Barbara Fields, *Slavery and Freedom on the Middle Ground: Maryland*

during the Nineteenth Century (New Haven, Conn.: Yale University Press, 1985); Joel Williamson, *The Crucible of Race: Black-White Relations in the American South since Emancipation* (New York and Oxford: Oxford University Press, 1984); Howard N. Rabinowitz, *Race Relations in the Urban South, 1865–1890* (New York: Oxford University Press, 1978); Edward Ayers, *Promise of the New South: Life after Reconstruction* (New York: Oxford University Press, 1993); Orville Vernon Burton, "Race and Reconstruction: Edgefield County, South Carolina," *Journal of Social History* 12 (1978): 31–56. Overall, these historians' understandings characterize the Jim Crow South as a time when white southerners tried to place themselves within a modernizing economy while maintaining political power.

5. Stanley J. Tambiah, "A Performance Approach to Ritual," in *Readings in Ritual Studies*, ed. Ronald Grimes (Upper Saddle River, N.J.: Prentice Hall, 1996), 497; Catharine Bell, *Ritual Theory, Ritual Practice* (New York: Oxford University Press, 1992), 37–39. This ritual united whites along class lines, allowing lower-class whites to commit acts of violence that would go unpunished, creating an illusion of their own power (Brundage, *Lynching in the New South*, 15). Grace Hale argued that lynchings functioned for white adults to strengthen segregation by helping create "a collective, all-powerful whiteness." In addition, communal lynchings would not have been possible without the consent and often the participation of the social elite (Hale, *Making Whiteness*, 237).

6. Elizabeth Fox-Genovese, "Between Individualism and Community: Autobiographies of Southern Women," in *Located Lives: Place and Idea in Southern Autobiography*, ed. Bill J. Barry (Athens: University of Georgia Press, 1990), 87. Katherine Du Pre Lumpkin's parents also enrolled her in the children's Ku Klux Klan. There she, with help from her mother, made robes from old sheets with cheesecloth crosses. The children held secret meetings and planned imaginary violence against African Americans (Katherine Du Pre Lumpkin, *The Making of a Southerner* [Athens: University of Georgia Press, 1991], 136).

7. Anne Braden, *The Wall Between* (New York: Monthly Review Press, 1958), 19–21.

8. Will D. Campbell, *Brother to a Dragonfly* (New York: Continuum, 2000), 61–64.

9. Junius Irving Scales and Richard Nickson, *Cause at Heart: A Former Communist Remembers* (Athens: University of Georgia Press, 1987), 47–48.

10. Melton McLaurin, *Separate Pasts: Growing Up White in the Segregated South* (Athens: University of Georgia Press, 1998), 37–40.

11. Lillian Smith, *Killers of the Dream* (New York: Anchor Books, 1963), 74.

12. Bertram Wyatt-Brown, *Hearts of Darkness: Wellsprings of a Southern Literary Tradition* (Baton Rouge: Louisiana State University Press, 2003), 154; Leon F. Litwack, *Trouble in Mind: Black Southerners in the Age of Jim Crow* (New York: Knopf, 1998), 288.

13. Interview with Marion Wright by Jacquelyn Hall, 8 March 1978, 9; Interview with Marion Wright by Arnold Shankman, 11 March 1976, 8, both in Southern Oral History Program Collection, Southern Historical Collection, University of North Carolina, Chapel Hill. Most biological rituals focus primarily around female, not

male, entrance into adolescence and sexuality; see Ronald L. Grimes, *Deeply into the Bone: Re-Inventing Rites of Passage* (Berkeley: University of California Press, 2000), 108.

14. Rollin Chambliss, "What Negro Newspapers of Georgia Say about Some Social Problems" (M.A. thesis, University of Georgia, 1934), 5, 8.

15. "Mob Trails Man Who Escaped and Then Lynch Him: Local Dailies Attempt to Write Humorous Stories of the Orgy," *Chicago Whip*, 20 August 1927, File: Lynching: Bailey, N.C., 1927, Group I, Series C, Box 363, NAACP Collection.

16. Litwack, *Trouble in Mind*, 286–88; Michael Hatt, "Race, Ritual, and Responsibility: Performativity and the Southern Lynching," in *Performing the Body/Performing the Text*, ed. Amelia Jones and Andrew Stephenson (New York: Routledge Press, 1999), 77; Royster, ed., *Southern Horrors and Other Writing*, 92.

17. Orlando Patterson, *Rituals of Blood: Consequences of Slavery in Two American Centuries* (Washington, D.C.: Counterpoint, 1998), 204; James Allen, ed., *Without Sanctuary: Lynching Photography in America* (Santa Fe, N.Mex.: Twin Palms, 2000), photograph 57. Before the lynching, the police escorted Stacy to Jones's home where "the Jones children ran excitedly to inform their mother of the black man's arrival. One little girl reportedly exclaimed to her mother 'There he is!' and all of the other small children began screaming as they scurried from one window to another"; Walter T. Howard, *Lynchings: Extralegal Violence in Florida during the 1930s* (Selinsgrove, Penn.: Susquehanna University Press, 1995), 75, 77.

18. Hale, *Making Whiteness*, 203–10. Awareness of the camera helped to enact whiteness and exhibit it to the larger audience of the nation (Mary Esteve, *The Aesthetics and Politics of the Crowd in American Literature* [New York: Cambridge University Press, 2003], 141). The exhibit-turned-book *Without Sanctuary* contains a collection of souvenir lynching postcards that underscore this point.

19. Phillip Dray, *At the Hands of Persons Unknown: The Lynching of Black America* (New York: Random House, 2002), 136; Hatt, "Race, Ritual, and Responsibility," 77. This postcard image is in Royster, ed., *Southern Horrors and Other Writings*, 118. Mob violence against African Americans often took on the veneer of a "Sunday outing" or a "celebration, with hundreds of men, women, and children in attendance" (NAACP, *Burning at the Stake in the United States* [Baltimore: Black Classic Press, 1986], 21).

20. "A Bill to Assure to Persons within the Jurisdiction of Every State the Equal Protection of the Laws and to Punish the Crime of Lynching," S. 1978, Hearings Before a Subcommittee of the Judiciary, United States Senate, 73rd Cong., 2nd Sess. (Washington, D.C.: United States Government Printing Office, 1934), 231. See also Paul Ortiz, *Remembering Jim Crow: African Americans Tell about Life in the Segregated South* (New York: New Press, 2001).

21. "Bill to Assure to Persons within the Jurisdiction of Every State the Equal Protection of the Laws and to Punish the Crime of Lynching," 43; Freeman, report, 1. Most inquiries into lynching concluded they occurred at hands of "parties unknown," despite obvious evidence to the contrary; see Dray, *At the Hands of Persons Unknown*.

22. "Bill to Assure to Persons within the Jurisdiction of Every State the Equal Protec-

tion of the Laws and to Punish the Crime of Lynching," 174; Terence Finnegan, "Lynching and Political Power in Mississippi and South Carolina," in *Under Sentence of Death: Lynching in the South*, ed. William Fitzhugh Brundage (Chapel Hill: University of North Carolina Press, 1997), 201; Litwack, *Trouble in Mind*, 288.

23. "Belleville Is Complacent over Horrible Lynching," *New York Herald*, 9 June 1903, quoted in Ralph Ginzburg, *100 Years of Lynchings* (Baltimore: Black Classic Press, 1988), 51; "Mob Overcomes Nat'l Guard to Lynch Accused Rapist," *Atlanta Constitution*, 1 June 1930, quoted in Ginzburg, *100 Years of Lynchings*, 185; Lawrence H. Larsen and Barbara J. Cottrell, *The Gate City: A History of Omaha* (Lincoln: University of Nebraska Press, 1997), 171; Royster, ed., *Southern Horrors and Other Writings*, 202.

24. Larsen and Cottrell, *Gate City*, 170; "Huge Mob Tortures Negro to Avenge Brutal Slaying," *Atlanta Journal*, 21 June 1920, quoted in Ginzburg, *100 Years of Lynchings*, 133.

25. In performing acts of violence that were sexual in nature, white men linked racial superiority to masculinity. In taking away black male sexuality, white males furthered the idea that African Americans were an inferior and unmanly race, unable to, like white men, protect themselves or their families (Gail Bederman, *Manliness and Civilization: a Cultural History of Gender and Race in the United States, 1880–1917* [Chicago: University of Chicago Press, 1995], 49–51).

26. Interview with Alice Spearman Wright by Jacquelyn Hall, 28 February 1976, 49, Southern Oral History Program Collection.

27. Arthur Franklin Raper, *The Tragedy of Lynching* (Baltimore: Black Classic Press, 1933), 323–24.

28. James Cameron, *A Time of Terror: A Survivor's Story* (Baltimore: Black Classic Press, 1994), 66.

29. *Lynchings and What They Mean* (Atlanta: Southern Commission on the Study of Lynching, 1931), 39; Raper, *Tragedy of Lynching*, 323.

30. It is important to note that African Americans resisted white attempts at lynchings or violence. In 1906, members of the Wiggins, Mississippi, African American community exchanged more than five hundred shots with a white mob attempting to punish some blacks who had prevented the lynching of a "bad nigger." The more typical response to white lawlessness was to remain in the relative safety of the community or to migrate (Neil R. McMillen, *Dark Journey: Black Mississippians in the Age of Jim Crow* [Urbana: University of Illinois Press, 1989], 225–27).

31. "Boys Unsex Negro before Mob Lynches Him," *Chattanooga Times*, 13 February 1918, quoted in Ginzburg, *100 Years of Lynchings*, 114. Joel Williamson, in a psychosexual interpretation of lynching, argued that whites projected their sexual fears onto African Americans; see *The Crucible of Race: Black/White Relations in the American South since Emancipation* (New York: Oxford University Press, 1984), 119–24.

32. Royster, ed., *Southern Horrors and Other Writings*, 116; "Souvenir Hunters Loot Ruins of Slain Pair's Home," *Journal and Guide* (Norfolk, Va.), 23 May 1936, Group I, Series C, Box 370, File: Lynching, Gordonsville, Va., 1936–37, NAACP Collection.

33. Orlando Patterson, *Rituals of Blood: Consequences of Slavery in Two American Centuries* (Washington, D.C.: Counterpoint, 1998), 182–83; Allen, ed., *Without Sanctuary*, 8–9. Anxious customers in Pennsylvania bought some of Zachariah Walker's remains from resourceful boys (Dennis B. Downey and Raymond M. Hyser, *No Crooked Death: Coatesville, Pennsylvania, and the Lynching of Zachariah Walker* [Urbana: University of Illinois Press, 1991], 38–39).

34. *Chicago Record*, 27 February 1901. Orlando Patterson has argued that such actions were perhaps a form of communal rape upon African American men (Patterson, *Rituals of Blood*, 174).

35. "An Act to Assure to Persons within the Jurisdiction of Every State Due Process of Law and Equal Protection of the Laws, and to Prevent the Crime of Lynching," H.R. 801, Hearings before a Subcommittee on the Judiciary, United States Senate, 76th Cong., 3rd Sess. (Washington, D.C.: United States Government Printing Office, 1940), 42.

36. McMillen, *Dark Journey*, 225, 227; "Lynch Negro at Laurens: Mob Storms Jail for Victim, Who Wounded Three White Boys," *New York Globe*, 2 April 1920, Group I, Series C, Box 366, File: Lynching, Laurens, S.C., 1920–21, NAACP Collection; "Special Investigation of the John Carter Lynching, Little Rock, Ark.," 10, Group 1, Series C, Box 349, File: Lynching, Little Rock, Ark., 1927, NAACP Collection.

37. S. D. Redmond, attorney at law, Jackson, Miss., to Walter White, 14 August 1934, Group I, Series C, Box 360, File: Lynching, Pelahatchee, Miss., 1934, NAACP Collection.

38. Brundage, *Lynching in the New South*, 1–2.

In Defense of "This Great Family Government and Estate":
Cherokee Masculinity and the Opposition to Allotment

Rose Stremlau

In 1896, Samuel H. Mayes wrote an impassioned letter in which he described his countrymen as the quintessence of virtuous, modern manhood. He used evocative words with strong connotations to convey his pride: these men were "sober," "industrious," and "independent." He explained that although the common men he lived among humbly "earned [their] daily bread by honest labor upon the soil," each was "an equal participant in God's great gift of liberty." Mayes went on to assure his readers that, in time, the men of their nation could become upright citizens in the model that he had just described. He urged them to open their minds and accept the superiority of his way of life, and he further suggested that their assimilation promised the "one solution to the many vexed problems already upon [them]."[1]

Writing in the heyday of the movement to assimilate Native Americans into American society, Mayes was not a reformer peddling the benefits of Anglo-American culture to Indian people. Instead, Mayes, the principal chief of the Cherokee Nation, wrote this letter to the U.S. Congress in response to their on-going critique of tribalism. In other words, Mayes offered to acculturate Americans into Cherokee society, which he believed to be superior. He maintained that Cherokees surpassed Americans in the arts of civilization because their custom of communal land ownership produced more patriotic citizens and principled men by fostering generosity and reciprocity while their adoption of a republican political system further nurtured these ancient values.

Mayes and his fellow Cherokee statesmen were prolific writers in defense of their nation. They communicated regularly with their citizenry through annual state-of-the-nation addresses and the tribal newspaper, the *Cherokee Advocate,* published in their capital, Tahlequah, Indian Territory. They reached out to American audiences though petitions, editorials, lobbyists, and speeches. In some documents, elected officials responded to specific charges; in others, they comforted Cherokee people as the prospects of national survival appeared bleak. All of these sources contributed to the larger debate about the kind of people that Indians were and the kind of people that assimilationist policies promised to make them. The Cherokees were not unique in their opposition to detribalization. Many Indian leaders protested ethnocentric policies and explained that while they understood what the advocates of assimilation asked of them, tribal officials, representing the wishes of their communities, preferred traditional ways. Likewise, those Native statesmen open to change nonetheless sought to shape its direction and pace. What makes Cherokee leaders unique, then, was that they debated the critics of tribalism on the intellectual merits of assimilation through the American press and in the halls of government. In particular, Cherokee statesmen critiqued Anglo-American manhood, defended their civilization, and defined a positive, alternative view of tribal manhood.

Prior to contact with Europeans, Cherokees had a unique conception of appropriate gender roles. Selu and Kanati, the first Cherokee woman and man, embodied the egalitarian division of labor that characterized relations among Cherokees. Selu, whose name means corn, maintained the home and tended the fields, and Cherokee women took on their work in matrilineal households of extended female kin. Kanati, in contrast, wielded power in the world beyond the home and fields—the hunting grounds, the council house, and the battlefield. Like the first hunter, Cherokee men provided meat for their families that complemented the fruits of women's labor, primarily corn, beans, and squash. Although Cherokee men and women occupied separate spheres, their obligations to each other reinforced and extended the ties of kinship. Formal political power descended through men through the maternal line, meaning from uncle to maternal nephew, but women influenced decision making, particularly through the contribution or withholding of their resources, namely their foodstuffs and labor. Women and men worked independently of each other in Cherokee society, and yet their families only survived through reciprocal giving and receiving among them. It was a system that mitigated social tension and reduced the likelihood of starvation by enabling the utilization of a broad range of resources and created extended social ties.[2]

Late nineteenth-century American reformers struggled to solve what they called the "Indian problem," the inability or refusal of Native American people to assimilate. These non-Indian advocates for the right of Indian people to adopt Anglo-American culture represented the best and worst characteristics of the era. Typically white, educated Protestants of the middle and upper classes, they believed that Indian people should be helped to survive in modern America but concluded that so-called primitive cultures had no place. Although these self-designated "friends of the Indian" claimed to speak with authority, most lacked any firsthand knowledge of Native life. Cherokee principal chief William Potter Ross dismissed them as "self-constituted guardians and interested intermeddlers." Regardless of their questionable credentials as experts on Indian affairs, reformers rallied Americans to their cause of emancipating Indians from tribalism, and they founded organizations such as the Women's National Indian Association and Indian Rights Association that became influential philanthropic engines of change, urging politicians in Washington, D.C., to overhaul federal Indian policy. Even those most concerned with Indian women's status, the Women's National Indian Association, recognized the importance of Indian men to the success of reform efforts as the organization committed itself to "[raising] the Indian into his true and rightful manhood and citizenship through legislation."[3]

By the 1880s, reformers had reached a consensus about the necessity of urgent action designed to redress a fundamental flaw undercutting all other efforts toward assimilation, such as Christianization and education. They believed that tribal land bases enabled Native people to circumvent meaningful, systemic change. Specifically, reformers agreed that communal resource ownership created a cyclical pattern trapping Indian people in dependency and disorder, most visibly manifested in their supposedly dysfunctional families. The critique fell particularly harsh on Indian men because reformers reasoned that common property discouraged them from working to attain self-sufficiency by preventing the accumulation of wealth. Reformers theorized that Indian men, lacking the status associated with capital, failed to assume a proprietary interest in their wives and children, which, in turn, led to anarchy. As Commissioner of Indian Affairs Ezra Hayt remarked, "The system of title in common has also been pernicious to them, in that it has prevented advancement and repressed that spirit of rivalry and the desire to accumulate property which is the source of success and advancement in all white communities." Reformers commonly spoke of Indian men in terms of buzzwords like "idle" and "lazy."[4] A century before "welfare queens" were the talk of the 1980s, Indian men were the "welfare kings" of the 1880s.

Having diagnosed communal resource ownership as the source of tribal people's social sickness and Indian men's pecuniary impotency, reformers prescribed private resource ownership as the obvious cure. They designed a policy that would subdivide tribal land among individuals and break up Native communities that defied discipline and hierarchy. Their plan also would dissolve tribal governments resisting changes in land tenure. Reformers called it "allotment"; William Potter Ross called it "a nut without a kernel."[5] Throughout the 1880s, reformers lobbied Congress with promised magical results if individual Indian men were forced to own land. Western businessmen, eager to profit from the development of tribal land, needed no encouragement to advocate for the dismantling of Indian nations. These unlikely allies committed themselves to allotment with energy reminiscent of abolitionism. They would, they vowed, emancipate Indians from tribalism and make them men!

Men's assumption of their proper role as heads of households and providers was essential to Indian assimilation and the goal of allotment. Reformers likened Indian communities to fleets of ships with no captains, and they specified that *individual* Indian men must lead *individual* nuclear families. Ideally, allotment provided each Indian man with his own 180-acre homestead on which he labored to support his wife and biological children. Lobbyist C. C. Painter of the Indian Rights Association explained the importance of allotment to reformers' goal of assimilating Indians into Anglo-American gender roles: "The fact is, we have entered upon the beginnings of a new dispensation, and we shall find it necessary that all things in the methods and machinery of our Indian policy, shall be made new and adapted to the growth and development of men."[6] This goal seemed not only laudable but plausible, and yet it involved transforming Native societies in fundamental ways. Among non-Indians, few dissented or questioned the morality or possibility of this monumental task.

In response, Cherokee leaders called into question the concept of an "Indian problem" and suggested that the source of Indians' troubles did not reside in Indian Country. As William Potter Ross put it, "The ambition of aspiring men, the cupidity of soulless corporations and combinations of whatever name, or the mistaken philanthropy of the uninformed" threatened his nation. Cherokee principal chiefs critiqued their critics and had few kind words for American men, who, above all, failed to keep their word. Ross attributed this to a collective lack of will and wisdom.[7] Over generations, Cherokee statesmen had learned that federal officials did not honor treaties. Leaders of the allotment era did not have to remember far back for the most egregious example: the fraudulent Treaty of New Echota. In 1836, against the will of the majority of the Cherokee people and their elected officials, Congress ratified this treaty made with a minority faction of the nation. This group traded what remained of the Cherokees' ancient homeland in Georgia for land in Indian Territory, which is modern-day Oklahoma. While the illegitimate signers immediately relocated, most Cherokees refused to leave until President Andrew Jackson ordered General Winfield Scott to round up and march the approximately seventeen thousand remaining Cherokees west in 1838. Heartbroken over the loss of their homeland, sick due to exposure and lack of supplies, and grieving over the estimated several thousand who died along the way, Cherokees remembered the journey as "the trail where we cried." Non-Indians typically refer to it as the Trail of Tears. Notably, the men who led the Cherokee Nation during the allotment crisis either had survived the trail as children or were born shortly after the reestablishment of the Cherokee Nation in Indian Territory. Likewise, many experienced the bloody guerrilla war that divided the Cherokee Nation during the Civil War as tribesmen fought for both the Union and the Confederacy. Some of these statesmen even participated in the negotiations resulting in the unfavorable Treaty of 1866 through which the United States punished the Cherokees for secession by further reducing their land base in Indian Territory.

Cherokees treasured their remaining land, and treaties were their sole guarantee of ownership. For this reason, Cherokee delegates to Congress assumed the role of moral chastisers by repeatedly scolding their colleagues for abrogating agreements. In petitions to Congress, in other words, Cherokee representatives did not beg American leaders for assistance. Rather, they reminded politicians of obligations by recounting solemn promises constitutionally made between governments. Those who stood by treaties were those who "[had] the manhood" to do so, according to Principal Chief Joel B. Mayes. American leaders changed Indian policies when expedient, but Cherokees considered each promise made and honored in good faith. Consequently, Cherokee statesmen sometimes lost their patience with American politicians. In a letter to President Benjamin Harrison, Mayes related that Cherokees "have souls and are responsible for their conduct to the law of God and man. Do you," he questioned, "keep your word only to greed?"[8]

At the same time, Cherokee statesmen valued their relationship with the U.S. government, explained it to politicians unfamiliar with the history thereof, and demonstrated their extensive knowledge of American and Cherokee political cultures. Cherokee leaders contextualized the breaking of treaties in the larger history of Indian affairs, arguing that the promises made by previous generations dishonored those who had made the treaties and well as those who broke them. Samuel Mayes put it bluntly when he stated that his contemporaries in Congress insulted the legacy of the Founding Fathers. In doing so, Mayes held American statesmen up to their own ideal and found them wanting.[9]

Cherokee statesmen also characterized American politicians as ineffective and unqualified to represent their people's wishes or guide them in making wise decisions. According to Cherokee political tradition, leaders did not command absolute authority. Instead, they governed through influence and consensus, and in this system, the citizenry had a direct relationship with leaders who did as they willed. Cherokee statesmen, then, mocked American leaders for making laws that no one followed and policies that failed to serve public interest. Late nineteenth-century Cherokee chiefs pointed to two specific crises that demonstrated federal impotence: the railroads and the intruders.

In the unfavorable Reconstruction treaty signed in 1866, Cherokee representatives consented to allow railroads to run lines through their nation, and the federal government interpreted those reluctant signatures as permission for the corporations to operate without tribal regulation yet with access to tribal resources. Cherokee statesmen disagreed and haggled with railroad owners and federal officials because they held to a belief not unfamiliar to American statesmen: all powers not expressly given to the federal government in their treaties were reserved to the Cherokee Nation. For this reason, tribal leaders sought to regulate the railroads; charge them for using tribal resources, particularly timber; and profit from their presence in the nation. They emphasized that ceaseless vigilance against encroachment sapped their energy and generated fear among the population, discouraging further development. Principal Chief Dennis Wolf Bushyhead was pointed in his condemnation and suggested that by representing corporate interests, the federal government set an unfortunate precedent: he predicted that "gigantic corporations and federations of corporations" would grow more powerful than the states and even the federal government, and they would prove a greater menace to progress than the relatively weak Indian nations that businessmen blamed for obstructing western development. American leaders, he insisted, demonstrated a lack of foresight in failing to defend tribal nations' right to exist.[10]

Likewise, although the influx of intruders, or non-Indian homesteaders, into the Cherokee Nation also violated treaties, the federal government proved unable and unwilling to stop its citizens from entering Indian Territory and to remove those who settled illegally. Following the Civil War, non-Indians increasingly squatted in Indian Territory. The Cherokee Nation was powerless to remove squatters because they were beyond tribal jurisdiction. Instead, the federal government, having assumed responsibility for its citizens in treaties, which included provisions for the prosecution of criminals and the removal of intruders, refused to act. Politicians would not remove intruders because doing so would deny American citizens their property rights to improvements made on Cherokee land—a stance unpopular with American voters who had no appreciation for treaty rights and a great interest in ensuring a steady supply of cheap land. This impossible situation robbed the Cherokee Nation of resources and its leaders of energy.[11]

During the late nineteenth century, Cherokee statesmen constantly communicated with the president, Congress, and Indian Service regarding the removal of intruders but soon realized that the federal government was unable to control its citizens and unwilling to enforce its laws. The situation became severe during the 1880s. As a result, statesmen worked to defend their borders from illegal immigration. Although the men expressed frustration, the diversity of their responses suggests that they felt far from powerless. Dennis Wolf Bushyhead attempted to coordinate efforts among the governments of Indian Territory. Joel Mayes urged the use of force. Principal Chief C. J. Harris laid the legal groundwork for the seizure of intruders' property.[12] Most commonly, Cherokee statesmen attempted to use tribal laws to discourage intrusion while enabling needed laborers to immigrate and work in the Cherokee Nation. Despite their many attempts, however, the Cherokee government could not stop the influx and attempted to use the crisis as a bargaining chip in allotment negotiations. When accused by reformers of encouraging lawlessness and corruption in their nation, Cherokee statesmen calmly explained that white men, particularly bandits escaping federal marshals, were responsible for outrages against innocent people in Indian Territory. Then they reminded reformers about the federal promise to remove intruders.[13]

Although non-Indian reformers and policy makers distinguished between themselves and the class of people whom they characterized as intruders, Cherokee statesmen did not make such distinctions. Instead, they identified a common motivator behind American men's behavior: greed, or as Chief Samuel Houston Mayes put it, "gain, so evidently the ruling passion of your civilization." As early as 1869, Principal Chief Lewis Downing revealed the fundamental difference between Indian and non-Indian cultures that created discord in the Indian Territory as non-Indians clamored for its development: the "idea of accumulation" failed to appeal to Cherokees as it did to Americans. Every late nineteenth-century Cherokee chief identified American covetousness as the greatest threat to their survival. Of course, the reformers' goal was to use private landownership to teach Indian men this very characteristic—"to keep," in the words of reformer Henry Dawes.[14]

Lust for gain, Cherokee statesmen believed, prompted non-Indians to falsely represent them as inferior men. Most commonly, reformers charged the Cherokee government with allowing monopolization of its resources by a "mixed-blood" minority, oppressing the "full-blood" majority, poorly administering civic duties, and encouraging lawlessness. Cherokee statesmen challenged this information and urged Congress to take their word instead, offering themselves, their government, and their society as evidence of their civilization. As Cherokee congressional delegates asked, "Is it to be doubted that a people fostering and encouraging such institutions have all the finer sensibilities of education and Christian manhood that will be found among similar communities in the United States? Could a nation of irresponsible, corrupt, criminal people produce such conditions?" Pride in their way of life was evident, and Cherokee statesmen's boasting offered an alternative version of late nineteenth-century Indian life that called reformers' accusations into question and gave another view of Cherokee civilization and the men who governed it.[15]

In contrast to reformers who equated communalism with savagery, Cherokee statesmen explained that common resource ownership provided the foundation of their superior civilization by enabling self-sufficiency while fostering shared interests. Collective independence was the heart of Cherokee culture. Ironically, communalism guaranteed individual self-sufficiency and, in turn, independence, essential components of Cherokee manhood. Most Cherokee families farmed and raised stock, and common title guaranteed each citizen's access to the one thing needed to live in subsistence: land. As Dennis Wolf Bushyhead explained, Cherokees held to communal land ownership because "in this way every one of our citizens is sure of a home." They valued security for themselves, and they sought to guarantee it for their descendants. Delegates to Congress tried to explain this worldview: "Lands in common means perpetual homes to [Cherokees] and their prosperity, they know that under that system, they can never become homeless." Allotment threatened them with "certain loss of home if not to them certainly to their children and ultimate pauperism to their race, no thought troubles their hearts so much."[16] This fear of homelessness was not only an aversion to poverty but also to perpetual dependence. Turn-of-the-twentieth-century Cherokees recognized that communal land provided each working man with a degree of economic stability and independence unattainable to American contemporaries, particularly those in neighboring southern states whose poor crossed the borders of the Cherokee Nation to squat on tribal land.

Cherokees valued self-sufficiency in their government as well. Statesmen educated outsiders about their tripartite government, bicameral legislature, and system of common schools and institutions, maintained without assistance from the federal government. Throughout the late nineteenth century, Cherokee leaders struggled to collect the revenue needed to provide services, and like American politicians they experimented with various methods of revenue collection in hopes of enriching their treasury, but this was a difficult task. Self-sufficiency was a matter of national pride, however, even when it was barely or imperfectly attained. Praising his fellow citizens for working through a drought by pooling resources, which enabled the government to avoid selling land for relief money, Dennis Wolf Bushyhead commented, "Present industry and economy are our true and only certain refuge against the recurrence of bad seasons."[17] In their families, communities, and nation, Cherokees looked, above all, to care for themselves and their own.

Cherokees also valued hospitality, and reciprocal giving among families and communities complemented their self-sufficiency. Although scholars agree that the Cherokees' ancient kinship system had faded by the late nineteenth century, the obligatory and extensive sharing that characterized it was still a social norm. While reformers applauded Joel Mayes's claim that "charity is the greatest of virtues," they disapproved of the magnitude of Cherokee generosity because it prevented men from accumulating wealth. Cherokees, however, considered a virtuous man to be benevolent and understood hospitality as a process of giving and receiving that benefited both parties. In other words, accepting hospitality did not detract from one's manhood because it embodied the nurturance and maintenance of relationships central to Cherokee culture, such as those represented by Selu and Kananti.[18]

In response to reformers' criticism of the liberality of tribal expenditures, Cherokee statesmen explained that a primary function of their government was to extend hospitality to their citizenry. In other words, communal landholding engendered a political ethic and concern for social welfare that distinguished the Cherokee Nation from its American and European counterparts. Joel Mayes explained, "The greatest purpose for which all government can thus extend over its citizens is a protecting hand, thereby creating in the citizen a feeling of security and contentment." Decades before the federal government committed itself to social welfare, Cherokee statesmen, representing the wishes of their citizens, fostered the common good as their primary duty.[19]

In addition to enabling self-sufficiency, Cherokees believed that common title also fostered shared interest. As C. J. Harris explained, "Land in common is common interest, and common interest implies equal benefits whenever the people as a community demand their share of equal rights and benefits in the common property." This economic arrangement, they argued, logically complemented their republican political system. Cherokee statesmen praised their forefathers for including communal resource ownership in the Cherokees' first written constitution, adopted in 1827, which they described as progressive and forward-thinking, promoting harmony in an increasingly diverse society.[20]

In the 1820s, Cherokee leaders had consolidated their nation in response to the threat of removal from Georgia to Indian Territory, and they adopted elements of constitutional government and adapted them to their political tradition. Cherokees did not borrow from Americans to assimilate; rather, they did so to become better Cherokees and maintain independence. Republicanism offered a way to maintain the egalitarian harmony of their political system, which had been based on clan law, while strengthening it with centralized, representative authority. It seemed the best of both worlds, and Cherokees put their faith in this new path. John Ross, the famous Cherokee principal chief during the Removal Era, ruled as a traditional chief who brought the Cherokees towards republicanism at the behest of the more conservative members of his nation.[21]

A half century later, allotment-era Cherokee statesmen lauded their ancestors for adopting elements of constitutional government and thereby enhancing and perfecting their existing political traditions, particularly that of communal land ownership. C. J. Harris commented, "To my mind, the wisest provisions made by our fathers for their posterity was the dedication of the use only of the lands and the interest on the invested funds to each succeeding generation." Cherokees emphasized the dual heritage of their government, and in describing their government to non-Indians, they explained that the Cherokee Nation combined the best of what Creator had chosen for them in primordial time—communal resource ownership—with representative democracy introduced to them by the United States. As William P. Ross bragged, Indians governed themselves by both written law and ancient custom.[22] In no way did Cherokee statesmen think that their adoption of a republican government replaced tribal traditions. Instead, they argued that by adapting, they evolved.

Although modeling their system of government after their American counterpart, Cherokee leaders retained the communal nature of their political system. Reformers accused the Cherokee government of corruption because of leaders' close ties with communities, but this reflected the grassroots nature of the Cherokee republic. Cherokees believed that tribal government was accountable to them, and final authority on important decisions, such as land sales, rested with the people. For example, although elected officials regulated the occupancy and use of land, all decisions relating to title belonged to the people rather than the tribal council. Statesmen endorsed the idea of putting matters directly before their citizens, particularly in matters of local concern, such as education, and regional expertise, such as the census.[23]

While reformers in the United States would not create a social welfare system until well into the twentieth century, late nineteenth-century Cherokees invested in their public institutions as a manifestation of shared interests and a means to connect their national government to local communities. In particular, Cherokee statesmen considered their common school system to be the logical complement to communal land ownership. The average Cherokee man, Samuel Mayes wrote, "believes in common education; such as is natural with his ideas of common property." He emphasized that this system existed as a priority of the majority of Cherokees, and a substantial financial commitment over several generations proved that the average Cherokee was "he who loves his fellow man." The common school system was free to all Cherokee children.[24] Notably, Cherokees provided equal opportunity to male and female students, and Cherokee women had access to all levels of education, including the seminaries that served as normal schools. This commitment to common schooling and women's education was unequaled in Anglo-American society well into the twentieth century.

Cherokee politicians disagreed over methodology, but they agreed that the main purpose of public education was to inspire the mind and train the body. Although they realized that most Cherokee boys and girls would work on farms throughout their adult lives, statesmen had loftier goals than vocational training. They wanted their schools to build character, teach values that would enable students to live in harmony with other Cherokees, and prepare them to work honorably and profitably as adults. Above all, Cherokee statesmen believed that schools should train young Cherokees to be "useful" to their people, to serve national needs, and to defend Native rights. Education, then, not only improved the lives of individuals but also protected their interests as a people with common enemies: intruders, corporations, and the federal government.[25] Reformers who believed that education should train Indian children in Anglo-American culture interpreted the Cherokee school system as failing and could not appreciate the nation's pride in it.

Suggesting the extent of their interrelationship, however, Cherokee statesmen emphasized that homes functioned as the most important institutions in their society. To late nineteenth-century Cherokees, the word "home" conveyed two meanings, neither of which referred to the actual physical structure that reformers so closely equated with the attainment of civilization. "Home" referenced a permanent place of settlement, and it referred to collectively owned land.[26] Cherokee statesmen rarely used the word "home" for an individual household. More specifically, "homeland" conveys their meaning for "home."[27] Because they shared a common homeland, Cherokee statesmen conceptualized their government as a family, or as Joel Mayes put it, "this great family government and estate." He also referred to the tribal government as a "family" and a "household located on their [the Cherokees'] home." It was membership in and ownership of this home that enabled the Cherokees to govern themselves. Political power began with this common interest. Because Cherokees referred to their nation and land in familial terms, or as Dennis Wolf Bushyhead put it, "this great family of ours," they spoke of allotment as abandonment of their communal title and each other.[28]

Nurtured by a culture that embraced both self-sufficiency and hospitality, Cherokees considered themselves to be better citizens than white Americans. In particular, statesmen emphasized the centrality of independence to their conception of masculinity. Samuel Mayes wrote, "The common tenure of land makes every man independent—no paupers, no beggars, no patient worth forced by circumstances to bow the head to insolent success. Every man is a peer of his fellow-man, an equal participant of God's great gift of liberty." Independent men had something those bound to another by economic interest did not have: the ability to freely choose. Tied to one another in common property ownership,

Cherokee citizens looked to the public good and beyond the greed that statesmen believed corrupted men and crippled American society. The Cherokee homeland perpetuated a fellowship of self-reliant individuals by giving Cherokees the economic freedom to stand together by choice.[29]

Often speaking in patriotic turns of phrase that must have resonated with Americans, Cherokees equated their love of countryperson and homeland. Common property enabled everything that was of value to Cherokee people—their independence, their homes, and their nation. As C. J. Harris commented regarding the public domain in his 1893 address to the Cherokee people: "This [our communal land] means our country. It means everything to us—life, self control and prosperity. Without a country, we are simply a people without lands, we have no governments. Without homes, we are paupers and vagabonds. How jealous should we then be of our common property and how well we should guard it!" In other words, Cherokees believed the value system that enabled their higher civilization could not endure beyond their common homeland.[30]

Although their persistence against allotment confused and annoyed reformers, Cherokee statesmen explained their resistance as evidence of manliness and patriotism. As they had once taken up arms as warriors, leaders insisted that Cherokee men now defended themselves as statesmen. William Potter Ross wrote, "Distinguished for their valor, love of country and independence of character, no pallor has blanched their cheek in battle, nor whining despondency marked the hour of defeat." He continued, "Standing in the gateway to the Indian country it is no less reflection upon their neighboring brethren to say that they are second to none, and that their defense of their own rights and those common to all inhabitants of the territory has been constant, unflagging, and successful this far despite the powerful influence arranged against them." Other statesmen concurred with Ross's definition of Cherokee men. Those who served the interests of their fellow countrymen and women through public service in defense of their nation were valued in life and praised in death. Other Indian peoples recognized this quality of the Cherokees, and other tribal leaders deferred to Cherokee statesmen whom they believed would stand firmly in defense of tribal rights.[31]

Cherokee statesmen not only argued that they were the better men, but they suggested that they also proved the better heirs to America's Founding Fathers. Claiming republicanism as their own, they strongly identified with the Founding Fathers and claimed to share their vision: "The names of those great men are enshrined in our hearts; they are our heroes of liberty and truth, as well as yours." Cherokee statesmen liberally borrowed the words of the Revolutionary generation in defense of their nation and as an analogy explaining their own persistence. In a letter to reformers, C. J. Harris explained that Cherokees refused to acquiesce to allotment for the same reasons that the Founding Fathers would not bend to the demands of the Crown, and he invoked the Declaration of Independence in defense of Cherokees' "popular liberty" and "pursuits of happiness." In other words, as he had done for their Revolutionary American counterparts, God endowed Cherokees with certain inalienable rights.[32]

While Cherokees saw themselves as fellow participants in the republican experiment, they believed that their combination of communalism and republicanism created a society that the world's best minds could admire and in which suffering people could find hope. Communal resource ownership balanced individual gain with public good, enabling the success of the industrious while providing for the subsistence of those unable or unwilling to accumulate surplus. Communal resource ownership functioned, then, as a social welfare system of sorts by preventing profound poverty, fabulous wealth, and the social ills created by vast discrepancies in class. While poverty stalked the majority of Americans, delegates from the Indian Territory explained, "We have no rich men among the Indians, in the sense the word is now used in the United States. . . . Potter's fields and poor houses are unknown to our civilization." In other words, while reformers wrung their hands over the disorder they believed to be characteristic of Indian families, Cherokee leaders offered their society as the solution to the economic problems they knew to be the norm in America. For this reason, Cherokee statesmen believed that they must preserve their way of life, not only for their own benefit but for that of all humanity. Dennis Wolf Bushyhead wrote how "[o]ur system of government must be perpetuated. . . . The system is well worth preservation to mankind. The burden of other governments is the unequal distribution of their territory. Out of such injustice—a relic of times when might was right, a few men were absolute and many slaves—all sorts of evils have sprung and increased. The principle of common property in land is the principle of universal brotherhood and is the leading feature of our government. It recognizes the right of every citizen to his just share of the bountiful gifts of Providence to all—land being one. How to preserve this right to Cherokee citizens safely . . . is the problem we have to solve or go down as a nation."[33] This was the mission to which Cherokee statesmen committed themselves during the allotment era.

While visiting Washington, D.C., with a delegation of Cherokee statesmen, Samuel Houston Mayes wrote evocatively of the Cherokees' contribution to the Washington Monument—one plain white marble slab. Cherokees had paid for its carving, hauling, and engraving in honor of "that champion of liberty to the world." To Cherokee statesmen, disavowing their treaties and destroying their nation made as much sense as would removing one block of the Washington Monument. They were part, they insisted, of the great movement in governance that would uplift humanity—republicanism. At the end of the nineteenth century, they wanted only to continue their experiment in civilization.

The campaign for allotment gained momentum beginning in 1881, with debates leading to the General Allotment Act of 1887, or Dawes Act, which excluded Indian Territory because of legal technicalities related to tribal land titles. Reformers promised to pass legislation that included Indian Territory immediately, but Cherokee statesmen thwarted these initiatives until spring 1898 when Congress took up a series of bills concerning Indian Territory. They granted non-Indians the right to do business in the Indian Territory without regard to tribal law. Congress also compensated intruders. Prior to voting on an allotment bill, congressmen refused to hear any additional testimony on the Cherokees' treaties because they dismissed the documents as irrelevant. The House Committee on Indian Affairs denied the Cherokee delegation a hearing, and the House passed Senator Charles Curtis's bill to allot Indian Territory with less than two and one-half minutes of debate. After some discussion in the Senate, President McKinley signed the Curtis Act into law on 28 June 1898. Supporters of the Curtis Act believed that they had succeeded in opening up Indian Territory for development, which they predicted would take two years.[34] Cherokee statesmen stalled negotiations regarding implementation for four more years. Ultimately, the Cherokees were allotted under the Cherokee Agreement of 1902 a more favorable policy than the Curtis Act.

As they had been first in resisting the policy, they were the last of the Five Tribes of Indian Territory to concede to allotment. The tragedy of Cherokee allotment makes their resistance for over two decades no less remarkable. As the Cherokee Nation's tribal historian, Julia Coates, remarked, "Much as in the removal era, this most acculturated of the Five Tribes, with the highest proportion of mixed-race citizens, unexpectedly exhibited the most conservative behavior while also engaging in the most sophisticated legal/political battle of any of the Indian nations."[35] To any student of the well-known chief John Ross during the Removal Era, Cherokee resistance was not unprecedented or unexpected. For Cherokee statesmen, it was the only manly thing to do.

NOTES

The author thanks Mike Green and Theda Perdue for their comments and encouragement.

1. Samuel H. Mayes et al., "Cherokee Delegates," *Indian Chieftain*, 30 January 1896, Box M-50, Folder 37, S. H. Mayes Collection, Western History Collection, University of Oklahoma, Norman. S. H. Mayes, G. W. Benge, Roach Young, and Joseph Smallwood signed this letter to the Senate and House of Representatives in response

to a federal report that characterized the government of the Cherokee Nation as hopelessly corrupt and recommended the Indian republic's immediate dissolution.

2. The classic text on gender in Cherokee society is *Cherokee Women* by Theda Perdue (Lincoln: University of Nebraska Press, 1998).

3. William Potter Ross, speech, September 1874, Box 1, Folder 21, William Potter Ross Collection, Western History Collection; Women's National Indian Association, *Annual Report for 1884* (Philadelphia: The Association, 1884), 53. For an account of this reform movement and its goals, see Frederick E. Hoxie, *A Final Promise: The Campaign to Assimilate the Indians, 1880–1920* (Lincoln: University of Nebraska Press, 1984).

4. House Committee on Indian Affairs, Lands to Indians in Severalty to Accompany Bill H.R. 6268, 45th Cong., 3rd Sess., 1879, H.R. Report No. 165, 2.

5. Ross speech.

6. Lake Mohonk Conference of the Friends of the Indian, Proceedings for 1887, 4, Indian Collection, Hampton University Archives, Hampton University, Hampton, Va. Painter was on to something in noting this new trend in policy. Prior to this point, missionaries had focused assimilationist efforts on women and children, and this turn to men was a shift in Indian policy. This approach resonated with other mission movements. See John D'Emilio and Estelle B. Freedman, *Intimate Matters: A History of Sexuality in America* (Chicago: University of Chicago Press, 1997), 93.

7. Quoted in Craig Miner, *The Corporation and the Indian: Tribal Sovereignty and Industrial Civilization in the Indian Territory, 1865–1907* (Columbia: University of Missouri Press, 1976), 30; Ross speech.

8. Joel B. Mayes, Fourth Annual Message, 4 November 1890; Joel B. Mayes to President Harrison, 6 March 1890, both in Joel B. Mayes Collection, Western Historical Collection.

9. Mayes et al., "Cherokee Delegates"; C. J. Harris, Memorial, 3 January 1894, C. J. Harris Collection, Western History Collection.

10. Dennis Wolf Bushyhead, letter re: the Attempt of the Southern Kansas Railway Company to Build through the Cherokee Nation, 12 April 1886; Bushyhead, Third Annual Message of Dennis Wolf Bushyhead, 6 November 1881, Box 4, Folder 164, both in Dennis Wolf Bushyhead Collection, Western History Collection; William Potter Ross et al., Memorial Signed by Wm. P. Ross and Other Chiefs, 1870, Box R-36, Folder 3; W. P. Ross, Address to the House Committee on Territories, 1874, Box 1, Folder 14; "Native," letter to the editor (unidentified news clipping), 6 June 1874, all in William Potter Ross Collection; C. J. Harris, Annual Message of C. J. Harris, 6 November 1894, Box 56, Folder 19, C. J. Harris Collection.

11. See Nancy Hope Sober, *The Intruders: The Illegal Residents of the Cherokee Nation, 1866–1907* (Ponca City, Okla.: Cherokee Books, 1991).

12. Dennis Wolf Bushyhead, letter re: Compliance with Article 27 of the Treaty of 1866 Concerning Intruders, 15 April 1886, Box 3, Folder 134; Bushyhead, Second Annual Message to Congress, 11 November 1880, Box 4, Folder 162, both in Dennis Wolf Bushyhead Collection; Joel B. Mayes, Third Annual Message of Hon. J. B. Mayes,

principal chief of the Cherokee Nation, 6 November 1889, Box M-48, Folder 46, Joel B. Mayes Collection; C. J. Harris, Message of C. J. Harris, 6 November 1894, Box 56, Folder 19, C. J. Harris Collection.

13. C. J. Harris, et al., An Appeal for Justice by Delegates of Five Civilized Nations to the Congress of the United States, 1895, Box H-56, Folder 33, C. J. Harris Collection. Delegates from the Cherokee, Creek, Choctaw, and Chickasaw nations signed this memorial. Beginning in 1839, the Cherokee government defined citizenship and established a system through which noncitizens could live in their nation and work for citizens. The National Council constantly experimented with this system, which was at times strict and prohibitive while at other times lenient and open. For example, in 1878, the National Council taxed citizens twenty-five dollars per month for every noncitizen who worked for them, but in 1879, they reduced that tax to one dollar (Sober, *Intruders*, 26–41).

14. Mayes et al., "Cherokee Delegates"; quote from Miner, *Corporation and the Indian*, 19; Board of Indian Commissioners, Annual Report for 1883, 69–70, Indian Collection.

15. Mayes et al., "Cherokee Delegates." For examples, see C. J. Harris et al., "An Appeal for Justice"; C. J. Harris et al., Memorial Adopted by the International Convention of the Cherokee, Creek, Choctaw, Chickasaw and Seminole Indians," Box P-19, Folder 13, C. J. Harris Collection; William Potter Ross et al., Memorial Signed by William P. Ross and Other Chiefs, Box R-36, Folder 3, William Potter Ross Collection.

16. Congressional Record, 46th Cong., 3rd Sess., 1881, 781; C. J. Harris et al., "An Appeal for Justice."

17. Mayes et al., "Cherokee Delegates"; Dennis Wolf Bushyhead, Campaign Speech of D. W. Bushyhead to Friends and Fellow Citizens of the Cherokee Nation, 31 July 1879, Box IV, Folder 159; Bushyhead, Message of D. W. Bushyhead, 12 November 1885, Box III, Folder 115; Bushyhead, Fourth Annual Message of D. W. Bushyhead, 10 November 1882, Box IV, Folder 165, all in Dennis Wolf Bushyhead Collection; Joel B. Mayes, Third Annual Message; Joel B. Mayes, Fourth Annual Message; Samuel H. Mayes, First Annual Message of S. H. Mayes, 1895, Box M-50, Folder 26, S. H. Hayes Collection.

18. J. B. Mayes, Fourth Annual Message; Mayes et al., "Cherokee Delegates"; editorial on R. B. Ross, *Fairland* (Indian Territory) *News*, 1899, Box M-51, Folder 16, S. H. Mayes Collection; Ross speech. In present-day Cherokee communities, however, clans still retain relevance for practitioners of traditional Cherokee spirituality.

19. Mayes, Fourth Annual Message.

20. Harris, Annual Message for 1894; John F. Adair, editorial on John Ross and Sequoyah, *The Cherokee Advocate*, 14 November 1874, Box 1, Folder 27, William Potter Ross Collection.

21. John Gulick, *Cherokees at the Crossroads* (Chapel Hill: University of North Carolina for the Institute for Research in Social Science, 1960), 12; William McLoughlin, *Cherokee Renasence in the New Republic* (Princeton, N.J.: Princeton University Press, 1990); Thurman Wilkins, *Cherokee Tragedy: The Ridge Family and the Decimation of*

a People, 2nd ed. (Norman: University of Oklahoma Press, 1986), 275–76. Historian William McLoughlin believed that this move began with the 1808 National Council, which passed several laws to reorganize the Cherokee government. In 1810, the Upper and Lower towns coalesced to form a unified central government; see *Cherokees and Missionaries, 1789–1839* (New Haven, Conn.: Yale University Press, 1984), 54–81.

22. Harris, Annual Message; Ross speech; Mayes et al., "Cherokee Delegates." For another good example, see Ross et al., Memorial of William Potter Ross. Mayes and the delegates used this opportunity to humorously refute charges of incompetence and corruption. They told the congressmen that having adopted some elements of their government, it is understandable that they would struggle with the same evils the federal government did!

23. Mayes, Fourth Annual Address; Harris, Annual Message for 1894; Mayes, Third Annual Message. For an interesting commentary on accountability, see Mayes, First Annual Message; Harris, Memorial of C. J. Harris.

24. Mayes et al., "Cherokee Delegates"; Samuel H. Mayes, Message of S. H. Mayes, 1896, Box M-50, Folder 43, S. H. Mayes Collection.

25. For an example, see Dennis Wolf Bushyhead, Sixth Annual Message of Dennis Wolf Bushyhead, 13 November 1884, Box 4, Folder 167, Dennis Wolf Bushyhead Collection; Mayes, Third Annual Message.

26. Cherokee statesmen appeared to be referring to the language of their removal treaty, which referred to "a permanent home, and which shall, under the most solemn guarantee of the United States, be and remain theirs forever—a home that shall never in all future time be embarrassed by having extended around it the line or placed over it the jurisdiction of a State or Territory, nor be pressed upon by the extension in any way of any of the limits of any existing Territory or State" (Ross speech).

27. The first chief whose papers I read through, William Potter Ross, made this distinction in his public writings, and I speculate that subsequent leaders shared the same understanding of the word (Ross speech). For other examples, see Dennis Wolf Bushyhead, Letter of D. W. Bushyhead to Dr. M. Frazee, 1891, Box 3, Folder 157, Dennis Wolf Bushyhead Collection; Mayes, Third Annual Message; Mayes, Letter of S. H. Mayes to Grover Cleveland, 18 January 1896.

28. Mayes, Fourth Annual Message; Dennis Wolf Bushyhead, Fifth Annual Message of D. W. Bushyhead, 16 November 1883, Box 4, Folder 166, Dennis Wolf Bushyhead Collection; "Meeting of Representatives of Five Civilized Tribes," *Indian Journal*, 1894, Box H-56, Folder F-1, C. J. Harris Collection.

29. Mayes et al., "Cherokee Delegates"; Dennis Wolf Bushyhead, First Annual Message of D. W. Bushyhead, 26 November 1879, Box 4, Folder 160; Bushyhead, Letter of Acceptance, 1891, Box 3, Folder 156, Dennis Wolf Bushyhead Collection.

30. C. J. Harris, Message to the Honorable National Council, 11 November 1893, Box H-55, Folder 24, C. J. Harris Collection; Harris, Annual Message for 1894.

31. Ross speech. See J. B. Mayes, Fourth Annual Message of Hon. J. B. Mayes and Samuel H. Mayes, "Editorial on Message of S. H. Mayes," 1898, Box M-51, Folder 11,

S. H. Mayes Collection; "Meeting of Five Civilized Tribes," *Indian Journal*, 1894, Box H-56, F-1, C. J. Harris Collection.

32. Mayes et al., "Cherokee Delegates"; Ross speech; Harris, letter of C. J. Harris to Mess. Kidd and McKennon. See also D. W. Bushyhead, First Annual Message of D. W. Bushyhead; S. H. Mayes, Second Annual Message; Mayes, Message of S. H. Mayes for 1896.

33. Mary Jane Warde, *George Washington Grayson and the Creek Nation, 1843–1920* (Norman: University of Oklahoma Press, 1999); Mayes, et. al., Cherokee Delegates; Memorial Adopted by the International Convention of the Cherokee, Creek, Choctaw, Chickasaw, and Seminole Indians, 1895, P-19, Folder 13, Anne Ross Piburn Collection, Western History Collection; Bushyhead, Letter of Acceptance.

34. "The Five Tribes in Congress," *Claremore* (Oklahoma) *Progress*, 19 February 1898, Box M-50, Folder 59; "The Five Tribes in Congress," *Claremore* (Oklahoma) *Progress*, 9 April 1898, Box M-50, Folder 62; "The Five Tribes in Congress," 19 February 1898; "The Five Tribes in Congress," *Claremore* (Oklahoma) *Progress*, 23 April 1898, Box M-50, Folder 63; S. H. Mayes, Special Message of S. H. Mayes, 1898, Box M-50, Folder 6; "A Meeting of the Five Tribes in Congress," *Claremore* (Oklahoma) *Progress*, 15 January 1898, Box M-50, Folder 58, all in S. H. Mayes Collection.

35. Julia Coates, "'None of Us Are Supposed to Be Here': Ethnicity, Nationality, and the Production of Cherokee Histories" (Ph.D. diss., University of New Mexico, 2002), 142.

William Raoul's Alternative Honor: Socialism and Masculinity in the New South

Steve Blankenship

When, in 1908, William Greene Raoul Jr. decided he would "travel about, hobo if necessary, and find out what was being done in the socialist and working class world," he committed political and social apostasy and announced his voluntary descent down the ladder of the American hierarchy his father and grandfather had struggled to climb.[1] He lived at his father's elaborate mansion on Atlanta's Peachtree Street, reading Marx and giving lectures on working-class virility and the virtues of socialism at local theaters.[2] Raoul remembered, "What was I going to do? I certainly couldn't live off my father and work for the Socialist Party." He had been "brought up in the tradition of the self-made captain of industry. I must make a living, and a good one."[3] For Raoul, dependence was a feminizing attribute, a quality incompatible with his class and gendered expectations. And expectations were great for Raoul, as his father and maternal grandfather had both reached the apex of their professions. His family had settled in Atlanta, after all, because his father believed it the ideal city where his sons could cultivate the manly arts of commerce. Repeated failures in the business world, however, would push Raoul down a different path.

Raoul appeared to be a natural candidate for success. His grandfather, William M. Wadley, had guided the Central of Georgia Railroad throughout most of its history, except for brief appointments as an executive for other rail lines and a stint as the superintendent of transportation for the Confederacy during 1862–63. Wadley's handpicked successor, Greene Raoul, had married his daughter Mary just after the Civil War ended. Greene would become president of the Central before assuming command of the Mexican National Railroad, where he established himself as one of the most respected railroad men north and south of the Rio Grande. The William Raoul of this essay was the second of the couple's ten surviving children. Although his father's influence provided him with many connections across the business and political worlds of the South, Raoul's commercial life was erratic, and by his mid-thirties deemed a failure by himself, his family, and peers.

Raoul finally rejected the bourgeois values and masculine role of his conservative upbringing for a life lived on the radical fringe as a member of the Socialist Party and advocate of free love—ideals simultaneously subversive and emancipating for the failed businessman and frustrated lover. Driven to this alienation by an unsatisfying sexual life and financial dependence upon his father, he fashioned another sort of southern manhood that rejected the model of the "captain of industry" for that of an elite condescending to join an oppressed working class. Raoul crafted a version of masculinity that in some ways predicted that of the "modern man" who anticipates (and encourages) women's sexual expression. Raoul's failure to achieve the sort of masculinity valued by his father and peers made him an improviser of masculinities, shaping his life and gendered behavior along two distinct paths: aristocrat and radical.

The paradoxical title of Raoul's unpublished autobiography, "The Proletarian Aristocrat," suggests the parallel organization of his recollections. The "aristocrat" framed the events of a lifetime through a lens of honor—achieved by restraining certain masculine impulses on the one hand and avoiding dependency on the other. Raoul the "proletarian" portrayed masculine honor through an ideological retrospective whereby traumatic memories of disappointment and humiliation were refashioned to reflect not his shortcomings but the failure of capitalism.

Raoul's troubles began when he was expelled from the Lawrenceville School in New Jersey after being discovered in an illicit dalliance with a serving girl. His parents were aghast at this public embarrassment, and their subsequent admonitions about his emerging promiscuity convinced him to remain chaste. This self-imposed celibacy may have rendered Raoul a gentleman among his female peers, though their admiration came with a price. One of his lady friends announced to a gathering of their peers, "I could travel around the world with William, and sleep in the same room with him, and always feel safe." Raoul remembered how "uncomfortable" he felt receiving this ostensible compliment, which in his memory became a "jibe" since it called into question his presumed natural masculine desires.[4] Raoul's dependency, in contrast, left no ambiguity about his dishonored status. Indeed, his relationship with his father was damaged, if not irrevocably broken, by intermittent paternal interventions in his financial affairs.

Raoul's parallel memories juxtaposed aristocratic and radical recollections, and his conversion to socialism allowed him to reconstruct two versions of his past. His honor manifested itself in multiple masculinities: conservative and radical, traditional and modern, prude and libertine, aristocratic and working class.[5] For instance, Raoul defended the abuse of southern labor as traditional and necessary; next, he condemned the same as capitalistic exploitation while seeking to transform the passive southern working class into society's most virile force. He assigned women to the domestic sphere on the one hand, and liberated his lovers (and himself) from conventional sexual restrictions on the other. Raoul's fine clothes and superior temperament made him suspicious to his adopted working-class brethren; he appalled his elite peers by his enthusiasm for sharing the wealth.

After leaving the Lawrenceville School, Raoul joined the architectural firm of Bradford Gilbert (a friend of his father) in New York in 1891. But by 1893, he was back with his parents in Atlanta. That summer he attended the Columbian Exposition and World's Fair in Chicago. Returning to Atlanta that fall, Raoul struggled to establish a career in the booming cotton mill industry. Over the next fifteen years, he held leadership positions in an assortment of industries, from saw manufacturing to boxcar building. These responsibilities usually ended when Raoul refused to abide by his superior's wishes in reinstating an employee whom he had recently fired. Raoul would invariably resign his position rather than stain his honor by rehiring one whom he considered an unsatisfactory underling.

After his conversion to socialism, Raoul ventured westward to observe and participate in a variety of radical endeavors, from the single tax colony of Fairhope, Alabama, to the socialist administration of Butte, Montana. He established a homestead on the plains near the Canadian border before his father's impending death brought him back to Atlanta in 1912. By 1915, Raoul had embarrassed and alienated his family and community by his unorthodox behavior at one of the family's plantations in Millen, Georgia. The following year found him in Greenwich Village keeping company more congenial to his temperament. Raoul eventually retired to nearby Atlantic Highlands, New Jersey, where he reflected on his life in the New South during the depths of the Great Depression.

This essay examines four sites of memory and the stories Raoul associated with these places as he reconstituted his various masculinities in Chicago, Atlanta, Birmingham, and Millen. In Chicago, Raoul created an alternative working-class persona while visiting the Columbian Exposition and World's Fair in 1893, fifteen years before his socialist epiphany. In 1909, on the train home from Waycross, Raoul had a radical revelation that took shape in Atlanta, where he converted to socialism and became aware that masculinity assumed myriad forms. In Birmingham in 1910, soon after his socialist conversion, Raoul undertook a variety of masculine roles in which gender and class collided. In Millen, in 1914–15, he subverted the community's gender expectations by his ill-appropriate sexual relations and his opposition to a prospective lynching. These events led to his alienation from the land of his birth, but together they offer a better understanding of the complex ways that memory and masculinity functioned together in the New South.

Raoul depicts his deliberate descent into the working-class world not just as an adventurous bon vivant on an antivacation, but also as an apprentice anthropologist observing the underclass. Raoul's experiment among "this new world of the working class" hints of Columbian daring and was anticipated by other amateur ethnologists with alternative agendas. Their collective audacity created an unwitting partnership among early twentieth-century social investigators who chose to assume the guise of the working man for purposes of adventure, observation, and identity. Historian Frank Higbie argued that "social investigation literature . . . in which writers donned working-class clothes and lived a double life" presented problems for historians. On the one hand, they convey authenticity while on the other the resulting "texts are as much about defining differences between investigator and subject as they are about working-class life itself." Raoul would never escape this paradox: his descent into the working class was a quest for manliness more authentic (and accessible) than the privileged masculinity of his upbringing, yet the porousness of class boundaries brought into question Raoul's masculine character among his elite and working-class audiences. Higbie asserted "the middle- and upper-class social investigators who took on working-class identities were in a sense expressing uneasiness about their own and working men's manliness." Certainly, Raoul's sojourn among his laboring comrades often revealed the proletarian aristocrat as a stranger searching for alternative masculinities in an alien land.[6]

Sent by his father to the Columbian Exposition in Chicago to observe and report back on new technology, Raoul was soon both broke and hesitant to return home. He had promised his family and peers that he would remain in Chicago to seek employment there if he did not receive a summons for work in Atlanta. This vow led to a futile job search in depression-ridden Chicago and provoked him to assume an alternative masculine personality. Raoul's sartorial surface often undermined his working-class intentions, however. He complained that "people seemed to differentiate me from the usual workman." Fifteen years later, in his initial foray into radical politics in Atlanta, Raoul went to his first meeting of the Socialist Party and was received with "rather hostile looks." Of course, Raoul "was very well dressed. That was part of my job, and in considerable contrast with the membership." His fashionable dress prompted a member to make "a somewhat fiery speech about how, since the Socialists were becoming such a threatening force in society, the capitalists would soon be trying to break in so as to capture their organization, and he warned that great care should be exercised in taking in new members." Raoul was astounded by this hostile declaration, though very impressed with the local's "excellent and systematic methods of organization."[7]

Raoul's astonishment arose from the heretofore unimagined hostility of the working class to his sympathetic presence when, after all, he should have been greeted with gratitude for his thinly disguised paternalism on the one hand and authentic interests in their socialist ideas on the other. The confusion attendant to both sides—Raoul and his working-class audience for which he was essentially auditioning—reflected confusing masculine facades. Raoul came to this radical congregation as a novice, though possessed of the bearing and dress of a class enemy. To the socialist club he sought to join, his surface betrayed class antagonism by its easy confidence and its genuine upper-class countenance. The irony, of course, lay in Raoul's search for masculine authenticity among the blue collars combined with his rejection of the facile manliness of his peers. At play in Raoul's identity were (at least) three possible masculinities: the steely captain of industry (Raoul's father), the rich dandy ne'er-do-well (Raoul himself), and the rough-and-tumble working-class proletarian (Raoul's alter ego).

As a young man in Chicago in 1893, Raoul, having been caught in the wrong cultural clothing for workingmen's jobs, resolved to try a new masculine wardrobe in his forlorn search for work even as the Depression of 1893 began. He decided not to "waste any time on good jobs . . . After all, this was merely a demonstration, not the great career of captain of industry I would yet embark on." His high-sounding language of exploration revealed the state of desperation in which Raoul found himself unemployed in a Chicago bursting with out-of-work men. Various construction foremen told Raoul "in forcible and unmistakable language just how little they needed any men at all, particularly one such as I."[8] His daily deportment made his applications for work absurd in the eyes of men who had never done anything other than labor with their hands. Raoul's estimation of himself, fashioned in opposition to the blue-collar men he now sought to join, underwent seismic shifts as his borderline status rendered him useless to his class peers and ridiculous to the working class.

Raoul imposed a pattern of radical remembrances upon his difficult stay in Chicago. His decision to apply for work at every storefront along a prosperous-looking street meant, in retrospect, that Raoul "was going to *scab* it with a vengeance." He got a job selling life insurance door-to-door to people who viewed such products cynically as unattainable luxuries. His honor was called into question by a maidservant who scolded him for trying to sell her an insurance policy she could not afford. Raoul "flushed again at the memory" of being "set right on a point of common honesty and plain figures by a maid servant at a back door."[9] This attack on Raoul's honor, and his memory of it, revealed a young man uncomfortably trapped in a netherworld of malfunctioning masculinities: neither his elite status nor his pathetic earnestness made any impression on Chicago's bloated labor market.

Raoul tried to salvage his diminished honor by reinventing himself as a member of the working class. His "brilliant idea" resulted in a public résumé of sorts, a "postal card" displayed outside his rooming-house. This advertisement was signed "in a feigned hand" by a working-class persona created in Raoul's imagination, one "Tom Davis." He had never known "a man named Tom Davis, but that name brings to my mind a real personality, the man I was to be." Thus Raoul sought to create out of his own raw material what he fancied a working-class man might look like. Should anyone call on this fictitious "Tom Davis," Raoul informed his landlady that "I was he."[10]

Raoul's new masculinity grew tiresome after a day, and he stopped "impersonating Tom Davis" and reassumed his "own personality." He shed his working-class shirt and "dressed carefully in a cutaway coat and short fawn colored top box coat." Authenticity and artifice collided, however, when after retrieving his "fashionable derby hat" and gloves, his "enigmatic landlady" flung open the door and declared in an irritated tone: "Davis: someone to see you." "Paralyzed," Raoul hurriedly began to dismantle his elite masculine appearance by dropping the gloves and discarding the coat as "if I was going into action," thus linking physicality to a manliness he believed would be required in this surprise interview.[11] For Raoul, the difference between upper-class and working-class masculinities lay in his façade. He may have told his sister, Mary Raoul Millis, a different memory of this event. In her *Family of Raoul,* Millis described the dramatic scene absent the landlady as her brother descended "the dingy stairs" only to be confronted by "a burly Contractor" who announced that he was looking for Tom Davis, "the man who sent me this letter." Raoul, dressed as if on the way to a cotillion instead of a construction site, confirmed his false identity. The foreman's "glance wandered from top hat to patent leather shoes, in slow, inexpressible scorn . . . and without another word, he turned and left."[12]

In Raoul's version of the incident, he confessed the "crime" of impersonation in his memory while assuring the foreman of his qualifications. The foreman's questions were asked "sternly"; Raoul answered "feebly." He had been emasculated by a member of the working class and embarrassed by his dandified dress in the presence of a man bewildered by Tom Davis, the laborer, now inappropriately dressed as William Raoul, an elite without need of work and, indeed, probably a part of the exploitive capitalist class. When asked if he understood framing, Raoul, who "had never heard the word . . . rose to the occasion" and said "yes." When informed by the foreman that he should be ready to leave on the morning's five o'clock train, Raoul lost what was left of his composure. He did not have any money, tools, or skills. By this confession, he avoided the job. While writing his memories, Raoul reflected that he "should have plunged . . . [because] once out in the sticks he would have had to give me a fair trial."[13] The implication, of course, was that Raoul could represent a framer until he actually became one. Clearly particular masculinities corresponded to particular skills. With myriad masculinities available, Raoul had only to determine what unique qualities were required.

Raoul as a working man in disguise would reemerge in his adventures as a hobo and socialist proselytizer. He paid special attention to his appearance as an aristocrat on the one hand and as a member of the working class on the other. When he arrived in Birmingham, on the first leg of his journey through radical America, Raoul chose "a working shirt . . . instead of the white collar mark," making clear for all to see what sort of man was he. When offered an opportunity to return to Atlanta to look after his father's interest in the Associated Charities, he took a "recess" from his "working-class life," thus diminishing the authenticity of his life as a laborer. Looking for, and getting, work in Kansas, Raoul believed he was "well *disguised* as an amiable and capable farm hand." By the time he reached Butte, Montana, Raoul deliberately "dressed in corduroys and blue shirt, and a western hat, something on the cowboy order."[14] Raoul's attentiveness to dress and comportment revealed his bourgeois status. Genuine working class would not know or care about appearing in appropriate attire. Raoul was self-conscious about the numerous masculinities available to him.

Raoul's inability to find either work or suitable quarters convinced him to end his Chicago experiment and return to Atlanta. He sought financial help from two prominent Georgians staying in the city: future governor John Slaton and William Black, later a federal judge in New York. Both were ensconced in a Chicago hotel. The first time Raoul called upon them, he had to wait. Adding to his humiliation, he imagined the "bell hops had begun to be suspicious of me," a perverse inversion of honor as his social inferiors questioned his status as he loitered about the lobby. He returned the following morning and said to Slaton, "I hardly know you well enough to ask such a favor, but I would be most obliged if you would help me." Slaton was "most happy to accommodate" Raoul's financial needs, which amounted to $7.50 for a train ticket back to Atlanta.[15]

Raoul arrived back in Atlanta from Chicago before dawn and walked to his father's house at 708 Peachtree Street, just one door north of the city limit. It was early September 1893, and Raoul went to sleep in the hammock strung up in the backyard. At sunrise, he entered the house with the servants through the back door and went upstairs to the "boy's floor" where he bathed and made himself presentable at the family's breakfast table. After greetings were exchanged, Raoul remembered "no prying questions were asked, and I volunteered no information." He had "a feeling that I had been whipped, but hadn't had a fair deal, and that nobody would understand this." His sister Mary remembered Raoul's homecoming: he was received at breakfast "without enthusiasm. He was disgraced; but . . . was it *his* fault that men lay idle and hungry [in Chicago] . . . and could find no work to do?"[16]

Raoul's memories were often constructed with a caveat whereby his radical voice anachronistically imposed itself on events that occurred years before his conversion to socialism. This justified and made sense of his failures before his socialist enlightenment. He employed one when recalling this painful first morning home from Chicago. He blamed "this very family of mine" who "were part of that world which had gone all wrong," and that they were not "capable of understanding the spiritual revolution" that gripped him after this apparent defeat. He remembered a "misconception, disproved by my experience in Chicago, that all men who were willing to work could always find work . . . but I did not then realize" how false was the capitalist explanation of economic life. After breakfast, Raoul went to the Southern Iron Car Line and spoke to owners Eugene and Will Spalding, who were neighbors. He pleaded with Will Spalding. "I want work. I wanted work before I left [for Chicago three months ago], but now I just must have it. I will do absolutely anything, Mr. Will, at any price, or no price, but I just must have work."[17] Raoul, of course, was not begging for a living wage, but rather for a respectable masculinity.

Raoul's bad memories of his Chicago ordeal informed his conversion to socialism. Continued personal and business failure acted as a catalyst for transformation. Home from Chicago, Raoul wondered whether he was "the same stout heart" that had departed for the Columbian Exposition three months previous. Never personally religious, Raoul nevertheless may have borrowed this vocabulary from the evangelical ambience of the South. Personal failure was allayed by assigning blame on an exploitive system. He had been told that "every man who was willing to work [could] earn his living." This bromide "was a damned lie." On the verge of switching class allegiances, Raoul ruminated on how he had "nothing, or near to nothing" to show for his fifteen years of business endeavors. In that time, he had become a "rolling stone" without gathering "either the moss of business reputation or of financial power." In his memory, Raoul "always seemed, in some unaccountable way, to become the storm center of some question of policy or procedure, which eventually eliminated me from the picture." Self-doubt made him ask whether "there [was] a screw loose in Raoul?"[18] Raoul's anxious sense of his own unfulfilled masculine identity combined with his frustrated expectations to make a volatile mix. His sexual life had been narrowed to prostitutes after an unsatisfying marriage; his business career had been reduced to temporary positions without prestige and performed by one increasingly peripatetic. Thus, Raoul's two primary outlets for masculine expression, as a husband and as a businessman, had been thus far disappointing. An epiphany awaited that would provide an alternative path to gender happiness.

In Waycross, Georgia, in 1908, on a small accounting job, Raoul stayed for dinner with his Uncle John, then president of the First National Bank of Waycross. While "mixing toddies at the sideboard," the two discussed politics and economics "in an academic way." After an inebriated discourse on a subject lost to memory, his uncle characterized one of Raoul's ideas as "socialistic." An authority of these unusual politics was "a shoemaker here in town" who had given Uncle John some socialist literature. Raoul asked for the pamphlets. His Aunt Hennie, believing the material taboo, complied with the comment, "Here William, here they are, take the dirty things. I'll be glad to get them out of the house."[19] It would be interesting to know why Aunt Hennie had kept such forbidden material.

On the train home to Atlanta, Raoul began to thumb through the various pamphlets. He remembered the "ABC of Socialism" by someone named Clemons who turned out to be Mark Twain's brother. By the time he reached Atlanta, Raoul was in an "excited frame of mind," his imagination and reason "captured" by the various arguments. His "mind flashed back over the experiences of [his] life. Why was I not given work way back in Chicago when I was a beggar for it? Because the silly system had tied itself in a knot and no one could make a profit out of my labor." Raoul remembered his low wages in the Atlanta cotton mills and his high wages at the Lowell Mills in Massachusetts and realized that "one set of robbers could get more than another out of you, that was all there was to that."[20]

Back in his office in Atlanta, Raoul's "blood surged back into my heart as I paced the room." He was animated by "hope, fight, and defiance." He ordered socialist literature and read constantly. A light went on. "Maybe I was not a failure after all." He began thinking of "a better world" in which he could participate. Raoul was "reborn, transformed, exalted, with this vision of what might be." He began to regard his past values and behavior with contempt. This language indicated a genuine conversion. Raoul's epiphany transformed his narrow conception of proper masculine behavior and, perhaps more importantly, of how a southern gentleman could acquire honor in a society where masculine reputation accrued via business success. He seemed, suddenly, "to stand for the moment far and aloof from . . . this painful, humiliating, money grabbing ambition." He enjoyed, at least in memory, the irony of reading subversive literature at his "big comfortable desk in my comfortable office." His stenographer, Miss

Crosthwait, implored him in the feminized language Raoul reserved for nearly all women, "Oh, Mr. Raoul . . . if you would just put the energy in looking around for work that you do in reading those Socialist books, I know that you would get a lot to do." Traditional condescension fled in the face of uncharacteristic fury. Raoul turned "almost savagely" on his secretary: "Miss Crosthwait . . . just get this through your head. I have crawled around and begged for my last job. I'm going to sit here and read these Socialist books just as long as I want to, and when I get through doing that, I will be ready to tell you what I am going to do."[21] Miss Crosthwait, an idealized foil, and her impertinent advice, combined with his disgust of continued supplication, hastened Raoul's transition from a deskbound masculinity to one with (occasionally) calloused hands.

Raoul resolved to "make an honest living," to give up "reputation and influence" and depend, instead, on his "muscle and skill as a workman to supply my modest requirements." He substituted one set of masculine criteria for another. "An honest living" meant one more genuine since it would be procured with muscle. In contrast, "reputation and influence" were artifices of capitalism's exploitive system. Raoul would replace the artificiality of elite connections with the authenticity of manual labor, yet remnants of his aristocratic upbringing kept Raoul a figure on the fringe (in both his life and memories) easily able to penetrate the boundaries of whichever masculinity he chose to inhabit. He possessed little muscle and less skill as he embarked on his new masculinity; his "modest requirements" were not meant ironically. He had "begged and flattered and cajoled to get a chance to make a living for the last time." Henceforth, he "would quit lying about how prosperous [he] was and how bright [his] prospects." As for his peers, he remembered that he was "through with their standards, and through with them." Instead, he would venture into the working-class world, carrying the "lance of the proselyte."[22]

In this "exalted and rebellious state of mind," Raoul received a letter of complaint from a bank president whose books Raoul had examined. He was angry that his cashier had been stealing from him for years, and yet he, the bank president, had caught the thief instead of Raoul, the accountant. In the letter, he asked what good did it do him "to hire high priced accountants, if it is left to me to catch the defaulter?" Had such a letter arrived before Raoul's conversion, it would have thrown him "into a cold sweat. Now the privilege of answering it amused me immensely." Raoul wrote back that his advice "was to dispense with the accountants, and do all the work himself." Raoul, a new man, would no longer abide "lecturing from anybody."[23]

Raoul decided upon Birmingham to begin "earning my living as [a] journeyman." To do so in Atlanta "would savor too much of publicity seeking." Also, he wanted "to make a more complete severance with my inherited associations than would have been possible" in Atlanta. As if auditioning for a workingman's job, Raoul built an elaborate tool chest within which his new masculinity might be both demonstrated and contained. He arrived in Birmingham with the newly constructed chest and a "working shirt . . . instead of the white collar mark." Raoul remembered his earlier fashion imbroglios in Chicago and Atlanta. The chest, too, would soon be discarded for a "suit case" less heavy and more practical for a man on the move.[24] Raoul improvised his new masculinity.

In February 1910, only a month since his departure from Atlanta, Raoul wrote to his mother, "there is a movement on fire here to start a socialist paper." In March, he wrote that he had taken leave from work to arrange the first issue of *The People's Voice*. He would edit the paper without compensation and would like for his mother "to send us $1.00 for your subscription." Raoul believed that his mother would come to "understand" [him] by reading his paper. Judging from his next letter home, his mother apparently took the same dim view of socialist literature as had his Aunt Hennie. In a supplicating tone, Raoul wrote his mother that socialism seemed "so reasonable and noble and good to me and so free from all communism or servility, that it is hard for me to believe it can seem totally otherwise to those I honor and love." The utopian vocabulary of socialism sounded to Raoul "like those of a great patriarch or statesman." Raoul obviously received a rude reply as his next letter declared in an incredulous tone that, "I had no idea that I could go to editing a paper and you not wish to see it." For Raoul, editing a paper marked success; for his mother, the achievement was tainted by its subject matter. The pathetic tone of a disappointed schoolboy gave way to an indignant voice that did "not wish to change your views *one whit. I only wish that you could become acquainted with mine.*" The happy tone of his next letter was no doubt due to a check from his mother that was "certainly greatly appreciated" since it allowed him to "square" his debts and give more time to the "Voice."[25] The shame of financial dependence disappeared when the cause shifted from Raoul's personal failures to his noble quest to uplift the working class.

The People's Voice ran for less than a year, but before it ended, Raoul ran a story that forced him to revert to the paternalistic masculinity native to his temper. An explosion at a nearby mine prompted Raoul to visit the site, mingle with the miners, spend the night "around the pit head," and write an article published the following day. This piece did not "spare either owners or local managers or foremen." To make certain it was read by the miners, Raoul sent a bundle of papers with a miner to distribute them at the site. Receiving no reply to this provocation, Raoul went himself the next day to the camp and delivered his presumably accusatory story "from house to house."[26]

The results of Raoul's story, now widely disseminated within the mining camp, yielded quick consequences that tested its author's wits. Two men entered Raoul's Birmingham office the next day, "and as they seated themselves, the older man picked up the long shears lying on the desk, and kept possession of them. The younger man was a burly, grimy customer, and heavily under the influence of liquor." The latter informed Raoul that he was a mine foreman, that he did not appreciate the abuse aimed at him in the story, that, in addition, he was armed and "had come to town to have it out with me." To ratchet up the tension, the foreman, whose honor had been insulted, suggested that he and Raoul "shoot it out right then and there." Raoul portrayed his opponent in memory as "overwrought" with both "liquor and his grievance," while admitting that "things looked rather dangerous for me." His defense rested upon drawing the drunk foreman "into an argument" about the circumstances of the explosion while not "retracting" anything he had written. (Years before, as a cotton-mill manager, Raoul had made it plain that he would not accept threats of violence from the underclass, and that his code then was to shoot down any worker who transgressed and laid a hand upon him.) The ensuing argument only inflamed the mine foreman whose "voice became so loud, and his language so lurid, that two plain clothes men passing on the street came up and threatened to run him in for swearing in public."[27] Three competing (and ironic in the case of the first two) masculinities converged: Raoul the aristocratic editor of a radical paper; the working-class mine foreman, drunk and armed, and representing the capitalist's interests; and two Birmingham plainclothes policemen whose backgrounds are unknown but whose authority trumped all.

The policemen's intervention in this potentially violent affair provided Raoul an opportunity he would not miss. Instead of welcoming the authorities as a deus ex machina ready to snatch away the belligerent mine boss, Raoul said something so offensive to them that they now threatened to arrest him as well. At this juncture, Raoul "became . . . judicial." He explained the dispute "was merely a friendly difference of opinion" in which his friend, the mine foreman, "had forgotten himself." Raoul guaranteed "that he would not transgress again." His demeanor mollified both the police and the foreman: the former left satisfied that things were well in hand and the latter "was so impressed with my apparent magnanimity . . . that he proposed that we go to the nearest speakeasy and have a drink." Over shots of whiskey, Raoul promised the foreman he would return to the mining camp and if he discovered any editorial mistakes, he would correct them in the next edition of *The People's Voice*. No retractions were made. The foreman never returned. New editions of *The People's Voice* were met by "company guards on arrival and marched off the mining reservation without further ceremony."[28]

This incident demonstrated the variety of masculine roles at play and available to Raoul. As an ostensible member of the working class and a committed socialist, he instigated the drama on behalf of what he considered the most progressive—and exploited—segment of society. His readings of Marx and others had made plain the inexorable triumph of the proletariat, while his position as the vanguard of that movement allowed him to assume an ironic role as champion of the underclass against his own. By provoking the mine foreman into an argument, Raoul was able to temporarily forestall violence through question and rebuttal. When immediate gunplay was threatened, Raoul then came to the defense of his apparent class enemy against authorities of the law. He reconciled all parties to a solution of his construction, thus making plain his mastery of all the masculinities he surveyed.[29]

Raoul spent his final year in the South as an accountant, occasional overseer, and general troubleshooter at the family's plantation at the small southeastern Georgia town of Millen, equidistant between Savannah and Augusta. In 1914, immersed in self-doubt and depression after receiving his inheritance following his father's death, Raoul received a letter from his cousin Frank Wadley requesting his presence at the family's plantation in Millen where his accounting skills might help "in straightening out the books." This letter arrived "like a godsend." Raoul was "galvanized into action" and left for Millen. He met with his cousins (the estate's two principals and siblings) Frank Wadley and Florence Wadley Coleman to discuss his duties. Raoul was untroubled by impending gender subversion. Florence made plain that she would run the estate and that her brother, Frank, would be excluded from decision making as he was "a child in arms compared to Florence, in business and executive ability, and in shrewdness and singleness of purpose." Thus Florence assumed traditional masculine roles as Frank was assigned feminine subordination. Raoul would act as Florence's "ally in the undertaking."[30]

Raoul served briefly as plantation overseer and encountered myriad gender surprises in his management of labor, black and white, male and female. In his attempts to secure needed farmhands, Raoul had to reconcile paradoxical masculine impulses: to exploit labor as was expected from a white southerner, or to empathize with his various charges as a radical reformer. His experience as a manager of men had convinced Raoul that "sustained work cannot be gotten without a reasonable degree of contentment." For Raoul, "The plantation Negroes [were] handled a good deal like a lot of children . . . cajoled and flattered and pushed into carrying on their long and monotonous tasks." Similar to the feminization of Frank Wadley, African American labor was infantilized and their masculinity diminished, yet Raoul the radical remembered how "the plantation Negro is an entirely different breed of animal from the up-country white who worked in the cotton mills." He contrasted pliable white mill workers with recalcitrant African Americans who on the plantation "can sabotage more effectively than any workman that I know of." Thus the radical track of Raoul's memories mitigated his traditional contempt for African Americans. He admired the black laborer's capacity to disrupt, via sabotage or other means of resistance, a capitalistic system based on both class and racial exploitation. Raoul's aristocratic and radical memory paths intersected when he remembered how one of the family's long-term associates and onetime overseer, Joe Duberry, always referred to him as "Mr. Willie. This was in recollection of our childhood, and a compromise with our first names, which his class position did not permit him to use." Here indigenous paternalism (Raoul's easy acceptance of this hierarchy as natural) and acquired radical critique ("class position") combined to reinforce one another. In contrast, Raoul's radical memory recalled how Duberry's brother, another overseer, "had died from a wound inflicted with an axe by some irate Negro, whom he was doubtless abusing."[31] Raoul's adopted antipathy toward southern labor traditions made possible the juxtaposition of the African American murderer as victim and the white (and dead) overseer as aggressor. This line of reasoning would reappear when Raoul used race and gender to defend another black sharecropper accused of an assault against a white landowner.

Raoul imposed parallel memories on the masculinity and the management of African American labor. An earlier overseer had hired two "stalwart young Negroes as wage hands." These two settled into their sharecropper cabin with supplied provisions, worked a day or two, and then disappeared "up the railroad tracks." Raoul the aristocrat admired the overseer's ability to capture and return his truant labor to the field with the aid of the local sheriff. Raoul the radical deplored the tradition of placing these men "in debt" and the "illegal law" that required their labor in exchange for room and board.[32] Southern mastery of black labor exemplified white supremacy, a notion not unpleasing to Raoul, yet in his socialist memory the dignity of labor clashed with traditional southern exploitation of African American workers.

Raoul remembered another method by which white masculinity asserted its dominance over black manliness. He heard his cousin Frank Wadley tell an African American sharecropper, whom he had heard swearing at one of his mules, that he "did not allow anybody to curse any of my mules. It don't do any good, and besides, I just don't allow it on this plantation." Wadley objected to a black man cursing in his presence since such language implied an equality that did not exist. Wadley's qualification, "on this plantation," substituted spatial parameters for racial injunctions in this instance. Raoul admired Wadley's "tactful" method.[33] For Raoul, race would usually, but not always, trump class.

Feminine labor proved especially vexatious for Raoul the overseer. Once he had to settle the "debt" of a family who worked for a neighboring farmer to bring them to the Wadley plantation. The husband remained behind while the wife proceeded to unload all their worldly possessions in view of Raoul and another farmer who happened by. Raoul felt "guilty at sitting there in a buggy and watching that poor woman struggling with her household goods." In response to his suggestion that the two of them lend a hand, Raoul's neighbor "replied with condescending authority, knowing that I was a comparative stranger to the life," that he "couldn't think of doing anything like that." Should Raoul deign to help, warned his knowing companion, "[s]he wouldn't have any more respect for you."[34] Thus Raoul's inclination to assist the weaker sex was shot down by his neighbor's insight that any help would diminish his masculine dominance asserted across gender and class lines.

Crossing racial lines were as treacherous for Raoul as transgressing class lines in his quest for labor. He "scraped up . . . an exceptionally good looking mulatto" with a baby but without a man. After settling the two into their sharecropper cabin, Raoul brought supplies for the week and food for the evening. As he made to leave, "she looked up at me with a pathetic appeal." Raoul remembered her as two people in one, "just a child herself, but a woman, and beautiful to look upon." Perhaps this woman's racial ambiguity made easier Raoul's escape as he "hurried away in confusion. My God! What was I about to get into?" The young woman, both vulnerable and perhaps sexually available, complicated Raoul's masculine calculations, forcing him to waver between paternal restraint on the one hand and pent-up sexual desire on the other.[35]

Indeed, the confusion attendant to sexual choices made Raoul's stay in Millen especially problematic because his inclination to transgress traditional gender behavior alienated his family and community. Having turned forty-three while at the plantation, Raoul initiated a troubling relationship with eighteen-year-old Winifred Wadley, Raoul's cousin and the younger sister of Florence Wadley Coleman, his putative boss. Like the mulatto woman just mentioned, Raoul had a dual memory of Winifred as a "combination of baby, child, and voluptuous woman. She was small, and plump, with beautifully full and firm breasts . . . and a romping manner." Raoul enjoyed watching Winifred "break over foolish conventions" and the subsequent consternation on the faces of family and friends. Raoul's encouragement of Winifred's exaggerated feminine behavior, however ossified he believed traditional gender roles to be, angered both family and community. With young Winifred, pliable, rebellious, and alluring, Raoul proposed marriage "as a more satisfactory relationship than the one we had then entered into." In Raoul's mind, "more satisfactory" meant sexual access without necessarily committing to a permanent union as he coupled his proposal with the comment "that if, in the future, it became undesirable, it could be easily dissolved."[36]

Raoul's first marriage had been characterized by four years of dangerous pregnancies, fear of intimacy, abortions, miscarriages, ignorance of contraceptives, and, finally, the death of his wife Ruth Cunningham Raoul during childbirth.[37] He understandably complained that marriage did not guarantee a happy sexual union. On the Millen plantation, he created his own version of the "New Woman" by supporting Winifred's unorthodox behavior and dress.[38] In this way, he gained her confidence as prelude to possessing her body.

Married in January 1915, the newlyweds' connubial glow had already begun to dim by that spring because of Raoul's dalliance with Meta Sinclair Fuller, the wife of novelist Upton Sinclair. He had met her in New York after attending a socialist convention in Cleveland. Invited to the plantation, Meta promptly scandalized both the household and the community by her unorthodox dress and behavior.

Adding to these troubles was the shooting of a neighbor that, combined with Raoul's sexually charged relationship with Mrs. Sinclair, led to his permanent departure from the South. Ben Franklin, owner of a nearby plantation, was shot by one of his African American sharecroppers, Tom Campbell. Raoul received two stories upon the incident and later, in 1933, imposed his interpretation upon both narratives as he wrote his memoir. He heard the black version of the incident from the Campbell's fellow sharecroppers, and then two days later, he listened to the white side of the story from his cousin Frank Wadley, who had talked to Franklin's brother. The interpretation Raoul imposed on his memories combined elements of both his aristocratic and radical selves to manipulate these two narratives. His rendition demonstrated how masculine honor was too slippery to be easily categorized by race.

According to the African Americans, Franklin had gone to the Campbell home and became irate after finding the sharecropper's wife readying a shotgun for fishing (the blast stuns the fish and they float to the top). He complained about her laziness and of the work that needed attention. Furious, Franklin snatched the shotgun from Mrs. Campbell and aimed it at her while trying unsuccessfully to load a shell into the chamber. Leaving the yard in frustration, Franklin was accosted by Tom Campbell who "protested against this treatment, seized another gun, a single barreled shotgun . . . and emptied its contents into Franklin's back." This version of the episode exemplified the conundrum posed by W. E. B. Du Bois twelve years earlier on his tour of southern Georgia when he wrote of the black sharecropper's "careless ignorance and laziness here, fierce hate and vindictiveness there."[39]

Franklin was severely wounded, but lived; Campbell fled into the nearby swamps of Duck Pond to hide from the inevitable retribution of a lynch mob that began gathering "within an incredibly short time" from the "neighboring plantations and towns, and from other parts of the state." Vigilantes "came in automobiles, in buggies, and on horseback" while the local sheriff "brought the dogs from his convict camp for use in tracking Campbell to his hiding place." Georgia Governor John Slaton (who had paid for Raoul's dismal train trip home from Chicago in 1893) posted a reward for Campbell's capture. Thus an interracial conflict over two men's honor had mobilized "all the forces of law and lawlessness" that now "joined hands to take part in the man hunt."[40]

The other version of the story, the one related to Raoul by his cousin Frank Wadley, came secondhand from the victim's brother. It differed significantly and contained elements incompatible with Raoul's (aristocratic) estimate of Franklin's masculinity or his (radical) estimate of Campbell's honor. According to Franklin, he informed the Campbells that they had better get to work plowing instead of shooting fish. While crossing the yard to get his mule, Campbell said loud enough for Franklin to hear, "I b'lieve I'll jus' kill de son of a bitch now."[41] Alarmed at this threat, Franklin began to run until he was cut down by Campbell's shotgun blast to the back. Campbell's wife rushed at him with an axe as he lay prostrate, and his death was only prevented by the couple's excited children. According to Wadley, Franklin claimed to have never abused or touched the Campbell woman.

Raoul was incredulous and asked his cousin if he believed this tale. Wadley replied, "I have no reason not to believe it. I would take a white man's word before a Negro's every time." Truth, explicitly racialized, was now also implicitly gendered between distinct masculinities divided not only by race and class but also by implied essential differences between two types of men: a white landlord and a black sharecropper. Raoul, acutely aware of the nuances of white honor and masculine shame, critiqued Wadley's version of events. He pointed out that Franklin was not only a courageous man but a "high tempered one, and that it was not at all like him, or any other man, to run in the face of a threat from a Negro . . . that the natural course of any man in such a situation, would have been to go to the Negro to prevent his carrying out the threat."[42] Raoul dismissed his cousin's version of the story, in part, because it posited a white man fleeing a black man. Raoul's interpretation troubled Wadley because of its implications: Franklin had lied about his aggression to mitigate his share of the blame for the shooting that followed. Raoul was less interested in Franklin's defense than what he believed to be the honorable response of any white man confronted with black violence.

Frank Wadley became angry and ended the conversation by stating his preference for a white man's word over a "nigger," and that anyone who did not "would do himself no good in this part of the country."[43] Wadley did what Raoul refused to do: he willingly subordinated white honor to black guilt, a conclusion repugnant to Raoul's aristocratic calculations of white southern manliness.

Raoul believed that had Campbell been "captured in the next twenty-four hours he would have been lynched." He was captured five days later, however, after the excitement had died down and Franklin appeared well on his way to recovery. Both Campbell and his wife were charged with "assault with intent to murder" and jailed in Millen. Raoul visited the jail and spoke with the sheriff. A mutual friend asked the sheriff what he would do if men appeared at his jail with shotguns. The sheriff answered that he would "be somewhere else," thus signaling his acquiescence in vigilante justice.[44]

Raoul's interpretation of the Franklin-Campbell dispute made explicit what the rest of the white community ignored. He recognized that this incident inverted the usual southern narrative about racial violence. Here, a white man apparently assaulted a black woman instead of the traditional trope of black men attacking white women. In this case, instead of a white man defending the honor of his alabaster spouse, a black man came to the rescue of his threatened wife. Raoul argued "that *any man* would have shot Franklin under like circumstances," thus collapsing racial distinctions about masculine honor. Raoul's arguments affirmed that the dignity and motives of an African American man, in defense of his wife and home, were no different than that of a white man—that, indeed, black and white masculinities mirrored one another.[45]

Previous to his conversation with the sheriff, Raoul had "expressed [his] intention to be present in case of a lynching, and to put the mob on notice that [he] would stand as a reputable witness in prosecuting them." Alarmed for his safety, Raoul's family was also angry and confused at his ambiguous attitude. A younger cousin, Richard Wadley, told him that he had heard that Raoul would be shot and strung up "alongside the nigger" if he interfered with the lynching party. Raoul expressed "contempt of such mobs."[46] In the end, Raoul's calculations of white and black masculinities were too complex for a community that confined manliness to a narrow gamut dependent primarily on race. Raoul was a symptom of the New South's tentative steps into the twentieth century's often bewildering array of choices. His choice of socialism exemplified the proliferating, though only grudgingly recognized, masculinities in the New South.

Race, class, and gender were deeply conflicted issues as the New South underwent tremendous change. Raoul's anthropological assessments of class and gender, his class inversion and interests in socialism, his (self-serving) reformulation of gender and sexuality, even his attempts to envision a form of southern laboring-class masculinity that was able to transcend racial divisions are remarkable in their own right. But they are important for other reasons too: with Raoul we have a lens through which we can glimpse how these categories of identity that seemed too rigid and unchanging were in fact easily manipulated. As the aristocrat shifted into the socialist proletarian, Raoul did not abandon his patrician heritage; rather it remained, encoded in his behaviors and thoughts about race and class. As gender identities mutated and were "classed" and "raced," we see the twinning images, the parallel tracks that continued to inform Raoul's relations with those in his family and community. While Raoul seems aberrant in his path from aristocrat to worker, he in fact demonstrated that deep conflicts about class status were intertwined with serious reservations about how to construct and maintain a viable "southern" masculinity, a problem that transcends the narrow bounds of William Raoul's life and speaks to the broader historical transformations being felt across and through the New South.

NOTES

Many thanks go to Jared Poley and Krystyn Moon for their guidance throughout this project.

1. William G. Raoul Jr., "The Proletarian Aristocrat," 1933, Southern Historical Collection, University of North Carolina, Chapel Hill, 242. Thanks also go to Dr. Robert McMath who supplied this author with a copy of "The Proletarian Aristocrat," as well as his "From Captain of Industry to Sergeant of Socialism," in *Looking South: Chapters in the Story of an American Region*, ed. Winifred Moore and Joseph Tripp (New York: Greenwood Press, 1989), 171–89.
2. Located at 848 Peachtree Street, the Raoul residence was designed by New York architect Bradford L. Gilbert, with whom Raoul served for a year as an apprentice after leaving preparatory school. For Gilbert, see Henry F. Withey and Elsie Rathburn Withey, *Biographical Dictionary of American Architects (Deceased)* (Los Angeles: Hennessey and Ingalls, 1970), 233.
3. Raoul, "Proletarian Aristocrat," 2, 240. Raoul's self-imposed category of a particular style of manliness is reflected within the historiography of masculinities. See Michael Kimmel, *Manhood in America: A Cultural History* (New York: Free Press, 1996), 9; Elizabeth Pleck and Joseph Pleck, ed., *The American Man* (Englewood Cliffs, N.J.: Prentice-Hall, 1980), 21–28; Anthony Rotundo, *American Manhood: Transformations in Masculinity from the Revolution to the Modern Era* (New York: Basic Books, 1993), 7; Gail Bederman, *Manliness and Civilization: A Cultural History of Gender and Race in the United States, 1880–1917* (Chicago: University of Chicago Press, 1995); Lorri Glover, "An Education in Southern Masculinity: The Ball Family of South Carolina in the New Republic," *Journal of Southern History* 59 (2003): 39–71.
4. Raoul, "Proletarian Aristocrat," 8.
5. For the construction of honor in the antebellum South, see Bertram Wyatt-Brown, *Honor and Violence in the Old South* (New York: Oxford University Press, 1986), 3–120; W. J. Cash, *The Mind of the South* (New York: Vintage Books, 1991); Kenneth S. Greenberg, *Honor and Slavery* (Princeton, N.J.: Princeton University Press, 1996); Craig Thompson Friend and Lorri Glover, eds., *Southern Manhood: Perspectives on Masculinity in the Old South* (Athens: University of Georgia Press, 2004).

6. Raoul, "Proletarian Aristocrat," 238. See Walter Wyckoff, *A Day with a Tramp* (New York: Benjamin Blom, 1901); Nels Anderson, *The Hobo: The Sociology of the Homeless Man* (Chicago: University of Chicago Press, 1923); Frank T. Higbie, *Indispensable Outcasts: Hobo Workers and Community in the American Midwest, 1880–1930* (Urbana: University of Illinois Press, 2003), 68. Anthropologist (and Raoul's contemporary) Franz Boas, *The Mind of Primitive Man* (New York: Macmillan Company, 1911), 21, described how the assumed superiority of the investigating (or colonizing) group was often based on the "difference between its social status" with that of the subject people. Boas's protégé, Claude Levi-Strauss, *Structural Anthropology*, trans. Claire Jacobson and Brooke Grundfest (New York: Basic Books, 1963), 378, asserted that the anthropological method was marked by "distantiation" whereby the investigator and his subjects were "representatives of very different cultures."

7. Raoul, "Proletarian Aristocrat," 20, 238. John K. Turner, "Labor Union and Socialist Local Infested with Corporation Spies," in the 25 July 1914 *Appeal to Reason*, argued that "ever since the smoke began to rise from the tall chimneys at Akron, the Corporation Auxiliary Company has had scores of 'operatives' (pretended workingmen) in the factories 'inspecting,' reporting upon and discharging the rubber workers"; see John Graham, ed., *"Yours for the Revolution": The Appeal to Reason, 1895–1922* (Lincoln: University of Nebraska Press, 1990), 122. In the same collection is a confidential letter from the Corporation Auxiliary Company, Cleveland, Ohio, that promised to "eliminate the agitator and organizer quietly and with little or no friction, and further, through the employment of our system, you will now at all times know who among your employees are loyal and to be depended upon" (126).

8. Raoul, "Proletarian Aristocrat," 18. Walter Wyckoff, *The Workers: An Experiment in Reality, the West* (New York: Charles Scribner's Sons, 1899), an academic, undertook an adventure among the underclass similar to Raoul's. Like Raoul, Wyckoff did all he could "to keep a respectable appearance," though his eastern accent and polished manners made him appear alien to working-class types in Chicago (303). Wyckoff's *Day with a Tramp* was "without the smallest gift of mimicry" and imagined that western workers credited his otherness with being "an immigrant of a new and hitherto unknown sort" from "an island in distant seas, where any manner of strange artisan might be bred" (51). Raoul, like Wyckoff, little realized the "indelible marks of class, the speech, the manners, the habit of thought" that, according to a friend familiar with his elite background, made obvious the "ruling class written all over you" (Raoul, "Aristocrat," 248). Wyckoff and Raoul discovered while mingling among the working class that each possessed "inescapable, insulating cultural blubber" (Daniel T. Rodgers, "The Tramp and the Policy Doctor," *Princeton University Library Chronicle* 58 [1996]: 61).

9. Raoul, "Proletarian Aristocrat," 18, 20.

10. Ibid., 21. Jerry Seigal, "Problematizing the Self," in Victoria E. Bonnell and Lynn Hunt, eds., *Beyond the Cultural Turn: New Directions in the Study of Society and Culture* (Berkeley: University of California Press, 1999), 281–314.

11. Raoul, "Proletarian Aristocrat," 20–21.

12. Mary Raoul Millis, "The Family of Raoul: A Memoir," 1943, Raoul Family Papers, Manuscript, Archives, and Rare Book Library, Robert W. Woodruff Library, Emory University, Atlanta, 116.

13. Raoul, "Proletarian Aristocrat," 21.

14. Ibid., 244, 256, 270, 279. Anne McClintock, in *Imperial Leather: Race, Gender and Sexuality in the Colonial Contest* (New York: Routledge, 1995), argued that nineteenth-century English businessman Arthur Munby's long-term relationship and marriage with Hannah Culliwick (a maidservant) lay in the latter's ability "to switch from maid to mistress, wife to slave, nurse to mother, white woman to black man." Munby, like Raoul, was transfixed not so much by actual labor as by the "representation of labor . . . [of] labor of spectacle" (144–47).

15. Raoul, "Proletarian Aristocrat," 24–25. John M. Slaton (who as one of his final—and ultimately futile—acts as governor was to commute Leo Frank's death sentence to life in prison) was a lawyer whose residence on Courtland Street was just east of the Raoul's Peachtree Street address. William Black was also listed as an Atlanta lawyer. See *Atlanta City Directory,* 1894, Manuscript, Archives, and Rare Book Library, Robert W. Woodruff Library, Emory University, Atlanta, 456.

16. Raoul, "Proletarian Aristocrat," 26; Millis, *Family of Raoul,* 117.

17. Raoul, "Proletarian Aristocrat," 26–27, 48. Eugene Spalding was president and general manager of the Southern Iron Car Line. His address at 477 Peachtree Street put him one block away from the Raoul home (*Atlanta City Directory,* 1899, Manuscript, Archives, and Rare Book Library, Robert W. Woodruff Library, Emory University, Atlanta, 1213.

18. Raoul, "Proletarian Aristocrat," 23, 229–30, 233.

19. Ibid., 234–35.

20. Ibid., 235–36. Scott A. Sandage, *Born Losers: A History of Failure in America* (Cambridge, Mass.: Harvard University Press, 2005), discussed the flip side of the Gilded Age: "Even Mark Twain had to abandon a novel called *The Autobiography of a Damned Fool,* based on his elder brother Orion's hapless career as a lawyer, politician, inventor, land speculator, author, proof-reader, and chicken farmer. After giving up on *Damned Fool,* Samuel Clemons cruelly suggested that Orion himself write a memoir and call it *Confessions of a Life That Was a Failure*" (256).

21. Raoul, "Proletarian Aristocrat," 236–37.

22. Ibid., 242.

23. Ibid., 242–43.

24. Ibid., 243–44.

25. William Raoul to Mary Wadley Raoul, 22 February 1910, mss 548, box 19, folder 2; William Raoul to Mary Wadley Raoul, March 1910, mss 548, box 19, folder 2; William Raoul to Mary Wadley Raoul, 24 March 1910, mss 548, box 19, folder 2; William Raoul to Mary Wadley Raoul, 4 March 1910, mss 548, box 19, folder 2, (emphasis in original); William Raoul to Mary Wadley Raoul, 2 May 1910, mss 548, box 19, folder 3, all in Raoul Family Papers.

26. Raoul, "Proletarian Aristocrat," 249.

27. Ibid., 249–50.

28. Ibid., 250; Edward L. Ayers, *The Promise of the New South: Life after Reconstruction* (New York: Oxford University Press, 1992), 122. Ayers set the stage for a potential disaster like the one Raoul reported: The miners "began their work by 'undercutting,' digging out a cavity beneath the 'face' of coal at the end of the shaft with pick and shovel. This job took two or three hours. When they finished undercutting, the miners drilled a hole, loaded it with powder, and detonated the charge" (122).

29. Drew Gilpin Faust, *James Henry Hammond and the Old South: A Design for Mastery* (Baton Rouge: Louisiana State University Press, 1982); Greenberg, *Honor and Slavery*, discuss ideals of masculine mastery in the antebellum South.

30. Raoul, "Proletarian Aristocrat," 317–18, 323.

31. Ibid., 328–29, 331–32.

32. Ibid., 333.

33. Ibid.

34. Raoul explained that "you could not hire or contract with hands from another place, unless you first settled their debt. This was referred to as 'buying' the man. It was a rather delicate business, as it must be done without giving offence to your neighbor. Usually therefore you did not get an opportunity to buy anybody unless for some reason, not always plain upon the surface, your neighbor wanted to get rid of his man, and was glad to have you pay up his debt" (ibid., 334–35).

35. Ibid., 335.

36. Ibid., 341–42, 345–46, 359.

37. Franklin Garrett, "Necrology, 1822–1933" and "Obituary Abstracts, 1892–1896," 144, Georgia Department of Archives and History, Atlanta. Ruth Cunningham was born in 1875 and died at thirty years of age. She was the daughter of Judge John D. and Cornelia Cunningham and was raised in the West End suburb of Atlanta.

38. On their honeymoon in Atlanta, the Raouls stayed at the Georgian Terrace Hotel where Winifred lit a cigarette. Raoul quoted from a column called "Chatter by Polly Peachtree": "Imagine the thrill that swept over the assemblage when, breakfast being over, the groom took out his cigarette case and passed it over to his young wife, who promptly selected a nice little 'Philip Morris' and used it for what it was intended. Protestations, exclamations, defamations, declamations and ultimatums were hurled upon the manager, who Bryanized the situation by showing the ladies that he was not prepared for defense or offense—only to sit on the fence . . . the bride went on smoking whenever she wanted to, while the bridegroom looked on with pride—I almost said with fatherly interest, for he really was old enough to have known better and to have taught his very young wife more discretion" (Raoul, "Proletarian Aristocrat," 349).

39. Raoul, "Proletarian Aristocrat," 359–60; W. E. B. Du Bois, *The Souls of Black Folk* (1903; reprint, New York: Alfred A. Knopf, 1993), 104.

40. Raoul, "Proletarian Aristocrat," 360; Du Bois, *Souls of Black Folk*, 103; "Governor's Office—Rewards," 4 January 1920, unit 12, Georgia Department of Archives and History. An entry for 30 April 1915 noted Thomas Campbell's assault "with intent to

murder" Ben Franklin in Jenkins County. Governor Slaton offered a reward of $150 for aid in Campbell's capture.

41. Raoul, "Proletarian Aristocrat," 360.
42. Ibid., 361.
43. Ibid.
44. Ibid.
45. Ibid., 362.
46. Ibid.

Privilege's Mausoleum: The Ruination of White
Southern Manhood in *The Sound and the Fury*

Christopher Breu

O ne of the challenges to theorizing masculinity in relationship
to history is the way in which historical narratives are often implicitly gendered
as masculine. Typically, this gendering takes the form of allegory, in which the
imagined subject of a period is presented as implicitly or, less often, explicitly
male.[1] Such a subject, then, becomes the bearer of temporality in the narrative constructed by the historical text. The modern male subject, for example,
becomes imagined as exemplary of the universal modern experience. In such a
context, temporality and narrative history become gendered, and it becomes a
challenge to imagine other forms of historical experience without conceiving of
different temporalities and a different experience of the historical.[2]

In its representation of issues of history and temporality via the stream-of-
consciousness narratives of three brothers, William Faulkner's *The Sound and
the Fury* (1929) directly engages the gendering of time and history. Faulkner's
celebrated modernist novel focuses on the story of the Compson family and the
family of black servants who work for them. The first three parts of the story are
alternately narrated by the three Compson brothers. The first part of the novel
is narrated by Benjy, who suffers from a mental disability in which temporal
distinctions no longer exist. His narrative takes place on 7 April 1928, on the
family estate near the mythical town of Jefferson, Mississippi, and is notable for
the way in which it collapses past and present, perception and memory. The
second section of the novel is narrated by Quentin and takes place on 2 June
1910, in Cambridge, Massachusetts, where Quentin is attending Harvard University. Quentin's narrative focuses primarily on his incestuous obsession with
his sister Caddy and the final hours of his life before he throws himself into the

Charles River. Quentin's narrative alternates, sometimes in the middle of sentences, between his rather confused perceptions of the present and his obsessive preoccupation with the past. The third section of the novel is narrated by Jason and takes place on 6 April 1928, in and around the mythical town of Jefferson. This section recounts Jason's attempts to discipline and control Caddy's teenage daughter, also named Quentin, who was sent by Caddy to live with the family. The action of this present-oriented chapter revolves around Jason attempting and failing to catch Quentin with a carnival worker who she is dating for the day. The final section of the novel is set on 8 April 1928 and is the only section of the novel that is narrated in the third person. This section begins by detailing the Easter morning activities of Dilsey, the Compsons' main servant. Dilsey attends a black Baptist church service with her family and Benjy. The section next details the female Quentin's revenge on Jason's domineering ways: she absconds with money that is rightfully hers (it has been sent by Caddy for her) but which Jason has stolen for himself. The section and the novel end with a scene of the family going for a carriage ride around a Civil War monument and with Benjy wailing because, to his mind, they are circling the monument the wrong way. Thus the novel ends with an image of the family, as representatives of the fallen aristocracy of the South, circling painfully and pointlessly around the memorialized idea of the Civil War.

As this plot description already suggests, time and history are explicitly allegorized in Faulkner's novel; moreover, they are allegorized as male. Yet the brothers' masculinities that become the bearers of allegorical meaning are presented as thoroughly pathological. In presenting these allegorical figures in a less than affirmative light, Faulkner's narrative opens up a space for interrogating the conflation of southern masculinity and southern history.

Of course, Faulkner's engagement with issues of temporality and the writing of history was hardly unique in the modernist period. Time was a central preoccupation for the writers and artists of the early twentieth century. Literary and cultural historians have long identified an engagement with questions of temporality as one of the defining features of artistic modernism and, more generally, of the modernist period, yet the dominant historical accounts of modernism often unconsciously repeat Faulkner's gendering of time and history as masculine.[3] The male artist or thinker becomes exemplary of the modernist project in general.

Feminist critic and cultural theorist Rita Felski argues that it is the historiography of modernity (i.e., the way in which the history of modernity has been written), more than the art and artists associated with modernism, that privileges masculinity by allegorizing the process of modernization in masculine terms.[4] Felski demonstrates that women and representations of womanhood were central to various cultural constructions of the modern. Countering claims of the exclusion of women from the experience of modernity, even as she charts the unequal ways in which women and men experienced the modern, Felski's work asks an essentially historiographical question: how do the narratives of modernity that we construct implicitly privilege male experience and deprivilege that of women?

This essay draws on Felski's argument to ask a basic set of historiographical questions about *The Sound and the Fury*. Whereas Felski interrogates what the implicit masculinism of narratives of modernity means for the historical account of women's experience, the chapter asks what it means for the construction of masculinity in the modern era and specifically in relationship to the pathological forms of manhood dramatized in Faulkner's novel. Or, in other words, how does the very privileging of pathological masculinity (both historiographical and social—for the two are related) shape cultural conceptions of manhood and, more importantly, paradoxically open up a textual space for the interrogation of the very forms of male privilege that the narratives of modernity take for granted?

In asking this question, the work undertaken by this essay can be situated within the broad rubric of masculinity studies. One of the central axioms of masculinity studies is, as with whiteness studies, the interrogation of the dominant.[5] By treating masculinity and whiteness as ideological categories in need of critical analysis, rather than as unmarked universal dominants, these theoretical approaches seek to undo the historiographical and cultural logics of sexism and racism. They also work to historicize gender and racial formations that are often taken to be natural and immutable. Yet, even as much of the scholarship on white masculinity in the United States works to historicize various conceptions of male identity, the critical accounts of masculinity often revolve around the same set of descriptions regardless of the era. American masculinity is usually described as individualist, violent, and unemotional and is theorized alternately as ascendant, besieged, or in crisis.

Part of what is so distinctive about the representation of white masculinity in *The Sound and the Fury* is that the novel constructs a clear historical periodization of southern manhood, one that situates modern southern masculinity in relationship and reaction to the "aristocratic" ideal of manhood that preceded it.[6] This aristocratic ideal was largely an ideological fiction even in the period of its ascendancy, one organized, as historians Craig T. Friend and Lorri Glover argue, around the twin ideals of honor and mastery.[7] Yet, while largely fictional, this ideological construction was definitional in its impact upon southern manhood, and the novel presents modern southern masculinity as formed in relationship to the long shadow that it cast.

The novel dramatizes the story of three brothers—Quentin, Jason, and

Benjy—each of whom represents a distinct embodiment of modern masculinity. Through the representations of these three brothers, modern manhood is represented as both highly specific and variable, underscoring that it cannot be reduced to a singular, generalized conception, but instead must be understood in terms of a range of variable, often conflicting identities. Moreover, in focusing on three white brothers from the same declining, upper-class family, the novel suggests that this variation exists among those of the same class and race as well as between races and classes. Masculinity is neither a natural inevitability nor an invariable ideological given; it is specific and potentially malleable in its embodiments. The representation of this subjective agency is intimately bound up with the novel's engagement with history—specifically the postbellum history of the American South—and the subjective apprehension of time.

As with many modernist works, time and temporality are central preoccupations of *The Sound and the Fury*. No less a critic than existentialist philosopher Jean-Paul Sartre famously analyzed the apprehension of time in *The Sound and the Fury* as exemplary of modernist preoccupations with temporality. Literary critic Richard Godden argues that the novel's engagement with temporality needs to be contextualized in terms of narrative form and the novel's (re)construction of southern history.[8] The representation of these issues cannot be separated from the novel's figuration of masculinity. For part of what Faulkner suggests is that history and temporality cannot be separated from their subjective apprehension; moreover, such subjective apprehension cannot be separated from the specific embodiments, social positions, and psychological orientations of those who do the apprehending.

Faulkner employs this conjunction between historicism and masculinity in order to use one to critique the other and vice versa. Specifically, Faulkner presents each of the brothers as embodying a different pathological relationship to temporality and history. Moreover, these pathologies are presented as being integrally bound up with the forms of racial, gender, and class privilege that all three brothers enjoy. The pathologies that all three manifest can be situated as different subjective responses to the feared loss of the forms of upper-class, white, male privilege that was ideologically embodied in the figure of the antebellum southern planter. This rendering of dominant masculinity as pathological performs the work of what gender theorist Kaja Silverman theorizes as the "ruination of masculinity."[9] It is this work of ruination that Faulkner's text undertakes. White masculinity and the privilege that it enjoys are represented as either destroyed or self-destroying.

The apprehension of time and the construction of history in the novel are represented as inseparable from the various psychological pathologies manifested by the three brothers. Thus, Quentin is melancholically and finally suicidally obsessed with a nostalgic fantasy of antebellum aristocratic, paternalist manhood, while Jason's paranoia represents the anxiety-ridden attempt at the reconstitution of white male privilege in the future-oriented liberal ideology of the New South, and Benjy's schizophrenic subjectivity represents a form of subjective destitution that strips white masculinity of its privilege, a privilege built on systematic forms of race, class, and gender inequality, and reorients it towards the open present.[10] In presenting these various pathologies, Faulkner's text does not construct a contrast between pathological and ostensibly "normal" forms of identity; instead, it presents these subjective pathologies as the product of different forms of social pathology, from racism to sexism to class privilege. By linking the novel's representation of history and masculinity to these various pathologies, *The Sound and the Fury* enacts a critique of masculinist historicism and the dominant forms of manhood present in the South.

Of the narratives of the three brothers, Quentin's is the most retrospectively oriented. For him, the forward movement of time is the curse that his father, Jason Compson Sr., predicts it would be "[w]hen the shadow of the sash appeared on the curtains it was between seven and eight oclock and then I was in time again, hearing the watch. It was Grandfather's and when Father gave it to me he said I give you the mausoleum of all hope and desire; it's rather excruciating-ly apt that you will use it to gain the reducto absurdum of all human experience."[11] These famous opening lines of the Quentin section present time itself as a mausoleum. While they certainly lend themselves to an ahistorical, metaphysical interpretation of the type often championed by formalist critics (i.e., time as the conqueror of all things and thus the harbinger of death), this bleak perspective can also be understood as the product of a specific conjunction of historical forces and subjective experience.

Quentin's worldview, like that of his father before him, is essentially tragic: he is eternally at odds with the world in which he lives. His tragic perspective is intimately bound up with the narrative of southern history that he constructs. This narrative is one of the dominant ones of southern history in the period, positing the antebellum years as a golden era of southern history, one characterized by an organic social hierarchy oriented around the ideology of paternalism and a truly noble—and seemingly larger-than-life—southern "aristocracy." This larger-than-life quality suggests that this image of the southern aristocracy is a retrospective fantasy construction (as was often the claim to "aristocratic" heritage itself in the South), one that had little to nothing to do with the conditions of life in an agrarian-capitalist slaveocracy.

Or, in other words, the antebellum South, in which Quentin and his father and many other members of the New South believed, was essentially a myth that served specific political and historiographical ends. The myth served two interrelated purposes: first, it justified the current regime of Jim Crow by renaturalizing and rendering quaintly pastoral the racial hierarchies of the Old South; second, it worked to rescript the narrative and real trauma bound up with the loss of the Civil War by recasting the South as an unambiguous protagonist during the war and an equally unambiguous victim of "northern aggression" after the end of the conflict. As feminist theorist Wendy Brown notes, the problem with victim narratives, however justified (or otherwise), is that they can quickly turn from being liberating to paralyzing.[12] This paralysis is integrally related to the tragic worldview that Quentin and his father manifest. If the members of the twentieth-century South were victims, then they can only pale in comparison to the heroic stature of the antebellum southern aristocrats; moreover, if the world was a tragic one organized around loss and the disappearance of the ideal, the only position to occupy was one of melancholy victimhood. This victimhood represents the fear of a loss of privilege that lies at the heart of the fallen construction of southern history that Quentin articulates. The paralysis afflicts Quentin throughout his narrative. He lives in a modern shadow world, one that is hopelessly fallen in comparison to the golden age represented by the Old South. His existence in this shadow world is literalized throughout the narrative by the recurring image of his shadow, which haunts him throughout his last day.

As social theorist Walter Benjamin reminds us, historical narratives are conventionally written to empathize with the victors.[13] And we might add: even the history of defeat often focuses on the privileged in a given society. The narrative of southern history that Quentin ascribes to was composed primarily by and about the socially and ideologically dominant group in the New South: the upper-class, white, male descendants of the slaveholding class. They feared that the advent of the New South would produce a loss of the forms of race, gender, and class privilege that they had taken for granted for a long time. This fear had its grounding in the material transformations represented by various processes of modernization and the shift in ideology from paternalism to liberalism that the New South represented. In many ways, this fear was the product of fantasy. Gender and racial privilege may have changed shape in the transition from the Old South to the New, but the privileging of white masculinity itself altered very little in the movement from slavery to the Jim Crow South. Yet, the fear did have its grounding in the everyday life of the New South as well. It was around class, rather than race or gender, that this loss of privilege had its basis in everyday life, for the advent of modernization and the New South represented a shift in the dominant historical actors of the South from the members of the aristocratic plantation class to a new class of merchants, tradesmen, industrialists, and professionals. Still, this real loss of privilege was metaphorized in terms of race and gender.

Quentin thus experiences this fantasized and material loss of cultural privilege as a symbolic loss of manhood and the categories of honor and mastery with which it was associated. I pursue the specifics of Quentin's symbolic loss of manhood a little further on, but for now it is only important to recognize the way in which this loss is situated in relationship to the construction of history that Quentin articulates and the larger thematics of time with which we began our discussion. As literary critic Nathaniel Miller puts it, "Quentin's problem as a Southerner is that he is neither a new man nor an old one."[14] If the New South was a pale imitation of the Edenic world represented by the Old South, then Quentin's masculinity can only be understood as a pale imitation of the one embodied by his mythic forefathers. From this hopelessly retrospective point of view, time becomes the enemy, drawing Quentin further and further from the ideal form of manhood embodied by the antebellum southern aristocrat. Thus, while in the novel's parlance, time is the mausoleum of all desire, it is also privilege's mausoleum. The retrospective cast of Quentin's relationship to manhood means that he is unable to imagine a productive or progressive relationship to manhood in the present or future and informs the suicidal arc of his narrative.

Given its retrospective orientation, the form of masculinity that Quentin embodies is best described as a melancholic one.[15] Melancholia, the most retrospectively oriented of psychic disorders, is organized around an irresolvable sense of loss and a consequent interminable state of mourning, characterized by "a profoundly painful dejection, cessation of interest in the outside world, loss of the capacity to love, inhibition of all activity, and a lowering of self-regarding feelings to the degree that finds utterance in self-reproaches and self-revilings." It often is mixed with mania and ends in suicide. All of these symptoms are clearly visible in Quentin's narrative. Freud articulates that this loss in melancholia is typically of an abstract nature, either the loss of an abstract ideal such as nation or love, or the loss of an ideal conception of an individual, usually a loved one. In the case of Quentin, the loss he embodies draws a bit from both of these definitions. On one level, the loss he feels is clearly for the abstract ideal of the antebellum South, yet this ideal is also personified in the fantasy figure of the southern aristocrat and the larger-than-life form of manhood he embodied.[16]

Freud theorizes the irresolvable dimension of melancholia as produced by the unconscious resentment that the melancholic individual bears toward the lost object (however abstract) precisely because the object is lost or has not lived up to the fantasy that the individual has constructed of it. Because the individual loves and unconsciously resents the lost object, the form of pathological mourning that characterizes melancholia becomes interminable. The final dimension of melancholia articulated by Freud is the psychological internalization of the lost object. The melancholic individual tries to make up for the loss of the object by internalizing it and incorporating it into his or her ego, yet this incorporation produces an internalization of the resentment directed at the object as well, so the anger is turned around on the melancholic individual.[17]

All of these qualities are present in Faulkner's depiction of Quentin. Quentin clearly internalizes the fantasized ideal of antebellum manhood. Indeed, his obsession with defending his sister's "purity," in spite of all the evidence that Caddy neither wants her purity protected nor is particularly invested in the patriarchal category as such, indicates that Quentin is in thrall to the chivalric ideology associated with antebellum manhood.[18] This ideology was partially an invention of the antebellum period and partially a retrospective projection onto the antebellum period of the specific racial and gender politics of the post-Reconstruction South. As cultural theorists such as Robyn Wiegman and Angela Davis argue, the reactionary politics of the post-Reconstruction period were refracted through the ideological myth of the black rapist.[19] This myth drew upon the chivalric ideology of the antebellum South with its ideal of virginal women and gallant, paternalistic men to renegotiate power in the post-Reconstruction South by turning political and economic issues of black enfranchisement into psychosexual issues of purity and transgression. As its name suggests, the myth turned around the fantasy figure of the black rapist and the need of white men to protect the virtue of white southern women from this imagined threat. On a material level, the myth enabled the white South to justify a systematic campaign of disenfranchisement and racial terror against African Americans, rescinding rights that would only be restored with the end of Jim Crow in the 1960s.

The ideology of the black rapist and the more paternalist ideal of antebellum white manhood both inform Quentin's obsessive investment in protecting his sister's "honor," which under the ideology of paternalism is a cognate of his own. While the antebellum ideology seems more ascendant in Quentin's obsessions, traces of the post-Reconstruction ideology are detectable as well. Quentin's identification with the ideal of antebellum manhood is evident in a passage in which Quentin's memories mix indistinguishably with his fantasies of his interactions with his sister:

do you love him
    her hand came out I didnt move it fumbled down my arm and she held my hand
flat against her chest her heart thudding
    no no
    did he [Dalton Aimes, Caddy's main lover in her teenage years] make you then
he made you do it let him he was stronger than you and he tomorrow Ill kill him

I swear father neednt know until afterward and then you and I nobody need ever know we can take my school money we can cancel my matriculation Caddy you hate him dont you dont you

    she held my hand against her chest her heart thudding I turned and caught her arm Caddy you hate him dont you

    she moved my hand up against her throat her heart was hammering there

    poor Quentin

Here, Quentin clearly demonstrates his investment in the chivalric ideal of protecting white womanhood, even (or especially) when the woman in question does not seem to need or want protecting. The passage demonstrates the way in which Quentin's melancholia makes him a man out of time. Caddy clearly is living by the modern sexual morality of the early twentieth century, with its challenge to the prohibitions against casual sex and the autonomous expression of female desire, while Quentin is thoroughly caught up with the ostensibly heroic, yet antiquated ideals of antebellum manhood. Indeed, Quentin's modern take on traditional southern white manhood becomes unintentionally parodic. He offers to kill Caddy's defiler, thereby protecting her honor, yet Caddy refuses to play along with this narrative. Quentin wants to rescript Caddy's loss of virginity as rape, thereby casting himself in the role of the heroic protector/avenger, yet Caddy refuses to say that she did not want to have sex with her lover, nor will she claim here that she hates him. A little further on, she, at Quentin's insistence, does claim she hates her lover, but even this assertion is cast in the rhetoric of modern romance rather than Quentin's rhetoric of family honor and female purity: "yes I hate him I would die for him Ive already died for him I die for him over and over again everytime." In Caddy's romantic rhetoric, hate is merely another word for love and death is a euphemism for sex. This is decidedly not the heroic resonances of these words that Quentin means to invoke.[20]

Quentin's use of the rhetoric of rape turns implicitly on the ideology of the black rapist, albeit in displaced form. While Hilton Head, Caddy's fiancé and briefly her husband, is not black, he is a middle-class professional and thus is viewed by the aristocratic Quentin as a less than acceptable romantic choice for Caddy. Moreover, the incestuous quality of Quentin's investment in Caddy also suggests, as has been noted by a number of critics, a fantasy of maintaining blood-line "purity" by avoiding exogamy and that most extreme version of exogamy in the cultural imaginary of the South: miscegenation.[21]

The specific coordinates of Quentin's investment in the racial imaginary of the South is addressed more explicitly in other parts of his section. As with his gender investments, Quentin's racial investments are modeled melancholically on an antebellum ideal. This ideal is most explicitly thematized in a passage when Quentin addresses a black man sitting on a mule from a train car while the train is stopped:

> How long he had been there I didn't know, but he sat straddle of the mule, his head wrapped in a piece of blanket, as if they had been built there with the fence and the road, or with the hill, carved out of the hill itself . . .
>
> "Hey Uncle," I said. "Is this the way?"
>
> "Suh?" He looked at me, then he loosened the blanket and lifted it away from his ear.
>
> "Christmas gift!" I said.
>
> "Sho comin, boss. You done caught me, aint you."
>
> "I'll let you off this time." I dragged my pants out of the little hammock and got a quarter out. "But look out next time. I'll be coming back through here two days after New Year, and look out then." I threw the quarter out the window. "Buy yourself some Santy Claus."
>
> "Yes suh," he said. He got down and picked up the quarter and rubbed it on his leg. "Thanky, young marster. Thanky."[22]

The interaction between Quentin and the African American seems more lo-cated in a fantasy of the antebellum past than it is in the modern present—or, more precisely, presents—of the novel. Indeed, Quentin constructs the black man as being as ancient as the landscape itself: he is carved literally out of the hillside and as such predates both the fence and the road. His positioning on the mule as an earlier form of transportation in relationship to the modern locomotive also situates him as part of a fantasized premodern past. Moreover, their verbal exchange also appears oddly anachronistic. While such an exchange is certainly imaginable in the South of the early twentieth century with its continued adher-ence to racial hierarchy, the specifics of the interaction suggest that Quentin in particular is in thrall to a fantasy of antebellum race relations. Indeed, his state-ments to the African American reek of the kinds of condescending jocularity that were central to the planter-class ideology of paternalism. Interestingly, the passage indicates that the black man himself becomes aware of the anachronism of Quentin's discourse, shifting (in an attempt to placate the white interlocutor, a survival skill necessary to African Americans of the early twentieth century) from calling him "boss"—a term more associated with the post–Civil War cul-ture of sharecropping—to describing him as "young marster," thereby playing along with Quentin's fantasy of reanimating antebellum aristocratic manhood.

Of course, Quentin is finally not able to convincingly maintain this fantasy as most of the world that surrounds him refuses to conform to the dictates of his melancholic investments. Instead, Quentin's attempts to impose his nostalgic vision on the modern world only result in parody. When Quentin fantasizes that he is fighting a climatic duel with Dalton Ames, Caddy's primary lover, he is really engaging in a pointless and losing fight with a Harvard classmate. Moreover, while he tries to convince (or fantasizes telling—the line between fantasy and reality becoming increasingly blurred as Quentin's narrative progresses) his father that he and Caddy have had incestuous relations, his father merely laughs and dismisses the claim, recognizing that his obsession with Caddy's virginity is really in part a projection of his virginal status. As the disjunction between Quentin's fantasy investments and the world he lives in becomes more pronounced over the course of the narrative, the line between internal fantasy and external perception becomes increasingly blurred, finally resulting at the end of the narrative in the complete disintegration of Quentin's sense of self that immediately precedes his suicide.[23]

This disintegration is represented formally in the narrative by the complete disappearance of punctuation and capitalization, and particularly the capitalization of the first-person pronoun in Quentin's stream-of-consciousness narrative: "i was afraid to i was afraid she might and then it wouldn't have done any good but if i could tell you we did it would have been so and then others wouldn't be so and then the world would roar away and he and now this other you are not lying now either but you are still blind to what is in yourself to that part of general truth the sequence of natural events and their causes which shadows every mans brow." Here, the ruination of Quentin's identity is thorough. If, as psychoanalytic theorist Jacques Lacan argues, adult subjectivity is organized around its relationship to the symbolic system that is language, then the breakdown of conventional linguistic distinctions in this passage marks the disintegration of Quentin's identity.[24]

Markedly, this breakdown is accompanied by Quentin's first recognition that he did not sleep with Caddy. The coinciding of this recognition with Quentin's psychological disintegration underscores that his identity was predicated on the maintenance of his nostalgic fantasy of manhood. Thus Quentin's section, when read as a whole, stages the ruination of the melancholic manhood embodied by Quentin; more importantly, it suggests that this form of masculinity underwrites its own ruination with its inability to confront the exigencies of the modern present. Interestingly, the discussion of what "shadows" every man's brow in the above passage (and which seems to be spoken by Quentin's father—or at least Quentin's fantasy construction of his father) also indicates in displaced form (as does the image of the shadow, a conventional trope for blackness, that haunts Quentin throughout his narrative) the forms of racial exclusion and exploitation that form the unacknowledged underside to the rosy image of the antebellum South with which Quentin is obsessed. This is the part of himself that Quentin and others like him in the modernist period were "blind to" in their construction of the myth of the golden era of the Old South.

If Quentin represents a melancholic version of modern masculinity, one that is retrospectively focused on the image of the antebellum gentleman planter, Jason Compson embodies a much more present- and future-oriented version of modern masculinity. Jason's stream-of-consciousness narrative, unlike Quentin's, recognizes the transformations and modernizations that have produced the New South, even if he is equally unhappy about them. If Quentin turns away from the unbearable present toward the past, Jason immerses himself, obsessively, in the implacable workings of a present and future that he perceives as hostile to his interests as the twentieth-century heir to the aristocratic lineage of the past. Whereas Quentin's ideology can be allied with the residual belief system of southern paternalism, Jason's beliefs (while still invested in the privileges he ostensibly deserves because of his aristocratic lineage) can be situated squarely within what historicist literary critic Kevin Railey has described as the specifically southern version of liberalism that came to dominate the South in the early twentieth century.[25] This version of liberalism gave lip service to the egalitarian principles articulated by the Populist movement of the late nineteenth century, but was basically organized around rationalizing the government and providing social support for the already privileged middle classes as well as maintaining the privileges of white male supremacy against any political or social incursions made by African Americans and women. Jason's relationship to the present is as defensive as much as an aggressive one. Indeed, he imagines himself as continuously embattled in relationship to those who would lay present and future claim to the forms of class, race, and gender privilege that he sees as his birthright.

In psychoanalytic terms, Jason's embattled attitude can be theorized as a form of paranoia. In the famous Judge Schreiber case history, Freud defines paranoia in relationship to the dynamic of projection: "The mechanism of symptom-formation in paranoia requires that internal perceptions—feelings—shall be replaced by external perceptions. Consequently the proposition 'I hate him' becomes transformed by *projection* into another one: '*He hates me,* which will justify me in hating him.'"[26]

Projection in psychoanalytic terms is a dynamic in which those qualities or feelings that an individual represses from conscious recognition are transferred (or "projected") onto another. In paranoia, projection usually takes the form of hating or fearing in the other the very qualities that one possesses yet refuses to recognize in one's self. Freud also notes that paranoia is the most theoretically inclined of psychic disorders, suggesting that as a conceptual logic paranoia is not always fully distinguishable from critical thought.[27] As such, paranoia lends itself, as a logic, to larger forms of ideological thinking. Thus, Jason's paranoia is not presented as merely an individual symptom but as representative of the larger forms of economic, racial, and gender paranoia that characterized the ideology of southern liberalism.

Faulkner's depiction of Jason becomes another version of the ruination of southern manhood, one that in this case cuts against the grain of the historical record. While southern liberalism and the Jim Crow regime it underwrote remained in power until the 1960s, Jason as a representative of this ideology is presented in Faulkner's novel of 1929 as a figure of comic ineffectuality and delusion. As such, Faulkner, in a move that is partially prescient and partially historical fantasy, suggested that the defensive formation that was southern liberalism was finally doomed for failure. Of course, part of the particularly acute dimensions of Jason's paranoia come from his continuing psychological investment in the privileges of aristocratic birthright, even as he recognizes that the world does not work by the ideology of paternalism anymore.

Jason sees himself as still hemmed in by the responsibilities of paternalism, without any of its privileges. This attitude of burdensome paternalist responsibility is evident in Jason's ranting monologue about his niece, Quentin (named after his dead brother), to the owner of the store where he works: "Do you think I can afford to have her running about the streets with every drummer that comes to town, I says, and them telling the new ones up and down the road where to pick up a hot one when they made Jefferson. I haven't got much pride, I cant afford it with a kitchen full of niggers to feed and robbing the state asylum of its star freshman. Blood, I says, governors and generals. It's a dam good thing we ain't never had any kings and presidents; we'd all be down there at Jackson chasing butterflies." Even as Jason seems to mock his aristocratic heritage in this passage, he is also careful to invoke it. Moreover, he suggests that all that he has inherited from this aristocratic lineage is the responsibility (here presented as his paternalist responsibility to protect the honor of the white women he lives with—especially when they don't seem to desire such protection—and feed the "niggers" who work on the family estate) without any of the honor and privilege. Indeed, he suggests that such responsibility is difficult to "afford" in a modern South that only acknowledges money and not birthright. Jason also continuously marks that, unlike his older brother Quentin who was sent to Harvard, his birthright has been squandered and thus he is forced to make his way by the liberal ethos of the self-made man: "Well, Jason likes work. I says no I never had university advantages because at Harvard they teach you to go for a swim at night without knowing how to swim" [a sneering reference to his brother's suicide].[28]

Yet, for all his claims otherwise, Jason does not like work. Throughout his section, he continuously complains about how no one else works (especially the blacks he works with at his job, and the "New York . . . jews" who, from his paranoid vantage, control the stock market and "take the money away from us country suckers" who "work like hell all day every day"), yet he is presented as never doing a lick of work. This contrast between Jason's rhetoric and his actions reaches particularly comic proportions in a scene in which he berates a black worker for being lazy while the latter is doing a job (fixing cultivators) that Jason is also supposed to be doing:

> "Well," I says. "If you dont look out, that bolt will grow into your hand. And then I'm going to take an axe and chop it out. What do you reckon the boll-weevils'll eat if you dont get those cultivators in shape to raise them a crop?" I says, "sage grass?" . . .
>
> And then a Yankee will talk your head off about niggers getting ahead. Get them ahead, what I say. Get them so far ahead you cant find one south of Louisville with a blood hound. . . . Well, just about that time I happened to look up the alley and saw her [Quentin].

Jason spends the rest of the day shirking work by chasing Quentin and her date for the day.[29]

This passage suggests the bankruptcy of the rhetoric of southern liberalism in the early twentieth century. While, as an ideology, liberalism is committed to an ideal of meritocracy and advancement through hard work, the early twentieth-century southern version made explicit the way in which this rhetoric was contradicted by a set of class, gender, and especially racial exclusions that privilege the work (and even the lack of work) of middle- and upper-class white men against all others. While this contradiction is present to a greater or lesser degree within most forms of liberalism, it is explicitly marked and overt in the case of the South of the 1920s. The paranoia that Jason embodies is integrally bound up with the racism, anti-Semitism, sexism, and class privilege of a whole class of southern men. In the context of this paranoia, Jason projects onto various racial and gendered others the very qualities that he represses from representation as part of his own identity. Thus, blacks, not he, must be lazy and privileged, and Jews, not himself, must be living off the labor of others.

In his comic ruination of Jason's masculinity, Faulkner finally reveals as ineffective this paranoid subjectivity. Jason spends the rest of the section chasing, but never catching, Quentin and getting nothing out of it but a good beating and a massive headache. Jason's obsession with Quentin's promiscuity is also represented as a product of paranoia. While Quentin is certainly sexually active with multiple partners, Jason's obsession with her sexual liaisons displaces his own ongoing dalliances with a Memphis prostitute: it is Quentin who is a "damn little slut" and women in general who "dress like they were trying to make every man they passed on the street want to reach out and clap his hand on it," while Jason sees himself as a pillar of respectability who has no causal part in a sexual economy that constructs women as objects for male consumption.[30]

Faulkner completes his presentation of Jason as embodying an ineffective version of manhood by having Quentin permanently gain the upper hand at the end of the novel. She steals back the money that Jason stole from her by cashing the checks her mother had sent for her, and lights it out of town. This scene presents an image of subjective agency on the part of Quentin, albeit a limited one; the reader does not get a sense of her having many better options on her own in the resolutely masculinist South (and North) of the 1920s. However, it finalizes the novel's parodic representation of Jason's masculinity. This ruination of modern southern masculinity is more wishful thinking on the part of Faulkner than a historical reality, but the text does demonstrate the fragility of the paranoid logic that held together southern male hegemony in the modernist period. And while Faulkner's antipathy toward the form of liberal masculinity Jason embodies may have come, as Kevin Railey suggests, as much from his own investment in the archaic forms of paternalist masculinity that the male Quentin embodies as from any more progressive critique, the text's work of ruination remains open to more radical readings than is reducible to conscious authorial ideology.[31]

At their best, Faulkner's novels do a kind of critical work on the cultural unconscious of the modern South, revealing the contradictions, forms of violence, and utopian longings that represent the heterogeneous and repressed contents of such an unconscious. It is a mistake to read Faulkner's text as reducible to a conscious authorial ideology; it is instead a compendium of unconscious conflicts and yearnings, phobias and desires, or, as literary critic Philip Weinstein would have it, it is "a cosmos no one owns."[32]

Nowhere are the unconscious utopian yearnings of *The Sound and the Fury* more discernable in relationship to cultural constructions of manhood than in the Benjy section. At first, such a claim must seem counterintuitive. Benjy's subjectivity seems hardly stable enough to warrant description as masculine (or feminine). However, it is in the very negative work of almost complete ruination that Benjy's fragmented subjectivity represents the possibility of a more utopian, progressive construction of masculinity. It is as if the text has to reduce consciousness to a mere mechanism of perception and involuntary memory in order to imagine a different construction of male identity than the ones that were dominant in the early twentieth century. While traditionally Benjy, following Faulkner's usage in interviews, is described as an idiot, recent criticism has suggested the much more descriptive and less demeaning diagnostic terms of autism and schizophrenia to describe Benjy's subjectivity.[33] For, as his consciousness is presented in the novel, Benjy is far from lacking intelligence. Indeed, he is unusually perceptive at certain points (he often is more attuned to changes in social relationships than the other characters in the novel). It is just that his consciousness lacks any sense of temporal order and continuity; he is unable to separate immediate perception from memory and internal fantasy from external perception. The designation "schizophrenic" can be just as profitably applied to the textual logic of Benjy's narrative (and it is, after all, as a text that we encounter him).

Marxist cultural theorist Fredric Jameson provides perhaps the best description of schizophrenia as a form of textuality: "Very briefly, Lacan describes schizophrenia as a breakdown in the signifying chain, that is, the interlocking syntagmatic series of signifiers which constitutes an utterance or meaning. If we are unable to unify the past, present, and future of the sentence, then we are similarly unable to unify the past, present, and future of our own biographical experience or psychic life. With the breakdown of the signifying chain, therefore, the schizophrenic is reduced to an experience of pure material signifiers, or, in other words, a series of pure and unrelated presents in time."[34] Jameson's description of the breakdown of meaning and temporality in schizophrenia reads as if it could have been written with Benjy's narration in mind. Readers are unable to "unify the past, present, and future of the sentence," and thus the past, present, and future of Benjy's "biographical experience." Moreover, Benjy himself is unable to unify his own past, present, and future.

Of course, Jameson's account of schizophrenia was not written with Benjy's narration in mind; it is instead a key part of his larger account of postmodernism as both a cultural logic and a privileged aesthetic of the era of late capitalism. As such it may initially seem like a stretch to apply his comments to *The Sound and the Fury*, which is celebrated as one of the totemic texts of modernism. However, this discrepancy can be accounted for if we recognize that, for Jameson, textual styles, like modes of production, are overlapping and composite. What changes in the shift from modernism to postmodernism, as in the shift from realism to modernism, is which set of aesthetic practices are privileged as dominant. Thus, the schizophrenic narrative occupies a dominant position in postmodernism, while in a modernist text such as *The Sound and the Fury* it occupies a subsidiary or emergent position, one that seems to deviate from the aesthetic norms and conventions that are associated with modernism. As such, the use of schizophrenic narrative in a modernist text like *The Sound and the Fury* has the potential to be more disruptive than its use in a postmodern text in which it has become part of a dominant aesthetic.

In contrast to the representation of Quentin's and Jason's subjectivities in the other sections of the novel, Benjy's narration is indeed disruptive. While both Quentin and Jason are represented as embodying identities that are differently pathological, they are also relatively coherent and continuous. Benjy's subjectivity, in contrast, is represented as radically discontinuous:

> "I is done it. Hush, now." Luster said. "Aint I told you you can't go up there. They'll knock your head clean off with one of them balls. Come on, here." He pulled me back.
>
> "Sit down." I sat down and he took off my shoes and rolled up my trousers. "Now, git in that water and play and see can you stop that slobbering and moaning."
>
> I hushed and got in the water *and Roskus came and said to come to supper and Caddy said,*
>
> *It's not supper time yet. I'm not going.*
>
> She was wet. We were playing in the branch and Caddy squatted down and got her dress wet.[35]

This passage, as does any taken from the Benjy section, demonstrates the breakdown of temporality in his narration. The passage shifts without any warning but the orthographical indication of italics from the present of 7 April 1928 to a memory from Benjy's childhood. Immediate experience and memory are both understood by Benjy as part of a discontinuous present. Moreover, as this suggests, the line between internal and external perception is eradicated. The form of subjectivity embodied by Benjy thus represents the most extreme version of the ruination of conventional embodiments of modernist masculinity. Benjy literally represents the male subject stripped of history, memory, and authority.

Yet, it is in this very stripping away of the liniments of history and privilege that the utopian energy of Faulkner's narrative becomes evident. Such an energy is even detectible in the passage above. In contrast with Jason's and Quentin's differing obsessions with racial hierarchy, Benjy does not perceive race. Luster and Roskus, two of the Compson's black servants, are not marked as black in his perception (even the dialect that Luster speaks is hard to fully separate from the dialect spoken by working-class white characters in this text and many of Faulkner's other texts). Race does not seem to factor into his consciousness at all. Instead, the reader is left to glean the race of the characters in this opening section of the text by such more or less imperfect clues as dialect and social role.

While in our own post–Jim Crow present, the rhetoric of colorblindness has been appropriated by a right wing bent on eradicating social justice programs such as affirmative action by claiming that the only kinds of contemporary racism are of the so-called reverse variety, colorblindness in the Jim Crow era, with its explicit (rather than implicit) investment in white supremacy and racial hierarchy, took on a much more utopian and radical cast. What the text imagines in Benjy's refusal to see race is a form of white southern masculinity that is not predicated on white supremacy and one that can be open to the experiences and narratives of those who do not occupy a position of historical and social privilege. Colorblindness in this sense is not a refusal to see race or racism, but rather the refusal to treat privilege and inequality as either natural or justified.

While Benjy's consciousness genuinely seems to move outside of the usual dictates of white southern constructions of race, his perception of gender and gendered hierarchy is more complicated. At first glance, he seems to make note of gender only slightly more than race. Unlike race, gender is marked in Benjy's narrative though seemingly only in the most cursory of ways: via pronouns. However, as any number of critics have commented, Benjy seems to be strangely aware of Caddy's loss of virginity (she no longer "smelled like trees") and is adversely affected by it. Thus, even in the context of Benjy's radically alternative psychology, Faulkner could not seem to construct an understanding of manhood that is not in thrall to the virgin/whore dichotomy. Yet, even in the persistence of this ideological bugbear, Benjy's perception of it, in terms of whether Caddy does or does not smell like trees, suggests that his subjectivity in relationship to his sister is not Oedipalized in the conventional ways that are detectable in the subjectivities of his brothers. His construction of his sister's identity seems more associated with a strange set of metonymic associations with the earth and landscape that elude reduction to a conventional Oedipal narrative.[36] Thus, while in terms of gender Benjy's identity does not fully forego conventional forms of white male privilege and authority as it does in relationship to race (just as Caddy's narrative is never fully articulatable within the space of the novel), it still advances a very different conception of the relationship between male and female subjectivity than is conventional in the 1920s South.

Given the allegorical dimensions of Faulkner's portrayal of the different forms of manhood embodied by the brothers, the refusal of subjective authority in Benjy's narrative works on a larger symbolic level to deprivilege the white male subject as the central actor in the drama of modernity and southern history. This deprivileging enables the possibility of imagining a space in which other stories can emerge and other social actors can become visible, thus enabling different narratives of modernity than the ones that conventionally are told in our history books and theory texts.

The final section of *The Sound and the Fury*, the only one related via omniscient third-person narration, presents a suggestive image for allegorizing the potential emergence of these other narratives of modernity: the Easter Sunday church meeting attended by Benjy, Dilsey, and members of her extended family (who are also servants for the Compsons). Benjy's presence in this otherwise all-black meeting again suggests the difference he represents. Moreover, the churchgoers embody a collective, largely African American version of subjective experience that can be positively contrasted to the resolutely individualist and white forms of subjectivity narrated by the rest of the novel. And, while Faulkner's presentation of the preacher is, at best, ambiguous with its heavy emphasis on dialect and its repeated description of his appearance as "monkey"-like, the description of the effect of his voice points beyond such conventional racism toward forms of collective experience and desire that exceed the individualist narratives presented by the rest of the text: "And the congregation seemed to watch with its own eyes while the voice consumed him, until he was nothing and they were nothing and there was not even a voice but instead their hearts were speaking to one another in chanting measures beyond the need for words." The collectivity imagined in this passage suggests a very different subject of modernity than the privileged ones that form the greater part of the text.[37] Moreover, this collective subject is not merely a product of textual fancy, but one that has historical corollaries as well. From slavery forward, the black church often served as a site for antiracist organizing and activism. Such activism reached perhaps its greatest realization in the central role the church played in the emergence of the civil rights movement of the 1950s and 1960s, which ushered in the end of the Jim Crow era. It is perhaps not too much of a stretch to suggest that part of what is revealed within the regional unconscious engaged by Faulkner's text is the presence of this collective historical actor in an emergent form.

Yet this actor and its narrative only become detectable when modernity and southern history are no longer equated with a privileged construction of white masculinity. It is only through the work of ruination done by Faulkner's narrative that such histories, with their alternate temporalities, begin to emerge. In presenting the value of such a work of ruination, *The Sound and the Fury* suggests an allegory for our own time as well. If we are really committed to a just society in terms of issues of race, gender, and class, then those of us who are privileged must similarly make a mausoleum of such privilege and begin to truly attend to the alternate narratives and experiences that exist in our own contemporary moment.

NOTES

The author thanks Elizabeth Hatmaker, who read various drafts of this essay.

1. On the issue of the gendering of historical allegories, see Rita Felski, *The Gender of Modernity* (Cambridge, Mass.: Harvard University Press, 1995), 1–10. On the implicit privileging of men's experience in historical narratives, see Michael Kimmel, *Manhood in America* (New York: Free Press, 1996), 1–5.

2. This essay's engagement with questions of historiography, temporality, and allegory has been influenced by the following texts: Hayden White, *The Content of the Form: Narrative Discourse and Historical Representation* (Baltimore: Johns Hopkins University Press, 1990); Fredric Jameson, *The Political Unconscious: Narrative as a Socially Symbolic Act* (Ithaca, N.Y.: Cornell University Press, 1981); and Paul Ricoeur, *Time and Narrative*, vol. 1, trans. Kathleen McLaughlin and David Pellauer (Chicago: University of Chicago Press, 1990).

3. For accounts of modernism that focus on issues of temporality, see the following texts: David Harvey, *The Condition of Postmodernity: An Enquiry into the Origins of Cultural Change* (London: Blackwell, 1991), 10–39; Richard Terdiman, *Present Past: Modernity and the Memory Crisis* (Ithaca, N.Y.: Cornell University Press, 1993), 3–33; Fredric Jameson, *Postmodernism, or, the Cultural Logic of Late Capitalism* (Durham, N.C.: Duke University Press, 1991), 1–54; James McFarlane, "The Mind of Modernism," in *Modernism: A Guide to European Literature, 1890–1930*, ed. Malcolm Bradbury and James McFarlane (New York: Penguin, 1978), 71–94.

4. See Felski, *Gender of Modernity*, 1–34. For other feminist critiques of conventional narratives of modernity and of modernist artistic practice itself, see Sandra Gilbert and Susan Gubar, *No Man's Land: The Place of the Woman Writer in the Twentieth Century*, vol. 1: *The War of the Words* (New Haven, Conn.: Yale University Press, 1988); Alice Jardine, *Gynesis: Configurations of Woman and Modernity* (Ithaca, N.Y.: Cornell University Press, 1985), 31–49.

5. For a comprehensive account of masculinities studies, see Rachel Adams and David Savran, eds., *The Masculinities Studies Reader* (London: Blackwell, 2002). The field of whiteness studies involves the work of a range of different theorists but has been most closely associated with the writings of David Roediger. For an example of the critique of whiteness as an interrogation of the dominant, see Roediger, *The Wages of Whiteness: Race and the Making of the American Working Class*, rev. ed. (London: Verso, 2007).

6. In discussing Faulkner's novel in the context of southern history, I do not want to obscure its relationship to larger forms of national and indeed transnational history. Certainly, the questions of race and gender raised by the text have national and transnational implications as well. On the importance of reading Faulkner in a national context, see Ted Atkinson, *Faulkner and the Great Depression: Aesthetics, Ideology, and Cultural Politics* (Athens: University of Georgia Press, 2006), 1–15; Christopher Breu, *Hard-Boiled Masculinities* (Minneapolis: University of Minnesota Press, 2005), 115–41. For the importance of reading Faulkner within an international framework, see Edouard Glissant, *Faulkner: Mississippi*, trans. Barbara B. Lewis and Thomas C. Spear (Chicago: University of Chicago Press, 2000).

7. See Craig Thompson Friend and Lorri Glover, "Rethinking Southern Masculinity: An Introduction," in *Southern Manhood: Perspectives on Masculinity in the Old South*, ed. Craig Thompson Friend and Lorri Glover (Athens: University of Georgia Press, 2004), viii–x.

8. Jean-Paul Sartre, "On *The Sound and the Fury:* Time in the Work of Faulkner,"

in *Literary and Philosophical Essays*, trans. Annette Michelson (London: Rider, 1959), 79–87; Richard Godden, "Quentin Compson: Tyrrhenian Vase or Crucible of Race?" in *New Essays on* The Sound and the Fury, ed. Noel Polk (London: Cambridge University Press, 1993), 99–137. Godden argued that Sartre's philosophical engagement with the novel's construction of temporality misses the historical and social context in which this temporal obsession takes on material weight.

9. See Kaja Silverman, *Male Subjectivity at the Margins* (New York: Routledge, 1992), 214–97.

10. On the opposition between paternalism and liberalism as residual and dominant ideologies of the New South, see Kevin Railey, *Natural Aristocracy: History, Ideology, and the Production of William Faulkner* (Tuscaloosa: University of Alabama Press, 1999), 3–28.

11. William Faulkner, *The Sound and the Fury: A Norton Critical Edition*, 2nd ed., ed. David Minter (New York: W. W. Norton Press, 1994), 48. All grammatical variations in this and subsequent quotes are specific to Faulkner's text.

12. Wendy Brown, *States of Injury: Power and Freedom in Late Modernity* (Princeton, N.J.: Princeton University Press, 1995), 52–76.

13. Walter Benjamin, *Illuminations: Essays and Reflections*, ed. Hannah Arendt, trans. Harry Zohn (New York: Schocken Books, 1968), 256.

14. Nathaniel Miller, "'Felt, Not Seen, Not Heard': Quentin Compson, Modernist Suicide, and Southern History," *Studies in the Novel* 37 (2005): 39.

15. In developing my psychoanalytic reading of *The Sound and the Fury*, I am particularly indebted to the following texts, which advance differing psychoanalytic accounts of Faulkner's novel: John T. Irwin, *Doubling and Incest/Repetition and Revenge: A Speculative Reading of Faulkner* (Baltimore: Johns Hopkins University Press, 1975); André Bleikasten, *The Most Splendid Failure: Faulkner's* The Sound and the Fury (Bloomington: Indiana University Press, 1976); Minrose Gwin, *The Feminine and Faulkner: Reading (Beyond) Sexual Difference* (Knoxville: University of Tennessee Press, 1990); Elizabeth M. Kerr, *William Faulkner's Gothic Domain* (Port Washington, N.Y.: Kennikat Press, 1979), 53–73; Philip Weinstein, *Faulkner's Subject: A Cosmos No One Owns* (Cambridge: University of Cambridge Press, 1992), 1–10, 83–109.

16. Sigmund Freud, "Mourning and Melancholia," in *The Standard Edition of the Complete Psychological Works of Sigmund Freud*, trans. and ed. James Strachey, 24 vols. (London: Hogarth, 1958), 14:244–45. On melancholia as one of the defining features of modernist manhood, see Breu, *Hard-Boiled Masculinities*, 71–72; Greg Forter, "Against Melancholia: Contemporary Mourning Theory, Fitzgerald's *The Great Gatsby*, and the Politics of Unfinished Grief," *Differences: A Journal of Feminist Cultural Studies* 14 (2003): 134–70.

17. Freud, "Mourning and Melancholia," 247–51.

18. For a reading of *The Sound and the Fury* that convincingly locates Caddy's voice as resistant to the patriarchal desires of her brothers and the world in which she lives see Gwin, *Feminine and Faulkner*, 34–63.

19. Angela Davis, *Women, Race, and Class* (New York: Vintage, 1983), 172–201; Robyn

Wiegman, *American Anatomies: Theorizing Race and Gender* (Durham, N.C.: Duke University Press, 1995), 81–113.

20. Faulkner, *Sound and the Fury*, 95.

21. On the vexed relationship of incest and miscegenation to the South, see Godden, "Quentin Compson"; Irwin, *Doubling and Incest/Repetition and Revenge;* Eric Sundquist, *Faulkner: The House Divided* (Baltimore: Johns Hopkins University Press, 1983).

22. Faulkner, *Sound and the Fury*, 55.

23. Ibid., 104.

24. Ibid., 112; Jacques Lacan, *Écrits: The First Complete Edition in English*, trans. Bruce Fink (New York: W. W. Norton, 2006), 412–41.

25. Faulkner, *Sound and the Fury*, 23–28.

26. Sigmund Freud, "Psycho-Analytic Notes on an Autobiographical Account of a Case of Paranoia (Dementia Paranoides)," in Strachey, ed., *Standard Edition of the Complete Psychological Works of Sigmund Freud*, 7:63.

27. Faulkner, *Sound and the Fury*, 75–77. Commenting on the similarity between Schreber's delusions and his own theories, Freud puts it this way: "It remains for the future to decide whether there is more delusion in my theory than I should like to admit, or whether there is more truth in Schreber's delusion than other people are as yet prepared to believe" (Freud, "Psycho-Analytic Notes," 79).

28. Faulkner, *Sound and the Fury*, 123, 144.

29. Ibid., 144–47.

30. Ibid., 117, 145.

31. Railey, *Natural Aristocracy*, 45–46.

32. Weinstein, *Faulkner's Subject*, 1–10.

33. On Benjy as a schizophrenic, see Rupert Read, "Literature as Philosophy of Psychopathology: Faulkner as Wittgensteinian," *Philosophy, Psychiatry, and Psychology* 10 (2003): 115–24. Jeffrey J. Folks uses ideas of schizophrenia to (less persuasively, in my opinion) discuss Quentin's subjectivity in "Crowd and Self: Faulkner's Sources of Agency in *Sound and the Fury*," *Southern Literary Journal* 34 (2002): 30–44. On Benjy as autistic, see Sara McLaughlin "Faulkner's *Faux Pas*," *Literature and Psychology* 33 (1987): 34–40. For an occasionally too literal but otherwise provocative critique of the representation of Benjy from a disabilities studies paradigm, see Maria Truchan-Tataryn, "Textual Abuse," *Journal of the Medical Humanities* 26 (2005): 159–72.

34. Fredric Jameson, *Postmodernism, or, the Cultural Logic of Late Capitalism* (Durham, N.C.: Duke University Press, 1991), 27.

35. Faulkner, *Sound and the Fury*, 11 (italics in original).

36. Ibid., 31. For an account of schizophrenia that challenges its relationship to the oedipal narrative, see Gilles Deleuze and Félix Guattari, *Anti-Oedipus: Capitalism and Schizophrenia*, trans. Robert Hurley, Mark Seem, and Helen R. Lane (Minneapolis: University of Minnesota Press, 1983), 1–137.

37. Faulkner, *Sound and the Fury*, 182–83. On the significance of this passage in relation-

ship to the liberation rhetoric of the black church, see David Hein, "The Reverend Mr. Shegog's Easter Sermon: Preaching as Communion in Faulkner's *The Sound and the Fury*," *Mississippi Quarterly: The Journal of Southern Cultures* 58 (2005): 559–80. While I am not fully convinced by Hein's discussion of the relationship of the black Baptist church to the Catholic ideal of communion, I find compelling his discussion of the social and political significance of the black church.

The Cosmopolitanism of William Alexander Percy

Benjamin E. Wise

On 5 December 1910, William Alexander Percy toiled unhappily all day in his law office in Greenville, Mississippi. Twenty-five years old and a recent graduate of Harvard Law School, he had returned home to practice law with his father and write poetry. Greenville was a prosperous port city on the Mississippi River with its own opera house and a new four-story grand hotel. For a small southern town it was bustling and diverse. Russian and Greek and Chinese immigrants ran many of the storefronts downtown. Steamboats docked at the landing and offloaded whiskey and burlap and dry goods from New Orleans and Memphis. Blacks outnumbered whites eight to one in the surrounding countryside, where their labor on cotton plantations created wealth for families like the Percys. Will Percy's ancestors were among the first whites to settle in the Mississippi Delta in the 1830s and 1840s, and the Percys remained among Mississippi's foremost families. In 1910, Will lived with his parents in a mansion on a tree-lined avenue appropriately named Percy Street.[1]

The fifth of December that year was a gray and rainy Monday. In the mail, Will received word that Harold Bruff, his best friend and likely his lover from law school, was leaving the country. Will wrote in his diary that night that Harold was "to have six months vacation—without me—among divine places." He confided that he was "filled with longing" and stuck in "that old mood between exasperation and restlessness." A few days later, Will received another letter from Harold with details of his upcoming trip. Harold had been ordered by his doctor and his New York law firm to take six months of vacation to rest his ailing body. As Will read his letter, "it seemed to palpitate: poignant to the degree that rereading is almost an act of courage. He is going to *our* country. How I long to go with him." But demands of work and family made that impossible. Percy felt, though, that "there is compensation" in the knowledge that "Hal is almost all mine when he gets over there." That Sunday, 11 December, Percy spent two hours playing piano and took a walk alone on the levee overlooking the Mississippi River. He wrote in his diary that "Harold sailed yesterday to the lands overseas and the haven where I would be," and tried to redirect his focus on his legal work and his role in his father's campaign for reelection to the U.S. Senate.[2]

The events of early December 1910 illustrate the simultaneous sense of longing and belonging that shaped Will Percy as a southern man. Throughout his life, Percy longed to leave the South and be with Harold Bruff and other men, but he also felt a deep sense of obligation to his home and region. Percy, who lived from 1885 to 1942, witnessed and participated in a significant transitional period in southern history. During his life as a lawyer, plantation owner, and civic leader, the American South became increasingly enmeshed—through global markets, radio waves, and telephones, among other means—with a modernizing, global world. It was during the span of his lifetime that transportation technologies such as railroads, steamships, and automobiles transformed American life: local cultures like Greenville, Mississippi, became forever disrupted by the dramatic increase in the movement of people, goods, and ideas into and out of them. Though long interdependent with the global marketplace of capital and ideas, southerners became increasingly aware of their own connectedness to the rest of the world, even as they worked to construct a solid and enduring "southern" identity.

Percy's life reflected this tension between the local and the global: though he lived and worked and died in Mississippi, he also evinced a cosmopolitan sensibility. This cosmopolitanism—a style of living marked by regular travel and crossing of regional and national boundaries, and a way of thinking marked by openness to new ideas and discomfort with the received wisdom of a traditional society—shaped him in ways as significant as his regional experience in the American South. Percy traveled to five continents and lived for brief periods in Paris, New York, Japan, and Bora-Bora. His adopted son Walker Percy remembered that Will "felt more at home in Taormina than in Jackson," and though he could have "chucked it all, quit, cut out, and went to the islands," he always returned to the South. Will Percy wrote in his now classic memoir, *Lanterns on the Levee: Recollections of a Planter's Son* (1941), that as a child a distinctively southern mentality "seeped into me, colored my outlook, prescribed for me loyalties and responsibilities that I may not disclaim." All his life, though, "the sirens call and the flutes" never ceased to "sound over the hill," and he explained that he had a "reckless determination to spend every cent I earned on going places."[3] This space "over the hill," the world of international travel, is central to understanding Will Percy's sexuality and manhood. In addition, Will Percy's cosmopolitanism suggests important connections between modern mobility and the construction and performance of masculinity among affluent, educated men in the gay male world of the early twentieth century.

Despite his regular movement throughout the world, Will Percy has been characterized in media portrayals as a distinctly southern man. In many ways, Percy has been called on to speak for the South. "Mr. Percy," read his obituary in the New York *Herald Tribune*, "was born in the South, nurtured in its legends, and, to him, the Mississippi delta country was the only place in the world in which to live." Another obituary described him as an "exemplar of the best traditions that have come down to us from the Old South." Percy's life story "reeks of the Delta," one admirer wrote. "You cannot think of Will Percy apart from the Delta." When considering *Lanterns on the Levee*, reviewers portrayed Percy within a gendered context of his region: "Percy is the exemplar of the idealized Christian Gentleman of the Old South"; "Traditions of the Old South came naturally through his daily living"; "This book gives a perfect portrait of a Southern gentleman."[4] He was what it meant to be a southern man: white, aristocratic, provincial, articulate. Will Percy seemed to fit the bill, and has been largely imagined in those terms since his death.

In scholarly discourse too, understandings of Percy have been tethered to a localized understanding of the South. Scholars in southern studies have long been interested in the concept of "place," which has been used to explain the regional particularities that gave the South an exceptional role in American history. Place has traditionally been defined as the physical characteristics of a locale that give it distinctiveness and shape human relations: the architecture, the landscape, the weather, the various sights and sounds and smells that play a role in creating local identity. The artist Alan Gussow memorably defined place as "a piece of the whole environment which has been claimed by feelings."[5] More recently, historians and literary critics have looked to expand this idea of place beyond the local level and look for connections, overlaps, and interdependencies between the South and the rest of the world.[6] In these efforts, though, Will Percy continues to symbolize a provincial sense of place: critics Suzanne W. Jones and Sharon Monteith have noted that *Lanterns on the Levee* is "one of the most nostalgic (and reactionary) of place-defining memoirs," while Fred Hobson has suggested that Will Percy represents the "Old South" and should be contrasted with a newer South with "a more flexible idea of place."[7]

Will Percy's cosmopolitanism offers a corrective to this tendency to understand southerners and southern gender roles in solely regional terms. Geographer Doreen Massey has usefully connected the concept of place with the construction of gender. She insists that we view "the global as part of what constitutes the local, the outside as part of the inside," and within that framework, that we understand the construction of gender as a process that arises out of very specific spatial and temporal circumstances. Rather than what southernists have called a regional sense of place, then, it would be more appropriate to apply Massey's concept of a "global sense of place" to the study of southern men.[8] In moving throughout the world, both within and outside of the American South, Will Percy developed a cosmopolitan male sensibility. The outside world worked to construct his experience as a man in the South, and the South worked to construct his experience as a man in the global world. As a southerner abroad, he experienced a different and empowering sense of sexual freedom in places such as Paris and Capri; and conversely, his foreign encounters supplied him with a language and an imaginative space through which to write about sexuality while in the South. Indeed, this cosmopolitanism is perhaps the single most important concept in understanding how Will Percy managed living in the American South.

Examining southerners like Will Percy who regularly moved across regional and national boundaries creates an opportunity to highlight the ways in which information, identities, and ideas circulate across and between cultures.[9] The study of international travel is one way to demonstrate the reciprocity between global trends and local experiences and cultures. Indeed, this relationship between international travel and the local culture of the Mississippi Delta was central to William Alexander Percy's sexuality. Percy belies simplistic assignations such as "southern man," "Christian gentleman," and "Old South." He felt duty-bound to live out the masculine ideals of his father LeRoy in Greenville, Mississippi, but he also had a deep need to escape these strictures. Percy's access to mobility allowed him to experience his life as a man in different contexts, many of which were more conducive to his aesthetic and sexual desires. Percy traveled in order to experience a space in the world that legitimated and even valorized alternate versions of masculinity. That space was not delineated by regional or national boundaries, but by the possibilities afforded by modern cosmopolitanism.

Will Percy's travels should be placed in the context of his relationship with his father, LeRoy. A hunting buddy of Teddy Roosevelt, U.S. senator, and corporate lawyer, LeRoy overshadowed his son all of his life and created profound ambivalence at the center of Will's self-conception. Like his own father, LeRoy's perennial focus was on the Mississippi Delta—lobbying for better flood control, trying to get more cotton out of an acre, setting himself to solving the "labor problem" and the "negro problem." He didn't understand his son, or his son's avocations. Will preferred playing piano, translating French poetry, and tending his azaleas and roses and irises to LeRoy's diversions of hunting, poker, and drinking. LeRoy had another son, LeRoy Jr., who was killed in a hunting accident at age ten. Will Percy wrote that his brother was "all boy, all sturdy, obstreperous charm" and assumed that his father's "heart must often have called piteously for the little brother I had lost."[10]

Despite this sense of self-loathing that surfaces in his writing, Percy also found creative ways of achieving satisfaction and overcoming the strain of life under his father's roof. For one thing, he worked at his relationship with his father. Will lived in his parents' home all his life. He walked to and from work with LeRoy; he supported his father in his political and legal battles. When LeRoy died in 1929, Will commissioned a thirty-thousand-dollar statue to be placed on his grave. He loved his father and wanted to please him even though he rarely did. Rather than seeing Will as merely a victim of his father's disdain, it is important to understand the ways he worked against it, the ways he was wounded but not completely oppressed by it.

Another way Will Percy managed this constraint was to maintain regular distance from his father by traveling. Sigmund Freud's interpretation of travel sheds particular light on this aspect of LeRoy and Will's relationship. In 1937, Freud published an essay titled "A Disturbance of Memory on the Acropolis" in which he reflects on a trip he and his younger brother took to Italy and Greece in 1904. Although Freud addressed several psychological phenomena in the essay, in his conclusions he ventured a few suggestions as to why adults are compelled to travel, and whereby they gain pleasure or guilt from it. He suggested that the compulsion to travel is often rooted in painful childhood experience and fantasies of escape, and that "a great part of the pleasure of travel lies in the fulfillment of these early wishes, that it is rooted, that is, in dissatisfaction with home and family." However, just as this escape brings pleasure, it also creates guilt because, in Freud's reading, "a sense of guilt was attached to the satisfaction of having got so far: there was something about it that was wrong, that was from earliest of times forbidden. It was something to do with a child's criticism of his father." For Freud, whose father had never been to the Acropolis and furthermore did not have the education to appreciate it, guilt accompanied his pleasure at the top of the Acropolis because he had accomplished something his father could not have: "It seems as though the essence of success were to have gotten further than one's father, and as though to excel one's father were still something forbidden."[11]

One of Will Percy's own experiences atop the Acropolis, which he recounted in his autobiography, has instructive parallels with Freud's conception of travel, guilt, pleasure, and the figure of the father. Will and his family sailed for Greece after LeRoy Percy's painful political loss to James K. Vardaman in the 1911 U.S. Senate race. Though devastated by the recent loss, Will determined to recover his peace of mind during their trip abroad. Lying in bed on the first night in

Athens, he decided he "couldn't possibly wait until after breakfast to see the Acropolis, and besides it would be great fun to put one over on father and tell him all about Athena's Hill over coffee and rolls." He left the hotel at six in the morning and ran to the Acropolis. Near reaching the top, he stopped to catch his breath and heard a sound above him. Looking up, he saw that his father had beaten him to the enclosure atop the Acropolis. "The curative morning was flooding over him, and he laughed when he saw me."[12]

Although Freud's essay was published in 1937, it was not translated into English until 1941 so it is not likely that Percy had it in mind when he wrote this section of *Lanterns on the Levee*. Nonetheless, we can we read this episode in light of the phenomenon Freud described. Like Freud, for Percy the Acropolis was a site of escape even as it represented the dominating presence of his father in his life, both actually and symbolically. Unlike Freud, though, Will Percy never did "excel" his father, as symbolized by LeRoy's presence at the top of the Acropolis. The father always overshadowed the son, always dominated him, and never fully accepted him. In turn, Will never criticized his father, excepting veiled admirations such as, "It was hard having such a dazzling father."[13]

Yet, the first part of Freud's concept, that the compulsion to travel is in large part derived from the desire to escape home, is quite useful. Will Percy was fascinated with "travel and the thought of travel," and throughout his life, he wrote, travel was his "usual opiate" that he indulged at every opportunity. As he confessed, "Probably I had never been at peace. Probably I had always wanted to escape a life that had seemed to me filled with nothing and less noble than a human life need be." He spent much of his energy as an adult planning ways to leave Greenville, Mississippi, and the South. Richard King has pointed out that though Percy "presided over his own small realm in the delta, he felt no more sense of freedom in the world at large."[14] This, however, is exactly backward: while Percy is usually figured as someone rooted to his home, perhaps it would be more useful to see him as someone with a compulsion to escape his home.

Travel was more to Percy than just escape, however. Travel and the thought of travel, to use his phrase, served a crucial function in the formation of his masculinity and his ability to cope with the restrictive elements of southern society. Travel served as an outlet for his sexual expression, and indeed both in his material and imaginative life, the foreign served as a site of sexual, emotional, and artistic freedom. Far from believing that "the Mississippi delta country was the only place in the world in which to live," as some would have it, Will Percy fantasized about and experienced a life of freedom in other parts of the world. Shelby Foote, who knew Percy well, provided a more accurate reminiscence about Will's place in the world: "I sometimes speculate (impossibly)," Foote wrote to Walker Percy in 1980, "on whether he should have gotten the hell out of

Greenville, which he was always saying he loved yet really hated—I mean deep down. Of course he wouldn't, couldn't, but I sometimes wish to hell he had."[15] Foote's speculation was well received by Percy, who wrote back, "Re Uncle Will: You're right."[16] Inasmuch as Will Percy was animated by the local, drawn to live in and serve his hometown, and moved to write elegaically about the South, he was equally compelled to leave that place. His identity, as it were, was not merely "southern," but should be seen as a push and pull, a painful but often ecstatic set of journeys between the South and the world.

"From first childhood," Percy wrote in his autobiography, "I had saved every penny of birthday and Christmas money for a trip abroad. It was my obsession, my one mundane objective." After his graduation from the University of the South in 1904, Will Percy took his savings and left for a year in Europe. This was not the first time he had been to Europe, but in many ways it marked the beginning of his unique and lifelong relationship with international travel. Before this trip, his travels to Europe had been with his parents. Now he went alone. This year abroad, which lasted from June 1904 to September 1905, opened up a world of possibility and freedom.[17] He had to hide the freedoms enjoyed while traveling from those who looked to him to be a southern man in the vein of his illustrious father and grandfather. He shrouded his travels in secrecy, but there are clues in the historical record which indicate that Will Percy lived a distinctly different life in Europe than that of his common portrayal as a heterosexual, paternalistic Delta plantation owner.[18]

During his year abroad, Percy lived in the Latin Quarter of Paris in a four-room boardinghouse with a Polish medical student, a prostitute, and Marie, "the homeliest femme de chambre in Paris." He furnished his room with a piano. He read aloud to himself in French. To please his father, he took fencing lessons. He recounted that "[e]ven at this age I had great affection for the world and did not want to miss any of its beauties," and as such, he spent most of his time at the free Sorbonne lectures, the opera house, the Concerts Rouge, and the Luxembourg Gardens. He traveled regularly from his home base in Paris, even going as far as Egypt in January 1905.[19]

In his memoir, he portrayed his time in Europe as one of loneliness, but his letters home to his mother at the time suggest contentedness: "You mentioned something about my staying over here until next September. That would be great, grand, and glorious"; "I have been exceptionally gay and giddy, going to the theatre every night"; "There is hardly a day that I am not in the Louvre at least an hour and every time I discover something new."[20] Loneliness, however, is an important recurring element of *Lanterns on the Levee*: the things Will Percy cherished he lamented as gone and surrounded with sadness and silence. Loneliness did not always mean the absence of other people; rather, he used it as a trope to indicate his recurring sense of himself as an outsider. Percy was smart and charming, and was surrounded throughout his life with people who adored him. His loneliness was not physical as much as it was psychological, and it was abroad in 1904–5 that he directly confronted this aspect of his life. He also acquired a way of managing it: to create a divide between his life in Mississippi and his life abroad.

One aspect of this divide was the secrecy Percy exhibited regarding his travels. When an admirer of his poetry wrote him and asked if the poem "Sappho in Levkas," set in Greece, was modeled on personal experience, he answered, "I had not visited Greece when I wrote 'Sappho,' and I am afraid the scene of Sappho is Sewanee." Actually, Percy had been to Greece at least three times before the poem was published in 1915. In 1909, for example, he wrote home to his mother from Athens of the wonderful time he was having in Greece. "This morning I spent on the Acropolis," he wrote, "and thought again and again of how you, father and I enjoyed it all twelve years ago." Indeed, the poem may even have been written in Greece. Percy often spoke of how he wrote poetry—and particularly his long, narrative poems such as "Sappho in Levkas"—while on summer vacation. He explained to his friend William Stanley Braithwaite that he nearly always wrote his longer pieces outside the South "in the loveliest spot I can find," including Jackson's Hole, Wyoming, Taormina, and Capri.[21] For Percy, travel—and particularly his travels to Greece and Italy—was something he preferred remain distinct from his life in Mississippi. When he traveled, he journeyed alone or with friends not from Greenville. His most common American traveling companions were Harold Bruff (before 1911), Gerstle Mack, and Huger Jervey, all of whom lived in New York.

Harold Bruff in particular gives us some clues to the significance of the secretive nature of Percy's travels. Bruff and Percy met when they both entered law school at Harvard in the autumn of 1905 and immediately formed a deep bond. Percy reflects in his memoir that to sit at the symphony in Boston next to Harold Bruff was "ecstasy," and the two traveled to Europe together in 1907 and 1908 and visited frequently in New York after graduation. Will Percy felt free on these trips. In a moment of candor in 1907, he wrote home to his mother from Switzerland telling her a story of how he and Harold had met a group of delightful American girls. They were in a cheerful mood, and when they parted for the night, Bruff and Percy and the girls played a game whistling back and forth to one another from their hotel balconies. However, Percy wrote, "It all ended by my suddenly appearing on Harold's balcony clad in pink pajamas, with the moonlight a spot-light on me and imagining that I was completely hid by the shrubbery." The game ended, and the travelers retreated to their rooms "in a disgraceful anti-climax."[22]

Percy and Bruff's correspondence also indicates something of their intimate relationship, all of which took place in Boston, New York, and Europe. Bruff wrote affectionately and longingly to Percy during these years. Before Bruff had joined Percy in Europe in 1907, for example, he wrote to him, "Write soon Billy your inmost thoughts and even if it's a sonnet (an elegy or ode probably would be more polite) don't be afraid to pour it out." After their trip to Europe in 1908, Bruff wrote to Percy, who was still in Paris, "I have missed you tremendously and perhaps there is sour virtue in suffering in silence. Your letters have been whatever is appropriate to an aching soul—and I'm so glad for you that the trip has been a success and Italy is in sight. . . . You have done much for me in three years Bill, leading the way to something higher and the better things in life (and I don't mean morals) and you know that you have a place that no one else can ever quite fill."[23]

In the same letter, Bruff told Percy that while he had been enjoying his letters, he felt that Percy was not sharing everything with him. Harold had recently lunched with a mutual friend, who had just returned from Paris where he was with Will. Bruff commented that though they did not talk openly in the restaurant, "[h]e is going to take me out in his motor tomorrow and discourse on what modesty (?) made you omit." For Percy and Bruff, Europe was a site of sexual freedom. Even bohemian New York City felt confining. Bruff often wrote to Percy coaxing him to come visit, but also noted the lack of freedom there. "You must stay here many days," Bruff wrote in 1910. "I know N.Y. is not the place for *us* and there are so many distractions that seem to frighten away the desired mood but maybe—who knows?"[24] In one of the many tragedies in Will Percy's life, Bruff died shortly thereafter.

Percy never mentioned Harold Bruff again in writing, save for his brief recollection in his memoir and in a 1919 letter to his friend and mentor Carrie Stern, whom he trusted deeply. Another of Will's closest companions, Sinkler Manning, died in battle in World War I, and from France, Will wrote home to Carrie, "You, probably more than anyone else, know how much he meant to me: after Harold he was my best friend, one I understood and who understood me, one who I knew could never fail me."[25] Will Percy rarely spoke of people who understood him. He often spoke of loneliness. He often portrayed himself as a wanderer and a pilgrim. How hard it must have been for him to feel free in the company of others, how difficult to live on display as a man from a prominent family while trying to come to terms with his homosexual desire and poetic temperament in the patriarchal and philistine South of the early twentieth century. One way he managed this was to keep his life in Mississippi separate from his life of international travel—the provincial life a public one and the cosmopolitan life a private one. This was not easy, particularly for an intensely introspective person likely to fault himself for disingenuousness. Willful duplicity allowed Percy to experience rare moments of fulfillment even while it led to self-loathing. It helped him to manage life in the South by giving him access to a freer life in the larger world. But in the end, the balance rested on his ability to remain silent. He did so, but at great cost. He gave some clue to this inner torment in his poem "Safe Secrets," published in 1924:

> I will carry terrible things to the grave with me:
> So much must never be told.
> My eyes will be ready for sleep and my heart for dust
> With all the secrets they hold.
> The piteous things alive in my memory
> Will be safe in that soundless dwelling:
> In the clean loam, in the dark where the dumb roots rust
> I can sleep without fear of telling.[26]

It was abroad that Will Percy most often felt release from these torments. Between the two world wars, Percy involved himself with a group of British writers who left England to either travel extensively or set up residence abroad. Literary historian Paul Fussell has identified the international travel of such writers as Norman Douglas, Christopher Isherwood, Robert Graves, Somerset Maugham, Bertrand Russell, and others in this period as the "British literary diaspora," and argued that this movement was an essential component of modernism and the struggle for sexual freedom. For this group of writers, sexual freedom often meant homosexual freedom. Travel has always been considered romantic, but in this case the Mediterranean and Capri in particular was especially a site of erotic possibility as compared to the Victorian prudishness of England. (One contemporary observer noted in 1927 that "the Isle of Capri is a sodomic capital in miniature, the Mecca of inversion, a Geneva or a Moscow of the future internationalism of homosexuality."[27]) Writers such as Isherwood and Douglas in particular drew on the homoerotic literary tradition of Walter Pater and John Addington Symonds in order to portray the Mediterranean as a sexually uninhibited locale. According to Fussell, Isherwood's and Douglas's "sojourns abroad were inseparable from [their] erotic requirements and predicaments"; traveling and imagining travel were central to their sexuality. Will Percy became friends with Norman Douglas in Italy in the 1920s, and the two corresponded until Percy's death in 1942.[28] Douglas was fond enough of Percy to ask him to write a foreword to his book, *Birds and Beasts of the Greek Anthology* (1929).

Percy's involvement with this group provided him with sexual freedom and with an idiom with which to talk about that freedom. This literary idiom is especially evident in Percy's foreword to *Birds and Beasts*. Rather than introducing the book itself, which was a commentary on the natural history of the Greek anthology, Percy wrote a series of vignettes of Douglas. The first scene was in a café in Florence. Percy described Douglas's entrance as an almost regal event, and he did so in language that was undeniably sexual: "Norman Douglas appeared. . . . A person, a personage had entered, one whom Frans Hals would have walked miles to paint: the untidy room was galvanized, something robustious and electric accelerated the tempo of the waiters, stiffened the patrons into expectancy." When he entered the room, his booming voice ushered forth a greeting that "seemed an adequate climax." Two days later, Percy wrote, he met Douglas on a side street as he was headed to see the Giottos at Santa Maria Novella. When Percy asked him if he would care to join, Douglas declined, commenting with tenderness, "Two years ago . . . It's the most famous and convenient place in Florence for lover's meetings." Percy went alone but almost tripped over a step, he remembered, as he was "thinking of other things."[29]

In fact, the juxtaposition of aesthetic beauty and homoerotic feeling is a common element of Percy's work and much Victorian homoerotic writing. His discussion of colors in the landscape, museums, artwork, cathedrals, and other aspects of Mediterranean life often served to augment the sense of wonder and freedom to be found in the European South. In this respect, Percy utilized the idiom of Victorian writers who figured "friendship," "comradeship," and "companionship" in the context of this natural beauty to connote same-sex desire—a literary device well documented by historians of European literature and sexuality. Percy's foreword illustrates this well. In the next vignette, Percy and a companion, Berto, were walking along the Arno River in Florence at dusk, discussing Douglas. "Norman is amazing," Berto observed. "With him the end of a love affair is never the end of a friendship. The charming friends of his earlier years come back to him from all over Italy, in fact from all over Europe, for advice or merely to be shone on by his vitality. Of course you've recognized his terrific sunshine."[30] Natural beauty, friendship, and vitality: Will Percy found these things in the culture of the European South. He traveled there to experience them, and when absent he wrote about them. Percy's final vignette further illustrates this unique blend of artistry, beauty, and friendship that Percy found in Europe. Percy, Douglas, and another man named Carey were having lunch with one another when Will mentioned he spent his morning marveling at the Botticellis in the Uffizi gallery. "Isn't that sweet, Carey?" quipped Douglas. "Think, there are still persons who look at the Botticellis. I haven't seen one for twenty years." Douglas admonished Percy for being such a dilettante and suggested that if he wanted to see some truly beautiful works he should take the bus to Volterra to see the Etruscan art, which was "worth all your Michaelangelos and da Vincis and Botticellis put together." To Douglas, Volterra had an additional benefit:

"the charming boys there are all lightly powdered with alabaster dust, even their eyelashes. Exquisite! Like Pierrots!"[31] For many in this community of intellectuals, artistic beauty was inseparable from sexual desire, and sexual desire was inseparable from travel to Italy and Greece. Just as Douglas associated Etruscan art with its alabaster-dusted attendants, for Will Percy, the Mediterranean, artistic expression, and male companionship were intertwined. Percy's cosmopolitanism did not merely comprise travel and leisure; it was a method of managing constraint and experiencing sexual freedom. In Europe he encountered this new way of thinking about sexuality and found an outlet for sexual expression.

In addition, Percy's cosmopolitanism created an imaginative space that is central to his writing. In his autobiography, his travels play a dynamic role in his most intimate portrayals of himself. Critics have been correct to read *Lanterns on the Levee* as a book concerned with place, for geography and topography are central features of the text. Some of the most resonant moments in the book derived from local images: the Mississippi River and its levees and floods, the dark soil of the Delta, cotton, crawfish. But these descriptions, these local anecdotes, do not portray the *place* with which the book is concerned. *Lanterns on the Levee*'s presiding leitmotif is a series of travels away from Mississippi. Like Percy's life, his memoir is marked by the melancholic sense that the South was an inadequate home, and in turn Percy used the foreign as a template onto which he wrote his personal and emotional desire. He juxtaposed home and abroad to conjure a space of sexual freedom and personal wholeness.

Will Percy called his memoir a "pilgrims' script—one man's field notes of a land not far but quite unknown." It is a common trope in autobiography to describe one's life in terms of a journey or a pilgrimage, but in Percy's case this is instructive for two reasons. First, throughout the book, he portrayed his life as a series of journeys, both physical and metaphorical. It is not a book of stasis, but of movement—into and out of the South, toward Europe, to Japan, back to Mississippi. The pilgrimage was a concept that for Percy had more than vernacular significance: it was an essential component of his experience and imagination. Second, at the end of the book, he confessed the destination of his pilgrimage. After recounting his various failures in life, he described his vision of the afterlife and the vindication he hoped to receive for his "one tiny life." He saw himself on a road traveling toward heaven, and when the High God appears he demands, "Who are you?" "The pilgrim I know," Percy wrote, "should be able to straighten his shoulders, to stand his tallest, and to answer defiantly, 'I am your son.'"[32] Will Percy's pilgrimage would end, he hoped, with acceptance from a father. He never received it in his life, but in his most ardent hopes for the afterlife what he hoped to gain was sonship. It is ironic, then, that in the broadest terms, Percy's pilgrimage was toward his father, while in his life his journeys were away from him. In his life, his most fulfilling moments were when he was abroad; the moments of greatest freedom and self-realization he described in the book took place on foreign soil.

One of the most expressive and least guarded chapters of *Lanterns* is entitled "Jackdaw in the Garden." In this chapter, Percy assumed the role of the jackdaw, a type of crow that is noted for its quiet watchfulness. He perched in his garden, which he offered as a metaphor for his own struggle to flourish in a difficult environment. "The major moral afforded by a garden," Percy wrote, "comes from watching the fight for sunlight waged by those unhappy things rooted against their will in the shade." The Indica azaleas and the lilacs, for example, would prefer another climate, farther north. "They will exist if I take enough pains with them, but they are not happy and the meagerness of their bloom betrays their incurable nostalgia. The heart too has its climate, without which it is a mere pumping-station." Percy portrayed the aridity of Mississippi, the dryness of life, and his own efforts to reach for sunlight in spite of his rootedness in local soil. His shade plants "thrust emaciated feelers, gangling and scant of leaf, toward a spot of light. To escape the deeper shadow they twist themselves into ungainliness. Branches die so that the remnant whole may survive. They are bleached as by a sickroom." In the same way, such was life in Mississippi: "Standing at the post-office corner I recognize my poor sunless plants in the passers-by, sickly, out of shape, ugly with strain, who still search for a sunlight vital to their needs and never found, or found and lost."[33] The climate in Mississippi was not the climate for Will Percy's heart.

Having set up this guiding metaphor for the chapter, Percy described another reward of a garden: "It's a closed and quiet place, the best sort of Ivory Tower. . . . It's a starting point for thoughts and backward looks and questionings. . . . You sit there and think of the trip you have made, fifty-five years of trip, and you wonder what it totals up to."[34] As such, he set out to reminisce about his own life, its meaning, its occasional flourishes, and its constant struggle. But in an important change of tone, Percy wrote that rather than the struggle and the failures, he would write about the treasures in his heart. In a book dominated by self-deprecation and recounting of his various insufficiencies, he attempted in this section to record instances that represented his fullest experiences, "what was mine to possess utterly and sovereignly, without counterclaim . . . the jackdaw pickings of my curious and secret heart." "Now is the time," he wrote, "to spread my treasure out." For the remainder of the chapter, Percy told of what, when he looked like a jackdaw into his own heart, he found of value.

Percy's reminiscences have several repeating themes. The most striking is that each of Percy's treasured memories took place in a foreign setting. Moments of love between two people, moments of understanding, and moments of self-fulfillment took place in Spain, Greece, Turkey, Capri, Taormina, France, and on sea vessels approaching Bora-Bora and Rio de Janeiro. In addition to being geographically foreign, these moments were removed from time and set in a far-off, detached period. In each instance, Percy cast himself with another man or a group of men. Percy's expression of his homoerotic desire, his portrayal of those he was able to "love and understand," was carefully yet lovingly crafted. This was Percy's struggle, and likely the struggle of many with homosexual desire in the late Victorian South: how to both express this love honestly and articulate it in a way that would not end in public humiliation. Percy's solution was to cast the foreign as a site of sexual freedom and to adorn his homoerotic fantasies with exoticism and timelessness. The struggle, Percy wrote, "has all been good and worth the tears. I see it as a dream I long to hold, but not to relive. I hear voices unbelievably soft (whose are they, was it in Rio or Barcelona or the islands? No matter) that murmur: 'Don't go, don't leave me, I love you,' and I smile, knowing I will hear them no more and grateful for their music." In a series of vignettes, he laid his treasure out "for the mere delight of recalling," and in doing so provided clues as to how cosmopolitanism in life and imagination served a crucial function in navigating the constraints of the late Victorian world.[35]

Percy's first treasure centered on his encounter with a "satyr on the slopes of Parnassus." In Greek mythology, a satyr is often figured as an oversexualized man, but in this instance it was an antique and primitive "brown boy . . . hardly half as tall as the goat-herd's crook he carried." His hair was uncombed, he was wearing a goat-herd's skirt and tunic, and he had a conspicuous knife in his belt. Percy cast the shepherd boy as entirely premodern, and himself as a god, a "disengaged spirit" drinking in the splendor of the "high lost world" of a Greek dusk. The laughter and banter of village women below "were merely tinklings in the deepening silence." The boy stared at Percy "as though I were a mortal" and asked to see his watch. To emphasize the primal nature of the boy and the timelessness of the moment, Percy recounted that "he shook it and put it to his ear, but of course did not look at the time." The boy turned to one of his goats and from his throat "issued animal sounds, half cluck, half gutteral bleat," and the boy and the goat "danced together. The full moon and I saw them dance together." After this act of primal connectedness, the boy ran to Percy and took him by the hand. For a moment the two "walked in silence, hand in hand," but suddenly the boy looked at Percy and "smiled once—but it was like a gale of laughter—and was gone. And the night seemed suddenly bleak." The language of this encounter indicates the mystical possibilities the foreign held for Percy. Greece in Percy's imagination was "austere and primitive, antique and change-less," and as such offered unlimited possibility. Percy was free to script his desire in a playful and even joyful manner in a setting removed from his place and from his time. Nowhere else in *Lanterns* is a smile ascribed the power of laughter, nowhere else do mortals assume the properties of gods. Percy surrounded the moment with silence and sunset, and celebrated the possibility of connection between two humans even as he mourned its impermanence.[36]

Innocent and primitive love was a repeated theme in the memoir, and in another vignette set in the Anatolian headland of Turkey. In this instance, Percy was accompanied by another man on a picnic overlooking the sea, though we are not told the partner's name. The imagery of the passage is among the most colorful and positive in the entire autobiography. The sea and the sun were laughing, the sapphire water glistened below the clouds, the picnickers "seemed suspended magically" as they were bathed with "palest pink and lavender in the ecstatic light." "Except that it was live with rushing air," Percy wrote, "it would have seemed a fortunate bright dream. We lay on the ground in the penciled shadow, each in his own burnished reverie." As they lay looking out toward the distant horizon, they began to hear what sounded like singing in the water below them. They crawled to the edge of the cliff and peered over the edge, and in the water, "[a] young man, white and naked, with a mop of gold hair, was swimming beneath us, and as he swam he sang." In the silence, the young man was unaware of the onlookers and swam along playfully, "brimming with some hale antique happiness not ours to know." But, like the encounter with the satyr, the moment was brief. The swimmer disappeared from sight as "the dazzle hid him from us, but we still heard his voice." In this instance, Percy again emphasized the premodern disposition of the swimmer, him being possessed of an untouchable and momentary happiness unavailable to the Western watchers. Unlike the encounter with the shepherd, though, this memory was a voyeuristic fantasy. Though the vision of the young man was fleeting, in this moment Percy had a companion, quite possibly one whose loving whispering voice he recalled earlier in the chapter. Percy used the image of the naked boy to indicate that in their watching he and his companion experienced this ecstasy together. Though lonely and alone throughout his memoir, in this instance Percy revealed a fundamental connection with another that he experienced rarely in his life. When he did, he experienced it in Turkey, suspended in time as if dreaming.[37]

Yet Percy always had to reenter the world—these encounters were all marked by their brevity and volatility. The final vignette took place on the deck of a ship approaching Rio de Janeiro on a moonlit night. It was dark and silent, otherworldly: "Our ship receded from reality, became a tiny world abandoned to itself." Though ostensibly headed for Brazil, in this fantasy the ship became both placeless and without destination, for "despite the appeasing pathos of the moon, it seemed a lonely world, forgotten and adrift, pursuing some mysterious course that might not count a port." Percy was again a voyeur, this time watching the crew, an exoticized, all-male, working-class group of men from Portugal, Samoa, Finland, America, and Greece. In this detached but sexually charged setting, the men took on an ethereal beauty: "I watched them moving like somnambulists, the wind whipping their hair, the moonlight turning their bodies slender and unsubstantial, daubing their cheek-bones and shoulders, the arch of their chests or their buttocks with pallor, and a stillness was on them. They came on deck from the hatches in a sudden glory of light. . . . They came in all manner of garbs, in work clothes or stripped to the waist; mostly they came alone and kept to themselves." The men sat on the deck in silence as the wind muffled the occasional song or comment. Though the men were beautiful, Percy ascribed to them prescience of human limitation and the reality of pain. As they stood shrouded in moonlight, they gazed into the unending ocean. Percy suggested that they may have been thinking of many things, but likely they "were thinking each of the same thing . . . The patience of loneliness and the tranquility of unescapable pain were on their faces like grave beauty. I thought of a lost chart and an unknown port, and I too looked to the sea." The sea, the distant horizon, the endless night—these things suggest unlimited possibility. Unlimited possibility, like the destination of a ship bound for nowhere, was not a reality in Will Percy's world. But in another rare instance of optimism in a book marked by melancholic fatalism, Percy offered hope. As he and the sailors gazed out into the expanse, the night watchman clanged his bell to sound the hour and yelled to the captain, "in a voice piercingly young and full of hope, 'The lights are bright, sir!'"[38]

Throughout these vignettes, Percy demonstrated aspects of his cosmopolitan imagination. It was a moment in his memoir in which he became vulnerable, allowed himself to write more freely about the places and moments and people he valued. The instances he recorded are remarkable for their exoticism, magic, and detachment in place and time. In his most forthright expression of himself in his memoir, he sketched three homoerotic fantasies set in distant lands and removed from time. And in those instances in which he did mention his home and his region, he portrayed it as lifeless and dry. At the end of the chapter, after outlining his foreign fantasies, he returned to the local and, importantly, to the negative tone of the rest of the book. "These memories of mine," he writes, "lose nothing of their luster in this time of doom." Returned from the world of his imagination, he remembered again that "[a] tarnish has fallen over the bright world; dishonor and corruption triumph; my own strong people are turned lotus-eaters; defeat is here again." But sitting in his garden, reflecting and watching the vignettes of his remembered life, "the only treasure that's exempt from tarnish is what the jackdaw gathers."[39]

Will Percy's cosmopolitanism in life and imagination was crucial to his lived experience as a southern man. Rather than a regional assignation, then, such as "southern gentleman," perhaps it is most useful to characterize Will Percy as a traveler—as he himself did. Traveling outside the American South provided an opportunity for Percy to enjoy male companionship in a nonthreatening and often beautiful environment. He traveled often, and it was during these times that he most often experienced connection and understanding with another human. His experiences in foreign places comprised all of "the jackdaw pickings of [his] curious and secret heart," and Percy expressed those memories in language that indicates a freedom he never experienced in Mississippi. Despite Percy's deep connection and commitment to the American South, his relationships with other men—from his father to his traveling companions—depended largely on his ability to leave it.

NOTES

The author thanks Ann Ziker, Molly Robey, Gale Kenny, Caroline Levander, and the members of Southern Historians in New England, especially Bill Harris, Walter Johnson, Susan O'Donovan, and Claire Nee Nelson, for reading and commenting on drafts of this essay.

1. For background information on William Alexander Percy and his family history, see Bertram Wyatt-Brown, *The House of Percy: Honor, Melancholy and Imagination in a Southern Family* (New York: Oxford University Press, 1992); Jay Tolson, *Pilgrim in the Ruins: A Life of Walker Percy* (New York: Simon and Schuster, 1994); Lewis Baker, *The Percys of Mississippi: Politics and Literature in the New South* (Baton Rouge: Louisiana State University Press, 1984); Richard King, *A Southern Renaissance: The Cultural Awakening of the American South, 1930–1955* (New York: Oxford University Press, 1980), chap. 4; Fred C. Hobson, *Tell about the South: The Southern Rage to Explain* (Baton Rouge: Louisiana State University Press, 1983), chap. 4; McKay Jenkins, *The South in Black And White: Race, Sex, and Literature in the 1940s* (Chapel Hill: University of North Carolina Press, 1999), chap. 3; Scott Romine, *Narrative Forms of Southern Community* (Baton Rouge: Louisiana State University Press, 1999), chap. 3; James W. Silver, *Running Scared: Silver in Mississippi* (Jackson: University Press of Mississippi, 1984), Appendix H.

2. William Alexander Percy Diary, 5 December 1910, 8 December 1910, 11 December 1910, William Alexander Percy Papers, Mississippi Department of Archives and History, Jackson. On LeRoy Percy's 1910–11 senatorial campaign, see William F. Holmes, *The White Chief: James Kimble Vardaman* (Baton Rouge: Louisiana State University Press, 1970), and Albert D. Kirwan, *Revolt of the Rednecks: Mississippi Politics, 1876–1925* (Lexington: University of Kentucky Press, 1951).

3. Walker Percy, "Uncle Will," in *Signposts in a Strange Land*, ed. Patrick Samway (New York: Farrar, Straus, and Giroux, 2000), 55; William Alexander Percy, *Lanterns on the Levee: Recollections of a Planter's Son* (New York: Alfred A. Knopf, 1941), 73–74, 142.

For recent discussions of the contested concept of cosmopolitanism, see Kwame Anthony Appiah, *Cosmopolitanism: Ethics in a World of Strangers* (New York: W. W. Norton and Co., 2006); Gillian Brock and Harry Brighouse, eds., *The Political Philosophy of Cosmopolitanism* (New York: Cambridge University Press, 2005); Tom Lutz, *Cosmopolitan Vistas: American Regionalism and Literary Value* (Ithaca, N.Y.: Cornell University Press, 2004); Steven Vertovec and Robin Cohen, eds., *Conceiving Cosmopolitanism: Theory, Context, and Practice* (New York: Oxford University Press, 2002). My conception of cosmopolitanism especially draws from Ulf Hannerz, "Cosmopolitans and Locals in World Culture," *Theory, Culture and Society* 7 (1990): 237–51.

4. *Herald-Tribune* (New York), 22 January 1942; *Times-Dispatch* (Richmond, Va.), 23 January 1942; "Mississippi Writers Program for 1941," program pamphlet; *News and Courier* (Charleston, S.C.), n.d.; *Enquirer* (Cincinnati), 10 May 1941; *Book of the Month News*, April 1941; all in Alfred A. Knopf Papers, Harry Ransom Humanities Center, University of Texas–Austin.

5. Quoted in Peirce Lewis, "Defining a Sense of Place," in Peggy W. Prenshaw and Jesse O. McKee, eds., *Sense of Place, Mississippi* (Jackson: University Press of Mississippi, 1979), 40. For works dealing with the concept of place, see Louis D. Rubin and Robert Jacobs, eds., *The Southern Renascence: The Literature of the Modern South* (Baltimore: Johns Hopkins University Press, 1953); Louis D. Rubin, *The Faraway Country: Writers of the Modern South* (Seattle: University of Washington Press, 1963); Richard Gray, *Southern Aberrations: Writers of the American South and the Problems of Regionalism* (Baton Rouge: Louisiana State University Press, 2000); Martyn Bone, *The Postsouthern Sense of Place in Contemporary Fiction* (Baton Rouge: Louisiana State University Press, 2005).

6. See Houston A. Baker Jr. and Dana D. Nelson, "Preface: Violence, The Body, and 'The South,'" *American Literature* 73 (2003): 231–44; Michael Kreyling, "Toward a 'New Southern Studies,'" *South Central Review* 22 (2005): 4–18; *Global Contexts, Local Literatures: The New Southern Studies*, ed. Kathryn McKee and Annette Trefzer, special issue of *American Literature* 78 (2006); Leigh Ann Duck, *The Nation's Region: Southern Modernism, Segregation, and U.S. Nationalism* (Athens: University of Georgia Press, 2006); Jon Smith and Deborah Cohn, eds., *Look Away! The U.S. South in New World Studies* (Durham, N.C.: Duke University Press, 2004); James Peacock, *Grounded Globalism: How the U.S. South Embraces the World* (Athens: University of Georgia Press, 2007); Michael O'Brien, *Placing the South* (Jackson: University Press of Mississippi, 2007).

7. Suzanne W. Jones and Sharon Monteith, eds., *South to a New Place: Region, Literature, Culture* (Baton Rouge: Louisiana State University Press, 2002), 1–2; Fred Hobson, ed., *South to the Future: An American Region in the Twenty-first Century* (Baton Rouge: Louisiana State University Press, 2002), 5.

8. Doreen Massey, *Space, Place, and Gender* (Minneapolis: University of Minnesota Press, 1994), 5.

9. For examples of this type of work, see Brent Edwards, *The Practice of Diaspora: Literature, Translation, and the Rise of Black Internationalism* (Cambridge, Mass.: Har-

vard University Press, 2003); Dwight A. McBride, ed., *James Baldwin Now* (New York: New York University Press, 1999), esp. chaps. 6, 7, and 8; Michael O'Brien, "Italy and the Southern Romantics," in *Rethinking the South: Essays in Intellectual History* (Baltimore, Md.: Johns Hopkins University Press, 1988); Daniel Kilbride, "Travel, Ritual, and National Identity: Planters on the European Tour, 1820–1960," *Journal of Southern History* 69 (2003): 549–84. For work on the global South, see, for example, Peter Kolchin, *A Sphinx on the American Land: The Nineteenth-Century South in Comparative Perspective* (Baton Rouge: Louisiana State University Press, 2003): 3; C. Vann Woodward, "The Irony of Southern History," in *The Burden of Southern History* (Baton Rouge: Louisiana State University Press, 1970); Smith and Cohn, eds., *Look Away!;* James C. Cobb and William Stueck, eds., *Globalization and the American South* (Athens: University of Georgia Press, 2005); James L. Peacock, Harry L. Watson, and Carrie R. Matthews, eds., *The American South in a Global World* (Chapel Hill: University of North Carolina Press, 2005).

10. Percy, *Lanterns on the Levee,* 126.

11. Sigmund Freud, "A Disturbance of Memory on the Acropolis," in *Character and Culture* (New York: Collier, 1963), 319–20.

12. Percy, *Lanterns on the Levee,* 155.

13. Ibid., 57. This phrase comes after a fascinating moment in the text in which Will recounts a moment from childhood when he and his great Aunt Nana were reading a sentimental novel called *In Silken Chains,* which he refers to as "the most moving book ever written." LeRoy appears and demands to know why Aunt Nana is "'reading such trash to that child?' Aunt Nana was crushed, I was desolated, he was adamant. We asked weakly what please could we substitute, and unhesitatingly he answered: '*Ivanhoe.*' . . . He ruled as authoritatively as Moses that there would be no other novel-reading to poison my mind until I had finished Scott, Bulwer-Lytton, Dickens, and a little Thackeray." *Ivanhoe,* he confesses, produced unpredictable results: "I, far from being inspired to knightly heroism, grew infatuated with the monastic life, if it could be pursued in a cave opening on a desert" (*Lanterns on the Levee*), 56–57. In several instances like this one, when LeRoy Percy appears in the text of *Lanterns* he subverts Will's desires.

14. Percy, *Lanterns on the Levee,* 142, 158, 161; King, *Southern Renaissance,* 87.

15. Shelby Foote to Walker Percy, 6 September 1980, in Jay Tolson, ed., *The Correspondence of Shelby Foote and Walker Percy* (New York: Center for Documentary Studies in association with W. W. Norton, 1997), 267. I do not mean to suggest here that Will Percy's life in the American South was altogether void of sexual relationships, but that my focus in this essay is on the relationship between cosmopolitanism and masculinity. For scholarship on Percy's male relationships in Mississippi, see William Armstrong Percy III, "William Alexander Percy: His Homosexuality and Why It Matters," in John Howard, ed., *Carryin' On in the Gay and Lesbian South* (New York: New York University Press, 1997), 75–92; John Barry, *Rising Tide: The Great Mississippi Flood of 1927 and How It Changed America* (New York: Simon and Schuster, 1997), 296–301, 418–21.

16. Walker Percy to Shelby Foote, 10 September 1980, in *Correspondence*, 271.

17. Percy, *Lanterns on the Levee*, 105. Percy's travels were significant not only as detailed in this essay, but also in leading him to new ways of understanding and writing about sexual relations between men. While in Europe, where he encountered the intellectual context of homoerotic Hellenism exemplified by Walter Pater, John Addington Symonds, and Oscar Wilde, Percy absorbed and celebrated (especially in his poetry) the ideal of ancient Greece as the last authentic culture of sexual expression. See Benjamin E. Wise, "On Naïve and Sentimental Poetry: Nostalgia, Sex, and the Souths of William Alexander Percy," *Southern Cultures* 14 (2008): 54–79.

18. This is not to say that in Europe he lived the life of a "homosexual." The stark categories of "heterosexual" and "homosexual" are modern constructions of human sexuality that were just coming into use in Will Percy's era. See David M. Halperin, *One Hundred Years of Homosexuality, and Other Essays on Greek Love* (New York: Routledge, 1990); Halperin, *How to Do the History of Homosexuality* (Chicago: University of Chicago Press, 2002); Robert Padgug, "Sexual Matters: Rethinking Sexuality in History," in *Hidden from History: Reclaiming the Gay and Lesbian Past*, ed. Martin Duberman, Martha Vicinus, and George Chauncey (New York: NAL Books, 1989), 54–66.

19. Percy, *Lanterns on the Levee*, 106–7.

20. William Alexander Percy to Camille Percy, 15–17 November 1904, 22 December 1904, and 29 September 1904, all in William Alexander Percy Papers.

21. William Alexander Percy to Elizabeth Monroe, 29 January 1932; William Alexander Percy to Camille Percy, 16 and 17 June 1909, both in William Alexander Percy Papers; William Alexander Percy to William S. Braithwaite, 11 October 1922, Braithwaite mss, Houghton Library, Harvard University, Cambridge, Mass.

22. Percy, *Lanterns on the Levee*, 122; William Alexander Percy to Camille Percy, 21 August 1907, William Alexander Percy Papers.

23. Harold Bruff to William Alexander Percy, 1 July 1907; Harold Bruff to William Alexander Percy, 29 August 1908, both in William Alexander Percy Papers.

24. Harold Bruff to William Alexander Percy, 29 August 1908 (parenthetical question mark in original); Harold Bruff to William Alexander Percy, 8 September 1910, William Alexander Percy Papers (emphasis in original).

25. William Alexander Percy to Carrie Stern, 7 January 1919, William Alexander Percy Papers.

26. William Alexander Percy, *Enzio's Kingdom and Other Poems* (New Haven, Conn.: Yale University Press, 1924), 14.

27. Willy, *The Third Sex*, trans. Lawrence R. Schehr (Urbana: University of Illinois Press, 2007), 25.

28. Paul Fussell, *The Great War and Modern Memory* (New York: Oxford University Press, 1977), 115; Wyatt-Brown, *House of Percy*, 220.

29. Norman Douglas, *Birds and Beasts of the Greek Anthology* (New York: J. Cape and H. Smith, 1929), ix–xi. Douglas also briefly mentioned Percy in Norman Douglas, *Late Harvest* (London: L. Drummond, 1946), 26.

30. Douglas, *Birds and Beasts*, xi. On literary devices employed to connote same-sex desires, see Fussell, *Great War and Modern Memory*, 270–306; Timothy D'Arch Smith, *Love in Earnest: Some Notes on the Lives and Writings of English "Uranian" Poets from 1889 to 1930* (London: Routledge and K. Paul, 1970); D. H. Mader, "The Greek Mirror: The Uranians and Their Use of Greece," *Journal of Homosexuality* 49 (2005): 377–420; Robert Aldrich, *The Seduction of the Mediterranean: Writing, Art, and Homosexual Fantasy* (New York: Routledge, 1993); Wise, "On Naïve and Sentimental Poetry."

31. Douglas, *Birds and Beasts*, xi–xii.

32. Percy, *Lanterns on the Levee*, Foreword, 348.

33. Ibid., 333–34.

34. Ibid.

35. Ibid., 336–37.

36. Ibid., 337–40.

37. Ibid., 340–41.

38. Ibid., 342.

39. Ibid., 341–43.

A Subversive Savior: Manhood and African American Images of Christ in the Early Twentieth-Century South

Edward J. Blum

A religious revolution seemed to strike the United States in the mid-1960s. While the champions of civil rights blasted away at the legal, economic, and cultural bases of white supremacy, long-held conceptions of Jesus Christ came under fire. The notion that Jesus was white with blue eyes and blonde hair became anathema for many black power leaders. Long a dominant visual and sacred image in American culture, the white Christ now found himself besieged on all sides, especially in northern cities. On the streets of Detroit, bands of black men repainted statues of white Christs with black paint; black Madonnas emerged to symbolize Christ's nonwhite heritage. The popular magazine *Ebony* carried a story on the "Quest for a Black Christ" in April 1969, and on its cover a black, kinky-haired Jesus gazed past its readers to behold a new America in the making. The movement to blacken Christ inspired and drew inspiration from a vibrant black liberation theology fresh from the minds and pens of theologians James Cone, Albert Cleage Jr., J. Deotis Roberts, and William Jones. Their central aim was "to analyze the nature of the gospel of Jesus Christ in the light of oppressed black people so that they will see the gospel as inseparable from their humiliated condition, bestowing on them the necessary power to break the chains of oppression." These black theologians refused to believe that Christ or God was white. Instead, Christ looked almost like a Black Panther—a strong "Negro" man willing to do anything to help his community.[1]

What seemed novel, especially to many white Americans, was actually part of a long tradition in African American culture, one that was rooted in southern experiences of faith and frustration. Long had the white Christ been a subject of dedication, debate, dispute, and derision, and long had African Americans employed various depictions of Jesus to speak to their social, cultural, and political situations in the United States. The black Christ of black liberation theology emerged from more than a century of African American religion. He was first envisioned among southern slaves who crafted their own distinct faith, one that was informed by their West African traditions and by the Christianity they encountered from white missionaries and masters. In the nineteenth century, separate black religious congregations led by ministers like Richard Allan and Absalom Jones in the North taught that God had a special relationship with people of color, while abolitionists Frederick Douglass and Sojourner Truth assailed the idea that slaveholders could be true Christians. By the turn of the century, African Methodist Episcopal minister Henry Turner was convinced that if white people worshiped a white God, then black people should worship a black one. As part of an ideology of racial uplift, a God in their own image was necessary for social advancement and cultural recognition.[2]

In the twentieth century, black religious radicalism traveled North with the Great Migration. As thousands of black men and women left the rural and southern lands they had long inhabited and flooded to northern urban areas, a host of new religions emerged. These faiths prized blackness and associated it with the sacred. Whether it was the Nation of Islam's new global history that described whites as devils and blacks as true men, or Marcus Garvey's universal Afrocentric faith, these new "black gods of the city" tore apart the conflation of whiteness and godliness.[3] Then with the modern civil rights movement following World War II, racial integration and inclusion became paramount. Christ became a universal savior who taught all the children of the world to play together. Growing frustration with the slow pace of social change, coupled with economic deprivation in northern and western cities, however, led to another reconfiguration of Christ. This time, he was aligned with oppressed African Americans as a symbol of militant defiance to white supremacy.

The creation and ascension of the black Christ is an important historical narrative in American religion. But historians tend to neglect at least two important issues in their discussions. First, they often downplay competition and complexity of vision among African Americans in their depictions of Jesus. Conflicting portrayals of Jesus spoke to divisions within the black community, to divergent paths of social reform, and to distinct strategies of psychological and political resistance. It is not enough to set the black Christ in opposition to the white Christ alone; there is much to be understood about African American culture and religion by witnessing the internal dialogues over how to approach and conceive of Christ. Second, scholars often leap from the South to the North in the early twentieth century and then present black liberation theology as principally a phenomenon of urban and northern black culture. Scholars have failed to explore how the religious creativity of southern blacks presaged liberation theology or to provide a bridge across the sections. How did the various early-century black understandings of Christ inform the liberation movement? Was black liberation theology a distinct break from the southern and rural past or an extension of black religious cultures? What role did conceptions of Jesus play in southern African American life, culture, and experience?

Looking at depictions of Christ among some southern African Americans and at stories of Jesus set in the South during the early twentieth century, especially those narrated by everyday blacks and secular leaders Booker T. Washington and W. E. B. Du Bois, this chapter suggests that many of the elements of black liberation theology were floating around in the Jim Crow South. More specifically, this chapter maintains that diverse depictions of Christ reflected some of the conflicting and shifting notions of manhood for men and women of color. During these years, conceptions of manhood and masculinity were changing dramatically in American and African American culture. After the Civil War, emancipation, the industrial revolution, the emergence of the United States as a world power, the rise of consumer capitalism, and the creation of the "New Woman" led to a crisis in white manhood. No longer were white men defined by their economic independence or their mastery over African Americans and women of all colors. In response, white men looked to reassert themselves. Southern "redeemers" justified the purging of blacks from politics as a new manly imperative. Then through the lynching of black men, white men sought to prove their manliness in the defense of white womanhood and dominance once again over black bodies. Sometimes a gruesome element of lynchings, castrations heightened the symbolic and real unmanning of black men.[4]

For African American men in this environment, having their manhood recognized was a knotty problem. Masculinist power, such as in the form of champion boxer Jack Johnson, frightened and infuriated whites. In Johnson's case, his pugilistic skill and his penchant for marrying white women ultimately led to his arrest and undoing. Other aspiring black men, such as Du Bois, William Ferris, and Hubert Harrison, endeavored to establish their manhood through racial uplift, class differentiation, and patriarchy. Historian Martin Summers has identified a generational shift in notions of manhood and manliness among African Americans in the South and the North during the first decades of the twentieth century. Evidenced by changes in fraternal organizations, discussions in literature, and showdowns in southern black colleges over dress codes and courses, black manhood moved from a focus on the producer-oriented qualities of character, respectability, industry, and thrift to the consumer-oriented qualities of leisure pursuits, sexual virility, and material acquisition.[5]

Into this contested gendered and racial terrain, the image of Jesus Christ became a useful tool. As a historical model, as a sacred figure, and as an ethical archetype, Christ could be manipulated to serve a host of different functions. Throughout the centuries, Jesus has been a potent cultural and political symbol. He has been formed and re-formed to fit just about all circumstances, movements, and cultures.[6] Reconceptualizing Christ in the early twentieth century, a variety of African Americans provided models of manhood for consumption by other African Americans. Many everyday black men who remained in the South as thousands of their kin ventured to northern cities held onto visions of Christ and God that they had carried since the days of slavery. They imagined Jesus to be a small white man with impressive power, one who (although white) could undermine white supremacy. For the preeminent southern black leader of the era, Booker T. Washington, the image of Christ could be harnessed to his arguments for patient economic improvement and a reformation of the black clergy in the South. Washington expressed disdain for the mystical visions of common black men and women and for the otherworldly Jesus of black ministers. In the place of a little white Jesus, Washington looked to modernize and universalize Christ with a Jesus that encouraged bank accounts, cotton cultivation, thrift, and slow political change. In these ways, Washington hoped to use religious ideas in his efforts to modernize agrarian black life. Du Bois combated Washington with an image of Jesus as a puzzling and subversive radical. If Washington's colorless Jesus could allay the racial fears of whites, Du Bois's black Christ was an affront to white dominance. Although writing from the North (after his southern experiences), Du Bois looked to speak to the South. If Christ were to visit the southern United States, Du Bois declared, Jesus would align with African Americans, would challenge white hypocrisy and violence, and would become a symbol of ethics and manhood in death.

Although in conflict with one another, these images of Christ—the strong black lynch victim of Du Bois's imagination, the business leader of Washington's hopes, and the tiny white savior of everyday memories—provided approaches for resiliency and advancement in the Jim Crow South. The desired ends were almost always the same, and they were similar to those hoped for by later northern black liberation theologians. All sought the recognition of a sacred black manhood to resist and someday overcome white supremacy.

One does not have to look long or far to witness how agrarian southern African Americans imagined Christ. In fact, a host claimed to have seen him literally in their lives. This can be viewed vividly in the oral interviews conducted in the late 1920s by Andrew Polk Watson, an anthropology student at Fisk University in Tennessee. Compiled and published later as part of George Rawlick's edited *The American Slave: A Composite Autobiography* and separately as *God Struck Me Dead: Voices of Ex-slaves*, Watson's work relates the conversion narratives of a few dozen African American women and men. These men and women had remained in the South despite crop failures, disfranchisement, white violence, and the departure of thousands of other blacks. In their memories of slavery, emancipation, and southern society after the Civil War, they recounted visions of angels, demons, God, and Christ. These black women and men inhabited an enchanted rural world where the sacred routinely invaded their tangible and imaginary landscapes. Although most often used by historians for insight into slave religion, the accounts spoke at least as much to their conditions in the early twentieth century. The narrators described their encounters with the divine with freshness and vitality. As he or she related the incident, it seemed that the interviewee was almost beholding and feeling the images again. None of the participants discounted their tales of encountering God or the devil, and none claimed to have hallucinated or exaggerated. The sacred forces had immense power. They could enslave and destroy bodies and minds, free and unite families, heal medical ailments, and render white masters powerless. Within these stories, Christ was a deceptive model of manhood—seemingly innocuous, but extremely potent.[7]

It is easy to be struck by the prevalence of whiteness in these recollections. It was everywhere. One woman, for instance, recalled that Jesus "was standing in snow—the prettiest, whitest snow I have ever seen." And when she witnessed God, he was "sitting in a big armchair. Everything seemed to be made of white stones and pearls." One preacher told Watson, "I saw the Lord in the east part of the world, and he looked like a white man. His hair was parted in the middle, and he looked like he had been dipped in snow, and he was talking to me." Another interviewee remembered that "Jesus came to me just as white as dripping snow, with his hair parted in the middle just as white as snow." Another black man recalled, "I seen Christ with his hair parted in the center. He was white as snow." The Jesus of these imaginings was surrounded by whiteness, permeated by it, and in many ways defined by it. At first glance, these southern blacks appear to have accepted the association of whiteness with the sacred in American culture. Some black commentators, from the nineteenth-century minister Henry Turner to the twentieth-century literary critic Wilson Jeremiah Moses, considered such acquiescence to white-dominated faith to be harmful to the black psyche.[8]

Yet race was not the only factor of note in these recollections. The physical sizes of Christ and God's messengers were just as important as the surrounding colors or skin tone. On almost all occasions, the sacred was small. Repeatedly, interviewees reported seeing "a little man" who was God's herald. Sometimes the messenger was an angel, sometimes Christ, and sometimes God himself. One respondent remembered, "God came to me as a little man. . . . He was dressed in dark, but later he came dressed in white." A student at Fisk University told of a time when "a little child came to my bedside and got his hand in mine and said, 'Fear not, for lo! I am with you always." In this memory, the little child channeled the words of the biblical Christ.[9]

Although typically small of stature, the divine visitors sometimes appeared in military garb. Most of the warrior rhetoric was imported from the biblical book of Revelation. One angel, a "little man, very small and with waxen fire," carried on his shoulder "a spear, and on the end of it was a star that outshone the morning sun." Then, when Jesus appeared, he came "with great power, having on his breastplate, buckler, and shield. . . . He spoke, and out of his mouth came fire." Another responded that he saw God "sitting in a large armchair, his head up and looking into space . . . He wore a full armor, and across his chest was a breast-protector that shone as if it was made of bars of gold."[10]

Usually diminutive, usually white, and sometimes garbed for combat, this Christ character appears part of the broader culture of white supremacy that sanctified notions of black inferiority and ungodliness. Yet, if one listens to the interviewees, Jesus had a powerful impact on those he visited. He was a subtly subversive savior. Christ crossed the color line, and he did so not to dominate, rape, or exploit. By the time of Watson's interviews, segregation had become not only a legal bulwark in the South, but also an overarching culture. Churches and religious organizations were some of the most segregated places. Whites patrolled sacred space almost as militantly as they did white women's bodies.[11] Within this context, the interviewed black women and men recalled encounters with a white man—a white man who came to them for their benefit, rather than their harm. These were rebellious sacred memories in tenuous times. By describing and remembering mystical encounters with a white man, these African Americans subtly asserted that blacks and whites could share sacred space.

Several African Americans recounted feeling emboldened by their encounters with this sacred being. One former slave, who had long been whipped by his master and trembled in his sight, recalled that after being visited by the divine, "my master came down the field. I became very bold and answered him when he called me. . . . I told him that I had been talking with God Almighty, and that it was God who had plowed up the corn." The master was confused and seemed to sense that his slave "no longer dreaded the whipping I knew I would get." The rolls of the slave system became reversed; the slave was brave and the master afraid. "My master looked at me and seemed to tremble," this narrator boasted. Another black man who witnessed a small white Christ felt strengthened to become a preacher. His encounters with Christ led to a fixed belief that God would help men and women of color. "I believe that God heard my people when they called on him," he declared.[12]

Those interviewed by Watson did not provide uniform descriptions of God or Christ, but their recollections spoke significantly to the place of manhood and the sacred in their imaginations. For a handful, divine manhood was defined by militancy and the true God was a god of war who would battle against injustice. For most others, however, this sacred being was defined by his whiteness and his smallness. Akin to the Brer Rabbit tales where smallish and seemingly weak animals outwit and outmaneuver bigger and stronger foes, accounts of a white Jesus and God were deceptive.[13] What was small to the human eye might be huge in the sacred scope. With folklore and subtle sacred stories, southern blacks had long passed down traditions of cloaked personal and communal resistance. A white Christ who appeared before an African American was transgressing the color line, and by empowering the enslaved, he undermined the culture and structure of slavery and segregation. Everyday southern blacks found subversive manhood in an unlikely place—in the vision of a small white Christ who did not offend white supremacist culture but lurked around its edges undermining and challenging it.

For Booker T. Washington, the religious dreams, visions, and trances of rural and everyday African Americans represented a backward black culture that must be rejected. Washington crafted an alternative image of Christ and of true Christianity, one that defined true Christian manhood in terms of economic progress, moderation, and thrift. For Washington, black religion must discard both an uneducated ministry and the otherworldly faith of his sisters and brothers. This was imperative for the uplift of the race and for southern African Americans to convince northern business investors of their economic and social importance. Although historians have criticized Washington for advancing a social vision that "was consonant with the ethics of white Christianity" and for cherishing "the nonviolent, self-effacing, patiently-suffering white Jesus," Washington's characterizations of Christ were more complex and spoke to various aspects of race and gender in southern and northern culture. Washington's Jesus was a universal savior who had a clear message for southern blacks and northern whites. For African Americans, Christ should inspire hard work, slow and steady economic growth, business savvy, and courage. This Jesus was a means to attach the supposedly masculinist realm of business to the supposedly feminine realm of faith. To whites, Christ should inspire support for the uplift of blacks and the willingness to cross the color line. By presenting Christ as a modern capitalist, Washington foreshadowed and tapped into a nascent masculinist theme in early twentieth-century American religion. Combating the association of religion with women and femininity that dominated the Victorian age, Washington projected a religious vision that was shared by later organizations such as the Men and Religion Forward Movement, revivalists such as Billy Sunday, and religious writers such as Bruce Barton. As historian Ted Ownby has shown, southern religion was also marked by debates over the gendered meanings of faith and business. During the early twentieth century, business-oriented Christians endeavored to tie Protestantism to ideals of business management, the entrepreneurial spirit, and robust manliness as a way to take back the faith for men.[14]

Born into slavery but working his way to the headship of Tuskegee Institute in Alabama, Washington became the most powerful southern African American of the early twentieth century. He became the symbolic head of southern blacks in the eyes of many throughout the nation. By the time of his death in 1915, he was renowned throughout the world as a champion of black uplift, achieving national notoriety with his speech at the Cotton States and International Exposition of 1895 in Atlanta. Known for its acquiescence to southern whites, including a declaration that blacks should remain in the South, that they should accept social segregation, and that they should disavow political and legal struggles for civil rights, Washington's speech was precisely what southern and northern white businessmen wanted to hear. It promised harmony without substantive political upheaval and a southern black working class dedicated to their toil. The speech brought Washington unprecedented fame and power for a black man in the United States. Although not a minister, one critical aspect of his plan for economic and racial uplift was the remaking of black religion in part through the reconfiguration of Christ.[15]

Washington made it clear that he considered the Tuskegee Institute's work a Christian enterprise. In 1892, Washington told the Alabama State Teachers' Association that Tuskegee sought to aid in "the formation of a Christ-like character" within young black men and women. Then for the twenty-fifth anniversary of Tuskegee in 1906, he maintained, "'And Jesus said, I will make you fishers of men.' In the spirit of these words, the foundation of this institution was laid in 1881." The work of Tuskegee, he declared, was simple: "to fish for men."[16]

In speech after speech during the 1890s and the early 1900s in the South and the North, Washington attacked the otherworldliness of African American religion. To the Wizard of Tuskegee, the Jesus worshiped by most southern blacks lacked vigor, offered only a heavenly escape, and seemed a relic of their enslaved past. "There is one famous song sung by the colored people which says 'Give me Jesus and you may take all the world," Washington explained to a host of audiences (usually white ones in the North). This song epitomized the problem in black religion. Christ was a symbol of the internalized psychological forces that held back black communities. "The teachings of this they have been trained to follow for a number of years and the result is the Negro has been satisfied with 'Jesus' and the white man has gotten all the cotton." Washington lambasted black ministers who charmed their congregations with songs and sermons about a "great, big, white mansion" in the sky. In Washington's estimation, African

Americans would never achieve "Christian manhood" if they held onto their otherworldly Christ.[17]

Yet Washington did not dismiss Christ completely. Rather, he sought to replace this otherworldly and passive Jesus. Working harder, saving more money, acquiring more land—all of this would mean more Jesus, not less, for southern blacks. As Washington told a meeting of the National Education Association, "The number of valuable farms and other property that many wide awake colored people have bought and are improving with success and profit, go to show that they have already learned that the way to have the most of Jesus and to have him in the best way is to mix in a little land, and cotton." On another occasion, Washington claimed, "The way to teach them to have the most of Jesus in a permanent form is to teach them to mix in with their religion some practical ideas which will bring about an improved material condition." And then later, "The way to have the most of Jesus, and to have him in a substantial way, is to mix in some land, cotton and corn and a good bank account; and we find, by actual experience, that the man who has Jesus in this way has a religion that you can count on seven days in the week."[18] Blacks would become closer to Jesus, Washington proclaimed, by remaining in the South and by slow and steady economic uplift.

Christ also stood as a model of manhood because he obeyed worldly rules and regulations. "The law of God and nature is that every person shall tell the truth, not steal, and live in sexual purity," Washington told a group of Tuskegee students in 1891. "Let me leave you this thought, if we would live happily— live honored and useful lives—lives modeled after that of our perfect leader— Christ, we must conform to law." Obeying the law was imperative, he continued: "Learn that there is no possible escape from punishment that follows the breaking of the law. Growth in this direction cannot be completed in a day, but let us make one supreme effort." Christ was no law-defying radical who stood against established authorities and an oppressive government. He was a savior who played by the rules: he never lied, he never stole, and he was never sexually overactive. Washington's charge, especially to avoid sexual impropriety, could mean the difference between life and death for many young black men since accusations that black men raped or accosted white women provided the cardinal (albeit fraudulent) justification of lynching. The idea Washington posed was that if African Americans followed his image of Christ and obeyed the "law of God and nature," they would not only avoid the lynch mob but also achieve success in the United States.[19]

The Wizard of Tuskegee never commented on the race or physicality of Christ. In fact, Washington cherished the idea that Jesus transcended racial affiliations or prerogatives. Writing for the religious magazine *Our Day* in 1896, he characterized Jesus as one of history's great men who had embraced all races.

Discussing how he, Washington, refused to hate whites for their oppression of blacks, he then asserted: "It is only as the soul has opportunity unbounded and unfettered to its best that we have great and lasting deeds performed." "Take Whittier, Longfellow, Lincoln — and the name above all, Christ," Washington continued, "would their names live in all history had their sympathies been narrowed and confined to this or that race? I would permit no man to drag down my soul by making me hate him." For Washington, Christ's brilliance resided in his ability to embrace all peoples, not a select group.[20]

He also cast a vision for how whites could be more like Christ. If rural African Americans could achieve their manhood by obtaining an industrial education, by obeying the laws, by saving money, and by planting cotton, then white Christians could prove their manhood and emulate Jesus in two ways: contribute to African American education and cross the color line. Washington often declared that northern white businessmen who used their wealth for social good embodied Christ's spirit. He referred to them as "Christ-like philanthropists" who, especially in their giving to southern education, "have produced in a few years results that have not been surpassed in the history of the progress of the world." Washington lauded New York merchant and active Presbyterian William E. Dodge during a "Sunday Evening Talk" at Tuskegee in 1891. "He amassed a considerable fortune, but every dollar he got hold of he consecrated to the use of the Lord, to bringing about the Kingdom of Christ upon earth." Washington made it clear that "to become rich is not a sin . . . but if you make the mistake of trying to get this world's goods with a view to gratify yourself, you will find that your life will be miserable." White and African American men should emulate the Christian captains of industry, Washington explained, for men like Dodge, Andrew Carnegie, John D. Rockefeller, George Eastman, and Collis Huntington used their wealth to better the world.[21]

Washington had similar praise for whites who were willing to defy the culture of segregation in the North and South. In an open letter to the Christian Endeavor Society, an interdenominational youth movement founded in the 1880s, Washington underscored the religious hypocrisy that ran rampant throughout the country. "How often as a poor black boy have I passed the doors of churches and Sunday schools and heard the grand old song, 'Come to Jesus,' welling up from hundreds of throats, and at the same time if I, a poor black boy, had obeyed the command, and entered the church or Sunday school, I should have been put out by force if necessary." It would take "Christian courage" for white men to stand against Jim Crow in the house of Jesus Christ: "In many parts of our country it requires much courage for a Christian to take a poor black boy by the hand and lead him to the Sunday school or Christian endeavor society." Yet taking this action would be "heroic" and would help prove that "we are one in Christ."[22]

Washington's letter to the Christian Endeavor Society illuminated much of his gendered approach to race relations in American society and religion. He characterized African American men as "poor black boys" who needed the guidance of rich white men. While whites could prove their manhood and fellowship with Christ by helping African Americans, the black race was in its childhood and needed a helping hand. The white race had achieved maturity; the black race had not. On other occasions, Washington advanced a "romantic racialism" that identified "Negroes" as a "feeling" race and hence prone to otherworldly religion. "I believe that we can feel more in five minutes than a white man can in a day," Washington commented to a group of Unitarians in New York in 1894. "You can beat us in thinking, but we can beat you in feeling. We feel our religion, and when a black man becomes converted, and does not jump and shout, we say he has the white man's religion." Emotionalism, therefore, was indicative of immature faith, of a group in its infancy. It revealed a race that needed to grow up to achieve manhood.[23]

One should not overemphasize Washington's criticisms of black religion and his praise for some white Christians, though. In general, he maintained that blacks in the United States more authentically followed the teachings of Christ than whites. "There are thousands of white men North and South, who pray earnestly for the salvation and comfort of the negro's soul in the future world, who never think of turning over their hand to give the negro a chance to make his body comfortable in matters of public travel and accommodation in this world," Washington lamented. "Let us apply more and more the Golden Rule, 'as ye would have men do unto you do ye even so unto them.' I fear the negro is ahead of the white man in this."[24]

All in all, when discussing Christ as a model of manhood for whites and blacks, Washington overwhelmingly focused on the practical. Whether it was increasing one's bank account to have "more of Jesus" or extending a white hand across the racial divide as an expression of Christian courage, these were practical steps that Washington counseled. He expressed little concern for the emotional or psychological effects of faith. A little white Jesus who made one feel better with promises of rest and white houses in heaven would never help African Americans gain a mature manhood in American society.

While the Christ of Washington's program advocated building bank accounts and subsidizing black colleges, Washington himself became a messianic and religious figure. Responses to Washington's religious arguments varied greatly. To some African Americans, Washington seemed quite similar to the otherworldly Jesus that Washington himself castigated. After Washington dined at the White House with President Theodore Roosevelt in 1901 and southern whites excoriated both Roosevelt and Washington for the event, William H. Ferris, a northern black author and social activist, wrote to Washington to implore him to stand up to his critics. "Now Prof. Washington there are many colored people and a number of white people who think that you kiss the hand that smites your race too much," Ferris contended. "There is a time when patience ceases to be a virtue and when love for your enemies becomes a slave's love rather than a man's love. I wish you had less of the Christ and more of the John L. Sullivan." Juxtaposing the famous boxer John L. Sullivan with the seemingly passive Christ, Ferris presented Washington with a choice of manhoods. He could either turn the other cheek like the otherworldly Christ or be tough and aggressive in his defense of African Americans. To Ferris implicitly, the path of Christ was a path of nonviolence and patience.[25]

But a number of other African Americans and whites considered Washington an example of true Christian manhood and his work at Tuskegee a holy endeavor. Accepting a position as pastor and teacher at Tuskegee in 1888, Rev. John W. Whitaker wrote, "I make the change because I feel that I am going where I am needed and where I shall be able to do a great work for the Lord Jesus Christ. Ever since the call came, my mind has been more and more inclined to enter into the work. So in the name of Jesus I come to labor with you." Especially after a growing number of African Americans challenged Washington's acquiescence to whites and his dictatorial control over black expression, some of Washington's followers likened him to Christ. Writing in the *Colored American Magazine* in 1900, Pauline E. Hopkins contended, "Surely, whatever else he deserves, he does not deserve censure, criticism and calumny. Sad would it be, indeed, if it were said of him as it was said of another of earth's great benefactors 'He came unto his own and his own received him not.'" Six years later, another one of his defenders made it clear that he believed Washington was aligned with Christ. "I had heard you twice," Richard Carroll explained, "and endorsed every word that you said and that, if Jesus Christ came down from Heaven and was permitted to speak, I believe that he would have said just what you said in Zion church to the colored men." Even white minister Harry Emerson Fosdick, one of the forces pushing to masculinize Protestantism in the first half of the twentieth century by attuning to the "manhood" of Christ, invoked Washington's image and words when discussing Christ's "strength" in forgiveness. "When Booker T. Washington says, '*I will not let any man reduce my soul to the level of hatred,*'" Fosdick asserted, "he is reflecting the Master's spirit. Jesus held his own life in its inward friendliness and fellowship with God above the reach of man's hostility." If Washington was an emblem of the passive, otherworldly Christ to those like Ferris, to others he was a symbol of a Christian manhood that could overcome hate and violence.[26]

Taken together, Washington's characterizations of Christ proved a useful image in his social vision. On the one hand, he endeavored to reform the religious otherworldliness of southern rural African Americans—to convince them that having the "most Jesus" meant hard work, cotton cultivation, and a growing bank account. The Christ that promised white mansions in the sky should be abandoned, and men of color should follow a new model of Christ. This Jesus taught them to obey human and divine laws, to obtain economic solvency, and to uplift the race slowly. On the other hand, Washington offered white Americans Christlike roles as well. As benevolent businessmen who endeavored to help discriminated people of color, they could be just like Jesus. While perhaps unable to divorce himself from the concept that African Americans were a childlike race that needed the aid of whites to grow into Christian manhood, Washington nonetheless contributed to the making of a business-friendly, masculinized Christ that gained new force in the early twentieth century.

Washington's most prominent critic during the early twentieth century also spent a great deal of time recharacterizing Christ as part of a broader political and social agenda for racial uplift. W. E. B. Du Bois is usually depicted as far more secular than Washington and far more indicative of northern black culture than southern. Typically, scholars describe Du Bois as unreligious, irreligious, or antireligious and somehow out of touch with southern blacks. Only recently has there been new attention to the religious creativity of Du Bois and his many contributions to understanding faith and culture.[27] He actually expended far more literary time reinterpreting Jesus than Washington did, and in many ways, Du Bois bridged the divide between northern and southern African Americans. Born and raised in Massachusetts in 1868, educated at Fisk University, Harvard University, and the University of Berlin, a teacher and professor in Tennessee and Georgia, Du Bois became the most prominent black intellectual of the early twentieth century. He was a pioneer in urban sociology and a leader in black history, especially during his dozen years as a professor at Atlanta University. Having witnessed too much southern violence, Du Bois left Atlanta for New York to become a founder of the National Association for the Advancement of Colored People and editor of the NAACP's new magazine, *The Crisis*. He held that position until 1934.

During Du Bois's years at *The Crisis*, after his extensive time in Atlanta, he wrote a slew of short stories and poems reimagining Christ in the modern South. By situating Jesus in the South, he endeavored to draw attention to various aspects of the "race problem" to his northern and southern readers. Christ in the South would not only illuminate the hypocritical and violent elements of southern white society, but also provide a model and inspiration for southern blacks.

With fictive renderings of Christ in the United States, Du Bois echoed works by British journalist W. T. Stead and white American minister Charles Sheldon. During the late nineteenth century, Stead's *If Christ Came to Chicago* (1894) and Sheldon's *In His Steps* (1896) asked what Christ would think and how he would act if he were somehow transported to the contemporary United States. To Stead, "Citizen Christ" would lead political and social leaders in Chicago to uplift the unemployed, to ban the sale of alcohol, and to save women from prostitution. For Sheldon, this Christ would lead Protestants to ask themselves "what would Jesus do" when making a decision. Du Bois took these concepts and applied them to race relations and the American South: What would Jesus say to a southern lynch mob? How would Jesus treat rural men and women of color, and how would he inspire them? With whom would Jesus spend his time? What would Christ look like?

With his stories, Du Bois took part in a sweeping religious attack on the white Christ. He joined poets Countee Cullen, Claude McKay, and Langston Hughes in juxtaposing lynched black men with the biblical Christ; he shared with northern black leaders Marcus Garvey, Elijah Muhammad, Father Divine, Sweet Daddy Grace, and Noble Drew Ali the conviction that the divine must affiliate with blackness. Decades before liberation theologians James Cone and Albert Cleage Jr. depicted Christ as a black man, Du Bois and these others likewise presented Jesus as a model of black manhood—courageous and insightful. He refused to endorse crass materialism or to stand down against white supremacy. Christ was no capitalist; he was a communalist. He was no small white man; he was an intellectually and socially strong black man. He rejected raised bank accounts if they meant lowered group accountability. This dark messiah refused to wear a mask of racial subservience, and he implored all who would hear to smash their own masks and be set free.[28]

Du Bois longed for the birth of a black Christ who would right the wrongs of modern civilization and especially protect black women. In "The Burden of Black Women," first published in 1914 and then reprinted in 1920, he maintained that the "White World" was polluted by vermin, dirt, scum, and "spoilers of women." Du Bois fumed with hatred for whites who brought so much evil to society and did so little to aid African Americans:

> I hate them, Oh!
> I hate them well,
> I hate them, Christ!
> As I hate Hell,
> If I were God
> I'd sound their knell
> This day!

Only the birth of a black Christ could save the globe. Only a black Christ, Du Bois claimed, could lead all peoples to freedom and to genuine praise of God and humanity:

> And married maiden, Mother of God,
> Bid the Black Christ be born!
> Then shall the burden of manhood,
> Be it yellow or black or white,
> And Poverty, Justice and Sorrow—
> The Humble and Simple and Strong,
> Shall sing with the Sons of Morning
> And Daughters of Evensong.[29]

Du Bois then considered how different groups and individuals would respond to the black Christ's birth. In the short story "The Second Coming," a black Christ was born in Valdosta, Georgia. Three wise men—a black bishop, a white one, and a yellow priest, representing the major races of the world— traveled there to witness the birth. Upon their arrival, they "heard the faint wail of a child. . . . A white girl crouched before him, down by the very mules' feed, with a baby in her arms." The bishops were dumbfounded by this infant Christ. They expected Christ to return to the earth in apocalyptic glory as foretold in the book of Revelation. But even more shocking, at least to the white bishop, was the color of the baby: "*It was black!*" The white bishop refused to worship this creature. He refused to kneel and offer his gift. As Du Bois narrated, this bishop "stepped back with a gesture of disgust." The yellow priest proceeded to bow his head and to offer incense and gold to the young messiah, and the black bishop did likewise. The tale ended with the white bishop storming out of the stable, and the governor of Georgia, a modern-day Herod, trembling that this black Christ might undermine his authority. In this case, it was not a tiny white Christ that inspired grown-up black men; rather, it was a tiny black infant that had the power to terrify mature white leaders of church and state.[30]

Several of Du Bois's stories detailed the black Christ's teachings and experiences in the South. These tales highlighted Christ's relationship with poor and agrarian African Americans and his moral courage in the face of overwhelming odds. Although most of the tales portrayed him as black, in one story, "Jesus Christ in Georgia," also published with slight modification as "Jesus Christ in Texas," Christ's race was ambiguous. Although local whites believed that the Christ figure of the story was the product of mixed parentage—a mulatto— Du Bois described Jesus's dress and facial features in ways that pointed toward a Middle Eastern or Mediterranean ethnic background. As Du Bois portrayed this Christ, "He did not own the Negro blood. . . . He was tall and straight and the coat looked like a Jewish gabardine. His hair hung in close curls far down the sides of his face and his face was olive, even yellow."[31] Du Bois suggested that the racial phobias of southern whites and their ignorance of human diversity led them not only to confuse African Americans and Middle Easterners, but also to overlook the Son of God. In Du Bois's estimation, white Americans would consider a messiah of Middle Eastern descent as unthinkable as one of black heritage.

After displaying some willingness to heed Christ's teachings, southern whites in Du Bois's narratives either rejected the messiah or found themselves rejected by him. They could not accept a dark Christ, in part because he was a black man who refused to perform a subordinate manhood. In these stories, it was a black man that made sacred decisions, not whites or white culture. This black Christ attached true manhood to the willingness to voice his convictions in the face of opposition and violence. In "Jesus Christ in Texas," most of the white characters listened to the Christ's lessons to "love your neighbors as yourself," but when confronted with his nonwhiteness, they snubbed him. Concern for material goods or racial etiquette blinded the white characters from the true identity of Christ. Echoing the biblical claim of Jesus of Nazareth that many who professed to believe in him will not enter the kingdom of heaven, the black Christ in Texas responded to a white minister, "I never knew you." In other narratives, Du Bois described whites as openly hostile to the black Christ. In "The Gospel According to Mary Brown," whites "resented" that the black Christ "carried himself like a man." Likewise, in "Pontius Pilate," a crowd of whites denounced Christ for wanting "equality for Everybody—everybody, mind you . . . Turks, Jews, Niggers, Dagoes, Chinks, Japs, . . . everybody."[32]

Unlike pharisaical whites, African Americans in these stories recognized the black Christ as the Son of God and endeavored to follow his commands. The black Christ in the United States had a special bond with poor people of color, and his empathy was a hallmark of the manhood Du Bois endeavored to teach. Christ was not out for himself, but for his people. Whenever black characters witnessed Christ, they identified him as their distinct savior and friend. These fictive responses sounded similar to the conversion experiences recounted to Polk during his interviews. Jesus in the flesh had the power to transform their lives, yet for Du Bois it was Christ's ethics, not his miraculous actions, that had transformative power. In "The Gospel According to Mary Brown," Mary recognized that her son felt a special compassion for the downtrodden. He suffered "not simply in himself, but with every other sufferer. That he was wounded by every sin and bruised by every injustice. He was oppressed and he was afflicted." The black Christ's sympathy for exploited people led African Americans to worship him as their messiah. When Christ blessed a black servant in "Jesus Christ in Texas," the elderly man "paused in bewilderment, tottered, and then with sudden gladness in his eyes dropped to his knees." A black nursemaid then grabbed onto Christ's cloak in this story. As Du Bois wrote, she "trembled, hesitated, and then kneeled in the dust." This Christ touched her hand gently and encouraged her to "sin no more." Hope immediately filled the maid as never before. She let out a "glad cry" and left the plantation house. Christ subsequently ventured into the wilderness and encountered an African American convict who had escaped from prison. The black Christ instructed the convict not to steal and to obey the Lord's commands. The convict agreed, and the two men exchanged clothing. By having this Christ and the convict swap garments, Du Bois alluded to the instructions of St. Paul in his biblical letter to the church at Ephesus—that each believer must "put on the new man, which after God is created in righteousness and true holiness."[33]

Du Bois even rewrote Christ's Sermon on the Mount, a biblical passage usually considered evidence of Christ's passivity and meekness, with an edge to it. Recasting it in the American context, Du Bois not only underscored his conviction that Christianity was a religion of brotherhood and of liberation for the oppressed, but also opposed the conflation of manhood and individualistic economic accumulation. Amid the Great Depression, Du Bois endeavored to assault the notion that true Christianity was the handmaiden of capitalism. "Blessed are the poor," maintained the black Christ in "The Gospel According to Mary Brown": "blessed are they that mourn; blessed are the meek; blessed are the merciful; blessed are they which are persecuted. All men are brothers and God is the Father of all."[34] Du Bois went even further in "The Son of God," which he published in 1933 during the Great Depression. In this story, the black Christ revoiced the Sermon on the Mount in order to link the kingdom of God with suffering African Americans in opposition to rich whites. "Heaven is going to be filled with people who are down-hearted and you that are mourning will get a lot of comfort some day," the black Christ preached:

It's meek folk who are lucky, and going to get everything; and you that are hungry, too. Poor people are better than rich people because they work for what they wear and eat. There won't be any rich people in Heaven. You got to be easy on guys when they do wrong. Then they'll be easy on you, when you get in bad. God's sons are those that won't quarrel. You must treat other people just like you want to be treated. Let'm call you names. Listen! They have called some of the biggest folks that ever lived, dirty names. What's the difference? Which ones do we remember? Don't work all the time. Sit down and rest and sing sometimes. Everything's all right. Give God time. And say, you know how folks use to think they must get even with their enemies? Well, I'll tell you what: you just love your enemies. And if anybody hits you, don't hit 'em back. Just let them go on beating you. . . . [35]

Black liberation theologians in the 1960s would be hard pressed to articulate a clearer or more penetrating statement of their interpretation of Christ's affiliation with the truly disadvantaged or his challenge to unbridled capitalism. Du Bois's black Christ was far different from the business-minded Jesus of Booker T. Washington's imagination. Instead, Jesus was a folksy, radical man of the people.

Du Bois's black Christs usually found themselves crucified by southern white mobs. In "Jesus Christ in Texas," a group of whites hanged the messiah from a tree. Du Bois, however, transformed the scene of torture into one of sacred significance. As he described it, "There, heaven-tall, earth-wide, hung the stranger on the crimson cross, riven and bloodstained with thorn-crowned head and pierced hands." The Christ in the short story "The Son of God" became far too radical for white folk, especially since he had spent considerable time with Communists and white prostitutes. For this, a mob lynched him. The charges against him were unclear. Some claimed that he taught the people to worship a new God, while others asserted that he died because he had lived "with white women." Regardless, his social radicalism could not be tolerated.[36]

In most of his stories of black Christs, Du Bois ended the narratives with the crucifixion. He refused to offer readers the solace of a resurrected black Christ. "Jesus Christ in Texas" concluded with Christ crying out to the black convict, "This day thou shalt be with me in Paradise!" The story "Pontius Pilate" ended with the black Jesus shouting, "My God, my God! Why has Thou forsaken me!" In "The Son of God," Christ's mother continued to have faith in him after his death, but her only "Sign of Salvation" was a noosed rope. In the confines of this story, her son did not return. Only in one of Du Bois's stories, "The Gospel According to Mary Brown," did the crucified Christ return from the dead.[37]

Du Bois's neglect of the resurrection fit with his general erasure of supernatural biblical events in his tales of Jesus in America, an aspect of his religious approach that conflicted with the enchanted worlds of many rural southern blacks. The black Christ of Du Bois's creative renderings performed no deeds of superhuman ability. He turned no water into wine. He healed no hemorrhaging women. He exorcised no demons. He raised no people from the dead. The ethics of the Sermon on the Mount and the self-sacrifice of the crucifixion were the central elements of Christ's spirit, according to Du Bois. By minimizing the supernatural aspects of the biblical stories, Du Bois drew attention to his view of Christianity as an ethical system and to his insistence that African Americans rely on themselves, not on divine intervention, for their liberation. Hope in the miraculous—a hallmark of rural black religion—was not a lesson Du Bois gleaned from biblical texts or sought to inculcate in his readers. To be a true black man was not to walk on water, but to speak the truth, support the community, and be willing to die for justice.[38]

The black Christ was a model for black men, in Du Bois's estimation, because he stood by his principles unto death. An overt opponent of capitalism and to the exploitation of black women and men, this Jesus was quite distinct from that of Booker T. Washington or those of the *God Struck Me Dead* conversion narratives. Du Bois brought Christ into his political vision as a figure who strove for radical social change in the United States and the world. Of these Christ images, Du Bois's most presaged the Christ of black liberation theology during the 1960s. All of the depictions, however, demonstrated a reliance on Christ to obtain black manhood within the white supremacist culture of the United States.

When black liberation theology hit the streets and the minds of black America in the 1960s, it emerged from the various visions of Christ felt and expressed in the decades prior. It was not a strictly northern phenomenon, although the particulars of 1960s liberation theology may have spoken to the conditions of northern urban African Americans. The ideas and themes were rooted in southern black experiences and efforts to assert black manhood. African Americans have never all shared the same view of Jesus. At times, he has been a small white man with brown parted hair. At other times, he has been a universal savior who cared for all peoples. At other times, he has been a strong black man willing to live and die for his people. Whether a white man crossing the color line, a thoughtful economic planner, or a black man on the streets preaching a gospel of Christianity and communism, the Christ of black imaginations has been innovative, subversive, and a motivational force. The aim has always been the same—to assert manhood in a nation that seeks to take it, exploit it, destroy it, and profane it. By sanctifying black manhood through associations with Christ, black men and women found images of Christ particularly useful. He was, for many, a subversive savior.

NOTES

The author thanks Sarah H. Blum, Brian L. Johnson, and Kathleen Clark for their comments on drafts of this essay.

1. "The Quest for a Black Christ," *Ebony*, March 1969, 170–78; "Artists Portray a Black Christ," *Ebony*, April 1971, 177–80; Kelly Brown Douglas, *The Black Christ* (Maryknoll, N.Y.: Orbis Books, 1994), 53–77; Gayraud S. Wilmore, *Black Religion and Black Radicalism: An Interpretation of the Religious History of Afro-American People* (1973; revised, Maryknoll, N.Y.: Orbis Books, 1994), 192–242; C. Eric Lincoln, *The Black Church since Frazier* (New York: Schocken Books, 1974), 135–52; James Cone, *A Black Theology of Liberation* (Philadelphia: Lippincott, 1970); J. Deotis Roberts, *A Black Political Theology* (Philadelphia: Westminster Press, 1974); William R. Jones, *Is God a White Racist? A Preamble to Black Theology* (Garden City, N.Y.: Anchor Press, 1973); Albert B. Cleage Jr., *Black Christian Nationalism: New Direc-*

tions for the Black Church (New York: W. Morrow, 1972); Cleage, *The Black Messiah* (1968; reprinted, Trenton, N.J.: Africa World Press, 1991); William L. Eichelberger, "A Mytho-Historical Approach to the Black Messiah," *Journal of Religious Thought* 33 (1976): 63–74.

2. Douglas, *Black Christ;* Lincoln, *Black Church since Frazier;* Dwight N. Hopkins, *Shoes That Fit Our Feet: Sources for a Constructive Black Theology* (Maryknoll, N.Y.: Orbis Books, 1993); Dwight N. Hopkins, *Introducing Black Theology of Liberation* (Maryknoll, N.Y.: Orbis Books, 1999); Stephen Prothero, *American Jesus: How the Son of God Became a National Icon* (New York: Farrar, Straus and Giroux, 2003), 200–228; Richard Wightman Fox, *Jesus in America: Personal Savior, Cultural Hero, National Obsession* (San Francisco: HarperSanFrancisco, 2004), 359–90.

3. Milton C. Sernett, *Bound for the Promised Land: African American Religion and the Great Migration* (Durham, N.C.: Duke University Press, 1997); Randall K. Burkett, *Garveyism as a Religious Movement: The Institutionalization of a Black Civil Religion* (Metuchen, N.J.: Scarecrow Press, 1978); Arthur Huff Fauset, *Black Gods of the Metropolis* (1944; reprint, New York: Octagon Books, 1970).

4. Grace Elizabeth Hale, *Making Whiteness: The Culture of Segregation in the South, 1890–1940* (New York: Vintage Books, 1998), 199–240; Philip Dray, *At the Hands of Persons Unknown: The Lynching of Black America* (New York: Modern Library, 2003); Jacquelyn Dowd Hall, *Revolt against Chivalry: Jessie Daniel Ames and the Women's Campaign against Lynching* (New York: Columbia University Press, 1993); James W. Messerschmidt, "'We Must Protect Our Southern Women': On Whiteness, Masculinities, and Lynching," in *Regulating Difference: Race, Gender, and Punishment in America*, ed. Mary Bosworth and Jean Flavin (New Brunswick, N.J.: Rutgers University Press, 2005); Steve Estes, *I Am a Man! Race, Manhood, and the Civil Rights Movement* (Chapel Hill: University of North Carolina Press, 2005).

5. Gail Bederman, *Manliness and Civilization: A Cultural History of Gender and Race in the United States, 1880–1917* (Chicago: University of Chicago Press, 1995); Estes, *I am a Man!;* Martin Summers, *Manliness and Its Discontents: The Black Middle Class and the Transformation of Masculinity, 1900–1930* (Chapel Hill: University of North Carolina Press, 2004); Geoffrey C. Ward, *Unforgivable Blackness: The Rise and Fall of Jack Johnson* (New York: Knopf, 2004); Michelle Mitchell, *Righteous Propagation* (Chapel Hill: University of North Carolina Press, 2004).

6. Jaroslav Pelikan, *Jesus through the Centuries: His Place in the History of Culture* (New Haven, Conn.: Yale University Press, 1985).

7. Clifton H. Johnson, ed., *God Struck Me Dead: Voices of Ex-slaves* (1969; reprint, Cleveland: Pilgrim Press, 1993); George P. Rawick, ed., *The American Slave: A Composite Autobiography*, 19 vols. (Westport, Conn.: Greenwood Press, 1974), esp. vol. 19. For other analyses of the interviews in *God Struck Me Dead* or uses of their narratives, see Jean E. Friedman, *The Enclosed Garden: Women and Community in the Evangelical South, 1830–1900* (Chapel Hill: University of North Carolina Press, 1985), 72–80; Alonzo Johnson, "'Pray's House Spirit': The Institutional Structure and Spiritual Core of an African American Folk Tradition," in *"Ain't Gonna Lay My*

'Ligion Down': African American Religion in the South, ed. Alonzo Johnson and Paul T. Jersild (Columbia: University of South Carolina Press, 1996), 8–38; Jocelynn Moody, Sentimental Confessions: Spiritual Narratives of Nineteenth-Century African American Women (Athens: University of Georgia Press, 2001), 153–70.

8. Johnson, ed., God Struck Me Dead, 59, 74–75, 109, 168. Interestingly, visions of Christ from common folk in the American colonial period seemed to be dominated by visions of "light," rather than whiteness. See Susan Juster, Doomsayers: Anglo-American Prophecy in the Age of Revolution (Philadelphia: University of Pennsylvania Press, 2003). For more on the association of whiteness with godliness and African American assaults upon it, see Edward J. Blum, Reforging the White Republic: Race, Religion, and American Nationalism, 1865–1898 (Baton Rouge: Louisiana State University Press, 2005); Edward J. Blum, W. E. B. Du Bois, American Prophet (Philadelphia: University of Pennsylvania Press, 2007); Wilson Jeremiah Moses, Black Messiahs and Uncle Toms: Social and Literary Manipulations of a Religious Myth (University Park: Pennsylvania State University Press, 1982), 68–85.

9. Johnson, ed., God Struck Me Dead, 63, 91, 96, 143, 148.

10. Ibid., 101, 145.

11. On church segregation, see Michael O. Emerson and Christian Smith, Divided by Faith: Evangelical Religion and the Problem of Race in America (New York: Oxford University Press, 2001).

12. Johnson, ed., God Struck Me Dead, 16, 83.

13. Lawrence W. Levine, Black Culture and Black Consciousness: Afro-American Folk Thought from Slavery to Freedom (New York: Oxford University Press, 1978); William Courtland Johnson, "Trickster on Trial: The Morality of the Brer Rabbit Tales," in Johnson and Jersild, eds., "Ain't Gonna Lay My 'Ligion Down," 52–71.

14. Gayraud S. Wilmore, Black Religion and Black Radicalism: An Interpretation of the Religious History of Afro-American People (1973; rev. ed., Maryknoll, N.Y.: Orbis Books, 1994), 140; R. Drew Smith, ed., New Day Begun: African American Churches and Civic Culture in Post–Civil Rights America, vol. 1: The Public Influences of African American Churches (Durham, N.C.: Duke University Press, 2003), 29; Ted Ownby, Subduing Satan: Religion, Recreation, and Manhood in the Rural South, 1865–1920 (Chapel Hill: University of North Carolina Press, 1990); Prothero, American Jesus, 87–123; Fox, Jesus in America, 304; Ann Douglas, The Feminization of American Culture (New York: Farrar, Straus, and Giroux, 1998); Gail Bederman, "'The Women Have Had Charge of the Church Work Long Enough': The Men and Religion Forward Movement of 1911–1912 and the Masculinization of Middle-Class Protestantism," American Quarterly 41 (1989): 432–65; Blum, Reforging the White Republic, 209–43; Richard M. Fried, The Man Everybody Knew: Bruce Barton and the Making of Modern America (Chicago: Ivan R. Dee, 2005); Lyle W. Dorsett, Billy Sunday and the Redemption of Urban America (Grand Rapids: William B. Eerdmans, 1991).

15. The best biographical sketches of Washington remain Louis R. Harlan, Booker T. Washington: The Making of a Black Leader, 1856–1901 (New York: Oxford Uni-

versity Press, 1972), and Harlan, *Booker T. Washington: The Wizard of Tuskegee, 1901–1915* (New York: Oxford University Press, 1983). For more on religion in Washington's life, see Booker T. Washington, *Working with the Hands* (New York: Doubleday, Page and Company, 1904), 193–205,m and W. Fitzhugh Brundage, ed., *Up from Slavery by Booker T. Washington with Related Documents* (Boston: Bedford/ St. Martin's Press, 2003), 47.

16. "An Address on the Twenty-fifth Anniversary of Tuskegee Institute," 1906, in Louis R. Harlan, ed., *The Booker T. Washington Papers*, 14 vols. (Urbana: University of Illinois Press, 1972–1989), 8:561–68; "An Address before the Alabama State Teachers' Association," 1892, in Harlan, ed., *Booker T. Washington Papers*, 3:235.

17. See "A Speech before the Boston Unitarian Club," 1888, in Harlan, ed., *Booker T. Washington Papers*, 2:505; "A Speech before the National Unitarian Association," 1894, in Harlan, ed., *Booker T. Washington Papers*, 3:477–78; "An Address before the National Education Association," 1896, in Harlan, ed., *Booker T. Washington Papers*, 4:194–95; "A Speech before the New York Congregational Club," 1893, in Harlan, ed., *Booker T. Washington Papers*, 3:284. This tale was so stirring that the young Claude Bowers, who would later become a leading journalist, diplomat, and historian, wrote in his diary of its moving and stirring power. See "An Excerpt from the Diary of Claude Gernade Bowers," 1897, in Harlan, ed., *Booker T. Washington Papers*, 4:331.

18. "Boston Unitarian Club Speech," 1888, in Harlan, ed., *Booker T. Washington Papers*, 2:505; "An Address before the National Education Association," 194–95; "A Speech before the National Unitarian Association," 476–79.

19. "A Sunday Evening Talk," 1891, in Harlan, ed., *Booker T. Washington Papers*, 3:138–46.

20. "A New Emancipation," 1896, in Harlan, ed., *Booker T. Washington Papers*, 3:125.

21. "A Speech before the Alabama State Teachers' Association," 1888, in Harlan, ed., *Booker T. Washington Papers*, 2:429; "A Sunday Evening Talk," 1891, in Harlan, ed., *Booker T. Washington Papers*, 3:130.

22. "A Statement to the Christian Endeavor Society," 1896, in Harlan, ed., *Booker T. Washington Papers*, 4:208.

23. "A Speech before the National Unitarian Association," 1894, in Harlan, ed., *Booker T. Washington Papers*, 3:477–78. For more on romantic racialism, see George M. Fredrickson, *Black Image in the White Mind: The Debate on Afro-American Character and Destiny, 1817–1914* (New York: Harper and Row, 1971).

24. "Our Next Door Neighbor," 1896, in Harlan, ed., *Booker T. Washington Papers*, 4:166–67.

25. William H. Ferris to Booker T. Washington, January 1902, in Harlan, ed., *Booker T. Washington Papers*, 6:384–86.

26. John W. Whittaker to Booker T. Washington, 6 July 1888, in Harlan, ed., *Booker T. Washington Papers*, 2:464; quoted in Hanna Wallinger, *Pauline E. Hopkins: A Literary Biography* (Athens: University of Georgia Press, 2005), 71; Richard Carroll to

Booker T. Washington, 22 October 1906, in Harlan, ed., *Booker T. Washington Papers*, 9:99–100; Harry Emerson Fosdick, *The Manhood of the Master: The Character of Jesus Christ* (1913; reprint, Seattle: Inkling Books, 2002), 31.

27. See Blum, *W. E. B. Du Bois, American Prophet*, 3–19.

28. Michelle Kuhl, "Modern Martyrs: African Americans Responses to Lynching, 1880–1940" (Ph.D. diss., State University of New York at Binghamton, 2004); Prothero, *American Jesus*, 65, 87–90; Alan C. Braddock, "Painting the World's Christ: Tanner, Hybridity, and the Blood of the Holy Land," *Nineteenth-Century Art Worldwide: A Journal of Nineteenth-Century Visual Culture* 3 (2004), http://19thc-artworldwide .org/autumn_04/articles/brad.html; Mary Beth Culp, "Religion in the Poetry of Langston Hughes," *Phylon* 48 (1987): 240–45; Countee Cullen, "The Black Christ," in *The Black Christ and Other Poems* (New York: Harper and Bros., 1929), 67–110; Claude McKay, "The Lynching," in James Weldon Johnson, ed., *The Book of American Negro Poetry* (New York: Harcourt, Brace and Company, 1922), no. 73; Qiana Whitted, "In My Flesh Shall I See God: Ritual Violence and Racial Redemption in 'The Black Christ,'" *African American Review* (2004): 379–93; "Christ Jesus Not White," *Cleveland Gazette*, 16 December 1893, 1; W. L. Hunter, *Jesus Christ Had Negro Blood in His Veins* (Brooklyn: W. L. Hunter, 1901); E. Franklin Frazier, *The Negro Church in America* (1963; reprint, New York: Schocken Books, 1974), 52–69; Randall K. Burkett, *Garveyism as a Religious Movement: The Institutionalization of a Black Civil Religion* (Metuchen, N.J.: Scarecrow Press, 1978); Arthur Huff Fauset, *Black Gods of the Metropolis: Negro Religious Cults of the Urban North* (1944; reprint, New York: Octagon Books, 1970).

29. W. E. B. Du Bois, "The Burden of Black Women," *Crisis*, November 1914, 31. Also published as "The Riddle of the Sphinx," in W. E. B. Du Bois, *Darkwater: Voices from within the Veil* (1920; reprinted, Mineola, N.Y.: Dover Publications, 1999), 30–31.

30. Du Bois, "The Second Coming," *Crisis*, December 1917, 59–60; also in Du Bois, *Darkwater*, 60–62.

31. Du Bois, "Jesus Christ in Texas," in *Darkwater*, 70–77; Du Bois, "Jesus Christ in Georgia," *Crisis*, December 1911, 70–74; also in Phil Zuckerman, ed., *Du Bois on Religion* (New York: Altamira Press, 2000), 91–98.

32. Du Bois, "Jesus Christ in Texas," 72–73; Du Bois, "The Gospel According to Mary Brown," *Crisis*, December 1919, 41–43; also in Zuckerman, ed., *Du Bois on Religion*, 143–46; W. E. B. Du Bois, "Pontius Pilate," *Crisis*, December 1920, 53–54; also in Zuckerman, ed., *Du Bois on Religion*, 157–60.

33. Du Bois, "Gospel According to Mary Brown," 41–43; Du Bois, "Jesus Christ in Texas," 70–77; Ephesians 4: 24 KJ.

34. Du Bois, "Gospel According to Mary Brown," 41–43.

35. W. E. B. Du Bois, "The Son of God," *Crisis*, December 1933, 276–77; also in Zuckerman, ed., *Du Bois on Religion*, 181–86.

36. Du Bois, "Jesus Christ in Texas," 76–77; Du Bois, "The Son of God," 276–77.

37. Du Bois, "Jesus Christ in Texas," 76–77; Du Bois, "Pontius Pilate," 53–54; Du Bois, "Son of God," 276–77; Du Bois, "Gospel According to Mary Brown," 41–43.

38. Minimizing the supernatural elements of the Bible did not necessarily position Du Bois in the agnostic or secularist camp. Rather, it showed that he was a religious modernist. See William R. Hutchinson, *The Modernist Impulse in American Protestantism* (Cambridge, Mass.: Harvard University Press, 1976).

Memory and Masculinity: Arthur Ashe in Word, Deed, and Monument

Matthew Mace Barbee

On 6 February 1993, Arthur Ashe died due to complications from HIV/AIDS. The tennis champion, activist, writer, and Richmond, Virginia, native was forty-nine years old. National newspapers reported his passing with pronounced mourning and loss. Along with a standard obituary, the *Washington Post* recalled Ashe in an editorial as "a legendary figure in modern American history." The *Post*'s Tony Kornheiser lauded Ashe as "my hero. He was a man of grace, of intellect, of moral purpose, of courage and integrity." Kornheiser's fellow sports columnist Michael Wilbon wrote that "nobody brought more dignity or honor than Arthur Ashe" and defined his passing in terms of great loss and confusion: "Arthur Ashe is dead, and anybody who ever cared about fairness and enlightenment and the betterment of humanity is worse off. There must be some way to mourn his passing, while celebrating the many gifts he left us."[1]

Wilbon's call for a new form of mourning, one that would mediate the breadth of responses to Ashe's passing, points to the complexity and gravity of the persona Ashe presented in life and in death. In these editorials and in much of the elegiac writing that celebrated his life, Ashe's "grace," "honor," "moral purpose," and "dignity" justified mourning, remembering, and learning from his life. Through these tropes of mourning, Ashe was presented as an ideal example of personal behavior and gentle manliness.

Yet, in the arena of southern public memory, Ashe's character and legacy were more contested. Immediately after his death, Richmond's City Council explored possible ways to memorialize Ashe within the landscapes of the former capital of the Confederacy. Those explorations culminated in a June 1995 decision to place a statue of Ashe on Monument Avenue, the New South–era boulevard named for the memorials of Confederate leaders that dotted its median. From that decision through the unveiling of the statue in July 1996, Richmond struggled with the meaning and appropriateness of honoring an African American man associated with the civil rights movement alongside men who, in an earlier age, had fought against the extension of citizenship and human rights to Ashe's ancestors. As a model citizen, Ashe had stood for the highest ideals of liberal democracy; in the Ashe Monument, Richmond found an ideal subject to commemorate the political and economic changes wrought by the long struggle for full civil rights. If we turn our attention toward the subject of the statue, his life, and his connection to his hometown, we gain a deeper understanding of the legacies of race and racism enforced under Jim Crow legislation and which continued to structure notions of masculinity and identity during and after the civil rights movement.[2]

As an athlete who willfully embraced being a role model, Ashe's actions were constantly on display and subject to scrutiny. Throughout his long career on and off the court, he handled this attention and scrutiny through a carefully formulated persona drawn from lessons learned through Richmond's harsh segregation of the 1940s and 1950s. In his three cowritten autobiographical works—*Portrait in Motion* with Frank Deford (1975), *Off the Court* with Neil Amdur (1981), and *Days of Grace* with Arnold Rampersad (1993)—and John McPhee's biographical profile of Ashe, *Levels of the Game* (1969), Ashe's memories of masculinity under segregation informed and supported the pragmatic and graceful persona he honed as an athlete and activist.[3] The elegiac writing occasioned by Ashe's death built upon these precedents and drew readers' attentions to a self-sustaining narrative of an honorable life, one on which to write out larger national struggles. Throughout his life, Ashe consciously drew upon his childhood in articulating and deploying a personal politics of morality, pragmatism, and moderation. His politics were not atypical; rather, they were representative of the larger cultural systems that informed Ashe's racial and gender identities, impressed upon him by his earliest male role models: his father Arthur Ashe Sr. and his first tennis coach, Dr. Robert Johnson.

Ashe gained national prominence in the summer of 1968 when, as an amateur, he won the inaugural U.S. Open. As the rare African American player in a predominantly white sport, Ashe and the manner and poise with which he carried himself stood in stark contrast to the violence and unrest of a spring and summer defined by the assassinations of Martin Luther King Jr. and Robert Kennedy, riots in major American cities and at the Democratic National Convention, and the public political stances of athletes such as John Carlos and Tommie Smith of the 1968 U.S. Olympic team as well as former Olympic gold medalist Muhammad Ali. Unlike other nationally recognizable African American men, Ashe avoided engaging in the increasingly tense world of political activism, and while

Ashe soon became involved in some aspects of civil rights and human rights activism, he did so in ways that often drew criticism from political activists.

One year after Ashe's U.S. Open victory, in 1969, John McPhee celebrated Ashe as a patient, moderate, and pragmatic man. Through this account, the nation was first introduced to Ashe, his potential as a national role model, and his commitment to the masculine ideals that informed his childhood. Writing in the *New Yorker*, McPhee profiled Ashe and Clark Graebner's semifinal match in a two-part story later published as *Levels of the Game*. The setting is the inaugural U.S. Open championship, and Graebner and Ashe are the last Americans standing — the contestants in the other semifinal are from Australia and the Netherlands. The winner of this match is the last chance for the United States to win its national championship. Ashe and Graebner's common purpose, however, belies the stark contrasts in their appearances, styles of play, and backgrounds. Graebner was a large, lumbering, powerful man who "looks exactly like — that is to say, he bears something far more precise than a striking resemblance to — Clark Kent" and played efficient, if conservative, tennis.[4] Ashe, in contrast, was graceful and lithe, a physical presence that masked his slight, almost scrawny build and his streaky, inconsistent, nervous play on the courts.

In the beginning pages, as he developed his characters in contrast to each other, McPhee described how Ashe planned a trip to Kenya, his first such visit to Africa. Linking national pride to Ashe's interest in Africa provided a 250-year narrative detour in which McPhee traced Ashe's family history back to the 1735 arrival of a nameless, enslaved African woman who became the Ashe family matriarch in Virginia and North Carolina. McPhee ended his two-page description of Ashe's family history with the remark that "Graebner has no idea whatsoever when his forebears first came to this country."[5] The irony of this juxtaposition drew readers' attention to the assumed uniqueness of the inherited social codes and family bonds of working-class African Americans that defined Ashe's identity.

Ashe's family tree immediately set him apart from Graebner and other suburban whites but also from other African Americans. The social and political exclusion of African Americans historically prevented the development of traditional family bonds and continues to frustrate the full documentation of familial histories. The family's history, however, has been carefully recorded and preserved in a six-by-seven-foot rendering of the family tree with each member represented by a leaf on the tree. One leaf, labeled Arthur Ashe, is painted gold. Ashe's intricately traced family tree stands as a textual and visual delineation of an African American family, fixing its pasts in distinctly national time and space. McPhee described Ashe's early ancestors, when the family exited slavery, and how they came to have the surname of Samuel Ashe, an early governor of

North Carolina. Ashe knew his past and knew the wide-reaching permutations of his family and its uniquely American characteristics. It stretched across Virginia and North Carolina, included whites and African Americans, and extended deep into the national memory. Ashe, the golden leaf, was a culmination of the American past.

His American past, however, was one that grew in the shadows. The anonymity of his first American ancestor reinforces the wholly American roots of Ashe's family while pointedly indicating the legacy slavery had on familial identity. Through the physical representation of the family tree McPhee claimed an ascendant, shadow memory of the national past. The amnesia of Graebner's middle-class, suburban family contrasts starkly with the cultivated memories of the Ashe family. These memories enabled Ashe a deep sense of his own identity and the material with which to express that identity. As such, they are the stories that McPhee used to contextualize Ashe's fight to win the first U.S. Open.

Ashe was deeply influenced by the example of his father, the early loss of his mother, and the tutelage of his first tennis coaches, Ronald Charity and Dr. Robert Johnson. Arthur Ashe Sr. was one of nine children who grew up on the family's small farm outside South Hill, Virginia. Barely literate, the elder Ashe left home in the 1930s at age twelve to seek his living in Richmond. He worked part-time odd jobs before, at thirteen, he got a driver's license and became a chauffeur-butler for wealthy white families. His employers were, for the most part, Jewish business owners, including the Schwarzchilds, who owned a chain of jewelry stores; the Thalhimers, who owned a chain of local department stores; and Daniel Schiller, who acted as the treasurer for the Thalhimers.[6]

In 1960, Thalhimers' department store became the focus of an important boycott in the Richmond civil rights movement. While the business practices of the Thalhimers' became the subject of later political struggles, their personal politics and their personal responses to acts of anti-Semitism cultivated Arthur Ashe Sr.'s ideas on proper masculinity. He often repeated a story about taking the family patriarch, William, to see a man about a piece of land. The man did not want to sell the land; he especially did not want to sell the land to a Jewish man. The seller insulted Thalhimer in every imaginable way, but in the end, the deal was finished. Privy to the conversation, Ashe Sr. asked his employer why he had endured the onslaught of insults and slurs. Thalhimer replied that he had come to purchase the land; he had bought the land and it was now his; the seller could go on cursing him as long as he wanted because, in the end, Thalhimer had won. Arthur Ashe Jr. explained that "this incident had a major impact on my father. It deepened his pragmatic sense; it made him see the world in a different way."[7]

His father's pragmatism was also rooted in the material and political demands on working-class African American men in Jim Crow Richmond. Ashe Sr. responded to these demands through hard work and a rigid sense of appropriate behavior rooted in familial responsibility. When Ashe Jr. was a small child, his father took a job as a special police officer for the Richmond City Police. Charged with patrolling and maintaining an African American park, Brook Field, his father was a combination night watchman, groundskeeper, and equipment and facilities manager. In this job, he "spent half his time encouraging athletic games and the other half breaking up crap games."[8] The family lived in the middle of the park, located at the heart of the closely knit African American neighborhood Jackson Ward and next to the historically black Virginia Union University; Brook Field was the best-equipped African American park in segregated Richmond, and was filled with fields, playgrounds, pools, and courts; it was the center of play and sport among African American Richmonders.[9] As a child Ashe lived at the athletic epicenter of a threatened yet proud African American community that for one hundred years had been among the most affluent in the South. The elder Ashe's dedication to hard work manifested in his sense of familial responsibility and the rearing practices he used with his sons, Arthur Jr. and John.

A key moment in the Ashe family history took place in 1950, when Arthur Jr. was seven and John was one. Their mother, Mattie, passed away due to complications from her third pregnancy. In McPhee's telling, her death altered the family structure. No longer a traditional dual-parent household, the family became a single-parent, wholly masculine environment. Young Arthur had no memories of his mother, save one: a week before her death, he remembers her standing by the door in a bathrobe as she was taken to the hospital. Though the household always had a live-in female housekeeper, and Ashe Sr. soon remarried and brought a stepmother and stepdaughters into the family, Arthur Ashe Jr.'s childhood, as told to and written by McPhee, was one of a father and two sons caring for and tending to each other.

In this narrative, the rigors of being "a lone parent seemed to increase in Arthur's father his already rigorous sense of discipline." Rigid rules and absolute maxims ruled Arthur's childhood. He was never allowed to tarry, never allowed to stray far from home, and was kept on a tight schedule. Explaining his philosophy on parenting, the elder Ashe told McPhee that "a parent has got to hurt his own child, discipline him, hold him back from things you know aren't good for him." Referring to himself as "a 'crooked-knees' Negro, which he define[d] as someone who has no class at all," Ashe Sr. expressed faith in the values of self-sufficiency, restraint, respect, and law and order. In McPhee's hands, these values are expressed in maxims that Ashe Sr. "bellows": "You respect everybody whether they respect you or not!"; "Never carry a grudge! I've seen Negroes wreck their lives through hatred of whites!"; "There's a certain class of people—there's a certain class of people you've got to handle by judge"; "I don't have any picks and pets. . . . I make everybody come by me, rich or poor"; and, finally, "I just want people to treat me as a human being. I'm sure my son is the same." The picture McPhee paints of the Ashe family home is one of political and personal moderation, one in which the reality of racism is acknowledged yet deflected by the shields of self-control and self-confidence. These politics did not ingratiate Ashe Sr. with his peers. A man who, as Dr. Johnson described him, "once had a reputation for being strictly Uncle Tom," Ashe Sr. was "one of the few blacks on the police force" and in a unique position to patrol and monitor the entire African American community. Ashe admitted that his power and the success of his son bred jealousy and discontent among his peers.[10]

Despite criticism from other African Americans, values of self-reliance and discipline were further cultivated by Ashe's early tennis coaches, some of whom were deeply invested in the symbolic power of African American athletic success. Ashe first learned of tennis by watching Virginia Union University students play on the courts at Brook Field. When he was six he became intrigued with one student in particular, Ronald Charity, who was, in Ashe's eyes, "the best in the world." Charity was, by his own estimation, the best African American player in Richmond. A self-taught player, he soon passed his lessons on to the very young Ashe. A natural athlete and, due to his father's strict rules, an attentive and responsive student, Ashe very quickly developed into a solid player. Charity recounted that Ashe was the ideal student: "He was a quiet child, observant. He took in everything, and read a lot. He was very disciplined."[11]

Impressed with Ashe's progress, Charity suggested that he enroll in Dr. Robert Johnson's summer tennis academy. A former football player at historically black colleges such as Shaw, Virginia Union University, and Lincoln, Johnson had attended medical school and set up a practice in Lynchburg, one hundred miles west of Richmond. After taking up tennis as an adult, Johnson became a regular champion in the American Tennis Association, the fledgling national body for amateur African American tennis players. Tennis was not a widely popular sport among African Americans, and Johnson dedicated his free time and finances to improving the ATA and the quality of its players.

In 1949, Johnson attended the national junior championship, held in Charlottesville. Impressed by the quality of the tennis and encouraged by the fact that tournament directors allowed African American players to enter, Johnson dedicated himself to the development of young male African American players. The next year, Johnson brought two entrants to the tournament. They were nowhere near as talented as the white youth players and did very poorly in the tournament. Embarrassed by the defeat and angered by the prevailing logic that

African Americans lacked the finesse necessary to succeed at tennis, Johnson set about to cultivate players who could win the national junior championship.[12]

In the summers, Johnson's impressive Lynchburg home became a camp for his protégés. The players lived in his house and trained on his personal court with coaching from him and his adult son. The training was rigorous. Before being allowed to handle a racket, Johnson's charges had to become proficient at hitting a tennis ball, suspended on a string, with a broom handle. And every day before breakfast they were required to hit a ball against a backboard five hundred times. In exchange for room, board, instruction, and transportation to and from tournaments, the young athletes worked as gardeners for the doctor, weeding his flowerbeds, trimming his boxwoods, clipping his rosebushes, and spraying his apple trees.[13]

In addition to tennis instruction and their chores, Johnson taught his athletes certain principles and manners. Because Johnson viewed the project as "an assault on a sport as white as tennis," he insisted that his players be prepared for adversity and the racist treatment they would assuredly face. Because junior tennis players often stayed at the homes of other players or in dormitories, Johnson taught, demanded, and got proper manners. His players learned to make their bed every day. They always hung up their clothes. When a woman entered a room they stood. They were taught the table etiquette of knives, forks, spoons. Johnson defended these rules to McPhee and recounted that he would tell his students, "I want you to be accepted without being the center of attention. . . . I want you to be able to take care of yourself in any situation where habits or manners are important, so that you don't stand out."[14]

Manners carried onto the court and into tennis games. Players were taught, above all, self-control. In the heat of competition, an athlete naturally becomes tense, aggressive, and reactionary. Johnson's players learned to control behavior no matter the situation. They would not question the judgment of an official, they would not holler or yell, and they certainly would not throw their rackets. And because in the early rounds of junior tennis tournaments players are responsible for calling shots in or out, Johnson insisted that his players call any questionable shots in the favor of the *other* player; further, they were instructed to return any shot that was less than two inches out of bounds. This way, Johnson reasoned, there would be no chance his players could rightly be accused of cheating. Certainly, there would be unsubstantiated accusations, but through carefully practiced restraint, there would be no proof, and Johnson's players would be able to succeed solely on their success as athletes.[15]

The strict training cultivated Ashe's inchoate skills, and in 1961 he became the first African American male to win the national junior championship, fulfilling one of Johnson's goals. However, while Ashe had gained success on the national stage during the summer, local segregation prevented his full participation in tournaments at home. He was barred from open tournaments in Richmond, and his high school had no team. His competition vastly limited, he had no equal and no challenger capable of pushing him to develop. To expand his game, Johnson arranged for Ashe to spend his senior year of high school in St. Louis, which was relatively integrated compared with Richmond. Ashe lived with friends of Johnson and attended an integrated school where he was able to compete on the tennis team and win a high school state title.

After his year in St. Louis, Ashe went on to college at UCLA, where he eventually won an NCAA title. Los Angeles was another step removed from the strict segregation of Richmond. Ashe socialized with whites and explored a loosely defined social hierarchy. He later described this time in his life as one of freedom and exploration. It was his first experience outside the authoritarian rules of his father and his first exposure to radical approaches to race and racism. However, it is important to note that Ashe experienced this liberation in a very controlled setting, limited as he was to the affluent Westwood area around the UCLA campus.[16] His isolation from the diversity of Los Angeles replicated in his continuing isolation due to the rigors of highly competitive athletics. As a champion player at the junior level, Ashe had been given rare access to a predominantly white world. And, at least for Johnson, his success in that sphere had political ramifications. His victories were symbolic, demonstrations that an African American man could succeed where least expected. As he gained more and more success, Ashe's isolation—as the rare African American man within the white, and increasingly international, world of tennis—deeply influenced his identity. Symbolic victories espoused by Johnson became the space in which Ashe expressed himself and responded to the pressures of his being the sole African American in a predominantly white world and the gendered expectations of his athletic performance.

The larger expectations of Ashe's success were palpable in 1968. As McPhee notes, "Because Ashe is black, many people expect him to be more than a tennis player—in fact, demand that he be a leader in a general way." The African American press had criticized him for not being more visible and vocally involved, and some activists demanded that he resign from the army and the Davis Cup team. Stokely Carmichael had been upset at Ashe's frequent refusals to participate in marches and protests. This lead to accusations and name calling and "inevitably, they have called him an Uncle Tom." [17] But, for Ashe, the demands of others were not enough to change the pragmatic approach to race and politics he learned from his father and the measured and subtle politics he learned from Johnson. Confessing to McPhee that he disapproved of militant groups and felt that the appeal of leaders such as Carmichael was the identity it gave to poor

African Americans, Ashe espoused a slow approach, one founded on education and symbolic victories. He saw his life as the realization of a politics in which all people are treated equally regardless of class or race. His father's pragmatism, forged in the strictly segregated worlds of Virginia, had filtered through the isolating experiences Ashe had as a tennis champion. He was given unique access to white worlds because of his personal skills and achievements. As in childhood, he had to practice the cool calm taught by Johnson, which opened doors for the symbolic power of athletic excellence.

As McPhee's account winds down, he tracks the last points of the match. As Ashe brings the victory to a close, McPhee jumps forward to the finals, where Ashe defeated Tom Okker, before returning to the victory over Graebner. Thus, the reader knows the ultimate outcome of the tournament with the final strokes of the Graebner-Ashe match. In rich prose, McPhee described the final point of the championship round and the way Ashe immediately turned to his father and Johnson, sitting high in the stands, and bowed to them. Their tears are enjoined by a three-and-a-half-minute standing ovation that, McPhee tells us, Ashe received that night in the West Point dining hall.[18] It is a moving paragraph, the culmination of 140 pages of subtle tension that reaches deep into the concerns of the nation. The reader's emotional response to an image of filial love and the success of the long struggles of three pragmatic, cautious African American Virginians—Ashe, his father, and Johnson—draws to a close a rumination on the future of race and politics in the United States. While McPhee's immediate audience was, undoubtedly, engrossed by the fears of 1968 and 1969, he gave them hope for the future, a faith in symbolic victories.

These symbolic victories began to echo through Ashe's direct involvement in social and political activism. Looking back with the hindsight of thirteen years, Ashe described 1968 as a turning point as he became involved in activism; however, rather than working alongside civil rights activists in the United States, Ashe turned his attention to a place far from home. Since 1964, South Africa had been barred from the Olympics, and numerous international sports organizations banned its athletes from competition. Tennis was one of the few sports in which individual South Africans competed. In 1968, pressure grew to bar South Africans from international tennis competitions and to boycott the South African Open, which was, at the time, one of the premier tournaments in the world. Ashe became intrigued by the tournament. Curious if he—the recent U.S. Open champion and top-ranked player in the world—would be allowed to play, he began to ask his South African colleagues on the tour for their opinions. Cliff Drysdale, Ashe recalled, made it very clear that while he would be permitted to enter the tournament—the sports association was invested in maintaining symbolic integration—Ashe would never be allowed to enter South Africa because the South African government would not award him a visa. The next year, Ashe began an annual tradition of applying for a visa to South Africa to play in the top tournament hosted by the apartheid government. He was continually rebuffed, but he continued to apply until 1973.

Ashe also chose to document 1973. Working with *Sports Illustrated*'s Frank Deford, Ashe kept a diary that Deford then turned into a memoir, *Portrait in Motion*, in which the biographical materials that were used in *Levels of the Game* were recycled and reinvented. Ashe's childhood and the lessons learned in Jim Crow Richmond appeared as defining moments, ones that drove and motivated his personal and political life and his engagement with South Africa.

Portrait in Motion begins, appropriately enough, with Ashe in motion; in London to prepare for Wimbledon, Ashe was summoned back to Richmond for the funeral of his maternal grandmother, whom he referred to as Big Mama. As a professional tennis player, Ashe traveled across the globe; in the book's preface he calculates that in 1973–74 he "played on five continents, made 129 airplane trips, slept in 71 different beds and traveled 165,000 miles." His journey back to Richmond for his grandmother's funeral and many subsequent trips across the globe and back to Richmond reinforced the identity that Ashe formed through his documentation of his international life. Big Mama's funeral enabled Ashe to foreground his dedication to family and his childhood in Richmond as central aspects of his persona.[19]

Ashe's physical and mental movement between home and memories of his childhood and the tense, international world of tennis and politics structured his diary. Over the course of the year, he made sporadic visits to Richmond to hunt and fish with his father. Like Big Mama's funeral, these trips became chances to extol the values he learned from his father and his early coaches, Charity and Johnson. While the diary begins with his breaking down in tears at the loss of one of his heroines, this reminder of the struggles of southern black women provides background material for his own masculine struggle for personal freedom and racial justice. Complemented by his grandmother's and mother's experiences, in *Portrait in Motion* Ashe's childhood remains one dominated by strong-willed, patient men—especially his father and Johnson—who, in what are remembered as wholly masculine environments, taught Ashe to believe in himself and the importance of slow, steady gains.

The prime example of that pragmatic approach was Ashe's success at entering South Africa and making what he hoped was a symbolic showing on the tennis courts. In 1973, Ashe received a visa to enter South Africa and became the first person of color to play under apartheid. Eager to have one of the world's best players and, it was assumed, a token black person play in the tournament, South Africa allowed Ashe to enter the country on the condition that he not make political statements. Ashe agreed to play on four conditions: he could come and go around the country as he pleased; the stands and the spectators be integrated for Ashe's matches; a conscientious effort be made to arrange a meeting between Ashe and South African Prime Minister Vorster; and Ashe be given a visa as a black man and that the government not give him temporary honorary white status. This last stipulation was important for Ashe; he told the South African government that he could not stomach the idea of being accepted through the purposeful alteration of government documents.[20]

While in South Africa, Ashe made it to the semifinals of the singles tournament and won the doubles tournament with his partner, Tom Okker.[21] However, the bulk of the trip was spent exploring the segregated worlds of South Africa. Through meetings with apartheid apologists and government officials, Ashe learned firsthand the logics and tensions that underlay white minority rule. He became discouraged by the unexamined racism and capitulation to history and social pressure that propped up the regime. He also, through the freedom granted by the government, visited Soweto and other townships in which black South Africans lived. The journey was, as he tells us, eye opening and painful.

Ashe made a journey that few Americans or athletes did. His personal experience allowed him to see and speak with those trapped within and those benefiting from apartheid, and he used these experiences as the basis for later educational endeavors. For example, he hoped to produce a film documentary about his trip and eventually set up a foundation to fund tennis clinics for nonwhite South Africans.[22] Furthermore, his presence on the courts was, for some, an important symbolic act. Nelson Mandela, still in prison, expressed his gratitude to Ashe in a note smuggled out in the hands of his wife, Winnie Mandela. She passed it on to Ashe as he boarded an airplane back to the United States. However, the benefits of his trip were drowned out by South African and African American criticisms. In Soweto, crowds of young people surrounded him and berated him for coming to their country. Many militant African Americans criticized the trip, calling him an Uncle Tom who bolstered the image of the apartheid state. When Ashe set up his foundation to help residents of Soweto, an African American newspaper writer denounced him for not "providing for the tennis players of Harlem first."[23]

In *Portrait in Motion*, Ashe responded to these criticisms by invoking Dr. Johnson and the importance of cultivating young athletes in South Africa.[24] His overall approach to apartheid—of making slow symbolic steps that would lead to incremental change and engaging politics through personal mediation—are hallmarks of the pragmatic approach he learned from his father. The national dialogue of 1968 had called for a patient and admirable role model. But, for the critics of his trip to South Africa, what was needed was not patience but a direct challenge affected through racial solidarity and aggressive political action.

Ashe quickly defended and reinvested himself in his approach. While he attempted to shrug off criticism, it is probable that, given the attention he paid to defending himself, *Portrait in Motion* can be understood as a memoir of self-defense. Throughout the diary, Ashe argued for his right to dissent from the prevailing logic of African American political action. Fearing this logic was too unified, Ashe argued that African Americans would not arrive "in politics until [they] start[ed] publicly disagreeing with each other." African American politicians lacked direction. "Too often, I'm afraid, some of us blacks in this country are more interested in methods than objectives. There is much rhetoric without any follow-up. . . . Some blacks—and some whites too—get mad at me because they feel I don't make enough waves."[25] He defended his trip to South Africa on the grounds that rather than pay lip service to global civil rights, he went out and did something. Furthermore, Ashe defended the global reach of his political interests and his relative lack of involvement in the American civil rights movement. Through careful crafting of his experiences in South Africa, he created a public image that created positive change.

In the second half of the 1970s, Ashe's career quickly declined. Despite winning Wimbledon in 1975, injuries limited his playing time and a 1979 heart attack prematurely ended his career. While recuperating from open heart surgery, Ashe decided to write a proper memoir, one that set the bits and pieces of his life in a coherent narrative. Considering his posttennis life, Ashe saw himself taking on new responsibilities, new projects, and new political and social work based upon and developed out of his life story. While this narrative had been told and retold, Ashe felt that it needed a linear retelling, one that would help people "understand how Arthur Ashe came to be who he is."[26] *Off the Court* traces the familiar development of his pragmatic approach to race and politics grounded in his childhood in Richmond.

However, while *Off the Court* emphasizes the masculine environments of his childhood, this iteration of Ashe's life emphasizes his new role as a husband as a stabilizing, fulfilling aspect of his future life. In the penultimate chapter, Ashe describes his relationship with his wife, Jeanne Moutoussamy-Ashe. His romantic life had been a minor subject of previous books; although Ashe had not been reticent in discussing his relationships or the sexual behavior of professional athletes, he never dwelt on discussions of sex. In *Portrait in Motion*, Ashe presented an image of a generally traditional, heterosexual man who longed to find his ideal soul mate. Jeanne Moutoussamy was just this woman. Ashe described his initial attraction to her as rooted in her physical features and her professional talent as a photographer. But in the soul-searching narrative of *Off the Court*, Ashe found other, more psychological reasons for his attraction to her as well. When she first met his father, we are told, Ashe Sr. looked at if he would faint and "just stood there and stared at Jeanne" because, he told his son, she looked just like Ashe's mother, Mattie.[27] The physical resemblance mirrored what Ashe described as the psychological resonance imparted by Moutoussamy-Ashe's presence. She was the first woman to whom Ashe felt spiritually close; she was capable of helping him grow and develop as a person. In *Off the Court,* Ashe acknowledged that while his father had been a wonderful parent, the early loss of his mother left him emotionally stunted. It was his wife who filled that gap and helped him move beyond his early loss. The memories and masculinities that had dominated his documented life up until then were now supplemented by a maternal presence that enabled him to move forward.

Ashe's personal transformation empowered him: "I feel this is a good time to offer some strong observations about trends and practices that I feel strongly about." Ashe offered a lengthy explication of the ways tennis, as he played it, is a metaphor for life. The game takes patience, can turn quickly, and is something one learns over time. Ashe used this metaphor to justify his political stances. While he remained committed to ending South African apartheid, he argued that it must be done slowly, patiently, and through established political channels.[28] Engagement with the political would come to define the last decade of Ashe's life, as he spent the 1980s engaged in issues of human and civil rights, most especially apartheid in South Africa and the treatment of Haitian refugees in the United States.

His advocacy was augmented by his work as a writer. In 1988, after seven years of research, Ashe published a history of African American athletes, *A Hard Road to Glory,* which provides an overview of the contributions of African Americans to various sports, many of whom have been long lost to historical knowledge.[29] Influenced, in part, by his own experiences as a solitary African American, Ashe sought out those athletes who had faced similar challenges. While primarily concerned with chronicling their contributions, Ashe's overall argument is one of faith in the symbolic value of athletic victory. He recounted the slow progress made by individual athletes; he demonstrated the unique challenges they faced and the tight line they walked. In his chapter on tennis, Ashe focused almost wholly on Althea Gibson and himself, reminding readers that like eighteenth-century boxers and nineteenth-century jockeys, Gibson and Ashe operated in difficult settings that forced a particular politics upon them.

Ashe's empathy for the hard road that African American athletes faced translated through his own experiences, enabling his readers to better understand the complex nexus of sport and society. His project was furthered through the occasional column he began writing for the *Washington Post* in 1981. Through these columns, Ashe comes across as a somewhat conservative voice in debates over standards of behavior for male athletes. He often criticized recognizable athletes, such as Mike Tyson, for failing in their duties as role models for young African American males. However, Ashe carefully placed the behavior within the contexts of the social and economic challenges facing African American athletes. He was especially critical of the questionable academic standards college athletes faced and the limited opportunities for nonathletic success facing all African Americans. Ashe saw these problems as rooted in the downfall of African American families and the discipline they had historically enforced, and he even went so far as to call for a national service program along the lines of the Civilian Conservation Corps.[30] He remained steadfast in his belief that escape from the dual oppressions of racism and poverty lay in the discipline and self-sufficiency that could be learned through the example of male role models. Rarely in these discussions did Ashe comment on the challenges facing African American women or the lack of female role models. He empathized with male African American athletes and adolescents and expounded the nation's debt to them and their importance to African Americans. He endorsed a national service program, in part, because it would teach young African American males discipline and self-respect, qualities they needed to be caring, supportive fathers.

Faith in the role of the father and the traditional family is underlined throughout Ashe's columns by his grounding arguments through his father's examples. Ashe's own experiences were exemplars and his voice became the voice of reason and gravitas, one that related the weight of the heavy historical burden he consciously carried. His use of personal weight and pain to expound on the virtues of the family and the importance of fathers became more deeply and intimately pronounced in the last year of Ashe's life. While Ashe embraced being a role model and advocate for particular social issues, he avoided until late in life acknowledging his own relationship to one of the most pressing concerns of the 1980s: the rising toll of HIV/AIDS.

On 7 April 1992, Ashe was approached by childhood friend and *USA Today* sportswriter Doug Smith who had been sent to verify rumors that Ashe had contracted HIV/AIDS. Confronted with the prospect of being outed by a national newspaper, Ashe elected to make the announcement himself at a press conference the next day, marking a crucial turning point in Ashe's life.[31] Thrust into a new spotlight, Ashe now negotiated a world in which his life was now defined by his looming death and pervasive, lingering doubts over the nature of his body. As Ashe articulated his AIDS status, he reaffirmed the value and importance of his life and the stability of his athletic, masculine body. This experience was not unique among African American athletes, and it is important to consider the ways Ashe's infection was handled in comparison with other HIV/AIDS-positive athletes and within the contexts of black masculinity, homophobia, and national response to HIV/AIDS.

As cultural and literary scholar Philip Brian Harper demonstrates in *Are We Not Men? Masculine Anxiety and Problem of African American Identity*, black masculinity is constantly challenged by the perceived threats of "rampant black male sexuality that constitutes so much sexuopolitical structure of U.S. society." Oftentimes, anxieties associated with transgressing sexual boundaries and the stigma of being homosexual prevent the frank discussion of sexuality and its affect on African American men. Through a close reading of the treatment of HIV/AIDS in the coverage of the death of television anchorman Max Robinson and the retirement of basketball superstar Earvin "Magic" Johnson, Harper argues that suppressed discussion frustrated efforts to provide information on HIV/AIDS to African Americans.[32] While Robinson's death and Johnson's announcement could have produced fruitful media through which to challenge heterosexist assumptions regarding the nature of HIV and its transmission, both occasioned the reaffirmation of African American masculinity as built upon eloquence, intelligence, heterosexuality, and attractive, athletic bodies. The discourse emphasized the promiscuous heterosexual activity through which Robinson and Johnson acquired HIV. After Robinson's death, Jesse Jackson continued to reaffirm that it was promiscuity not homosexuality that led to Robinson's death from AIDS. Johnson's initial announcement was followed by public appearances and media campaigns that attested to his rampant heterosexual habits. The unwillingness of Robinson, Johnson, and Jackson to address the realities of HIV/AIDS further suppressed discussion of African American sexuality, reentrenched images of African American masculinity, and homosexuality among African Americans.

We cannot know the precise rationale for Ashe's decision to remain silent after he learned he had AIDS. Certainly, the milieus of his life in the late 1980s would have frustrated a frank and open dialogue regarding his status. Effectively silenced by the suppression of discussions of African American sexuality and the structures of masculinity, Ashe avoided disclosing his health to anyone but his doctors, family, and close friends. It is safe to assume that his silence was a personal coping mechanism, a mode through which to limit potential criticisms and threats associated with his condition. And when he was finally forced to publicly acknowledge his status, Ashe both challenged and colluded in the perpetuation of these structures. While he questioned heterosexism's effect on the treatment of those living with HIV/AIDS and gave his name and body to efforts for HIV/AIDS education, he remained deeply concerned with his legacy and the impact it would have on his family.

When he finally went public, Ashe explained his infection without resorting to boasts of promiscuity. He carefully indicated the 1983 blood transfusion as the source of his infection. Media coverage emphasized this infection as accidental and unfair. Major newspapers emphasized that blood supplies were not tested for HIV until eighteen months after Ashe's infection. Many papers made much of the fact that less than five thousand of all documented HIV cases—only 2 percent—could be tracked to transfusions of blood, blood components, or other tissues; and that since screening of blood supplies began there were only twenty documented cases of infection through transfusion.[33] This pales in comparison to the 23 percent of infections through intravenous drug use and the 58 percent of cases through sexual contact between men. Ashe became the pitiable victim of chance and poor planning on the part of others; his infection was not the result of homosexuality or promiscuous sexual behavior, and was not his fault.

Media coverage of Ashe's infection quickly turned to the ways the information was disseminated. In his announcement, Ashe indicated his awareness that many in New York's medical community and the international tennis community knew about his infection but remained silent. This fact is corroborated, in part, by former tennis players who recounted widespread speculation and rumors that circled tennis tournaments for years. This willful silence contrasted with what Ashe saw as the mean-spirited actions of the person who "ratted" him out to *USA Today*. As media coverage exploded in the days after his announcement, most newspapers quickly bypassed speculation as to the origins of his infection and engaged in the big story of whether or not it was right for *USA Today* to expose his medical secrets.[34] While most columnists and editorial pages acknowledged that they would have behaved in the same way, others, especially Anna Quindlen in the *New York Times* and Jonathan Yardley in the *Washington Post*, expressed frustration and outrage at the prevailing journalistic ethics that stressed the scoop over the privacy of a person's medical records. Such debates skirted central issues such as the stigmas associated with HIV/AIDS, preventing intervention in the discussion of sexuality that was central to HIV/AIDS. Because Ashe had unfortunately been infected by the rare chance of receiving a tainted blood transfusion, this juxtaposition underlined his heterosexuality, further reinforcing the prevailing heterosexist discourses that forced him to remain silent.

Ashe's wife and daughter—both of whom were HIV-negative—figured heavily as he negotiated the next turn in his life. He emphasized his right to privacy and his family's desires to keep his infection quiet so as not to cause problems for the young daughter, Camera.[35] This turn to his family characterizes the last period of Ashe's life. While his identity as a role model had been borne out of his relationship to his father and, we learn in *Off the Court*, had been augmented and fulfilled by his partnership with his wife, in his last act, Ashe defined himself through his relationship with his daughter.

In the last eight months of his life, Ashe worked to secure his legacy within the United States and in Richmond. He founded a nonprofit tutoring organization, Virginia Heroes, which worked with young people in Richmond and began raising funds for an African American Sports Hall of Fame that was to be built in Richmond. In the last weeks of his life he collaborated with Richmond sculptor Paul DiPasquale on a statue of himself that was intended to be placed outside that hall of fame. Ashe gave DiPasquale his approval for such a statue on the grounds that it depict Ashe surrounded by children, holding a tennis racket and books, wearing his tennis warm-ups. He also specifically requested that DiPasquale depict Ashe as he looked in 1994 when he was near death from HIV/AIDS. The resulting statue shows a wan, sick Ashe, far removed from the healthy, smiling figure familiar to tennis fans in the 1970s.

This work occurred as Ashe completed the draft of a final memoir. Cowritten with Arnold Rampersad, who is best known for his biographies of Jackie Robinson and Langston Hughes, *Days of Grace* finds Ashe rehearsing his life experiences and offering a set of lessons that come from beyond the inevitability of assured death. What sets *Days of Grace* apart from Ashe's earlier memoirs is the readers' knowledge of Ashe's impending death. The fact that the book was posthumously published underlay the gravity of Ashe's life and work. This possibility was not lost on Ashe. *Days of Grace* is one of those rare texts that literary theorist Thomas Kane has theorized as automortography, or "the attempted representation of one's own death" in which the writer, aware or assuming that death is near, uses the knowledge of his imminent mortality to become an exemplar and agent for change.[36] Confronted with death, Ashe reiterated his life's story with an emphasis on imparting his belief in pragmatism to his daughter. In the final chapter of *Days of Grace*, "My Dear Camera," Ashe addressed a letter to his daughter in which he stressed that despite the challenges facing all African Americans, he hoped she would draw from the rich history of the Ashe family and dedicate herself to helping others.

Ashe's life ended with the reaffirmation of his faith in patience, pragmatism, and personal responsibility. While early in his career he had resisted politics, he had become a recognized role model and authority of issues pertaining to race in U.S. culture, especially sports. This status as a national role model occasioned the extraordinary mourning at his death and underlay the debates over Richmond's Ashe Monument. While his life took him far from the segregated playgrounds of Richmond, the logics and patterns of Ashe's life and work continually returned to the masculine ideals of his childhood in an intensely segregated society. His engagement with racial politics—as an athlete, activist, and writer—were defined by the examples set by his father and his early coaches, and throughout his life he explained and justified his actions by making appeals to his roles as a son, husband, and father. These memories and their use in structuring his masculine identity defined Ashe for a rightly celebratory public.

That celebratory public, however, was conflicted as to the appropriate ways to celebrate Ashe's life and legacy in Richmond. Though now a fixture in Richmond's memorial landscape, the Ashe Monument was subject to intense debates. There is not space here to address the long history of Monument Avenue and the Ashe Monument's role in altering Richmond's symbolic landscape. It is important to note that between 1890 and 1922, when the original core of Confederate monuments were erected, some African American civil leaders criticized the celebration of the Lost Cause. That criticism bubbled up during the 1960s, when local leaders of the civil rights movement, such as lawyer and politician Henry Marsh, criticized efforts by anti-integrationists, many affiliated with the segregationist U.S. Senator Harry F. Byrd Sr., who attempted to place new Confederate memorials along the boulevard's central median. As a site of contestation in the struggle for and against African American civil rights, Monument Avenue became a key site of symbolic change for a generation of African American political leaders who came of age in the 1960s and gained significant political influence in the 1980s.[37] Most influential of those African American political leaders was Doug Wilder, who served as governor of Virginia from 1990 to 1994. Wilder and others had long called for the placement of a statue of an African American leader, such as Martin Luther King Jr., on Monument Avenue.

In 1994 the sculptor DiPasquale completed a model of his Ashe Monument and in December was joined by Wilder at its unveiling. Wilder, building off of his own political capital and Ashe's legacy, publicly called for the city to place the Ashe Monument on Monument Avenue. Over the next eighteen months, Richmond's city government and public discourse engaged in at times volatile debates over placing Arthur Ashe alongside Robert E. Lee, Jefferson Davis, and other Confederate leaders. While the Ashe Monument was ultimately unveiled on 10 July 1996, the debates leading up to it point to the complexity of southern masculinity and the place of African American men in the modern South.

Wilder's desire to honor Ashe on Monument Avenue quickly gained the support of the Richmond City Council, many of whose members were, like Ashe and Wilder, African Americans who had grown up during the last days of Jim Crow segregation. However, widespread criticism of the Monument Avenue location arose. While white supremacists and some Confederate/southern heritage groups attacked the Ashe Monument because it meant the "integration" of Monument Avenue, the majority of critics attacked the statue because it would alter the temporal focus of Monument Avenue or because Ashe's contributions to Richmond and the United States were not considered sufficient for memorialization. Some groups, especially conservative pundits writing in the *Washington*

Times and those affiliated with Confederate heritage groups such as the Heritage Preservation Association, saw the Ashe Monument as an attack on white southern heritage. These groups often argued for the specialness of Monument Avenue's Confederate theme and suggested that a more appropriate memorial would be one to African Americans who fought for the Confederate Army. One very telling statement was the critic who wrote to the Richmond City Council that "the statues on that street are dedicated to one cause, a single cause," and that by adding a non-Confederate statue, the city would delegitimate Richmond's existing historical identity. Similarly, these and other critics questioned Ashe's historical importance. Writing to the Richmond City Council, another critic of the Ashe Monument complained that "Arthur Ashe, by most accounts, was a nice boy and a good tennis player. I would stop short of calling him a hero for being nice. A hero by most definitions is one who saves another's life." This critic went on to say that the city should erect a statue of Thomas Jefferson, James Madison, John Tyler, or Woodrow Wilson, all of them presidents from Virginia who "changed the course of history."[38] Lastly, the Ashe Monument was criticized by local arts patrons who questioned the statue as a piece of art. Led by gallery owner Beverly Reynolds, the group Citizens for Excellence in Public Art attempted to replace DiPasquale's statue with a statue of Ashe by a more well-known sculptor.[39] Attacking DiPasquale's statue on aesthetic grounds, CEPA was bothered by the casual nature of the statue and the depiction of Ashe's sick body.

These criticisms are bound together by the common thread of discomfort caused by Ashe's status as a new model for southern masculinity. As an African American man most often associated with the civil rights era, Ashe broke from longstanding ideals of southern masculinity based on whiteness and a connection to the Confederate past that had found their highest articulation in the "heroes" of Monument Avenue, most especially Robert E. Lee. That discomfort over a masculinity built upon new racial and temporal models worked alongside discomfort with Ashe's contributions as an agent for symbolic change through athletics and as a writer and activist for human rights. In addition, CEPA's dislike of the statue on aesthetic grounds reminds us that southern masculinity is intimately tied to the body. While Ashe had been a world-champion athlete, by celebrating his life through the image of his sick body, DiPasquale's monument undermined standing notions of physical perfection as a prerequisite for masculinity.

Despite these criticisms, the Ashe Monument was completed and stands at the western end of Monument Avenue's complex of memorials. This enshrinement is evidence not only of the changing nature of southern masculinity but also of the permanence of those ideals Ashe embraced and celebrated and upon which he built his life and legacy. While presenting a stark challenge to the racial, temporal, and physical standards of southern masculinity, Arthur Ashe reaffirmed the importance of pragmatism, self-sufficiency, restraint and, most importantly, fatherhood in the crafting of the ideal southern man.

NOTES

The author thanks Bill Albertini and Chadwick Roberts, who helped shape the arguments of this essay; Phil Terrie who provided editorial guidance; and the author's family for their support and encouragement.

1. "Arthur Ashe," editorial, *Washington Post,* 8 February 1993; Tony Kornheiser, "A Lone, Clear Bell, Mournfully Ringing," *Washington Post,* 8 February 1993; Michael Wilbon, "An Athlete Only Incidentally," *Washington Post,* 7 February 1993.

2. For thorough analysis, see Matthew Mace Barbee, "Race, Memory, and Communal Belonging in Narrative and Art: Richmond, Virginia's Monument Avenue, 1948–1996" (Ph.D. diss., Bowling Green State University, 2007); Jonathan Leib, "Separate Times, Shared Spaces: Arthur Ashe, Monument Avenue, and the Politics of Richmond, Virginia's Symbolic Landscape," *Cultural Geographies* 9 (2002): 286–312; Leib, "The Witting Autobiography of Richmond, Virginia: Arthur Ashe, the Civil War, and Monument Avenue's Racialized Landscape," in *Landscape and Race in the United States,* ed. Richard Schein (New York: Routledge, 2006), 187–212; Tony Horwitz, *Confederates in the Attic: Dispatches from the Unfinished Civil War* (New York: Vintage Departures, 1998), 247–52; John T. Kneebone, "Location, Location, Location." *Cultural Resource Management Online* 22 (1999), http://crm.cr.nps.gov/archive/22–9/22–09-01.pdf. For an analysis that places the Ashe Monument alongside larger debates over memory and heritage in modern Richmond, see Marie Tyler-McGraw, "Southern Comfort Levels: Race, Heritage Tourism, and the Civil War in Richmond," in *Slavery and Public Memory: The Tough Stuff of American Memory,* ed. James Oliver Horton and Lois E. Horton (New York: New Press, 2006), 151–67.

3. Arthur Ashe and Frank Deford, *Arthur Ashe: Portrait in Motion* (Boston: Houghton Mifflin, 1975); Arthur Ashe and Neil Amdur, *Off the Court* (New York: New American Library, 1981); Arthur Ashe and Arnold Rampersad, *Days of Grace* (New York: Alfred A. Knopf, 1993); John McPhee, *Levels of the Game* (New York: Bantam, 1969).

4. McPhee, *Levels of the Game,* 31.

5. Ibid., 13. In these early days of professional tennis most players had nonathletic careers; tennis was not yet the full-time commitment that other sports were. Graebner worked as an assistant to the president of the Hobson Miller division of Saxon Industries, and Ashe was a lieutenant in the U.S. Army stationed at West Point where, from 1965 to 1969, he worked in the office of the U.S. Military Academy's adjutant general and coached the cadet tennis team. Ashe had participated in ROTC at UCLA. The army secured this particular post for him so that he could pursue his tennis career. A benefit of this post was that Ashe would not have to serve in Vietnam. A

drawback was that he could not receive prize money from tennis tournaments. At the time, Ashe was also a part-time employee of Richmond-based Philip-Morris, a relationship that would continue for most of his adult life.

6. McPhee, *Levels of the Games*, 61; Ashe and Rampersad, *Days of Grace*, 162.

7. Lewis A. Randolph and Gayle T. Tate, *Rights for a Season: The Politics of Race, Class, and Gender in Richmond, Virginia* (Knoxville: University of Tennessee Press, 2003), 180–90; Ashe and Rampersad, *Days of Grace*, 162.

8. McPhee, *Levels of the Game*, 65.

9. Brook Field, Jackson Ward, and V.U.U. were clustered together in a manifestation of the spatial effects of racial segregation. It is also important to note that though tightly knit, this area of Richmond was threatened and eventually torn apart by city zoning practices during urban renewal in the 1950s and 1960s. When the Ashe family lived in Brook Field it was encircled by light industry, including a bottled gas plant. The development of Interstate 95 razed a large swath of Jackson Ward and cleaved this historic neighborhood in two. By 1968, Brook Field's trees and playgrounds had been torn down, and the site had been turned into general post office; see McPhee, *Levels of the Game*, 64–65.

10. Ibid., 63, 79–81; Ashe and Amdur, *Off the Court*, 22.

11. McPhee, *Levels of the Game* 36–37.

12. Ibid., 23–28.

13. Ibid.

14. Ibid., 29.

15. Ibid., 28–29.

16. Ashe and Amdur, *Off the Court*, 61.

17. McPhee, *Levels of the Game*, 143.

18. Ibid., 149.

19. Ashe and Deford, *Arthur Ashe*, viii.

20. Ibid., 18.

21. Ibid., 138.

22. Ibid., 143.

23. Ibid., 136, 143.

24. Ibid.

25. Ibid., 94, 151.

26. Ashe and Amdur, *Off the Court*, vii, 219.

27. Ibid., 181.

28. Ibid., 209–10.

29. Arthur Ashe, *A Hard Road to Glory: A History of the African-American Athlete, 1619–1918* (New York: Warner Books, 1988).

30. Arthur Ashe, "It Doesn't Take an Army to Discover Young Blacks' Choice for Role Models," *Washington Post*, 11 February 1991; Ashe, "True Test for NCAA: Turn False Step into Learning Process," *Washington Post* 13 February 1983; Ashe, "NCAA Propositions Itself over 42," *Washington Post*, 20 January 1990; Ashe, "Somewhere, a Wrong Turn," *Washington Post*, 6 January 1991; Ashe, "Heroes: Thomas vs. Ty-

son; Sadly, It's No Contest for Many Young People," *Washington Post*, 15 September 1991; Ashe, "Can a New 'Army' Save Our Cities? With Discipline and Training, Our Alienated Young Could Find News Lives," *Washington Post*, 10 May 1992.

31. Ashe and Rampersad, *Days of Grace*, 3–32.
32. Philip Brian Harper, *Are We Not Men? Masculine Anxiety and the Problem of African American Identity* (New York: Oxford University Press, 1996), 10. Natives of Richmond, Robinson and Ashe knew each other from childhood.
33. Lawrence K. Altman, "Ashe Received a Transfusion before Blood Supply was Tested for H.I.V.," *New York Times*, 9 April 1992; Mike Freeman, "Arthur Ashe Announces He Has AIDS; Tennis Greats Transfusion after '83 Surgery Blamed," *Washington Post*, 9 April 1992; Robin Herman, "In 1983, HIV Blood Screening Was Nonexistent," *Washington Post*, 9 April 1992; Loverro Thom, "Ashe Reveals He Has AIDS; Tennis Great Points to '83 Transfusion," *Washington Times*, 9 April 1992.
34. Christine Brennan and Christine Spolar, "Ashe Told Friends in '88; Stan Smith Says Media Forced Public Disclosure," *Washington Post*, 9 April 1992; Tony Kornheiser, "A Tear for a Hero," *Washington Post*, 12 April 1992; Richard Cohen, "Did We Have to Know?" *Washington Post*, 10 April 1992; Alex S. Jones, "Debate on Privacy v. Press Freedom Divides Media," *Chicago Daily Law Bulletin*, 1 May 1992; Howard Kurtz, "*USA Today* Lobs a Tough One," *Washington Post*, 9 April 1992; Robert Lipsyte, "Do We Need to Know that Arthur Ashe Has AIDS?" *New York Times*, 10 April 1992.
35. Ashe and Rampersad, *Days of Grace*, 3–33.
36. Thomas Kane, "Mourning the Promised Land: Martin Luther King Jr.'s Automortography and the National Civil Rights Museum," *American Literature* 76 (2004): 549–77.
37. See Barbee, "Race, Memory, and Communal Belonging in Narrative and Art," chaps. 2–4 for a lengthy discussion of this history.
38. Brian Pohanka, "Monument to a Richmond Hero," *Washington Post*, 21 December 1994; Andrew Cain, "Ashe to Join Lee and Jackson; Statue Approved for Richmond's Monument Avenue," *Washington Times*, 20 June 1995; "Arthur Ashe Joins the Confederacy?" *Washington Times*, 21 June 1995; Samuel Francis, "Virginia's Integrated Statuary," *Washington Times*, 23 June 1995; quoted in Gordon Hickey, "Statue's Path Wasn't Smooth; Debates Focused on Symbolism, Heroes, Justice, Site, Sculptor," *Richmond Times-Dispatch*, 8 July 1996.
39. Sibella C. Giorello, "World-Class Statue Sought," *Richmond Times-Dispatch*, 15 December 1995.

Southern Sodomy; or, What the Coppers Saw

John Howard

With voyeuristic delight, I ask you to picture, dear readers, two sexual acts that American legal officials have zealously attempted to suppress and that liberal reformers have consistently tried to obscure: oral and anal sex between men. Let's look together, if you will, at two particular instances: a gay Atlantan giving a blowjob to a friend and a gay suburban Houston couple having intercourse. These are two particularly important instances, for each resulted in a United States Supreme Court ruling of sweeping significance. The first, *Bowers v. Hardwick* (1986), upheld the constitutionality of state sodomy laws. The second, *Lawrence v. Texas* (2003), overturned them and was declared "the most momentous civil rights decision since *Brown v. Board of Education* outlawed school segregation" based on race.[1]

Debating a narrow right to privacy—assuming, with unexamined class privilege, that all of us have a room of one's own in which to do it—jurists and journalists alike effaced the most provocative aspects of late twentieth-century southern queer cultural practice. A drinker, drug-taker, and "practicing homosexual," Michael Hardwick was a Georgia scene queen, an unattached urbanite of promiscuous pleasures. Likewise residents of a state that forbade miscegenation until 1967's *Loving v. Virginia* decision, Texans John Lawrence and Tyron Garner were not only an interracial couple but also a nonmonogamous, cross-class, intergenerational pair; a fifty-five-year-old white medical technician and a thirty-one-year-old African American described variously as unemployed, a shipyard worker, or roadside barbecue vendor.[2]

Turning a blind eye to the behaviors in question, the Supreme Court and its commentators instead constructed a recalcitrant South in need of external supervision and, ironically, a noninterventionist state. Of numerous parallels to the *Brown* decision of 1954, one was unusually apropos. Just as the NAACP benefited from City University of New York professor Kenneth Clark's expert testimony about the adverse psychological consequences of segregation, the *Lawrence* legal team capitalized upon a friend-of-the-court brief coauthored by outside specialists, ten historians of sexuality. The brief, cited repeatedly in the majority opinion, evidenced the historical variability of the category of sodomy and demonstrated southern states' discriminatory application of the label to particular sexual acts between men. As a result, the Court intervened, effectively kicking southern law enforcement officers out of gay men's bedrooms.[3]

But how, you might ask, did they get there in the first place? How did sheriff's deputies happen into the bedroom of Lawrence at the very moment of intercourse with Garner? How did Officer K. R. Torick come to gaze upon the entangled bodies of the aptly named Hardwick and his mate? What exactly were these bedfellows doing? The answers to these questions are central to understanding the stakes involved for queers in the United States. I want to know what the cops *saw;* don't you? And through an analysis of those unelaborated forbidden acts—the ways they were represented and regulated—I offer a window onto contested southern and American norms around masculinity, race, and sexuality since the rise of identity politics.

Examining legal and popular discourses of sodomy in the South and mapping local sites of queer pleasure, this essay describes a renegotiation of ideas about region, sexuality, and privacy. First, through a close reading of the amicus brief and reports about its role in the *Lawrence* decision, it charts the continuing construction, at the national level, of a backward South requiring professional guidance. It reveals a willingness by federal authorities to selectively intercede in state policy making on behalf of duly recognized minority groups over the second half of the twentieth century. Second, it shows that by mandating a hands-off approach—slightly expanding a right to privacy not explicitly articulated in the Constitution and its amendments—the Court paradoxically foreclosed the articulation of sexual issues long at the fore of public debate. The landmark *Lawrence* ruling in fact delineated a narrow band of acceptable lesbian and gay comportment, in line with dominant notions of white middle-class respectability and far removed from the world Michael Hardwick inhabited. Finally, by reconstructing the circumstances leading to Hardwick's arrest—and, importantly, its immediate cultural contexts—this essay offers comment on contemporaneous queer sexual ethics and proposes a more emancipatory vision for current-day queer politics.

Originating in Western Christianity generally and sixteenth-century English law in particular, sodomy statutes were adopted in all thirteen original American states, with the harshest sentences sometimes meted out. One year after penning the Declaration of Independence, that great lover of liberty (and slaveholder) Thomas Jefferson put forward the progressive notion that sodomites should no longer be punished by death, but more humanely by castration. Statutes outlawing sodomy were on the books in all fifty states as of 1961, banning varied forms of "unnatural intercourse" or, in the words of the Mississippi Code, "the detestable and abominable crime against nature committed with mankind or with a beast." (Substitute the religio-juridical phrase "crime of sodomy" with the 1533 English Reformation Parliament's "vice of buggery," and you have the exact same statute.) Whereas France and Holland had decriminalized sodomy in the early nineteenth century, Scandinavian countries and much of the rest of a secularizing Europe had done so by the mid-twentieth. If Britain seemed a laggard, finally legalizing *some* sexual acts between men in 1967, then near the end of the millennium the United States looked positively retrograde, with its intractable sodomy laws. Though the Supreme Court reaffirmed them by a scant 5−4 margin in *Bowers* in 1986, future prospects dimmed. In the District of Columbia, liberal insiders glumly measured prevailing political currents against actuarial tables, calculating that aging justices who did not outlive Ronald Reagan, the oldest president, would be replaced by even more conservative appointees. Queer activists despaired, while enterprising gay attorneys urged a growing client base to rely on individually tailored contracts, instead of collectively appealed case law, in attempts to secure protections in housing, employment, survivorship, and the like. "Until this happens," one midwestern firm advertised, with a doctored Supreme Court portrait including a preposterously out-of-place drag queen, "call us."[4]

Sodomy statutes persisted longest "below the Mason-Dixon line, where hostility toward gays fed on the 'good ol' boy' southern syndrome of exaggerated masculinity," as one political scientist put it. By the time of the *Lawrence* case, sodomy laws remained on the books in Alabama, Florida, Louisiana, Mississippi, North and South Carolina, Texas, and Virginia, as well as Idaho, Kansas, Missouri, Oklahoma, and Utah. As John D'Emilio has shown in his brilliant essay, "Capitalism and Gay Identity," modern gay cultures emerged in the late nineteenth century in tandem with industrialization and urbanization, with cities serving as important sites for the development of gay identities, communities, and political movements. The population concentration of cities alone was enough to ensure that sexual outcasts formed a critical mass conducive to the eventual growth of bars and other commercial establishments, gay print media, and additional cultural institutions. Sexual migrants from the countryside further were attracted to the wage labor necessary for independent living, the freedom from so-called small-town values, and the relative anonymity that often fostered sexual experimentation. So whereas queer sexual practices flourished in rural areas—indeed, had motivated, in part, the establishment of sodomy laws—the visibility of gay enclaves and the outness so prized by gay identity politics from the 1970s focused attention—and police regulation—on cities. Thus, when considered alongside the greater evangelical and fundamentalist religiosity of the South and an antigay reaction dating from the 1960s and 1970s, it is not surprising that the two principal Supreme Court challenges would originate in two of the section's largest metropolitan areas.[5]

I never dreamed I would live to see the demise of American sodomy laws, much less play a role in it, however small, with the 2003 *Lawrence* decision—after only seventeen years, a swift reversal of precedent. "What happened to make assumptions that were obvious to one judicial generation so obviously wrong to the next?" the *Washington Post* asked in its big Sunday edition. "Credit the scholarly efforts of a group of history professors, toiling away in the nascent and controversial field of gay studies." "In Changing the Law of the Land," the *New York Times* headline chimed on the following Sunday, "Six Justices Turned to Its History." Indeed, our friend-of-the-court brief, with George Chauncey as lead author, focused upon *American* history. For at the same time that Republican Representative Walter Jones of North Carolina convinced an Iraq War–mongering U.S. Congress to rename their cafeteria French toast "freedom toast" and their French fries "freedom fries," my chief suggestion—that we place sodomy restrictions and, hopefully, their lifting within the comparative context of modern European decriminalization just outlined—was not taken up. The brief, however, did win over the Court with the sort of social constructionist reasoning that had been the hallmark of breakthroughs in queer theory and history. "*Bowers v. Hardwick* rests upon a fundamental misapprehension of the history of sodomy," the first of our three arguments went. The monolithic "millennia of moral teaching" that Chief Justice Warren Burger had invoked in *Hardwick* was in fact a varied, uneven history, during which different jurisdictions had defined sodomy in different ways: ranging across nonprocreative sexual acts from solitary or mutual masturbation to oral and anal sex between men, between men and women, and—less so—between women. It had often been equated with bestiality and had even been applied to the speech act of blasphemy. Through the years, state sodomy laws usually had been interpreted to cover oral-genital and anal-genital contact between opposite-sex as well as same-sex pairs, though they had been disproportionately enforced against the latter. "It was only beginning in the 1970s," our brief showed, "that a handful of States, including Texas, passed legislation specifying homosexual sodomy while decriminalizing heterosexual sodomy."[6]

This was but one example to support our second argument: a purportedly timeless animus and "discrimination on the basis of homosexual status was an unprecedented development of the twentieth century." We pointed up a bedrock assumption of queer history, found in Michel Foucault's *History of Sexuality,* volume 1: "the sodomite had been a temporary aberration; the homosexual was now a species." Put another way, in the past, anyone might have been tempted by sodomitical acts and thus engaged in them. Only in the late nineteenth century, with the advent of specific legal and especially sexological formulations, did the modern homosexual emerge, a person whose very being was characterized by and structured around related sorts of desires and behaviors. "The phrase 'homosexual sodomy' would have been literally incomprehensible to the Framers of the Constitution," we noted, "for the very concept of homosexuality as a discrete psychological condition and source of personal identity was not available until the late 1800s." So, whereas sodomitical *acts* had been punished in the past, homosexual *persons* now had become the target. Though true in some sense, I regret our emphasis on this idea and on the third and final argument of our brief, likewise accurate: "Tolerance toward homosexuals has increased, resulting in acceptance by many, but not all, mainstream institutions."[7]

By perpetuating the acts/identity, behavior/being dichotomy and by highlighting the second half of the equation—engaging in what many of us activist intellectuals have forthrightly called "strategic essentialism"—we participated in the hardening of a discrete social category. Dozens of times in the brief, we use the word *gay* either as a noun, as in "gays and lesbians," or as an adjective to describe not gay sex, but "gay men," "gay individuals," "gay persons," "gay people," "gay life," "gay subcultures," "the gay world," "gay entertainers," "gay characters in the movies and on television," "gay heroes of September 11," "gay residents," "gay partners," "gay parents," "gay families," "gay employees." If turn-of-the-twentieth-century sexologists had been instrumental in the construction of the modern homosexual, then after roughly one hundred years of homosexuality (also the title of a book by leading constructionist David Halperin) we historians had certainly done our bit in the invention of the modern gay male at the turn of the twenty-first century. Yes, one must assert the existence of a "gay employee" before one can protect that person from an all-too-obvious systemic discrimination in hiring, promoting, and firing, legitimized with reference to sodomy laws. But the emphasis on upstanding gay professionals perpetuates the myth of gay wealth—the powerful pink pound and almighty gay dollar—so roundly put asunder by lesbian economist Lee Badgett. The gay subject invented by historical treatises such as our amicus brief—a respectable gay protagonist held up for protection by LGBT legal strategists—is an enormously problematic one.[8]

In a world of representation, whether derogatory televisual stereotype or adversarial courtroom archetype, it is easy to depict the enemy of the American gay as the bigoted southern sheriff or the bellicose southern demagogue. Forget the born-again Georgia Baptist Jimmy Carter; a new religious right composed largely of southern fundamentalists came to prominence during the Reagan-Bush administrations and created a discourse of "traditional family values" that singled out homosexuality as the most baleful social evil. Donald Wildmon's fanatical American Family Association of Tupelo and Charles Stanley's reactionary InTouch Ministries of Atlanta garnered a fresh respect. Virginia preachers Jerry Falwell and Pat Robertson supplemented growing televangelism networks with influential political action committees, known as the Moral Majority and the Christian Coalition, respectively, alongside alternative tertiary education for young recruits in the form of Liberty University and Regent University. But southern zealots should not be understood as simple killjoys, for they have perverse pleasures all their own. Building upon the thinking of Randolph Bourne, scholar Allen Tullos has written that "in the puritan's renunciation of the world, the flesh, and the devil comes a paradoxical pleasure through the satisfaction taken in renunciation, in conspicuous humility, in the pleasure of acute self-control, and in the power to enforce these stern virtues and habits in others."[9]

Truly, gay writers have had good reason to excoriate southern politicians, if not send them up in high camp fashion. Hailing *Lawrence* as "seminal, landmark, a sea change," a decision to "go get yourself all wet with," San Francisco journalist Mark Morford described successive Senate floor leaders Trent Lott of Mississippi and Bill Frist of Tennessee as at the center of "the Right's political oligarchy, the sneering Republican apocalyptics who are right this minute scrunched and apoplectic and immediately proposing a major change to the U.S. Constitution to block gay marriage forever, to try and protect the 'sanctity' of God-given man/woman missionary-position 50-percent-divorce-rate marriage in this country."[10]

Marriage, the Constitution, and the South are indeed crucial here, but in ways that many have overlooked. Long before civil unions were pushed to the top of the so-called gay agenda, LGBT reformers had used the "miscegenation analogy" to craft legal arguments against sodomy restrictions and to build political support for equal rights. If straight citizens should be allowed to associate and procreate with any adult partner of their choosing, regardless of race—as *Loving v. Virginia* affirmed in terms of marriage rights—then why should gay or bisexual citizens not have the right to masturbate and copulate with any adults of their choosing, regardless of gender? Constitutional specialist Janet Halley has said that such "like race" comparisons have so structured sexual-orientation advocacy in the United States that it is now difficult to conceive of arguments without them. However, queer activists in and outside the South are increasingly looking elsewhere in the Constitution—and beyond it—to make compelling claims for sexual freedom predicated upon other principles, American and otherwise.[11]

The *Lawrence* legal team downplayed the cross-racial character of the arrestees, not to mention the sexual act itself, forbidding interviews with their clients in the lead-up to the Supreme Court hearing. As scholar Siobhan Somerville has noted in her skillful essay "Queer *Loving*," "the racial identities [were] unmarked in the official documents related to the . . . decision." So what happened to the second litigant Tyron Garner, effaced as well by the legal abbreviation of the case name? How were Garner and others viewed through the eyes of Harris County neighbors and arresting officers? Sophisticate Hendrik Hertzberg of the *New Yorker* advised keeping not just the state but all of us outside of an abstracted zone of privacy: "What the officers found Lawrence and Garner doing is really none of our business, any more than it was Texas's." I beg to differ.[12]

Joseph Quinn, William Lilly, and fellow deputies were dispatched to the leafy, three-hundred-unit, East Houston apartment complex where John Lawrence lived after a false report of a weapons disturbance, phoned in by a man later arrested himself. This particular ruse capitalized upon a knee-jerk suburban association of blacks with violent crime and guns. Further, interracial homosexual intercourse proved uniquely anathema in a southern legal universe still federally supervised in its dismantling of Jim Crow segregation, yet rapidly falling into line behind the constitutionally dubious 1996 federal Defense of Marriage Act signed by Bill Clinton, with state statutes and constitutional amendments reiterating it in a panicky political overkill. Whereas more than twenty nations in Europe had adopted some form of civil partnership or marriage legislation for lesbian and gay couples by the early twenty-first century, twenty American states had adopted these antigay marriage provisions, again predominating in the South, with Mississippi—ever the extremity—passing its measure by an unmatched 86 percent of the electorate. Not since the civil rights era had the South mounted such massive resistance to social change.[13]

Thus, residents of the apartment community may have feared less that Lawrence had invited a black trick into his home than that Tyron Garner would become a long-term thing. As the 2000 U.S. Census demonstrated, lesbians and gay men were twice as likely as married heterosexuals to live with a partner of a different race. But there would have been speculation about the act itself. We can imagine the gossip as people gathered around the squad cars that warm September evening in 1998. If they assumed that their older white neighbor, dragged out in his underpants, had been anally penetrated by the younger black man—it seems it was the other way round—then they would have ruminated upon southern social hierarchies most reprehensibly upended: the surrender of white male privilege, the giving up of racial and gender dominance.[14]

In mainstream print media, the racial analogy was pursued on both sides of the sodomy debate around *Lawrence*. Echoing states rights arguments from roughly 50 and 150 years before—that is, from the civil rights and Civil War eras—conservative white editorialists for the *Richmond Times-Dispatch* and *Birmingham News* argued not that police get out of gay couples' bedrooms, but that the Supremes stop interfering in southern lawmaking. By contrast, northern writers—and even liberal columnists for the *Tuscaloosa News* and Memphis *Commercial Appeal*—praised the passing of outdated codes and the securing of due process for lesbian and gay people, with repeated references to *Brown*. The legal invocation of the Reconstruction-era Fourteenth Amendment in attempts to establish lesbians and gays—like American populations of African descent—as a class of citizens deserving of rights, helped to secure their fundamental "homosexual status," to use the words of the historians' brief. Instead of Fourteenth Amendment equal protection claims and broader right-to-privacy arguments, which would further avert our eyes from specific "homosexual conduct," litigants could have chosen to describe sentences of up to twenty years for consensual sex as "cruel and unusual punishment" under the Constitution's Eighth Amendment, as legal scholar Nan Hunter and others have suggested. A closer examination of the *Lawrence* case, as well as the *Hardwick* case and its antecedents, exposes and elaborates queer practices of the sort gay lawyers assiduously cover up with their references to—and their reverence for—a gay male private space. It also undermines the assumptions governing that imagined space.[15]

Nowhere inscribed in the Constitution or its amendments, a right to privacy developed through case law and judicial interpretation. As historian Marc Stein has shown, in a series of rulings from the 1950s through the 1970s addressed to obscenity, contraception, immigration, and abortion, the Supreme Court embarked upon a sexual revolution that was essentially conservative, "reject[ing] a libertarian and egalitarian vision of sexual citizenship." A legal notion of privacy was established, a realm into which the state ostensibly would not tread, with privacy rights ascribed most readily and in tightly delimited ways to heterosexual, usually marital relations. Norms of white middle-class respectability were maintained. Noting a similar pattern in the United Kingdom, theorist Merl Storr—building upon the work of Gayle Rubin and Lauren Berlant—argued that "for those who fall outside the bounds of married and/or heterosexual acceptability, the best that one can hope for is that one's sex acts . . . will enter the 'zone of privacy' by becoming decorporealized. In other words, the condition of tolerance is the desexualization of one's sexual identity."[16]

This is precisely what reform-minded gay attorneys have dictated to their clients. To some, *Lawrence* seemed a "dream case": two men involved in consensual sexual intercourse, unpaid, in a private home, in a state that had rewritten its sodomy law to apply only to homosexual acts. In the end, though the Court equivocated on Fourteenth Amendment equal protection of the laws to lesbians and gays, they nonetheless expanded the zone of privacy to encompass them. But at what cost? One need look no further than the *Lawrence* case itself. For the details that gay attorneys suppressed reveal a great deal about what they and the Court endorsed and what they would not.[17]

The scene at the East Houston apartments was far more complicated than appellate courts and advocates could countenance. The bogus 911 pay-phone weapons complaint came not from a homophobic neighbor, as many journalists rushed to conclude, but from another older gay white male, Robert Eubanks, described in one account as Lawrence's friend and Garner's boyfriend. However, such pat distinctions are never so clear, especially in nonmonogamous queer cultures that value multiple intimacies and recreational sex. Eubanks and Garner were visitors in the Lawrence home, and it seems all were drinking to excess. Eubanks decided to leave; Garner chose to stay. Eubanks, characterized as "sort of a redneck," purportedly departed in a fit of jealousy, precipitating the phone call. Lawrence and Garner promptly began—or resumed—sexual activity, which the deputies soon discovered. I might choose to view this, as seemingly no other writer has, as a threesome gone wrong, except that deputies claim not only to have found pornography strewn about the place but also a mysterious fourth man representing yet another racial identity, thirty-six-year-old Ramon Pelayo-Velez, whom they never charged.[18]

The so-called facts grow ever more murky and unreliable. In a rare post–Supreme Court interview with a favorably disposed, gay-identified legal scholar, Lawrence, nonetheless accompanied by his own attorney, claimed not to know Pelayo-Velez. So as a journalist and local activist speculate, since "Lawrence was apparently in the habit of taking friends in for shelter, [Pelayo-Velez may have] just let himself in that night." The inconsistencies and incredulities of the deputies' accounts led another legal scholar to conclude they may not have witnessed any sexual act at all. Indeed, given deputies' distortions and advocates' elisions, one right-wing conspiracy theorist, former Harris County Judge Janice Law, reckoned that the instigating phone call to the sheriff's office could only have been a setup by conniving gay activists. As with any narrative—journalistic, historical, legal, or otherwise—what the coppers saw is ultimately unknowable: partial, selective, incomplete. But what all this looks like is less a gay legal strategist's dream of two adults in the "privacy of their own bedroom" and more a multiracial, intergenerational, cross-class, gay sex party.[19]

Let's note now how similar this is to the "crime scene" in the earlier *Hardwick* incident. Hardly the "perfect test case" that his legal team claimed, Michael

Hardwick's arrest—and the complex circumstances surrounding it—had to be tidied up to make it comport with arguments about privacy and respectability. Yes, Hardwick was arrested for engaging in consensual sexual activity with another adult in his own bedroom. The illegal act was straightforward enough. But in Rosa Parks fashion, the lawyers wanted to characterize Hardwick's civil disobedience as that of a role model. "College educated," according to one account, Hardwick was, more precisely, a college dropout. Less an entrepreneur, with failed attempts at a landscaping business and health food store, his consistent occupation was as a gay bartender. Yes, there was marijuana in his bedroom, his lawyers conceded—in part to ensure the case would not be thrown out—even as they glossed over his past as an acid and heroin user requiring drug rehabilitation. But, again, how did an Atlanta police officer come to be in that bedroom?[20]

Arriving at 8:30 A.M. on 17 August 1982 to deliver what proved to be a faulty warrant involving a prior offense, Officer K. R. Torick climbed the stairs up the steep lot and onto the front porch of the small two-bedroom house Hardwick rented, a 1925 bungalow at 811 Ponce de Leon Place, with a commanding view of Atlanta's gay-identified Midtown section. So even from the porch, the copper may have peered through the window into the living room, where an unnamed friend I'll call Thomas "was passed out on the couch." Severely hungover and startled by the police officer, Thomas was "freaking out." When queried about Hardwick's whereabouts, Thomas apparently pointed down the hall to the master bedroom. What the officer saw next is not in dispute: Hardwick engaged in "mutual oral sex" with yet another unnamed friend I'll refer to as Richard. Hardwick reckoned that Officer Torick stood near the doorway observing him and Richard for about thirty-five seconds, the time between Hardwick's first hearing a noise and Torick's announcing his presence. Torick did not contest this, but insisted that his eyes were adjusting to the darkness. This I find suspect, since the room not only had a north-facing window but also two large east-facing windows which, barring blackout curtains, would no doubt have emitted the early morning sun. The point is, Torick was wide-eyed, rapt at the various sights. As with the *Lawrence* arrest, the officer spotted intoxicants. He then arrested Hardwick and Richard and prepared to take them to jail. The commotion by this time surely would have roused Hardwick's housemate who, if not already at work, would have emerged from the second bedroom—a fourth man I'll call Harold. This possibility intrigues me: that what the copper saw, again, was not so much two men in private, but "party boy" Michael Hardwick, as the *Washington Post* later called him, alongside the proverbial Tom, Dick, and Harry.[21]

A married schoolteacher, Richard would not go forward with the legal action, a problem for strategists who wanted to paint the picture of a couple wronged.

Hardwick agreed to "keep a low profile because we did not want the personal aspects of the case to come into it." However, after the Supreme Court defeat, by then coached in legalistic protocols, Hardwick became a "spokesman," selectively revealing details of the case, with constant references to "my house" and "the privacy of my own bedroom." But even as he and liberal reformers attempted to construct a wholesome gay homestead to be shielded from state incursions, the unelaborated practices there rendered a queer private space impossible, illogical. Even if we assume that the state would leave us alone, in solitude, it is the very communal nature of much queer practice that draws its attention. Like John Lawrence, Michael Hardwick had something of an open-door policy, which he attempted to cast in the best possible, Good Samaritan light. Couch-potato Thomas had gotten drunk at the bar where Hardwick worked; Hardwick had taken away his car keys, called a cab, and packed him off not to his own home—assuming he had one—but to Hardwick's. Hardwick came home later with Richard, yet another houseguest, in town to search for work. About Harold, the housemate, we know nothing. His name has fallen out of the public record, like the names of so many one-night stands that fade from memory. All constituted a queer collective household of porous boundaries, fluid membership, and a capacious—but not anonymous—furtive sexuality.[22]

What did the larger context of Hardwick's arrest reveal about queer sexual cultures in Atlanta? Whether or not Hardwick and Richard's morning performance concluded an evening of several acts involving other men too, they nonetheless would have been viewed by police as linked to a decades-long tradition of illicit group sex. "Homosexual sodomy," Georgia Attorney General Michael Bowers warned the Supreme Court with Pandora's box reasoning, "leads to other deviate practices, such as sadomasochism," "transvestism," and—in a redundancy— "group orgies." Though Hardwick's supporters were quick to point out that he had been accused of none of these, local history proved all too telling.[23]

Referred to by postwar sociologists, psychologists, and legal authorities as "anonymous," "casual," "impersonal," or worse, queer recreational sex—except in the largest cities like New York—was anything but. Outdoor cruising grounds brought together friends, friends of friends, acquaintances, and acquaintances of acquaintances whom one could expect to see out and about repeatedly, in a camaraderie of infinite combinations and permutations. "They do it in twos and threes and sometimes fives," said a veteran of plain-clothes, vice-squad entrapment teams in Atlanta in the 1970s. Likewise, sex parties in private homes were a key means by which gay Atlantans expanded social circles and incorporated new sexual migrants from the countryside, as even the mainstream daily *Atlanta Journal* reported in 1967 of one get-together for twenty-five men.[24]

However, a private sex party put an extraordinary onus and expense upon the host, as the most popular gay sex manual from the period attested. If lacking in sufficient numbers or sexual versatility of former playmates to invite along, the host and a friend would first have to go out to the bars or baths to "round up likely candidates" or have to place classified ads in gay periodicals. To avoid guests settling in, chatting, and watching TV, the guide recommended that the host greet them at the door naked, provide the social lubricant of alcohol, joints, and poppers (amyl nitrate), and "instruct two or three lieutenants to start the ball rolling on a pre-arranged cue." The householder was also advised to "close off whichever rooms you don't want invaded; lock up your valuables; and place towels, lubricants and ashtrays in conspicuous places." Further, I would add, the host would have to accept that neighbors might witness a large number of men going into a single residence at night, perhaps resulting in a call to police, especially if the racial makeup of the group did not comport to local standards.[25]

Thus, even for those lucky individuals who had a home all to themselves, the interracial, cross-class contact that writer Samuel Delany saw as the admirable hallmark of public sex would be foreshortened. "If *every* sexual encounter involves bringing someone back to your house," he explained, "the general sexual activity in a city will become anxiety-filled, class-bound, and choosy." That is, individuals would tend to interact with and bring home only those people most like themselves. "This is precisely *why* public rest rooms, peep shows, sex movies, bars with grope rooms, and parks with enough greenery are necessary for a relaxed and friendly sexual atmosphere in a democratic metropolis."[26]

So, beyond the possible foursome found on the morning of 17 August 1982, what connects Michael Hardwick to the freewheeling sexual experimentation of these public and quasi-public commercial spaces? Before delivering the warrant to his house, Officer Torick had *first* arrested Hardwick in midsummer 1982 for violating the open container ordinance. At seven o'clock in the morning, at the end of a long night, Hardwick walked out of the gay bar where he worked and tossed the beer he was drinking into a garbage can. Driving through the area, Torick would have to have observed closely to witness this brief moment of imbibing out of doors, because the "trash can" was positioned right "by the front door." But then Torick *would* have been observing closely. As Hardwick concluded, based on the homophobic harassment he suffered that morning, the officer "knew it was a homosexual bar."[27]

But not just any homosexual bar. Since the 1960s, the Cove enjoyed a distinctive reputation in Atlanta, which all major gay tourist guides acknowledged. It was located farther north than the cluster of gay bars along Peachtree Street and Ponce de Leon Avenue in Midtown. And it stayed open later, until 8:00 A.M., drawing a raucous crowd fueled by narcotics and a last-ditch quest for sex. It flouted the South's notorious blue laws by allowing the brown-bagging of alcohol on Sunday mornings after 3:00. Occupying a detached building surrounded by a large parking lot, it hosted riotous outdoor charity carnivals that included kissing booths. Moreover, the Cove was situated adjacent to Piedmont Park, within a well-established gay cruising area, through which Hardwick was walking when arrested. None of this Hardwick or his legal team seems ever to have mentioned.[28]

A pernicious mythology holds that queer southerners of the mid- to late twentieth century readily accepted their inferior status, indeed were ignorant of and lagging behind gay developments elsewhere. Protestant fundamentalism held sway, and "Atlanta homosexuals . . . dared not pry the closet door ajar." True, along with black and white churches, both black and white Atlanta newspapers castigated lesbians and gays in the 1970s. The *Atlanta Daily World* faced down the "bold," "unashamed" demands of "male homos," editorializing against equal rights and discrimination protections. An ostensibly more earnest "series on the life-styles of . . . homosexuals" in the *Journal* reported on "the bizarre side of Gay Atlanta," including the "people who lurk in the dark for a little affection." With brusque condescension, presuming knowledge of another's lack of knowledge, liberal reformers and even gay lawyers have asserted that Michael Hardwick and his fellow southerners did not "giv[e] these matters a lot of thought." As Yale law professor William Eskridge—himself a native southerner—maintained, "these folks were unaware of the 1969 Stonewall riots" in New York, a pivotal moment in gay history. This assertion is, quite simply, inaccurate.[29]

Forcing us to reconsider the bicoastal bias in timelines of American gay organizing, gay Atlantans staged public protests of police harassment as early as 1947, when twelve activists picketed the home of Mayor William Hartsfield, including men fired and turned out of their own homes after press coverage of a raid on a private party. Following in that tradition, gay pride marches, held on the June anniversary of Stonewall, focused on political concerns both local and national. With forceful calls for equal rights, the 1971 march proceeded up Atlanta's main street, Peachtree Street, to Piedmont Park, and the Gay Liberation Front (GLF) of Georgia demanded justice for the two hundred people imprisoned under the state sodomy statute. The 1972 march, with three hundred participants, followed a similar route, culminating in a GLF rally in the park. Seeking to reclaim "the Hill," protestors condemned the police closure of a road into Piedmont Park as an attack on gay sociability, an affront to queer cruisers. Activists spoke out on TV and radio in support of the "innate rights of free and open expression." But this was only the latest in a series of large-scale battles over sexuality and public space in Atlanta, dating back at least to the 1950s.[30]

Over a one-week period in 1953, in the basement toilet of the Atlanta Public Library, police voyeurs used a two-way mirror to arrest twenty men having sex, in what one defense attorney called "the most famous case of the decade." Defendants' names and addresses appeared in the local press, they lost their jobs, and though only one served jail time, most were literally run out of town under court order. Meanwhile, the Atlanta City Council took a bold stand on the issue of intimate activities in racially segregated Piedmont Park. In 1954, in a progressive move that attracted international media coverage, they declared the Midtown park to be the city's official lovers' lane. They encouraged young white heterosexual couples—who had abandoned the porch-and-parlor court-ship of the private home to go out on the town in cars—to end their nights not on the dangerous dirty back roads but rather on the public terrain of Piedmont Park, where law enforcement could keep an eye on things—thereby taking over a responsibility previously left to parents. Cars were parked bumper to bumper, and under the phenomenon known as double dating, couples could be found in both the front and back seats—all of which we might think of in terms of state-sanctioned group sex. All was bliss until the Baptist Ministers Association intervened. The clergy publicly declared what many already knew: gay men also were having sex in the park. Methodist pastors and the PTA joined the outcry and pressured the police department to step up patrols after dark. The City Council approved massive expenditures for lighting systems to achieve what Mayor Hartsfield called a "near daylight" effect. Stings against men engaged in homosexual activity there continued through the 1990s.[31]

Scholar Mark Turner has creatively and effectively interrogated queer cruis-ing practices extending back to at least the eighteenth century. Turner positions the cruiser against the flaneur, that classic figure of urban modernity who ob-jectively surveys the city as he walks with confidence and purpose in a rational straight line, along the grid, from point A to point B. The cruiser, by contrast, meanders, wanders, "loiter[s] with intent," as Turner brilliantly described it, seeking to overcome modernist alienation, looking for connection in the eyes of strangers, moments of recognition that may or may not lead to sexual in-tercourse. But as we consider the mutually constituting relationship between sexuality and space, we see that, unlike the high-density foot traffic of New York and London, most cities and rural areas fostered twentieth-century cul-tures of cruising dependent foremost on the automobile. Here the reciprocal gaze of Turner's *Backward Glances* is often reflected in rearview mirrors, where one looks hopefully for the taillights of the car that has just passed, until both drivers tap their brakes, signaling their mutual desire. As should now be evident, police officers participated in the erotic gaze of cruising over time, endorsing some behaviors with a nod and a wink, while vilifying others with a search-light, handcuffs, and even more elaborate modes of surveillance. In the 1960s, Atlanta's sex offense registry—a regional model—recorded "known offenders" on three-by-five-inch index cards not only with physical descriptions, including age, race, and "type of perversion," but also, tellingly, with the "make and model" of their cars.[32]

During the 1970s and 1980s, after Atlanta police closed off Piedmont Park to automobiles after dark, car cruising diverted into neighboring streets and alongside smaller parks. Whereas sex workers tended to walk along Cypress Street, with drivers pursuing them in what policemen called the "Indianapolis 500," most cruising followed well-rutted streets from the west side of Piedmont Park to the east. Winn Park's "popularity as a gathering spot result[ed] in late-night traffic jams." And because cruisers abandoned their cars to slip down into the narrow, low-lying gardens just below headlamp sightlines, residents pressured the city to put "parking restrictions on Westminster Drive to the north of the small park and on one block of Lafayette Drive to the south." Continuing eastward, Westminster Drive crossed Piedmont Avenue and came to a dead end, deep in a ravine. There, cruisers walked along the railroad bed and had sex in the trackside wooded trails. Back in their cars, skirting north around the top of Piedmont Park, drivers came down Monroe Drive and into a small cluster of streets forming an ideal rectangular circuit known as Dutch Valley. "The Trails" along the railroad tracks could also be reached by footpaths leading downward from these streets. But more importantly, Dutch Valley Place and Dutch Valley Road led away from residential neighborhoods and into a small commercial and light industrial district with several one- and two-story detached office buildings and warehouses. Their grounds included small car parks, herbaceous borders, grassy lawns in front and—perhaps most importantly—wooded lots around back, where groups congregated. Instead of trespassing, we might think of cruisers as reappropriating these spaces, staking a legitimate claim to valuable urban lands otherwise un- or underutilized, for all of these businesses were closed in the evening and early morning hours—all of them except for a discreet S&M club without signage, along with Michael Hardwick's workplace, the Cove.[33]

Around the same time Michael Hardwick was arrested, in a speech addressed to "Racism in the Gay Male World," the multitalented historian, memoirist, playwright, and novelist Martin Duberman bemoaned "the gay movement's evolution from radicalism to reform . . . Originating in fierce anger and initially marked by broad-gauged demands for social change," it had degenerated into a "well-behaved, self protective association, and in the process abandon[ed] demands for challenging the vast inequities in our social system, substituting (at best) token liberalism." Indeed, speaking at the seventh annual benefit dinner for the Lambda Legal Defense Fund, key advocates in the *Hardwick* case, Duberman denounced "prosperous white male recruits who had previously disdained association with a movement then regarded as controlled by 'impractical,' noisome visionaries. The more those who earlier eschewed the gay movement have now joined it," he added, "the more their bland deportment and narrow social perspectives have come to dominate: they have 'upgraded' our image while diluting demands for substantive social change." Unsurprisingly, several black-tied white A-list gays walked out on Duberman's speech.[34]

Such misguided gay attorneys have pursued the withdrawal method of state sexual surveillance, advocating that the state pull out, beat a hasty retreat, once convinced that homeowning gays are reassuringly normal, respectable—indeed, perfect. Obviously, perfectionism always fails. And the bartered withdrawals are never complete, inclined as we humans are to peer into windows, look over the fence, and—like the Atlanta police officer—stand wide-eyed in doorways. Even when we don't actually see, we speculate, we compare, and—in the words of playwright Joe Orton—we judge the ostensibly "private" lives of others as "shocking." Such judgments, forever in gossipy circulation, should be made more not less explicit in public discourse. I would simply point to new criteria for judgment, based upon notions of consent, honesty, responsibility—and pleasure. Thus, those who want group sex—in survey after survey, the most popular sexual fantasy—would get it. And get safe public space for it.[35]

Geographically, the overlapping spaces with which Michael Hardwick was associated and through which he moved and was pursued—the house (811 Ponce de Leon Place), neighborhood (Virginia Highland), park (Piedmont Park), and cruising area (Dutch Valley)—demonstrate the fluidity of public/private boundaries. Characterized less by desires to forward the idealized, romanticized, long-term-committed dyad, they can make free, public, egalitarian group sex appear very appealing by contrast. Conceptually, given state surveillance there and potential state jurisdiction everywhere, they evidence the impossibility of queer private space. By imagining a legal zone of privacy—a sphere intimate and vulnerable, purportedly beyond state purview—jurists in fact affirm, quite explicitly, those people, practices, and places that the state supports, endorses, privileges, and protects. Less the cordoning off of a vacuous space apart from the state, the process involves the articulation of socially approved behaviors and attributes rewarded by the state—as with marital benefits, tax incentives for child rearing, general approbation. Practically, the American custom of knowing your neighbors' sex lives is older even than the nation. So we should give up the privacy trap.

In this sense, queer activists and intellectuals should advocate less a left coalition of essentialized identity groups based upon *who we are,* a set of marginalized *people* of color, women, gays, and the working-class—though such identity formations and coalitions have proven politically useful. Rather, we should advocate more a collective struggle based upon *what we do,* in support of particular ethical *acts,* personified by rough sleepers, squatters, and ramblers who—along with sexual adventurers—reappropriate underutilized private property, as well as by those who exchange money for sex, who cross-dress, who cross genders and, to move even further, free thinkers, radical conversationalists, dancers, ravers, and drug-takers who promote group bliss.

State sexual regulation, popularly conceived as a historical delimiting of space for sodomites, has in fact—with even greater diligence—proliferated spaces for particular sexual normativities, notably in suburbia. The state achieves this through marriage incentives, inheritance statutes, interstate highway acts, and subsidized mortgages, to name just a few measures. Thus, the state need not withdraw from the private bedrooms of sexual nonconformists, as these are the very individuals least likely to own such hallowed private property, given the decades of governmentally crafted disadvantage. Simply put, if we now recognize sexual pleasure as fundamental to human happiness, we must ask: Where are the homeless to have sex? What about those who live in crowded households with little if any privacy? What about that sixteen-year-old lesbian daughter in a xenophobic parental home? Determining how and, crucially, *where* these individuals are to attain sexual gratification is an urgent matter for state consideration—and action.

In the post-*Lawrence* South, arrests for sodomy may cease, with some decline in the attendant discriminations based on homosexual status, but arrests for sex-related "disorderly conduct" will surely continue in parks and other public spaces, especially if there are more than two individuals involved and if they are in other ways on the margins: indigent, homeless, involved in sex work. They will continue until southern queer activists articulate the historical and environmental rationales for public sex, as well as its ethical legitimacy. Often lacking adequate sexual education, not to mention frank discussions of homosexuality, so long taboo, men young and old have made outdoor cruising grounds a vital form of community initiation, imitation, and belonging, especially in warm southern climes and in poor and overcrowded environs where indoor space is unavailable. Valuing the giving and receiving of human pleasure, these men have evolved elaborate, subtle modes of communicating consent, even when there is no verbal exchange, as with the extended arm that either invites or blocks access, the change in stance that denotes interest or the lack thereof. In public discourse, candor about the joys of recreational sex increases the likelihood of "responsible" practices in the best moral (as opposed to moralistic) sense: foreseeing potential adverse consequences and acting to minimize them. Only when straitlaced gay advocates shake off mainstream worries of "promiscuity," abandon the respectable ideal of privatized coupledom, and actively proclaim the virtues of adventurousness, courage, experimentation, and fellow feeling in sexual activity can we begin to realize a viable and truly worthwhile political project of sexual freedom.

So I would encourage queer community activists to soft-pedal appeals to constitutional protections: negative freedoms *from* "government intrusion," *from* religious persecution—though a *real*, workable separation of church and state would help. I would appeal instead to those affirmative Jeffersonian ideals articulated in that other founding document, the Declaration of Independence: the notion that the state not just safeguard but support individuals and groups in their quest for life, liberty, and happiness. We'll have to undo generations of moral and economic thought that has perverted notions of the good life, equating the pursuit of happiness with the pursuit of property, resulting in a now trademark American acquisitiveness. Instead of the individual striving for and enjoying of possessions—literally, making a joy of things—we might imagine new ways of enjoying each other's company.

NOTES

Portions of this essay were presented in an inaugural professorial lecture at King's College London, 6 February 2007, and at the conference, Beyond *Brown:* How the Supreme Court Shaped the Modern South, University of Sussex, 24 March 2007. The title is adopted from the Joe Orton play, *What the Butler Saw* (London: Methuen, 1969). In it, a character proclaims, "Your private life is your own affair. I find it shocking nonetheless." The author thanks Tomas Georgiadis for the use of his Athens home, where the essay was drafted, September 2006, and is grateful to Cynthia Blakely and Wesley Chenault for pursuing leads in Atlanta and sharing their insights. The author is also indebted to Noeline Arnott, Susan Castillo, Michael Cowan, Nancy Koppelman, and those mentors, colleagues, friends, and acquaintances whose work is cited herein.

1. "What Gay Studies Taught the Court," *Washington Post,* 13 July 2003.
2. *Bowers v. Hardwick,* 478 U.S. 186 (1986), 188. See also Nayan Shah, "Policing Privacy, Migrants, and the Limits of Freedom," *Social Text* 23 (Fall/Winter 2005): 275–84.
3. Richard Kluger, *Simple Justice: The History of* Brown v. Board of Education *and Black America's Struggle for Equality* (New York: Random House, 1975), 315–39, 353–56.
4. Mark D. Jordan, *The Invention of Sodomy in Christian Theology* (Chicago: University of Chicago Press, 1997); David A. J. Richards, *The Case for Gay Rights: From* Bowers *to* Lawrence *and Beyond* (Lawrence: University Press of Kansas, 2005), 74; Jonathan Ned Katz, *Gay American History: Lesbians and Gay Men in the U.S.A.* (New York: Thomas Y. Crowell, 1976), 23–24; *Mississippi Code, 1972,* vol. 22, sec. 97–29–59; Johnson, Gulling, Heltzer and Burg, P.L.C., Attorneys at Law, "Until This Happens, Call Us," *Lavender Magazine* (n.p.: n.p., 1997).

5. Peter Irons, *The Courage of Their Convictions: Sixteen Americans Who Fought Their Way to the Supreme Court* (New York: Free Press, 1988), 385; John D'Emilio, "Capitalism and Gay Identity," in *Powers of Desire: The Politics of Sexuality*, ed. Ann Snitow, Christine Stansell, and Sharon Thompson (New York: Monthly Review Press, 1983), 100–113.

6. "What Gay Studies Taught the Court"; "In Changing the Law of the Land, Six Justices Turned to Its History," *New York Times*, 20 July 2003. The brief is reprinted, along with commentary by the lead author, George Chauncey, in "'What Gay Studies Taught the Court': The Historians' Amicus Brief in *Lawrence v. Texas*," *GLQ: Journal of Gay and Lesbian Studies* 10 (2004): 509–38. On related briefs, see Linda K. Kerber, "New Perspectives on Marriage in Early America: The Briefs of Historians for Same-Sex Marriage Cases," paper presented at the University of London, 30 October 2006. On the relationship between homosexuality and bestiality, see Jens Rydstrom, *Sinners and Citizens: Bestiality and Homosexuality in Sweden, 1880–1950* (Chicago: University of Chicago Press, 2003).

7. Chauncey, "What Gay Studies Taught the Court," 515, 520, 525; Michel Foucault, *The History of Sexuality*, vol. 1: *An Introduction*, trans. Robert Hurley (New York: Pantheon, 1978), 43.

8. Chauncey, "What Gay Studies Taught the Court"; Lisa Duggan and Nan D. Hunter, *Sex Wars: Sexual Dissent and Political Culture* (New York: Routledge, 1995), 155–72; David M. Halperin, *One Hundred Years of Homosexuality and Other Essays on Greek Love* (New York: Routledge, 1990); M. Lee Badgett, *Money, Myths, and Change: The Economic Lives of Lesbians and Gay Men* (Chicago: University of Chicago Press, 2001).

9. Didi Herman, *The Anti-Gay Agenda: Orthodox Vision and the Christian Right* (Chicago: University of Chicago Press, 1997); Allen Tullos, *Habits of Industry: White Culture and the Transformation of the Carolina Piedmont* (Chapel Hill: University of North Carolina Press, 1989), 38.

10. "How to Learn to Love Sodomy," *SF Gate* (San Francisco), 2 July 2003.

11. Kevin Mumford, "The Miscegenation Analogy Revisited: Same-Sex Marriage as a Civil Rights Story," *American Quarterly* 57 (2005): 523–31; Janet Halley, "'Like Race' Arguments," in *What's Left of Theory? New Work on the Politics of Literary Theory*, ed. Judith Butler, John Guillory, and Kendall Thomas (New York: Routledge, 2000), 40–74.

12. Siobhan B. Somerville, "Queer *Loving*," *GLQ: Journal of Gay and Lesbian Studies* 11 (2005): 346; "Unnatural Law," *New Yorker*, 16 December 2002, 33.

13. Andrew Koppelman, "Dumb and DOMA: Why the Defense of Marriage Act Is Unconstitutional," *Iowa Law Review* 83 (1997): 1–33.

14. Somerville, "Queer *Loving*," 346; Tavia Simmons and Martin O'Connell, "Married-Couples and Unmarried Partner Households, 2000: Census 2000 Special Reports, CEN-5" (Washington, D.C.: U.S. Bureau of the Census, 2003). One legal scholar suggested, by contrast, that Deputy Lilly would have been offended to see a fellow black man penetrated by a white man. The lead officer that evening, Deputy Quinn,

was white. See Dale Carpenter, "The Unknown Past of *Lawrence v. Texas,*" *Michigan Law Review* 102 (2004): 1503.

15. "Unaccountable Politicians: Court Usurped States' Legislative Role," *Richmond Times-Dispatch,* 6 July 2003; "High Court Decree Ends Morals Legislation," *Birmingham News,* 26 June 2003; "The Argument against the Recent Supreme Court Decision in Lawrence v. Texas Is Not New," *Tuscaloosa News,* 13 July 2003; "Intolerance Suffers a Judicial Setback," *Commercial Appeal* (Memphis), 28 June 2003; Duggan and Hunter, *Sex Wars,* 81.

Of syndicated columnists' views of the arrest, I particularly like that of humorist Joe Bob Briggs, UPI, 27 June 2003, the only one to meditate at any length on it: "John Geddes Lawrence and Tyron Garner are two of the unluckiest guys on the face of the planet. They were going at it one night—let's imagine they had soft lighting and incense and their moods were euphoric—but, unbeknownst to them, the Harris County police received a report of a 'weapons disturbance' in their apartment building. First unlucky fact: they forgot to lock the door. Second unlucky fact: the investigating cops were so gung-ho that they just barged in. Third unlucky fact: our two lovers were so oblivious to outside influence that they continued to shag even after the police entered the room. Fourth unlucky fact: one of the cops was such a good student at the police academy that he actually *remembered* the sodomy statutes. . . . Fifth unlucky fact: the cop is such a total Boy Scout that he decides to make an actual arrest. Sixth unlucky fact: the cop's captain lets the charges go through. Seventh unlucky fact: the judge fails to throw the case out. Because let's face it—how many *years* could go by before another gay couple was seen having sex in the privacy of their own bedroom by a duly constituted peace officer?" Briggs estimates fifty; the Supreme Court docket suggests seventeen; state case law shows it's much less. Joe Bob Briggs, "Sodomy Sodomy Sodomy," UPI, 27 June 2003.

About *Hardwick,* Nan Hunter has stated: "What brought us within striking distance on this case was the essential conservatism of the claim—a privacy argument based on the intersection of core values of individual identity and a-man's-home-is-his-castle locational sanctity" (Duggan and Hunter, *Sex Wars,* 81). For her further observations on the decision's equal protection and privacy implications, see *Sex Wars,* 96–100.

Two other scholars, examining the rhetorical strategies of the opinion, note an ill-disguised abhorrence of things queer. "The rhetoric of *Bowers v. Hardwick* is shot through with the traces of the homophobic passion whose relevance the Court's decision has taken such great pains to deny. That passion eclipses the cool constitutional reason by which the Supreme Court claims to be bound, and belies [Justice Byron] White's contention that the *Hardwick* decision has nothing to do with the 'imposition of the Justices' own choice of values regarding the legal regulation of gay and lesbian sexuality" (Kendall Thomas, "*Corpus Juris [Hetero]Sexualis:* Doctrine, Discourse, and Desire in *Bowers v. Hardwick,*" in *A Queer World: The Center for Lesbian and Gay Studies Reader,* ed. Martin Duberman [New York: New York University Press, 1997], 446). Never referring to Hardwick by name, the decision cast him as an "unsympathetic character . . . undeserving of constitutional recognition and protection." He was represented through an "ascribed voice as forceful and threatening, . . . an impertinent, aggressive deviant whose behaviors and beliefs threaten the traditions that have made the United States a great country." Of homosexual sodomy, Chief Justice Warren Burger's concurring opinion said that its "very mention . . . is a disgrace to human nature." For this and for further evidence of the silences around sexual acts, see Glenda Conway, "Inevitable Reconstructions: Voice and Ideology in Two Landmark U.S. Supreme Court Opinions," *Rhetoric and Public Affairs* 6 (2003): 489, 490, 502.

16. Marc Stein, "*Boutelier* and the U.S. Supreme Court's Sexual Revolution," *Law and History Review* 23 (2005): 500; Merl Storr, "New Labour, New Britain, New Sexual Values?" *Social Epistemology* 15 (2001): 124.

17. Carpenter, "Unknown Past of *Lawrence v. Texas.*"

18. Margot Sanger-Katz, "The Fourth Man: The Unsolved Mystery at the Center of a Historic Gay Rights Case," *Legal Affairs* 5 (2005), http://www.legalaffairs.org/ issues/July-August-2005/scene_sangorkatz_julaug05.msp.

19. William N. Eskridge, "'Dishonorable Passions': The Crime against Nature in America," paper presented to the University of Texas School of Law Faculty Colloquia, Austin, 6 May 2005; Sanger-Katz, "Fourth Man"; Carpenter, "Unknown Past of *Lawrence v. Texas*"; Judge Janice Law, *Sex Appealed: Was the U.S. Supreme Court Fooled?* (Austin, Tex.: Eakins Press, 2005).

20. Irons, *Courage of Their Convictions*, 382, 396–97; "The Hero Who Lost His Cause," *Atlanta Constitution*, 1 September 1986.

21. *Polk's Atlanta Directory, 1983* (Richmond, Va.: R. L. Polk and Co., 1983); Keller Williams Realty, "811 Ponce de Leon Place" sales sheet, 2006; Irons, *Courage of Their Convictions*, 395; "Another Hero," *Around the Clock* (Atlanta), 25 January 1985. Quoted in "Hero Who Lost His Cause," Art Harris further described Hardwick as "tall and trim, like a *GQ* model in jeans and bright Perry Ellis shirt unbuttoned to the waist."

   Hardwick said that Harold had left for work, but his great care in specifying the rationales for visitors' and residents' whereabouts suggests a legal coaching that I don't fully trust. Further, references to Harold as his "roommate"—not "housemate"— hold out the prospect of even more tenants in the two-bedroom house.

22. Irons, *Courage of Their Convictions*, 399, 403.

23. Ibid., 387.

24. The definitive sociological study remains Laud Humphreys, *Tearoom Trade: Impersonal Sex in Public Places* (1970; reprint, New York: Aldine de Gruyter, 1975); "Never Seen Anything Like That," *Atlanta Journal*, 2 October 1967. Describing a sharp reversal of the state optic and unwittingly revealing the careful maneuvers through which an often unspoken consent is negotiated in public sex environments, another Atlanta officer said cruisers "sometimes . . . look at you like you're not there. Other times, they'll jump out of bushes and from behind trees. Or you'll see them peeping out like scared rabbits" (*Atlanta Journal*, 13 May 1975). Certainly, cruisers

had reason to fear police. Officers' rhetorical dehumanization, indeed animalization, of them would be among their more benign forms of harassment.

25. Charles Silverman and Edmund White, *The Joy of Gay Sex: An Intimate Guide for Gay Men to the Pleasures of a Gay Lifestyle* (New York: Crown, 1977), 172.

26. Samuel R. Delany, *Times Square Red, Times Square Blue* (New York: New York University Press, 1999), 127.

27. Irons, *Courage of Their Convictions*, 394.

28. Ronnie Anderson, ed., *International Guild Guide, 1970: Gay Listing* (Washington, D.C.: Guild Publishers, 1970), 34, Hall-Carpenter Archives, London School of Economics, London, Eng.; *Bob Damron's Address Book '82* (San Francisco, Calif.: Bob Damron Enterprises, 1982), 167, 171; Frances Green, ed., *Gayellow Pages, The National Edition: USA and Canada, for Gay Women and Men* (New York: Renaissance House, 1982), 96; *Places of Interest, 1984: Gay Guide with Maps, USA and Canada* (n.p.: n.p., 1984), 87–88, GLBT Historical Society Library and Archives, San Francisco, Calif.; advertisement, *The (Atlanta) Barb*, September 1976.

29. Eskridge, "Dishonorable Passions"; "Why Homos?" *Atlanta Daily World*, 7 September 1978; "Homo Troubles," *Atlanta Daily World*, 28 December 1978; "Gay Can Be a Sad or Dangerous World," *Atlanta Journal*, 13 May 1975; Martin Duberman, *Stonewall* (New York: Dutton, 1993). On Atlanta churches, see John Howard, "The Library, the Park, and the Pervert: Public Space and Homosexual Encounter in Post–World War II Atlanta," in *Carryin' On in the Lesbian and Gay South*, ed. John Howard (New York: New York University Press, 1997), 107–31.

30. On the bicoastal bias, see John Howard, "Regional Distinctiveness in the Southern Lesbian and Gay Experience," paper presented to the American Studies Association, Nashville, Tenn., October 1994; Howard, "Library"; Jodie Lind Talley, "A Queer Miracle in Georgia: The Origins of Gay-Affirming Religion in the South" (M.A. thesis, Georgia State University, 2006), 55–57; "Gay Liberationists Plan March Here," *Atlanta Journal*, 25 June 1971; "Gay Group to March for 'Pride Week,'" *Atlanta Journal*, 23 June 1972; Cal Gough, "Atlanta's Gay and Lesbian Communities Since Stonewall: A Chronology, 1969–1989," unpublished manuscript, 1990, Atlanta-Fulton Public Library, Atlanta. Talley helpfully critiqued both contemporaneous and later historical accounts of the South before 1969 as a gay cultural wasteland—a "desert," a place of "darkness" (Talley, "A Queer Miracle in Georgia," 23–25).

31. Howard, "Library"; Beth Bailey, *From Front Porch to Back Seat: Courtship in Twentieth-Century America* (Baltimore, Md.: Johns Hopkins University Press, 1988); "Deviates Gain Tolerance," *Atlanta Journal*, 1 August 1968; "Gay Can Be a Sad or Dangerous World"; "Under Sodomy Laws," *Southern Voice*, 1 September 1994.

32. Mark Turner, *Backward Glances: Cruising the Queer Streets of New York and London* (London: Reaktion, 2003), 35; Earl C. Morgan, "Interim Report of Governor's Commission to Study Sex Offenses" (Birmingham, Ala.: District Attorney's Office, 1967), 6. On the dynamics of car cruising, see John Howard, *Men Like That: A Southern Queer History* (Chicago: University of Chicago Press, 1999), 99–115; Tim Retzloff, "Cars and Bars: Assembling Gay Men in Postwar Flint, Michigan," in *Cre-*

ating a Place for Ourselves: Lesbian, Gay, and Bisexual Community Histories, ed. Brett
Beemyn (New York: Routledge, 1997). Retzloff argued that "Homosexual men, and
bisexual men interested in homosexual encounters, met in locations marked as gay,
locations largely determined and significantly shaped by privately owned motor ve-
hicles. A homosexual milieu nearly invisible to heterosexual [citizens] took shape not
only in newly accessible gay and semi-gay bars, but literally on the streets, in moving
and parked cars" (228). He continued, "Like tearooms, baths, and bars before them,
car cruising, car sex, and homosexually active parking lots all became acknowledged
sites where gay and bisexual men could claim public spaces as their own. . . . By the
beginning of the 1970s, phrases such as 'car hop' (to solicit passing motorists from
the sidewalk), 'curb service' (a gay man on foot who cruises drivers), and 'road queen'
(a gay hitchhiker) were entrenched in homosexual argot" (244).

33. "Residents Protest Gays in Winn Park," *Atlanta Journal*, 28 November 1972; "Gay
Can Be a Sad or Dangerous World"; *ADC's Street Map of Atlanta and DeKalb County,
Georgia* (Alexandria, Va.: ADC, 1990), 19. Of course, Piedmont Park was a free alternative to the commercial space of the Cove. A source for the 13 May 1975 story, Fred
"used to go to Piedmont Park. He would nap until 11 at night, get up and stay in the
park all night, go home, take a shower, and go to work."

34. Martin Duberman, *Left Out: The Politics of Exclusion, Essays, 1964–1999* (New
York: Basic, 1999), 347–48.

35. In their pathbreaking essay, "Sex in Public," Lauren Berlant and Michael Warner
applaud transgressive sexual acts—scenes that intend "nonheteronormative worlds
because they refused to pretend that privacy was their ground; because they were
forms of sociability that unlinked money and family from the scene of the good life,
because they made sex the consequence of public mediations and collective self-
activity in a way that made for unpredicted pleasures; because, in turn, they attempted to make a context of support for their practices; because their pleasures were
not purchased by a redemptive pastoralism of sex, nor by mandatory amnesia about
failure, shame, and aversion" (reprinted in *Queer Studies: An Interdisciplinary Reader*,
eds. Robert J. Corber and Stephen Valocchi [Oxford: Blackwell, 2003], 179).

The Womanless Wedding: Masculinity, Cross-Dressing, and Gender Inversions in the Modern South

Craig Thompson Friend

When Dr. Rufus S. Rice died in March 1923, he left behind a most curious photograph in which he is decked out in a white bridal gown, complete with train and veil, white gloves, and patent-leather shoes. Born in 1863 Arkansas, Rice became a highly successful small-town physician, widely known for his mischievous sense of humor and his soft spot for treating local children to candy and sodas. He also, at least once, was the bride in a womanless wedding (see figure 1).

Photographs like Rice's may be found in family albums across the twentieth-century South and, to a lesser degree, throughout the United States. Sponsored by civic or charitable institutions, Womanless Weddings were (and are) organized fund-raisers in which men played all the roles. Individuals fondly remember their fathers, husbands, sons, brothers, and other male family members participating in these charades. As one person reminisced, "One of my most delightful childhood memories is of seeing my daddy in an evening gown at a 'Womanless Wedding' fund-raiser. Good thing mama was an excellent seamstress because he sure was a lanky, wide-shouldered bridesmaid." And then, sarcastically, she added, "I guess fifty years ago, country people were just too ignorant to know the mortal dangers of cross-dressing for fun one day a year."[1]

Indeed, the South's cultural climate has changed dramatically over the past half century, imbuing Womanless Weddings with gendered and sexual tensions that may have existed in the past but certainly went without public commentary. Before the 1960s, white men could be sure that their masculinity and whiteness granted them authority and license in southern society. They controlled family, politics, and economy; they established and sustained racial and gendered

Figure 1. Dr. Rufus Rice of Rogers, Arkansas, as the bride in a "womanless wedding" held by the Roger Elks Lodge in the early 1920s. Negative #N008205, courtesy of the Rogers Historical Museum, Rogers, Ark.

etiquette; and consequently, they could violate those socially constructed barriers at pleasure usually without censure. There was nothing untoward or questionable about civic and business leaders cross-dressing to perform for charity because they dictated the rules by which their actions were judged.[2]

In those decades, the Womanless Wedding was one of several carnivalesque "rituals of inversion," a longstanding tradition within Western civilization. As historian Peter Burke explained, such mock weddings were "a time of institutionalized disorder, a set of rituals of reversal" when "the bride might be a man or the groom a bear." In early modern Europe and early America, the participants were from the lower classes, and their targets were the status and pretensions of the upper class. The objects of their ridicule most often graciously accepted the frivolity as cultural recognition of their socioeconomic rank and as a much-needed "safety valve" to release social tensions in harmless ways. But nineteenth-century America witnessed a curtailing of uncontained and uncontrolled masquerade. From the charivarian carousing typically attached to weddings, the Womanless Wedding evolved as a more structured form of revelry.[3]

Although class tensions remained central aspects of such spectacles in the more democratic culture of the twentieth-century United States, the Womanless Wedding produced a different type of leveling experience. Instead of mockery by economic, gendered, or racial minorities, these rituals featured upper-class men of any given community parodying women and the lower classes. Like Dr. Rufus Rice, participants in Womanless Weddings were often socially prominent white men who found opportunity in the spectacle to mock those few aspects of southern society that tested their social strictures—strong-willed women, premarital pregnancies, effeminate men, unruly blacks. While audiences howled at prominent community leaders acting silly in women's clothing, the actors lampooned their wives, families, neighbors, and the very community standards that they represented.

If there is a litmus test for when the cultural challenges of the civil rights, feminist, and gay rights movements began to refashion white men's control of southern society, then it may very well be changes in the Womanless Wedding. By the 1990s, male cross-dressing no longer signified the freedom that accompanied uncontested masculinity and whiteness. Instead, performing in such an event forced participants to face their own anxieties over cross-dressing, same-sex intimacy, and homosexuality. In efforts to protect children from the ribald humor found in earlier versions of the Womanless Wedding, organizations produced more "family-friendly" adaptations that reinforced rather than mocked community standards of morality. In the wake of the civil rights and feminist movements, attacks on race and gender became taboo. And with the emergence of a visible gay culture, the sexual connotations of cross-dressing confronted organizers, participants, and audiences.

In the United States, the Womanless Wedding seems to have emerged from late nineteenth-century community festivals during which the event was occasionally, spontaneously, and rather informally performed by men assuming the male and female roles. Anthropologist James L. Peacock conjectures that the Womanless Wedding emanated from post–Civil War minstrelsy and reinforced white southern fears of the unity of the black male and white female through joining the blackface male and the transvestite bride on stage. Minstrelsy and vaudeville most certainly made gendered and racial impersonation an acceptable form of entertainment by the 1880s. Among the first, more organized Womanless Weddings was an 1890 performance at North Carolina's Trinity College, later Duke University. By the mid-1910s, the Womanless Wedding became somewhat standardized. Around 1918, two women—Bulamae Sympson of Bardstown, Kentucky, and Mrs. James W. Hunt of Franklin, Ohio—almost simultaneously wrote two separate and different Womanless Wedding play scripts. There are enough similarities, however, to suggest that they took their ideas from a common source: both called for small-built grooms and large, burly brides; both employed various stereotyped characters who work to disrupt the wedding ritual such as the groom's jilted girlfriend and uncooperative parents (Sympson chose to make the groom's parents "haughty" while Hunt had the bride's parents questioning their daughter's reasons for marriage); both presented a common black mammy character who insinuated herself into various aspects of the play for comedic effect; and both centered upon a common theme of gently mocking simple rural folk.[4]

The cast of characters provided the primary difference between the two scripts. Sympson created a strange amalgamation of national figures—for example, Andrew Carnegie, Henry Ford, actress Theda Bara, actor Charlie Chaplin, and the regional icons of the Kentucky Colonel and his Lady—and more general characters like the bride and groom, the best man and groomsmen, bridesmaids, flower girls, "bad boys," the bride's "weeping" mother and "comforting" father, the groom's "haughty" mother and father, an old-maid aunt, a country cousin, a butler, the village schoolmarm, a bishop, and guests like Sis Hopkins and Annie Laurie. A baby cries throughout the ceremony. "Negro mammy," "Sambo," and "Joe" fill out the cast, performed in the minstrel tradition of white actors in blackface.

Sympson clearly enjoyed developing irony with her characters and her actors. Sis Hopkins, a hillbilly icon who was the title character in a three-act musical comedy in 1900, becomes part of a play that ridicules rural folk. Annie Laurie, the pseudonym for journalist Winifred Black who, as a reporter for the *San*

Francisco Examiner, became widely known in 1900 for dressing as a man to report on the Galveston flood, was to be played by a man dressing as a woman. Sympson also reveled in creating contrasting characters and tense situations: a henpecked husband versus a devoted husband, the bride's emotional parents versus the groom's staid and standoffish parents, the flower girls versus the bad boys. The cast of characters, too, had a dramatic cosmopolitan-versus-colloquial tension to it.[5]

In contrast, Hunt's cast, created in the aftermath of World War I, is full of references to international politics and the recently ended conflict. Hunt presented the marriage of Miss Petite France to Mr. America, a "dreadful flirt" who could have "his pick of any of the girls." His jilted sweetheart, Miss Riga Russia, protests, "It's not fair! He was engaged to me for three years." The bride's parents are Mr. and Mrs. London England; her grandparents, Mr. and Mrs. Anglo Saxon. Aunt Africa, a mammy figure, promises the audience that "white folks in dis town ain't never seen sich a weddin' as dis am gwine to be." The script offers a rather folksy version of internationalism.[6]

A third version of the Womanless Wedding became available in 1920 in E. O. Harbin's *Phunology* (pronounced fun-ology). Harbin's goal was to instruct organizers on how to conduct successful social events for young people: "If the Church and the community do not provide their social life in other wholesome modes of expression, . . . young people will seek outside the Church for places, many of them undesirable, or positively dangerous." He borrowed directly from a folk production at the Broadway Church in Louisville, Kentucky. With a few intermittent and brief lines from several characters, the play was primarily a comedic monologue by the "minister" that reinforced traditional gendered roles. To the groom, the minister asks:

> Will you purchase for this spouse a machine of the latest model, with which she may while away her idle time? Either a "Singer" or "Wheeler and Whistle" will do. Will you promise . . . that you will not ask for an itemized account to show what became of the $1.30 you gave her the week before on which to run the house; and that you will take your turn when it comes to washing the dishes, including kettles and frying pans? And, furthermore, . . . that you will love and care for this young and tender Rosebud, and only her, even though the Daisies be plentiful?

To the bride, he turns and asks:

> Wilt thou promise not to go through the pockets of his trousers at midnight while he gently sleeps, in search of idle coins or souvenirs of bygone days? . . . Wilt thou give him hot rolls at least twice a year and pies like mother used to make on Thanksgiving Day? Wilt thou promise to make the fires, cut the wood, milk the

cow, drive the geese to water, never have company, and never refuse an invitation to tea?

Even as it poked fun at gendered roles in a marriage, the script certified that the husband's duty lay in providing and supporting, and the wife carried the responsibility of maintaining the home.[7]

While all three scripts became rather popular, Sympson may be credited with disseminating the standardized Womanless Wedding across the country. She arranged the first performance of her play around 1919 and with her sister, Marie, formed a theatrical troupe—the Sympson-Levie Company, stationed in Bardstown, Kentucky—with over thirty "directors" poised to help organizations produce shows with local male volunteers assuming the majority of roles. Among the earliest productions of Sympson-Levie's Womanless Wedding were shows in Royalton, Illinois (1926); Indiana, Pennsylvania (1929); and South Deerfield, Massachusetts (1931). By the 1930s, Marie and her husband, Thomas Levie, opened a second office and costume store in Jackson, Michigan, to meet the increasing demand for the play, including a 1932 production in Fillmore, New York. Womanless Weddings quickly became popular throughout the North, particularly in the upper Midwest.[8]

By 1930, however, the geography of the productions shifted southward as well. In 1923, the Elks Lodge in Rogers, Arkansas, sponsored a production (see figure 2). One woman remembered a late 1920s Womanless Wedding that she attended as a child in Spencer, West Virginia. A company (most likely Sympson-Levie) sent a director and "put these shows on and this director would pick out the local people that were to be in it and they'd have practices and they sold tickets and it was a big thing." In rural settings, both northern and southern, the arrival of outsiders to orchestrate a large communal event was particularly memorable. In most places, the men performed in local theater houses or large churches, making the ritual seem more authentic. After a Womanless Wedding at his church in Greenville, South Carolina, textile worker Paul Griffith felt rather romantic. His future wife, Pauline, recalled how it "was right funny that we was coming back from the womanless wedding and he decided he'd propose." Years later, she "got him all fixed up and put lipstick on him, and got him a pink hat and a pink dress" for his own participation in a Womanless Wedding; "I did fine, until I got down to his feet, and I couldn't find shoes big enough."[9]

Not all memories of the early years of the Womanless Wedding were celebratory, however. Lee Roberson, founder of the fundamentalist Tennessee Temple University, remembered his early appointment to a church in Germantown, Tennessee. Since the congregation could not afford his salary, members decided to host a Womanless Wedding to raise the money. When he arrived at the church,

Figure 2. Womanless wedding at the Elks Lodge, Rogers, Arkansas, 18 January 1923. Negative #N007562, courtesy of the Rogers Historical Museum, Rogers, Ark.

the organizers tricked him into donning a dress and playing the piano, or else he would not receive his wages. All he could imagine to play for the processional was "Tramp, Tramp, Tramp, the Boys Are Marching," a Civil War song that had regained popularity during World War I. Still, the memories were not fond to Roberson, who viewed all of this as too secular for his tastes. "I told you this just to show you that this is not God's way of doing God's business," he later wrote. "That was of the world, and it was wrong."[10] Roberson's reaction to the Womanless Wedding partially arose from his discomfort with this method of revenue making, but he also hints that there was something unseemly about dressing as a woman in a bawdy rendition of a sacred rite.

While Womanless Weddings were scripted, the local "charm" came from how the men flirted with the boundaries of the play, the community's moral standards, and individuals' reputations. Those participants dressed as women (and even some dressed as men) took liberty to "ham it up," kissing audience members of both genders, flashing garter belts, adjusting whatever passed as breasts, and in general just being naughty. They tried to embarrass each other as well. They would "get something ridiculous in the background of that person," recalled Daniel Stewart of an event in Harnett County, North Carolina, and "low rate [humiliate] them." While all three scripts suggested that the bride weigh over two hundred pounds, none recommended that she feign pregnancy. Still, in some presentations, the bride appeared in a notably "advanced condition," and her father followed behind the groom with a shotgun just to reinforce the reasons for this marriage. Harbin reveled in the spin that the Broadway Church put on its wedding: when the bride's former boyfriend objected to the ceremony, she fainted, forcing most of the wedding party to hold her up.[11]

As a central ritual in family and community life, however, marriage was not something to be taken so lightly. The mockery and silliness of a Womanless Wedding, especially when presented within the walls of a church, clashed with the conservative social values of fundamentalist Christianity. By the 1930s, fundamentalism had firmly rooted across the South, evidenced in part by the very public spectacle of Tennessee's Scopes Monkey Trial in 1925. Roberson's comments represented well the strict and serious bent of a Calvinist Protestantism intolerant of playfulness and just slightly more tolerant of elaborate ritual.[12]

What Roberson failed to grasp, however, was the role that the Womanless Wedding had in reinforcing familial and communal values. Rituals, like actual weddings, employ symbols to affirm, unify, and strengthen the ideal that a couple joins together spiritually and later physically to create the foundational unit of society. They relate what a community has determined ought to be the normative standards. So, at the simplest level, a Womanless Wedding promoted those values by reenacting the event. Clearly, Harbin grasped this point with his descriptions of husbandly and wifely duties in the wedding vows. But because it is parody, the event incorporates large elements of play, which typically mocks ritual. Play inverts reality, offering metaphoric images to comment on normative values and to imagine alternatives. In mocking the very ritual they found most central to communal stability, organizers and participants in Womanless Weddings raised questions about the society in which they lived. In the play, they called attention to real social change and its effects on marriage. In the late 1910s and the 1920s, for example, rural and small-town white southerners were unsure of the new corporate capitalist economy emerging across the South, and the weakening of Victorian family values that seemed to accompany it. More women found work outside the home; consumption rather than production became the primary economic role of the household; and growing numbers of young people were admitting to premarital sex. In the midst of socioeconomic changes that threatened their familial ideal, southerners found comfort amid laughter. Regardless of the script, the Womanless Wedding's basic plot remained the same— despite numerous distractions and diversions, the drama always culminated in a successful, community-affirming heterosexual marriage. Even as it reversed and violated the ideal, the Womanless Wedding replicated and buttressed reality.[13]

The participation of local civic and economic leaders, then, became crucial to the success of the Womanless Wedding. At base, it was just fun to watch distinguished men make fools of themselves. Sympson and Hunt specifically instructed organizers to recruit significant members of the community, recognizing the need for authority when testing the balance between play and ritual. "Special care should be exercised in the selection of the cast," Hunt cautioned organizers. "Use prominent men." To ensure that audiences did not interpret the play as subversive, she also encouraged organizers that "an alter [sic] draped in red, white, and blue is appropriate."[14]

Even with formal scripts, however, some aspects of the less formal Womanless Weddings of the minstrel days remained, especially racial ridicule. Mammy, Sambo, and Joe were done in blackface, and the dialogue was written in racist "Sambo" dialect. Of course, in its simplest form, the mockery of blacks was just that. Whites enjoyed laughing at the comical ways in which they interpreted black simplemindedness. Pauline Griffith remembered how "they had a black mammy and she 'Boo-Hooed' at the wedding. It was real funny." It is just as true that there was more than simple comedy involved in those characterizations. Representations of Mammy, Sambo, and Joe idealized the preindustrial South when docile blacks supposedly acquiesced to white society. As the rural South began to experience economic changes, white southerners sought to secure their social privileges and used a variety of methods to preserve the more familiar way of life, ranging from lynching and romanticization of the Lost Cause to Jim

Crow laws and political disfranchisement. Community customs like the Womanless Wedding contributed to the preservation effort by reminding individuals of the world they would lose if they did not remain vigilant.[15]

But when Mammy declared to the "white folks in dis town," the audience did not really see a black woman or the two black men with her; they saw white men "blacked up." As historian Eric Lott explained, "To put on the cultural forms of 'blackness' was to engage in a complex affair of manly mimicry." In white southern tradition and blackface representations, Mammy was largely an asexual being, indulging maternal rather than sexual fantasies. Black men, in contrast, had become so sexualized in the white southern imagination that even the insinuation of a black man's sexual involvement with a white woman provided justification for a lynching. In the early twentieth century, white men saw their masculinity as under attack from all sides. The masculine standard that had been in place since Reconstruction required that white men demonstrate "honor and virility, righteous adherence to biblical inerrancy in the forms of belligerent racism and an assertion of manhood over effeminacy and even women in general," as historian Bertram Wyatt-Brown put it. But the new century brought multiple challenges to that ideal. Not only were white women finding new opportunities outside the home and in the voting booth, but black male sexuality and manhood threatened white male identity. Sambo and Joe had no lines; they merely were there—silent, ubiquitous, watching, ogling. Those men who portrayed the two characters, then, assumed ambiguous racial personas in which they caricatured the ostensible black male threat even as they promoted white male dominance. The use of blackface in the Womanless Wedding, after all, emphasized *white* masculinity: the participants were white men, the audience was white and compliant to the authority of these men, and white masculinity mattered.[16]

In contrast to Womanless Weddings that had taken place prior to the 1910s, the Womanless Weddings of the late 1910s and 1920s were scripted and, in the South particularly where racial lines were most acute, carried significant social and cultural meaning in their innuendos and symbolism. Indeed, racial connotations, and even many of the gendered ones, were less pronounced outside the South. For example, in 1926, Leslie H. Carter published a script with a San Francisco publishing house. His version stripped the play of black characters and placed less emphasis on the gendered tensions of a wedding and marriage. Instead, he tapped into the consumer culture of the 1920s, particularly the new fascination with movie theaters and the silent film. In his directions to producers, Carter emphasized, "In advertising the play, feature the Movie Stars and the names of those playing such parts." Charlie Chaplin, Mary Pickford, Lila Lee, Pola Negri, Bebe Daniels, William S. Hart—the play was designed to spoof silent film stars rather than marriage.[17]

During the Depression, the draw of a community play that leveled social ranks lost much of its appeal. In small communities across the South, civic and business leaders no longer laid claim to the type of social status that could be parodied. The very tenuousness of their positions in the community made it more difficult for them to serve as symbolic foils. Still, the Womanless Wedding persisted, albeit in a different venue, with different types of performers, and for very different reasons. In 1933, members of the Civilian Conservation Corps presented a Womanless Wedding in Vernon, Tennessee. Whether the participants worked from a script or created their own, this event was quite different from its predecessors. The play's presentation did not center on parodying and laughing at well-known leaders or an established community; most of the participants were not even local residents. Additionally, the audience comprised other members of the CCC camp, all men and almost all unmarried. This presentation turned on gender issues. The audience came to laugh at cross-dressing. As a local newspaper reported, "The costumes were elaborate with full dress. The bridal gown of white with regulation veil and train and the gowns of the attendants, in pastel colors, created an effective picture as grouped before an alter [sic] of flowers and greenery." In this case, the Womanless Wedding engaged issues embedded within the community of American male heterosexuality, and the CCC camps embodied this community.[18]

In the 1930s, Civilian Conservation Corps camps cropped up across the South and throughout the nation, housing hundreds of thousands of young men who worked on projects in forests, parks, and recreational areas. Ranging between eighteen and twenty-five years of age, the young men found ways to contact local women, but overwhelmingly they operated in a homosocial atmosphere. Some were unemployed thespians who eagerly took to the makeshift stages of the CCC camps to perform plays and minstrel shows, and risqué and suggestive humor became a mainstay of these entertainments. After all, in the all-male world of the CCC camps, there was little reason to maintain standards of propriety that would have been requisite in front of mixed-gendered audiences. Instead, the players exaggerated their female attributes and mannerisms, using innuendos and double entendres to suggest moral laxity. This type of ribald humor situated women as sexually minded temptresses, and it permeated CCC culture, as evidenced in its national paper, *Happy Days.* "Little Audrey was walking in the wood when she saw a man with his arms around a tree," began one pun published in the paper, "but Little Audrey just laughed and laughed because she knew only God would make a tree." The joke not only poses that women's natural inclination is to think sexually, but it hints of the sexual loneliness faced by the men of the CCC.[19]

The emphasis on female sexuality in CCC productions became part of Hubert Hayes's script for a Womanless Wedding, printed in 1936 by a Boston printing house. In the midst of the Great Depression, it is no surprise that the cultural icons of previous versions disappeared from the stage. Instead, Hayes, a Duke University graduate and resident of Asheville, North Carolina, lampooned mountain folk and focused his parody on the families at the center of any given wedding. Of course, it was a shotgun wedding because that was the stereotype of hillbillies, as was the jug of moonshine that the father of the bride carried. All the characters—white and black—were to speak with a hillbilly dialect meant to imply simplicity and lack of education. As in the CCC performances, the women were sexually predatory, made easier by Hayes's casting of men as slow witted and henpecked.[20]

When a subculture such as the CCC camps performed mock marriages, they were not attempting to subvert as much as acknowledge the centrality of the wedding to American culture. But cross-dressing's power derives from the way it confuses boundaries and potentially threatens sexual identity. Men had to avoid acting their parts too naturally; instead, they protected their masculinity by insisting that, in performing female roles, they acted as good sports and team players.[21]

This proved most important in the 1940s when Womanless Weddings began to appear in another homosocial context—the U.S. military. In 1944, at a Japanese American relocation camp, the superintendent of the school played the groom and an aide to the camp kitchen donned the bridal gown. Historically, it is a very curious episode. Unlike the CCC camp productions, this one did have a leveling component, allowing the prisoners to ridicule those with authority. The Rowher Camp newspaper assured its readership that the participants were "masculine members" of the staff, "fittingly dressed for the roles." Reportedly, the audience was "rolling in the aisles." Equally important, however, was why the audience tumbled with laughter. Most certainly, there existed a cultural chasm between the white American participants and the largely urban Japanese American audience that had been relocated from the Pacific Coast to this remote southeastern Arkansas outpost. But watching grown men, rigidly and unmistakably masculine in their day-to-day military uniforms, dancing about a stage in drag was funny.[22]

When combined with the Womanless Weddings performed in CCC camps, the military version marked a dramatic shift away from the purpose of Womanless Weddings in the 1910s and 1920s. Rather than leveling social distinctions for a larger community audience, the performances of the CCC camps and the World War II military barracks and relocation camps were meant for internal consumption. While the audience at Rowher contained women and children, most wartime productions occurred in the largely homosocial environments of military camps. The Womanless Wedding was just one of many camp shows that featured cross-dressing. GIs regularly performed in drag, although three distinct styles emerged: comic routines with very unwomanly types playing for laughs; more talented and passable singers and dancers; and convincing impersonators. Womanless Weddings contained any mixture of the three, although at the most superficial level, the play was meant to be comical, particularly with its casting of big, burly men as the bride and bridesmaids.[23]

World War II was also the first war in which significant numbers of American women joined the armed services. While the USO shows provided occasional female entertainment for the troops, there was an official policy against WACs' involvement in soldier shows. If women were to be represented, the men were going to have to do it, and do it well. Womanless Weddings, therefore, also became tests of masculinity. Did a man have the nerve to cross-dress, and if he did, could he excel in his presentation while restraining himself from going too far? When *Newsweek* reported on a camp skit in 1944, the reporter assured his readership that the show featured a "traditional ensemble of husky, hairy-legged soldiers strategically padded as ladies of the chorus," protecting the performers from insinuations of effeminacy or homosexuality. As historian Allan Bérubé discovered, however, there were numbers of gay men in the armed forces who found these shows to be special opportunities to challenge heterosexuality. They hugged and kissed and sang love songs, not only to their fellow actors but to audience members as well, using the disguise of womanhood to tease and embarrass their commanding officers.[24]

Japanese American audiences and gay GI participants perceived the Womanless Wedding differently. As audience, the former viewed the mock ritual aesthetically, appreciating its comedy without necessarily grasping its social commentary. The Womanless Wedding was always foremost comedy, a mockery of heterosexual marriage by implied masculine straight men. As cultural anthropologist Clifford Geertz explained, however, participants find in ritualistic presentations "not only models of what they believe, but also models *for* the believing of it." Men who normally would have had to subsume their homosexual tendencies within the assumed straight arena of the military found opportunities in these productions to act out on their desires for same-sex love and intimacy. The groom and bride's kiss, flirting with audience members—such activities may have been solely funny, but they may also have been momentary manifestations of unstated longings.[25]

Yet such longings represented a very small number of those men who performed in Womanless Weddings. In his study of twentieth-century homosexual college men, Patrick Dilley argued that a Womanless Wedding performance at Texas's Baylor College in 1950 was "queer" because the "acts themselves were queer, and while they were engaging in them, the students adopted (and/or deployed) a queer identity; the image they understood to be projected was queer, even if their own personal self-definition might not be." But the Womanless Wedding was essentially heteronormative: it was a heterosexual parody of heterosexuality. While a few men with homosexual feelings may have imagined their images as queer, the majority of actors imagined their images as burly, masculine, comical, and fundamentally heterosexual.[26]

During and after the war, the Womanless Wedding traveled with GIs back to the rural and Sunbelt South and became more popular than ever. In 1949, a show in Mascot, Tennessee, drew more than four hundred people willing to pay thirty-five cents each (twenty-five cents for children) to watch local leaders dress like woman and act silly. Mountain City, Tennessee; Cumberland, Maryland; Cleveland, Mississippi; Seale, Alabama; Forest Park, Georgia; San Antonio, Texas; Wilson, Arkansas; Tazewell, Virginia—these towns and countless unknown others hosted Womanless Weddings in the 1940s and throughout the 1950s. Everywhere, the Womanless Wedding played on the same themes of rural stereotypes, romantic love, idealized marriage, heterosexuality, male authority, and class relations. In many places, after the main event, audiences attended receptions where the community joined in music, dancing, and fellowship.[27]

But possibly the most significant performance during these years took place in Frankfort, Kentucky, in 1943. Although most extant sources reveal the story of white Womanless Weddings, the events also were present in black southern culture. At first glance, they provided the same type of social leveling found in early twentieth-century white Womanless Weddings. The Hospital and Training School for Nurses, an African American organization outside Charleston, South Carolina, had its physicians play the roles in a fund-raiser during the 1920s. In the 1930s, anthropologist Hortense Powdermaker described a black Womanless Wedding in a Cottonville, Mississippi, church:

> The "Brideless Wedding" is a mock wedding in which all the parts are taken by men. The "hit" is the matron of honor, one of the foremost citizens. He is a large, portly man, costumed in a coverall apron, a kimono, and a broad-brimmed hat. As he walks up the aisle, hands clasped behind his back in his usual masculine fashion, he rouses shouts of laughter. The "groom" is the smallest boy that could be found and the "bride" the tallest. The parody is carried off with great gusto and *éclat*.

Both in Charleston and Cottonville, female impersonation by "foremost citizens" was the gag in these early shows.[28]

But Powdermaker made a careful observation about the show and other church-sponsored secular activities: "The church contributes to the sense of respect and esteem from others which is so essential to the self-respect of most individuals, and which is so consistently refused to Negroes by the white society which dominates most of their lives." In the southern white community, the performance of a Womanless Wedding required blackface and "rouge face" to mock African Americans and white women. In the southern black community, the very opportunity to perform beyond the eyes of the white community *was* the social inversion, empowering participants and audiences alike. Within churches, the only community-level venue in which blacks could freely congregate, the freedom to do as they pleased included cross-dressing, effeminacy, and silliness.[29]

The comical essence of the production remained, but the black Womanless Wedding differed from its white counterpart in its intent to inspire not only entertainment but pride. Whereas the Womanless Wedding functioned in white communities as an unstated affirmation of community norms, black communities sometimes made that role explicit. The Frankfort performance was advertised as "community building." A poster in Springfield, Missouri, proclaimed the Washington Avenue Baptist Church's Womanless Wedding as "something beautiful," "something unique," and "wholesome fun." When political scientist Curtina Moreland-Young returned to Cordele, Georgia, in the 1970s, she recalled her childhood there, "a world of 'Womanless' and 'Tom Thumb' weddings, homecomings, proms, Senior Deb and Esquires, and Silver and Green Teas" where the "legal manifestations of oppression had been discarded, and I was in a place where I felt empowered as an African American in a way I have never felt in any other region of this country."[30]

In many regards, the popularity of the Womanless Wedding in both the black and white Souths peaked between the 1920s and the early 1960s, culminating in 1963 with the most public of Womanless Weddings on *The Andy Griffith Show*. To keep wild mountain man Ernest T. Bass from interfering in Charlene Darling's wedding, Sheriff Andy Taylor had his deputy Barney Fife don the wedding gown. When Bass interrupted the wedding and stole the "bride" away, Charlene darted from the bushes, and the ritual was completed before Bass realized he grabbed the wrong "girl."[31]

The Andy Griffith Show drew upon notions of the folksy culture of the rural South and gently poked fun at it for a national audience, and the writers tapped into a common cultural experience, fully playing upon Hubert Hayes's hillbilly version. But promoters and participants of Womanless Weddings in the past had always "prepared" audiences by insisting upon the unquestioned masculinity of the players. Indeed, Fife reiterated to Taylor several times how foolish he felt in a bridal gown. Curiously, however, the final scene suggests that Bass failed to realize that the cross-dressing deputy was actually not a woman!

Womanless Weddings had typically cast large, burly men as brides so there would be no mistake that "she" was actually a "he." Don Knotts went against these norms. Physically slight—in fact, he and the actress who played the real bride wore the same gown in the episode—and having created a character known for his difficulties in mustering power and courage, Knotts was the antithesis of the traditional antibride. When he did drag, the image went to the heart of conservative southern concerns about Womanless Weddings—the chance of gendered confusion, especially for boys. "I say, I mean I didn't want to be in it," remembered Larry Lawhorne about his first Womanless Wedding as a child in 1950s Lynchburg, Virginia, "because they wanted us to dress up as little girls. . . . Because they made us wear lipstick and rouge and the whole thing. Sometimes we've got on stockings and our sisters' dresses—which was very traumatic."[32]

Gender bending had always been a part of the Womanless Wedding, but from the 1960s through the 1980s, it seemed to become more central to any given production. One of the first things to change was the character of the minister. In published scripts, the officiant had served as either a "straight" man for the antics around him or as a wise and even paternalistic figure, representing the community's oversight of marriage. By the 1960s, implying his effeminacy became common fare. Lois Connelly remembered a Gladys, Virginia, production in which the local Baptist preacher, playing himself, "came down the aisle just swi[s]hing from side to side . . . Well, that was amusing. It was surprising, but it was amusing." But with half the cast dressed in women's clothing, the real gender bending occurred between participants. Georgia humorist Merrill Guice remembered that when the bridal procession—"drunk, in drag, and covered with grease paint"—joined the men on stage, the "level of sexual aggression" was unmistakable. With "hairy pits, backs, and legs," the "women" were unmistakably men, but they acted as women, intimately touching and kissing the male characters. Still, this degree of gendered confusion was permitted and enjoyed because it was heterosexual silliness. Recalling the "better days," one blogger in Vaiden, Mississippi, noted that "when we saw someone wearing earrings, they were either women, or a man in a womanless wedding."[33]

Cultural changes were under way, however, that transformed the Womanless Wedding. In the early twentieth century, men were labeled "queer" or "fairy" only when they exhibited effeminate qualities that suggested homosexual tendencies. In other words, homosocial intimacy was not eyed so suspiciously when it happened between clearly "masculine" men because it implied nothing. Hence, although their actors dressed in womanly attire, promoters' insistence on the manliness of their Womanless Wedding actors enabled same-sex touching, kissing, and frivolity without critique. As historian George Chauncey has demonstrated, in the middle of the century, "The now-conventional division of men into 'homosexuals' and 'heterosexuals,' based on the sex of their sexual partners, replace[d] the division of men into 'fairies' and 'normal men' on the basis of their imaginary gender status." And as this shift occurred, gay men and culture became more public.[34]

With greater visibility, however, came more virulent resistance. Particularly in the South, where the civil rights movement was already challenging societal proscriptions, homosexuality was an unwanted distraction. Southerners had never been ignorant of its presence. "Even the most innocent Dear Old Thing knows what Town Fairy is and what he does," recalled feminist activist Mab Segrest about her southern town, "but the blue-rinse set simply refuses to think about it. Their blind spots are so calcified that eventually they actually forget that Town Fairy is Town Fairy." Blissful ignorance had always characterized southern communities. But New York's Stonewall Riots in 1969 pushed homosexuality onto the national stage. Significantly, news footage focused upon the drag queens at the center of the rioting. What did it mean to southern men who had always known but suddenly had to publicly recognize that cross-dressing was a staple of a hidden and "deviant" culture? While southerners were great defenders of individual privacy, as sociologist James Sears put it, they were more so "the great preservers of appearances."[35]

Yet, the Womanless Wedding had been about inverting appearances and challenging proscriptions. Increasingly, its cross-dressing and gender bending were interpreted as abnormal and suspicious. Straight men who enjoyed dressing in women's clothing had to be viewed as eccentric. One respondent to an Internet blog entitled "Do You Have Any Weird Family Members?" wrote, "Eep! I forgot about my uncle (yes, I do share this gene pool). He LOVES dressing up as a woman. Everytime there is one of the 'Womanless Wedding' things, he is right up there in line as a participant. He does NOT make a pretty gal, let me tell you." And when performance bubbled over into the audience, it really pushed the social boundaries. At a Kimesville, North Carolina, Womanless Wedding, the ushers offered their arms to male guests. "A lot of the men who came in were just flabbergasted," remembered the event organizer; "they didn't want to go in." After all, the original purpose of the Womanless Wedding had been not to mock men and push their limits but to lampoon women and the institution of heterosexual marriage. Now the play paralleled the intentions of gay drag shows that parodied femininity *and* heteronormativity.[36]

Ironically, as a tradition, the Womanless Wedding remained a feature of community life, bringing into direct collision its social parody with increasingly conservative southern views of masculinity. As one of James Sears's interviewees explained, "We were raised hard-core Baptists. They hate fags. But, they still have this nutty tradition in my church called 'the womanless wedding.' There is a bride, a groom, flower girls—everything except women. Dad's favorite part to play was the soprano soloist. He had this giant blonde wig and a purple sequined dress. It wasn't 'till years later that I realized that my dad did drag." Feminine and masculine had always been blurred in the Womanless Wedding. By the 1970s, heterosexuality and homosexuality threatened to follow suit.[37]

The Womanless Wedding remained harmless parody as long as it did not *inspire* homosexuality. But as in the World War II productions, the show did open up possibilities for men who did not know what to do with their sexual feelings. One man who grew up outside Wilmington, North Carolina, recalled how he awakened to cross-dressing as a boy when he played the flower girl, and how he became aware of his bisexuality years later as the bride. During the performance, he and his "husband" kissed: "I open[ed] slightly and he proceeded to place his tongue on mine and then kissed me. The audience cheered. When we danced, he held his hand close to the top of my fannie and told me I looked beautiful." Despite his insistence that "I am not gay," the writer described how he dated the young man who played the groom for over a year, doing "everything a man and woman do on dates."[38]

For heterosexual men, the allure of cross-dressing had to be distinguished from intimations of homosexuality. One man made sure to preempt any potential accusations about his participation in a Womanless Wedding: "We had dancing at the reception, and the feel of the lingerie as I moved was fantastic. Now I know what my crossdressing friends are so excited about. The only negative was the 2 or 3 times I had my bottom patted and grabbed. Also, whispers to the effect that I was lovely and that, upstairs, the gentleman would be glad to give me something special. I was mortified. . . . I did feel sorry for the two boys who were completely sissified as flower girls." While he was "mortified" by homosexual interaction, even in a playful sense, the "bride" still was manly enough to resist. It contrasts with his description of the boys as "sissified" and speaks to an important theme that has arisen since the 1970s about the suitability of the Womanless Wedding for children. Are cross-dressing, gender confusion, and insinuations of same-sex intimacy dangerous for children? Merrill Guice jokingly commented that "all this was deemed appropriate for children because we were too dumb to know what was really going on." In reality, however, when it came to stage plays, children's abilities to see through the charade had not changed that much over the course of the twentieth century; what had changed was what southerners feared "was really going on."[39]

While concerns over homosexuality and effeminacy increasingly characterized Womanless Weddings of the late twentieth century, in the black South, another theme emerged as well: black men's abandonment of their families. Folklorist William Wiggins described one of the play's "comical imbroglios as the groom's former wife and their children interrupting the marriage ritual by tearfully confronting the groom and begging him not to leave them." The jilted lover had always appeared as a former girlfriend or boyfriend; in Hayes's version, he only objected to the marriage because he had spent three dollars on the bride once. But this newer twist spoke more directly to late 1960s' and 1970s' social concerns. As Wiggins concluded, the lesson for the audience was that "social ridicule would be visited on any couple who breaks society's established sexual codes of behavior."[40] Moralizing through the Womanless Wedding was nothing new; recall Harbin's intentions to provide "wholesome forms of expression."

The Womanless Wedding of the late twentieth-century South retained many of the tropes found in the early twentieth-century form: premarital pregnancy, timid grooms, larger-than-life brides, and blackface. In the late 1970s, the Berean Baptist Church of Houston, Texas, put on a Womanless Wedding for its all-white, young people's Valentine Day party. The minister was portrayed in blackface and with exaggerated black strutting and dialect, particularly in his opening monologue:

How do ya'll? I's is the Reverend Leroy Bishop.

Tonights we's gonna have a wedding here in this here church.

'Less ya'lls don't know where you alls at, I'll tell you the name of this place. The name of this place is the First Sanctified Baptist Redeemed Spirit-Filled Progressive Non-Denominational House of the Living God and Jesus, Our Father and Lord and Savior Church. Now if you can't remember, just check it up in your Yellow Pages cause it's there on pages 15, 16, and 17. We's located at 4200 Dalling St. right in the downtown heart of Nig—, uh, downtown.

So just come on by anytime; the doors are always open cause we can't keep no locks on 'em. [audience roars with laughter][41]

The show did not follow a specific script, so in the absence of the traditional mammy figure, any overstated parody of blacks seemed sufficient for the organizers and audience.

For those who did stick to scripts, the presence of blackface posed new problems in the post–Civil Rights era. Both a 1980 Womanless Wedding at Pedlar Mills, Virginia, and a 1985 show at Snow Creek, Virginia, used the Hunt script, requiring them to put a mammy on stage. Rather than characterize her as a servant, however, they made her a nurse. Still, in the audience at Snow Creek were local African Americans who, in talking to the organizers after the show, "didn't seem to mind. They thought he was funny." Importantly, however, several also volunteered that "they would have done it for us." Since the 1950s, schools and diners were not the only venues that underwent desegregation. Community entertainments also became integrated, and as the producer of the Snow Creek Womanless Wedding came to realize, if anyone should look silly parodying a large black woman, it should be a large black man.[42]

With heightened awareness about race relations, homosexuality, and the social implications of cross-dressing, the sponsorship and scripts of Womanless
Weddings began to change as well. Dorothy Cundiff, a resident of Rocky Mount,
North Carolina, warned, "You *don't* want to bring anything into it of that nature
because, as I say, it's an entirely fun thing, and you wouldn't want to really ir-
ritate people or, most of all, your own principles, morals." By the turn of the
twenty-first century, to remain a viable "family entertainment," the Womanless
Wedding had to be stripped of its innuendos and ribaldry.[43]

First, any suggestion of gender confusion had to be eliminated. In January
2006, for example, promoters of a Womanless Wedding in Blooming Grove,
Texas, advertised it as a fund-raiser for a local volunteer fire department, Communities in Action library, and the Empty Stocking Fund. It is not that PTAs,
public libraries, high schools, and other organizations have ceased sponsoring
Womanless Weddings, but in promoting events, news reporters and advertisers
have emphasized that proceeds are going toward (and participants are drawn
from) fire departments, police units, rescue squads, and other examples of post-
9/11 masculinity. They also make sure to mention how aware participating men
are about the potential for confused gender identity. As one of the organizers of
a Greenville, Texas, event noted, "I did have to [do] some arm-twisting, though,
especially with my husband. Several men said that if my husband would do it
then they would, so my husband finally gave in." Even when agreeing to perform, many southern men avoid the female roles. "Thank God I was the groom,"
reminisced the former mayor of Ferriday, Mississippi. "Let's face it," explained
a fire and rescue squad member donning a lavender dress and pumps to southern
humorist Celia Rivenbark, "[y]ou have to be very sure of your masculinity to get
up there and do that."[44]

Second, attempts to ensure the hypermasculinity of participants has purged
the Womanless Wedding of ribaldry. For example, Dame Atena, an entertainment planner in Pensacola, Florida, advertises that "if you think a short, pudgy
little mechanic dressed as a flower girl is a funny sight, they you'll love a womanless wedding." Well, while cross-dressing can be funny in itself, the history of
the Womanless Wedding has shown that the hallmark of the show was not just
the appearance of gendered confusion but also the actions—kissing, swishing,
intimate touching, teasing, and intimations of same-sex intimacy. Atena, however, emphasizes the script as being "clean & church approved" and "family-
rated." A television reporter plays the emcee role, removing both the primary
dialogue and audience participation from the immediate wedding ritual. Atena
identifies the event with Christian morals: "CHRISTIAN FUNDRAISING? You bet!
When I was a kid growing up in the South, we used to hold a 'womanless wedding' every year to raise money for our gym. We cajoled the dads into being the

bride and bridesmaids and it was too funny. The girls had a blast 'dressing' their dads and putting make-up on them. (Who said Catholic schools have no sense of humor?) PS My dad was a boxer when younger and an electrician by trade, so not a wimpy guy!" Nothing here about script or humor; rather the point seems to be that strong parental relations and nonwimpiness equates with Christian morality and appropriate manliness.[45]

Third, fear of promoting homosexuality has become the primary reservation against offering Womanless Weddings. Celia Rivenbark discovered at a North Carolina production that a gospel singing group refused to perform at intermission "because they didn't want to give the appearance of endorsing homosexual activity." A 2006 Womanless Wedding at a Texas high school sparked a local debate over whether the event encouraged homosexuality, eliciting the following defensive response: "Although the participants in the wedding were dressed in the apparel of the opposite sex, it was not meant to promote cross dressing nor was there any vulgar dancing or any tastelessness, it was to show how unattractive a hillbilly family might be, not a gay-fest." Merrill Guice concluded, in the twenty-first-century South, "Mention 'womanless wedding' and people get apoplexy and start sputtering about homosexuals and call up their local newspaper and shout insensibly at the answering machine on the other end."[46]

In August 2004, the director of the Commerce, Georgia, Public Library related how a friend asked her: "When did we all get so cautious, so serious, so afraid of being silly?" The answer, of course, is complex. The librarian reflected:

It was a great question, maybe even an important question. And it led us to start reminiscing about the zany things people used to do. We recalled the "womanless weddings" that took place in the old auditorium, with prominent and dignified local gentlemen—doctors and lawyers and bankers and so on—dressed up as bridesmaids, not to mention the bride her/himself. Two of us recalled seeing Dr. Joe Griffeth on that same stage, along with a couple of other upstanding citizens, all of them clad in grass skirts and doing the hula, with big funny faces painted on their stomachs. Apparently people weren't allergic to being foolish back them, especially if it was for a good cause, and sometimes they did it just for plain old fun. So maybe y'all can tell me: has something changed? Are we afraid, these days, of being politically incorrect or insensitive, and having fun in a way that hurts someone? Could the womanless wedding, in today's culture, be taken as a slam at transvestites? Or the hula as a satire of Hawaiian-Americans?[47]

Well, certainly a conservative form of political correctness has had a role in transforming the event, but the possibility of transvestites or Hawaiians attending a southern white Protestant heterosexual fund-raiser is remote.

Throughout the twentieth century, the Womanless Wedding, like all plays of social inversion, made sport of what its audience feared. It was a safe space in which to mock the very things that threatened masculinity and therefore family and community—unexpected pregnancy, overpowering women, effeminate men, drunkenness, black male sexuality (for white audiences), unfaithfulness (for black audiences). As J. W. Williamson analyzed, the Womanless Wedding acted out "for our enjoyment the very antithesis of what we believed ourselves to be." In the twenty-first-century South, where premarital pregnancy and interracial sex have become common, the thing that many southerners now interpret as a threat to masculinity, family, and community is homosexuality. Yet, rather than explicitly incorporate that into the parody, as previous generations had done with the challenges of their days, the current backlash against the ribald humor, the innuendos and double entendres, and the hints of gendered confusion threatens to make the Womanless Wedding imitative of life, not a parody of it.[48]

In the South, the Womanless Wedding has always been understood as more a curiosity than a true theatrical performance. People attended to watch the eccentricities of prominent men—their neighbors and community leaders—on display. Julia Sugarbaker, Dixie Carter's character on the sitcom *Designing Women*, once mused about southerners, "We're proud of our crazy people. We don't hide them up in the attic. We bring 'em right down to the living room and show 'em off." The Womanless Wedding permitted even the most upright persons to show off their craziness, and southerners accepted it. But that was once upon a time. When Lee Roberson critiqued the Womanless Wedding, his words forewarned of conservative religion's reaction. With the rise of the Religious Right in the 1980s, southern men and boys faced extreme pressure to conform to rigid masculine roles. More socially conservative than the white church throughout the twentieth century, the black church's Womanless Weddings, with its moral lessons of husbandly faithfulness and premarital restraint, evidenced the direction in which socially conservative religion would push the parody. The political correctness that transformed the Womanless Wedding was one that preached that men and boys had to fit very carefully designed gender roles. Still, Womanless Weddings that have not been drained of parody continue to appear annually across the South, serving as a reminder that there is an undercurrent of healthy humor, crucial social commentary, and opportunity to stretch beyond limiting constructions of masculinity.[49]

NOTES

1. Plox [pseud.], post to Mind and Soul discussion list, 17 November 2004, http://www.suite101.com/discussion.cfm/mindandsoul/107351/.

2. Pete Daniel, *Lost Revolutions: The South in the 1950s* (Chapel Hill: University of North Carolina Press, 2000), 158–59.

3. Peter Burke, *Popular Culture in Early Modern Europe* (Aldershot, Eng.: Ashgate, 1990), 185, 190; Jean Duvignaud, "Festivals: A Sociological Approach," *Cultures* 3 (2004): 19; J. Yinger, *Countercultures: The Promise and Peril of a World Turned Upside Down* (New York: Free Press, 1982), 154; E. O. James, *Seasonal Feasts and Festivals* (London: Thames and Hudson, 1961), 280; Hal Rammel, *Nowhere in America: The Big Rock Candy Mountain and Other Comic Utopias* (Urbana: University of Illinois Press, 1990), 99; Lauren Senelick, *The Changing Room: Sex, Drag, and Theatre* (New York: Routledge, 2000), 352. Other examples of nineteenth- and twentieth-century American "rituals of inversion" were Christmas, Halloween, Sadie Hawkins Day (when women asked men out on dates), Tom Thumb weddings (in which children played all of the roles), and, of course, blackface minstrelsy (in which whites acted as black stereotypes).

4. Mrs. James W. Hunt, *The Womanless Wedding* (Franklin, Ohio: Eldridge Publishing Co., 1918), 6; Jane Xenia Harris Woodside, "The Womanless Wedding: An American Fold Drama" (M.A. thesis, University of North Carolina, 1987), 17–22; Nora Campbell Chaffin, *Trinity College, 1839–1892: The Beginnings of Duke University* (Durham, N.C.: Duke University Press, 1950), opposite 44; Anthony Slide, *The Vaudevillians* (Westport, Conn.: Arlington House, 1981), 50–53. There seems to be no surviving copies of the Sympson script. Susan Stewart, *On Longing: Narratives of the Miniature, the Gigantic, the Souvenir, the Collection* (Durham, N.C.: Duke University Press, 1993), 123–24; James L. Peacock, *Consciousness and Change: Symbolic Anthropology in Evolutionary Perspective* (Oxford, Eng.: Basil Blackwell, 1975), 209.

5. Jere C. Mickel, *Footlights on the Prairie: The Story of the Repertory Tent Players in the Midwest* (St. Cloud, Minn.: North Star Press, 1975); Joe Saltzman, "Sob Sisters: The Image of the Female Journalist in Popular Culture," the Image of the Journalist in Popular Culture Project, Annenberg School for Communication, University of Southern California, http://www.ijpc.org/sobsessay.pdf; Frances Boyd Calhoun, *Miss Minerva and William Green Hill* (1909; reprint, Chicago: Reilly and Britton Co., 1915), 97.

6. Hunt, *Womanless Wedding*, 5–6, 9.

7. E. O. Harbin, *Phunology: A Collection of Tried and Proved Plans for Play, Fellowship, and Profit* (Nashville: Methodist Episcopal Church, South, 1920), 317–21. The Sympson, Hunt, and Harbin scripts initiated a flurry of mock wedding scripts in the 1920s and early 1930s; see Elizabeth Freeman, *The Wedding Complex: Forms of Belonging in Modern American Culture* (Durham, N.C.: Duke University Press, 2002), 199, 257n47.

8. Lorelei F. Eckey, *1,001 Broadways: Hometown Talent on Stage* (Ames: Iowa State University Press, 1982), x–xi; "The Royal Theater Presents 'A Womanless Wedding," http://www.royaltonillinois.com/wwed.html; Grace United Church History, photographs, http://www.indianagrace.org/; "If You Can't Laugh, Don't Come to See the Womanless Wedding," broadside, 1931, Pocumtuck Valley Memorial Associa-

tion, Deerfield, Mass.; *The New Enterprise,* electronic newsletter, The History Club, Fillmore, N.Y., http://www.thenewenterprise.org/. I am most grateful to Nancy Buckhead of the Jackson (Mich.) District Library for assisting my research.

9. Chuck Holmgren interview with Julia Ramsey, 25 November 2002, http://xroads .virginia.edu/~MA03/holmgren/papers/julia.html; Allen Tullos interview with Paul and Pauline Griffiths, 30 May 1980, Southern Oral History Program Collection, Southern Historical Collection, Wilson Library, University of North Carolina, Chapel Hill.

10. Lee Roberson, *The Faith That Moves Mountains* (Murfreesboro, Tenn.: Sword of the Lord Publishers, 1984), 491.

11. Jane Xenia Harris Woodside interview with Daniel Stewart, 13 August 1983, quoted in Woodside, "Womanless Wedding," 16.

12. Frank E. Manning, *The Celebration of Society: Perspectives on Contemporary Cultural Performance* (Bowling Green, Ohio: Bowling Green University Popular Press, 1983), 20–27.

13. Ibid.; Don Handelman, "Play and Ritual: Complementary Frames of Metacommunication," in *It's a Funny Thing Humour,* ed. N. J. Chapman and H. Foot (London, Eng.: Pergamon, 1977), 185–92; Elaine Tyler May, *Great Expectations: Marriage and Divorce in Post-Victorian America* (Chicago: University of Chicago Press, 1980), 51, 63, 92; Michael S. Kimmel, "Men's Responses to Feminism at the Turn of the Century," in *The History of Men: Essays on the History of American and British Masculinities* (New York: State University of New York Press, 2005), 79; Woodside, "Womanless Wedding," chap. 2.

14. Hunt, *Womanless Wedding,* 2.

15. David E. Roediger, *The Wages of Whiteness: Race and the Making of the American Working Class* (New York: Verso, 1991), 117; Loretta T. Johnson, "Charivari/ Shivaree: A European Folk Ritual on the American Plains," *Journal of Interdisciplinary History* 20 (1990): 380, 385–86; Bertram Wyatt-Brown, *Southern Honor: Ethics and Behavior in the Old South* (New York: Oxford University Press, 1982), 435–61.

16. Roediger, *Wages of Whiteness,* 117; Eric Lott, *Love and Theft: Blackface Minstrelsy and the American Working Class* (New York: Oxford University Press, 1993), 52–53; Gail Bederman, *Manliness and Civilization: A Cultural History of Gender and Race in the United States, 1880–1917* (Chicago: University of Chicago Press, 1995), 1–5; Bertram Wyatt-Brown, *Shaping Southern Culture: Honor, Grace, and War, 1760s– 1880s* (Chapel Hill: University of North Carolina Press, 2001), 293; Eve Sedgewick, *Between Men: English Literature and Male Homosexual Desire* (New York: Columbia University Press, 1985), 1–27.

17. Leslie H. Carter, *The Womanless Wedding: An Entertainment in One Act for Male Characters* (San Francisco: Banner Play Bureau, 1926), 2. For other examples of Womanless Wedding scripts that deemphasized race and gender conflicts, see Theodore Johnson, ed., *Baker's Stunt and Game Book* (Boston: Walter H. Baker Co., 1938), 103–4; Arthur M. Depew, *The Cokesbury Party Book* (New York: Abingdon-Cokesbury Press, 1932), 143–45.

18. "ccc Members in Burlesque Wedding," clipping from unknown newspaper, http://
     dickson-online.com/Category18.html.

19. Alfred Emile Cornebise, *The CCC Chronicles: Camp Newspapers of the Civilian Con-
     servation Corps, 1933–1942* (Jefferson, N.C.: MacFarland and Co., 2004), 207–8,
     215–16. The Little Audrey joke came from a Bashrop, Texas, ccc camp; reprinted
     in Cornebise, ccc *Chronicles*, 208.

20. Hubert Hayes, *A Womanless Wedding* (Boston: Baker's Plays, 1936).

21. Senelick, *Changing Room*, 352–53; Garber, *Vested Interests;* Julia Epstein and Kris-
     tina Straub, eds., *Body Guards: The Cultural Politics of Gender Ambiguity* (New York:
     Routledge, 1992), 9; Lenard R. Berlanstein, "Breeches and Breaches: Cross-dress
     Theater and the Culture of Gender Ambiguity in Modern France," *Comparative
     Studies in Society and History* 38 (1986): 338.

22. Brock Thompson, "Black Lace and Blackface: The Politics of Performance in South-
     ern Drag," paper presented at the Manchester Conference of the British Association
     for American Studies, 15–18 April 2004, Manchester, Eng.; *The Rowher Outpost*,
     quoted in Thompson, "Black Lace and Blackface," 2–3; William G. Anderson,
     "Early Reaction in Arkansas to the Relocation of Japanese in the State," *Arkansas
     Historical Quarterly* 23 (1964): 196–211; Russell E. Bearden, "The False Rumor of
     Tuesday: Arkansas's Internment of Japanese-Americans," *Arkansas Historical Quar-
     terly* 41 (1982): 327–39.

23. Allan Bérubé, *Coming Out Under Fire: The History of Gay Men and Women in World
     War Two* (New York: Penguin Books, 1991), chap. 3; John Howard, *Men Like That:
     A Southern Queer History* (Chicago: University of Chicago Press, 1999), 116–17.

24. "This Man's Army Makes Its Own Fun Thanks to Special Services Division," *News-
     week*, 7 August 1944, 72, 74.

25. Clifford Geertz, "Religion as a Cultural System," in *The Interpretation of Cultures:
     Selected Essays* (New York: Perseus Books, 1973), 112–15.

26. Patrick Dilley, *Queer Man on Campus: A History of Non-heterosexual College Men,
     1945–2000* (New York: RoutledgeFalmer, 2002), 214.

27. James Dahir, *Region Building: Community Development Lessons from the Tennessee Val-
     ley* (New York: Harper and Bros., 1955), 38; Jean Haskell, "Community Gatherings,"
     in *Encyclopedia of Appalachia*, ed. Rudy Abramson and Jean Haskell (Knoxville: Uni-
     versity of Tennessee Press, 2006), 166–67; "Womanless Wedding—Mountain City,
     Tennessee," Prints, Sketches, and Drawings Undated, John Biggs Alderman Papers,
     1918–1983, Archives of Appalachia, East Tennessee State University, Johnson City;
     John Martin and Lurther Brown, "Delta Photo Road Show: Discovering the Un-
     known Photos of the Mississippi Delta," Delta State University, 8, http://www
     .deltastate.edu/images/capps_archives/RSfinal.pdf; "Womanless Wedding," Her-
     man and Stacia Miller Collection, Department of Community Development, Cum-
     berland, Md.; Louise B. Leslie and Terry W. Mullins, *Tazewell*, Images of America
     series (Charleston, S.C.: Arcadia Press, 2006), 99; "Womanless Wedding, Seale High
     School, 1948," photograph, http://seale.sketchbook.com/scrapbook/wedding.htm;
     "Womanless Wedding as PTA Fundraiser," photograph, Forest Park, Ga., ca. 1940,

Georgia Archives, Morrow; *San Antonio Register,* 8 April 1949; Daniel, *Lost Revolutions,* 160; Richard Carlin and Bob Carlin, *Southern Exposure: The Story of Southern Music in Pictures and Words* (New York: Billboard Books, 2000), 85; Chris Goertzen, "George Cecil McLeod, Mississippi's Fiddling Senator, and the Modern History of American Fiddling," *American Music* 22 (2004): 355.

28. Howard, *Men Like That,* 51–52; "McClellan Banks legacy to be honored in exhibit, reception," *Catalyst Online,* 25 February 2005, Medical University of South Carolina, Charleston, http://www.musc.edu/catalyst/archive/2005/c02-25mcclennan .htm; Hortense Powdermaker, *After Freedom: A Cultural Study in the Deep South* (New York: Viking Press, 1939), 283.

29. Powdermaker, *After Freedom,* 285; Bérubé, *Coming Out under Fire,* 79–80.

30. Mary E. Winter, *Community Memories: A Glimpse of African American Life in Frankfort, Kentucky* (Frankfort: Kentucky Historical Society, 2003), 5; Womanless Wedding poster, Stella Anderson Collection, Springfield History Museum, Springfield, Mo.; Curtina Moreland-Young, "Reflections of a Southern Woman," River of Song project, Smithsonian Institution, http://www.pbs.org/riverofsong/index.html.

31. Episode #94: "Mountain Wedding," Film F-4697/98, Andy Griffith Papers, 1949–1997, Southern Collection, Wilson Library; Ken Beck and Jim Clark, *The Andy Griffith Show Book* (New York: St. Martin's Press, 1985), 157.

32. Beck and Clark, *Andy Griffith Show Book,* 157; Woodside interview with Larry Lawhorne, Lynchburg, Va., 15 August 1985, quoted in Woodside, "Womanless Wedding," 90.

33. "Remember When," http://www.vaiden.net/remember_when.html; "Womanless Wedding," The Ladonia Historical Preservation Society, Fannin County TXGenWeb, http://www.rootsweb.com/~txfannin/werdlad.html; Woodside interview with Lois Connelly, Gladys, Va., 23 October 1985, in Woodside, "Womanless Wedding," 130; Merrill Guice, "Womanless Wedding," 12 February 2003, http://www .thegoosesnest.com/.

34. George Chauncey, *Gay New York: Gender, Urban Culture, and the Making of the Gay Male World, 1890–1940* (New York: Basic Books, 1994), 12–16, 359.

35. Howard, *Men Like That,* xv; Mab Segrest, *My Mama's Dead Squirrel: Lesbian Essays on Southern Culture* (Ithaca, N.Y.: Firebrand Press, 1985), 158; James T. Sears, *Growing Up Gay in the South: Race, Gender, and the Journeys of the Spirit* (New York: Haworth Press, 1991), 190.

36. Sglandon [pseudo.], post to the New Kitchen Table discussion list, 24 January 2006, http://www.annemccaffreyfans.org/forum/archive/index.php/t-8701.html; Marjorie Garber, *Vested Interests: Cross-dressing and Cultural Anxiety* (New York: HarperCollins, 1992), 10; Laurel Horton and Paul Jordan-Smith, "Deciphering Folk Costume: Dress Code among Contra Dancers," *Journal of American Folklore* 117 (2004): 431–32; Tri-Ess, "What Crossdressers Are Not," http://www.tri-ess.org/; Woodside interview with Deborah Black and Joanne Clapp, Kimesville, N.C., 14 September 1983, in Woodside, "Womanless Wedding," 109.

37. Sears, *Growing Up Gay in the South,* 247.

38. "Amy's Immersion into Bridal Bliss," post to First Encounters: Grabbing the Ring discussion list, http://www.pettipond.com/ring.htm.

39. "Steve #2's 'Male' Wedding Event," post to First Encounters: Grabbing the Ring discussion list, http://www.pettipond.com/ring.htm.

40. William H. Wiggins Jr., "The Black Folk Church," in *Handbook of American Folklore*, ed. Richard M. Dorson (Bloomington: Indiana University Press, 1983), 152; Wiggins, "Pilgrims, Crosses, and Faith: The Folk Dimensions of *Heaven Bound*," *Black American Literature Forum* 25 (1991): 94.

41. "The Womanless Wedding," video, http://x-celenterprises.com/Videos.htm.

42. Woodside interview with Shelby English, Glade Hill, Va., 17 July 1985, in Woodside, "Womanless Wedding," 82.

43. Woodside interview with Dorothy Cundiff, Rocky Mount, N.C., 25 June 1985, in Woodside, "Womanless Wedding," 114.

44. "'Womanless Wedding' will be Saturday," (Greenville, Tex.) *Herald Banner*, 25 April 2007; "'Womanless' crown up for grabs," *Natchez* (Miss.) *Democrat*, 4 October 2006; Celia Rivenbark, *Bless Your Heart, Tramp* (Wilmington, N.C.: Coastal Carolina Press, 2000), 87.

45. "Womanless Wedding Promises to Be a 'Fun Time' for All," *Corsicana* (Tex.) *Daily Sun*, 25 January 2006; "Fundraising Event-in-a-Box," http://www.iwantfundraising.com/index.htm.

46. Rivenbark, *Bless Your Heart, Tramp*, 85; WordDoHurt [pseudo.], post to NeoTribune discussion list, 27 December 2006, http://www.neotrib.com/index.php; Guice, "Womanless Wedding."

47. Susan Harper, editorial, *Commerce* (Ga.) *News*, 1 September 2004.

48. J. W. Williamson, *Hillbillyland: What the Movies Did to the Mountains and What the Mountains Did to the Movies* (Chapel Hill: University of North Carolina Press, 1995), 16.

49. "Bernice's Sanity Hearing," *Designing Women*, dir. David Trainer (Studio City, Calif.: CBS Television Studios, 1989).

A New Kind of Patriarchy: Inerrancy and Masculinity in the Southern Baptist Convention, 1979–2000

Seth Dowland

In 2003, Southwestern Baptist Theological Seminary President Paige Patterson identified a "war against boys" as "America's No. 1 problem." He made this comment at an Arkansas evangelistic meeting on a stage flanked by animal trophies. A noted hunter and gun enthusiast, Patterson began his talk by regaling the all-male throng with tales of African safaris. But he quickly moved to his main point: American culture, said Patterson, pressed parents "to make little girls out of your little boys." Feminist-inspired developments, including the vilification of superheroes and the eradication of playground games, threatened to eliminate differences between the sexes. Patterson would not abide that. He encouraged fathers to provide their sons with "a big dog" and "a real gun." Only the strong response of men could staunch the feminization of the next generation. And nothing, according to Patterson, was more worthy of men's attention.[1]

Patterson's sentiments paralleled those of many southern evangelicals at the dawn of the twenty-first century. Weaned on devotional books like John Eldredge's *Wild at Heart*, conservative Christians came to believe that innate differences between men and women demanded that humans observe the gendered order God had created. These evangelicals cast men in the role of protector and provider, and they argued that God had ordained men to lead families and churches. Feminist campaigns for women's full and equal participation in all roles of civilized society—including as ordained pastors—struck some conservative Christians as an assault on the created order. They fought these campaigns strenuously.

While feminism had raised concerns about the erosion of gender norms, the belief that God had laid out different roles for men and women was hardly new. Since the early nineteenth century, white southern evangelicals had crafted a Christianity that reinforced existing social hierarchies, including both patriarchy and white supremacy.[2] The linkage between masculine privilege and white supremacy persisted well into the twentieth century. But by the late 1960s, a majority of white southern evangelicals had grown increasingly skittish about theological defenses of racial segregation, at least publicly.[3] They had not, however, abandoned belief in divine hierarchy. God did not intend society to be an undifferentiated mass of humanity. Rather, God had ordained means of order to govern human communities.

Specifically, God had decreed that men lead families and churches. Conservatives in the 1970s and 1980s thereby introduced a new kind of patriarchy.[4] Unlike older patriarchies, which relied on social custom and unspoken guidelines to maintain order, this new patriarchy sanctioned masculine privilege through explicit reference to scripture. In fact, defenders of the new patriarchy placed adherence to biblical gender norms at the heart of theological orthodoxy. That helps explain why men like Patterson considered a war on boys "America's No. 1 problem." By arguing that gender differences were culturally determined, late twentieth-century feminism rejected the notion of manhood (and womanhood) as created by God. In response, white southern evangelicals articulated a theological defense of manhood that made male leadership normative and assigned women to submissive roles.

One of the most notable instantiations of the new patriarchy occurred in the Southern Baptist Convention (SBC), which in the 1980s endured a decade-long controversy pitting conservatives against moderates for control over the denomination. Beginning in 1979, a cadre of hard-line conservatives orchestrated the election of an unbroken string of conservative presidents, who used their appointive powers to reconfigure the political makeup of SBC boards and agencies. The "conservative resurgence," which revolutionized the nation's largest Protestant denomination, stands as the most important development in post–Civil Rights southern religious history.[5] This essay examines the SBC controversy in order to display how southern conservatives instituted the new patriarchy through resolutions and policy statements that reaffirmed male leadership and rejected women's ordination.

Throughout the 1970s, a faction of SBC conservatives coalesced in opposition to increasing liberalism in the SBC. In 1973, conservative leader W. A. Criswell said, "I have the feeling that there are elements in the Convention—and this is just a feeling, an intuitive judgment—that are definitely turning toward a more conservative theology."[6] Moderates may have dismissed Criswell's feeling as a baseless dream, but Criswell helped create the networks that facilitated the rise of

SBC conservatives. From his pulpit at First Baptist Dallas, which for many years was the largest Southern Baptist congregation, Criswell mentored several young Baptists who would emerge as leaders of the conservative resurgence, including Richard Land, Jimmy Draper, and Paige Patterson. Within the circles created, in part, by Criswell, young Southern Baptist conservatives lamented the direction of SBC seminaries, which they felt taught liberal and even heterodox theology. The SBC sponsored six seminaries scattered across the country, and budding pastors hoping for a prominent pulpit had to attend one of them. Though none of the Southern Baptist seminaries were considered liberal in the wider academic world, their faculties endorsed positions that upset conservatives (including the belief that the Bible supported women's ordination). Given Southern Baptist polity, which ascribed ultimate authority to the local congregation (rather than to a bishop or denominational agency), pastors commanded considerable power in shaping the religious world that Southern Baptists inhabited. As long as those pastors apprenticed under moderate seminary faculties, conservatives worried that a subtle but inexorable liberal drift would detach the denomination from its theological moorings.

Beginning in the late 1970s, SBC conservatives implemented a plan to reshape SBC agencies and seminaries. They drew on the strategy of Bill Powell, a conservative who edited the *Southern Baptist Journal.* Powell realized that control of the SBC presidency would enable conservatives to reconfigure the denomination. The president held power to appoint a certain fraction of the boards of trustees for all Southern Baptist institutions. If messengers to the annual convention could elect conservative presidents for ten consecutive years, and if those presidents reliably appointed only conservatives to seminary and agency boards, conservatives would constitute 60 percent of trustees at these institutions. The majority could then ensure that faculties and denominational officers complied with conservative teachings. Powell hatched his plan in the early 1970s, but he lacked the funds and support to implement it.[7]

Paige Patterson and Paul Pressler did not. Patterson, who taught at Criswell College, and Pressler, a Texas judge, launched the conservative resurgence at the 1979 convention in Houston. They nominated Memphis pastor Adrian Rogers as president. Through several preconvention "spontaneous" meetings, word of Rogers's candidacy had spread among denominational conservatives, and they delivered him a remarkable 51 percent majority in a field of six candidates. (No other candidate mustered more than 23 percent.) The political infighting that characterized the 1979 convention marked a departure from precedent. Messengers even passed a resolution "disavowing overt political activity and organization as a method of selection of its officers."[8] But conservative leaders made no apologies. In 1980, Pressler told reporters, "We are going for the jugular. We are going for having knowledgeable, Bible-centered, Christ-honoring trustees of all our institutions."[9] Pressler's comment, which became the most famous statement of the controversy, infuriated moderate denominational leaders. But they could not stop Pressler's plans. Since 1979, moderates have failed to recapture the SBC presidency.

After the 1985 convention in Dallas, where more than forty-five thousand messengers shattered attendance records (the previous high had been twenty-two thousand) and elected a conservative (Charles Stanley, in this case) to the presidency for the seventh consecutive year, conservatives could claim success. Moderates vowed to continue the fight, but they recognized that a return to power required an unlikely string of convention victories. A "Peace Committee," chartered by the convention to reconcile moderates and conservatives, exhorted presidents to appoint trustees "drawn in balanced fashion from the broad spectrum of loyal, cooperative Southern Baptists, representative of the diversity of our denomination."[10] Yet moderates charged that the Peace Committee was a conservative-controlled farce. Convention presidents continued to appoint only conservative nominees to boards of trustees. Those trustees asked seminary faculties to teach conservative theology, and in the early 1990s, their demands resulted in painful faculty turnover at Southern Seminary (in Louisville, Ky.) and Southeastern Seminary (in Wake Forest, N.C.). Moderates saw this "fundamentalist takeover" as a hijacking of the denomination and a renunciation of Baptist principles, which ascribed autonomy to local churches and freedom of conscience to each believer. Conversely, conservatives believed that upheaval in the SBC was an unfortunate but necessary byproduct of a long-overdue return to theological orthodoxy. Amid bitter disagreement, moderates and conservatives agreed on one thing: by the dawn of the twenty-first century, Southern Baptist conservatives had radically transformed their denomination.[11]

Among the issues that motivated Southern Baptist conservatives to battle moderates, biblical inerrancy—the belief that the Bible was "truth without any mixture of error"—stood paramount.[12] Though Southern Baptists had affirmed that definition of inerrancy since the 1920s, they had not participated in the fierce debates over inerrancy that had divided other American denominations. During the nineteenth century, biblical scholars began treating the Bible as they would any other historical document, pointing out the contingencies, apparent inconsistencies, and social contexts of scriptural texts. This "historical criticism" of the Bible caused many Christians epistemological problems. After all, if Matthew and Mark did not agree on a minor detail, how could one trust their reliability in more substantive matters? Questions like these cropped up with increasing frequency around the turn of the twentieth century. Many American churches split into two camps: fundamentalists (determined to defend biblical infallibility) and modernists (willing to read scripture through the lens of modern science and historical criticism). The fundamentalist-modernist controversy polarized several American denominations.

Southern Baptists, however, never experienced the fundamentalist-modernist controversy, at least not in the same way that northern churches did. Historian Bill Leonard, among others, has identified a "Grand Compromise" that characterized the SBC for most of the twentieth century. In this compromise, centrists exercised enough power to prevent any political faction, right or left, from taking control. A strain of fundamentalism certainly existed within Southern Baptist life, perhaps best embodied by Fort Worth pastor J. Frank Norris, who railed against modernists from his Texas pulpit. Yet, Norris's fundamentalism did not characterize the vast majority of Southern Baptists, mostly because the threat of modernism in the SBC was negligible. As Timothy Weber, a northern evangelical who taught a short stint at Southern Baptist Seminary in Louisville, put it, "I don't think most Southern Baptists would know a liberal if he or she was right in front of them, because liberalism in the South looked a whole lot different than it did in other places."[13] For most Southern Baptists in the early twentieth century, the fundamentalist-modernist controversy—if they even knew about it—seemed a distant threat.

By 1979, that had changed. Southern Baptist conservatives had developed a deep sense of cultural crisis that resembled the position of 1920s fundamentalists. Whereas an earlier generation of Baptists had lived "at ease in Zion"— that is, in a region saturated with (if not controlled by) Baptist culture—late twentieth-century Southern Baptists had grown "uneasy in Babylon."[14] Increasing diversity and political revolutions in the South had caused the region's culture to seem threatening to many Southern Baptists. This sense of cultural estrangement impelled a cadre of Southern Baptist conservatives to engage American culture. They argued that "liberals" threatened the denomination's reliance on scriptural authority and would hasten the SBC's demise.[15]

Southern Baptist pastor Harold Lindsell, editor of evangelicalism's flagship journal *Christianity Today*, made the issue of biblical inerrancy central to the debate between conservatives and moderates. In 1976, he published *The Battle for the Bible*, which accused some evangelicals of believing "the Bible has errors in it." Specifically, these people thought that in matters of history, geography, and science, scriptural texts were not always as reliable as contemporary academic research. Lindsell argued that this position put noninerrantists in an untenable position. "The best that can be said," he wrote, "is that some who hold to errancy do not go beyond errors of science and history," yet they had started down a slippery slope. Lindsell believed that the gap between evangelicals who maintained a belief in inerrancy and those who did not "will become enormous in due season, and the differences will increase as other doctrines, now believed, are tossed overboard, discarded with the doctrine of infallibility."[16] Lindsell thought that abandoning inerrancy would lead to loss of faith.

Lindsell's book occasioned an outpouring of comment. *Christianity Today*, not surprisingly, carried advertisements for *The Battle for the Bible* that urged evangelicals to "read it and act!" Critics worried that Lindsell's book would launch a second fundamentalist-modernist controversy. Indeed, the very title of his book suggested that inerrantists welcomed a fight. Donald Dayton, another evangelical professor, penned a critique of *The Battle for the Bible* in the *Christian Century.* "Evangelicals," said Dayton, "are jittery, feeling that the book might herald a new era of faculty purges and denominational splits." Dayton's words proved prophetic, as the SBC divided over inerrancy in the decade following publication of *The Battle for the Bible.* Lindsell did not apologize. In a subsequent book he wrote, "If to stand for the truth of Scripture is divisive, than I am divisive. So be it."[17] Lindsell divided evangelicalism into two camps: those who believed in inerrancy and those who did not.

This bifurcation helped conservatives who relied on divisive rhetoric in order to end the era of the "Grand Compromise." Whereas previous generations of Southern Baptists had tolerated some level of disagreement about the nature of scripture in the name of cooperation, Lindsell challenged people to decide. One either affirmed biblical inerrancy or rejected it. According to inerrantists, conditional endorsements of biblical inerrancy simply masked heresy. Moderates like Dayton complained that Lindsell "ignores contrary evidence" and "shows little awareness of the blurring of lines," yet Dayton's position proved more difficult to defend rhetorically. Moderates did not want to appear to doubt the Bible's trustworthiness, yet they also wanted to deal forthrightly with some of scripture's apparent inconsistencies. Their claims to believe in the Bible's authority necessarily entailed more nuance than Lindsell's simple statement, "All scripture must be true."[18] Inerrantists characterized their position in rhetorically favorable ways that made opponents seem hostile to scripture.

The SBC Pastors' Conference, held immediately prior to the national convention, became an important venue where conservatives spread their message. By the late 1970s, conservative preachers dominated the lineup at these annual gatherings. In one of the most notable Pastors' Conference sermons, Oklahoman James Robison lambasted SBC professors, labeling those who did not subscribe to inerrancy as the unwitting agents of Satan. "Have you ever noticed how many of these instructors look like they've been embalmed with the fluid of higher education?" he asked. They "look like a God-forsaking corpse. Pickle!"[19] Robison went further than most conservatives in bashing SBC moderates, but he captured the tone that characterized the SBC during the 1980s. Conservatives tabbed anyone who tried to qualify scriptural inerrancy as a liberal who did not uphold biblical authority.

In the face of criticism from men like Robison, SBC moderates contended that they could maintain a high view of scripture alongside their refusal to affirm its inerrancy. In the 1960s and 1970s, several denominational leaders—seminary professors notable among them—dismissed inerrancy as an outmoded way of viewing scripture. That did not mean moderates had withdrawn belief in the divine inspiration of scripture. In fact, they argued that their understanding of the Bible differed little from that of conservatives. In 1986, the presidents of all six SBC seminaries signed the "Glorietta Statement," which declared, "We believe that the Bible is fully inspired. . . . The sixty-six books of the Bible are not errant in any area of reality. We hold to their infallible power and binding authority."[20] The Glorietta Statement presented an unequivocal affirmation of the Bible's divine origin. Some moderates felt it represented a capitulation to conservatives.[21] Others said it simply captured their high view of scripture, hardly distinguishable from that of conservatives. As Fisher Humphreys, a professor at New Orleans Baptist Seminary, put it, "I am unable to detect any substantial differences between [inerrancy] and the high view of Scripture offered by many noninerrantists. I regard the Southern Baptist controversy as unnecessary and unfortunate." Humphreys' conservative theology predisposed him to believe in the divine inspiration of the Bible, yet he could not in good conscience affirm inerrancy, which he perceived as simplistic and anachronistic.[22]

Yet for Southern Baptist conservatives, affirming biblical inerrancy became the signal of orthodoxy on other positions, notably opposition to women's ordination. The decade between 1975 and 1985 had witnessed a dramatic upsurge in the number of ordained women within the SBC. Women like Nancy Sehested, who served as pastor for SBC churches in Georgia and Tennessee, argued that the ordination of women signaled an overturning of sinful patriarchy and improper scriptural interpretation. Conservative Southern Baptists disagreed. "I believe there are many opportunities for women to be engaged in ministry and serving the Lord," said conservative leader Morris Chapman. "It's simply that I believe the Bible teaches that . . . the role of pastor in the church [is] to be a male."[23] Opposing women's ordination emerged as the foremost marker of the new patriarchy, as conservative Southern Baptists inscribed a vision of manhood that made men the only legitimate leaders of their churches.

The centrality of women's ordination to the inerrancy debate revealed the ways conservatives favored a masculine approach to scriptural texts. Whereas moderates argued for contextualized interpretation, which treated the Bible as a historical document situated in first-century Palestine, conservatives preferred a populist interpretation of scripture. This populist hermeneutic privileged the simplest, most direct interpretations of scripture. Conservatives allowed little room for gray areas, preferring instead an unflinching confrontation with God's revealed word. For instance, moderates viewed Paul's blunt directive, "I do not permit a woman to teach or to have authority over a man," as a culturally specific command that did not apply to twentieth-century believers. Conservatives, conversely, saw Paul's words as a timeless statement of divine hierarchy that placed men above women. Moreover, they charged moderates with unwillingness to face up to the hard realities of scripture. "What do you think?" wrote one conservative about the passage. "Is verse 13 hard to understand? Or are [moderates] unwilling to accept what it says?"[24] Conservatives never missed an opportunity to use masculine pronouns for God, even though they admitted that God possessed no gender. And they portrayed biblical writers—especially Paul—as men unconcerned about being politically correct. In short, defenders of the new patriarchy read the Bible in particularly "masculine" ways, promoting verses that ascribed authority to men and interpreting scripture in the most direct manner possible.

Conservative Southern Baptists' interpretive certainty—the lack of doubt they displayed about the teachings of the Bible—aligned them with earlier generations of conservatives who had associated liberalism and uncertainty with effeminacy. Effeminacy went hand in hand with uncertainty, and uncertainty led to a loss of faith in scripture. Christianity itself, said evangelist Billy Sunday, was not a "pale, effeminate proposition." Rather, it involved commitment to Jesus, "a robust, red-blooded man." Conservatives trumpeted their masculine stripes by displaying surety, and liberals who waffled on the Bible and encouraged theological innovation came across as weak and effeminate. By displaying certainty, then, conservative Southern Baptists stood in a tradition that associated firmness with masculinity.[25]

While conservative arguments against women's ordination relied mainly on scriptural passages proscribing women's role in the church, conservatives also thought that the Bible simply affirmed the reality of creation. They believed that God commanded men to lead churches because men were better suited to the task. Sehested argued that conservatives had so biased Southern Baptists against the idea of female pastors that a woman hearing God's call to the pulpit would not know what to think. "WHO, ME?" asked Sehested's hypothetical woman. "You gotta be kidding! I'm a woman! I've got a high voice and no hair on my chest. I'm emotional, I cry, and I can't think straight." Sehested's parody caricatured conservative gender norms, but it nonetheless revealed a fundamental reality: SBC conservatives believed men were uniquely gifted to lead their churches. "Pastors must make their personal identity appealing," wrote one conservative, "by emphasizing their own masculinity."[26]

Southern Baptists' privileging of male leadership resonated with conservatives who felt increasingly alienated in the 1970s and 1980s, when feminists and gay rights activists made inroads into mainstream American culture. Southern Baptist conservatives referenced the increasing power of these movements in order to portray a society in decline. Morris Chapman, the CEO of the Executive Committee of the SBC, identified feminism (through its support of abortion) and gay rights (through its denial of the "traditional" family structure) as the key agents in diluting America's religiosity. "The fabric of America is the family unit, the husband, the wife, the mother, the father, the children," he said.[27] His colleague Mark Coppenger agreed: "Feminism is a galloping huge thing in America," he said, and "the homosexual agenda is huge."[28] Southern Baptist conservatives viewed the rise of feminism and gay rights with disdain. The two movements imperiled the survival of Christian social teaching and emasculated southern society.

In response, SBC conservatives celebrated "traditional" families, in which men led the family and worked outside the home, while women cared for children and tended to domestic duties. SBC conservatives repeatedly praised this family structure. Delegates to the 1987 convention meeting even passed a resolution that "honor[ed] the rich and valuable contributions of full-time wives and mothers who through their service and self-sacrifice have strengthened their families, enriched our nation, and pleased our God by honoring His purposes in their lives."[29] The resolution represented a direct assault on feminists who fought for recognition of American women's advances outside the home.

Southern Baptist conservatives couched their opposition to feminism and gay rights in their reading of the Bible. Whereas political action groups like Jerry Falwell's Moral Majority employed rhetoric designed to reach Christian, Jewish, and secular conservatives, Southern Baptists focused their debates on scriptural teaching. For instance, when convention messengers passed a resolution that called wives to "graciously submit" to their husbands' authority, conservative leader Dorothy Patterson said, "Our only intention was to try to put on the table what the Bible says." Patterson referred to Ephesians 5, which instructs wives to *submit* to their husbands, while asking husbands only to *love* their wives.[30] Conservatives thought a straightforward reading of this passage made clear God's intention for men to govern their families. They used this and other passages to claim biblical sanction for the new patriarchy.

Conservatives' institution of the new patriarchy reified the definition of "inerrancy." Al Mohler, the president of Southern Baptist Theological Seminary, delineated how this happened. Mohler believed that throughout the denomination's history, rank-and-file Southern Baptists "believed in biblical inerrancy [and] wouldn't understand why anyone wouldn't believe in biblical inerrancy."

But prior to the 1970s, few issues emerged to test that view. That changed when abortion and gay rights became prominent political debates. "Mr. and Mrs. Baptist," he said, "may not be able to understand or adjudicate the issue of biblical inerrancy when it comes down to nuances, and language, and terminology. But if you believe abortion should be legal, that's all they need to know. . . . That puts you outside the pale." Likewise, said Mohler, "If you believe that homosexual marriage should be recognized by the state, that tells them a whole lot more about what you understand about life and the most basic issues thereof."[31]

Mohler highlighted a basic issue in the "battle for the Bible": inerrancy became an issue only when cultural developments and political debates brought it into focus. As he pointed out, believing the Bible to be without error became synonymous with opposition to abortion and gay rights. To be sure, conservative leaders (including Mohler) gave extensive and nuanced presentations that defended inerrancy with linguistic and historical evidence, yet their arguments gained traction among rank-and-file Southern Baptists only when it became clear that moderates' reading of scripture coincided with liberal social and political positions. Mohler recalled that when he was a seminary student, moderate professors mocked letters from laypeople that asked them to make definitive statements about key political issues. Mohler thought, "You don't get it. [Grassroots Southern Baptists] don't care what else you believe if you're wrong on these issues."[32] Mohler's comments revealed the cultural resonance of Southern Baptists' debate over inerrancy. SBC conservatives called inerrancy the central issue in the controversy, but they did not view scriptural inspiration as an academic problem. One's stance on biblical inerrancy mattered because of the worldview it signaled. Believing in inerrancy came to coincide with belief in "biblical" notions of manhood that ascribed authority to (heterosexual) men and rejected attempts to normalize female leadership or alternative sexualities.

Southern Baptist conservatives felt a particular burden to codify biblical manhood because a movement known as evangelical feminism had grown in stature throughout the 1970s. Taking some cues from the secular women's movement, evangelical feminists advocated for the full and equal participation of women in all aspects of contemporary life. They argued that women could occupy all the offices that men currently controlled, and they wanted equality of representation and compensation in American government and business. Yet, unlike most of their secular counterparts, evangelical feminists anchored their advocacy in a particular reading of scripture, and they did not consider Christianity a hopelessly patriarchal religious tradition. Evangelical feminists favored egalitarian readings of scripture and campaigned for women's ordination, and they made both implicit and explicit charges that conservatives misrepresented biblical teaching.[33]

Just as Lindsell's *Battle for the Bible* served as a foundational text for inerrantists, Letha Scanzoni and Nancy Hardesty's 1974 book *All We're Meant to Be* supplied evangelical feminists with their own first principles. Scanzoni and Hardesty's book traded in some familiar feminist arguments, such as the contention that cultural conditioning instead of biology played the largest role in creating notions of "masculine" and "feminine." But unlike most feminists, Scanzoni and Hardesty enlisted the support of the Bible. They wrote that "from the beginning" of the church, "women participated fully and equally with men." The church must thereby "face up to the concrete implications of a gospel which liberates women as well as men."[34] Although Scanzoni and Hardesty's conclusions parroted the claims that feminists had been making for years, their use of biblical arguments in support of "women's lib" awakened Christians to the possibility that scripture might support feminism.

All We're Meant to Be launched a movement that grew and diversified over the next decade, attracting support from evangelicals of all stripes. By the mid-1980s, a growing number of conservative Christians considered themselves "egalitarians," who believed that the Bible ordained equal roles for men and women (even if they shied away from calling themselves "feminists"). Many egalitarians congregated in a group known as Christians for Biblical Equality, which attracted support from evangelical intellectuals and helped Christians in various denominations advocate for women's ordination. For instance, Southern Baptists witnessed a twentyfold increase in the number of ordained female pastors between 1974 and 1983.[35] Timothy Weber, an evangelical theologian, believed that in the early 1970s "[n]early all conservative Christians had concluded that a high view of the Bible and 'women's lib' were essentially incompatible." But by 1989, Weber thought, "It will not be long before the majority of evangelicals are egalitarian." Weber rooted his confidence in the belief that a proper reading of scripture showed that "its ultimate aim is to promote egalitarianism in Jesus Christ." He expected that evangelicals, who listed a high view of scripture among their most important beliefs, would increasingly see that the Bible supported the fundamental aims of feminism.[36]

Weber's expectation assumed that the reading of scripture used by evangelical feminists would convince a majority of conservative Christians to follow their lead, but it did not, at least not among Southern Baptists. This resulted largely from a division between egalitarians and conservatives over the nature of the Bible. Two major disagreements about scriptural interpretation separated SBC conservatives and egalitarians. First, egalitarians believed that a holistic reading of scripture demonstrated that early Christians rejected the prevailing patriarchal gender norms of first-century Judaism, whereas conservatives believed a straightforward reading of Pauline texts showed that scripture endorsed male leadership. One feminist author argued that "no well-informed ecclesiastic or church body has today the right to proclaim that 'Scripture irrevocably condemns' birth control, abortion, homosexuality, or women's equality to men."[37] Evangelical feminists believed that responsible interpretation of scripture must account for the ways Jesus and Paul relied on women in ministry and challenged the patriarchal culture in which they lived. But SBC conservatives focused on seemingly straightforward Pauline passages that called for females' submission to male authority.

Second, and more important, SBC conservatives believed that scripture endorsed hierarchy, whereas egalitarians read the Bible as, well, egalitarian. In *All We're Meant to Be,* Scanzoni and Hardesty connected conservative defenses of gendered order to past hierarchical arrangements. "Those who declare that the gospel offers women spiritual equality in Christ but not in this world," they wrote, "find themselves arguing along with [those] who wrote in defense of slavery." Timothy Weber agreed, though he avoided a direct reference to slavery. "The debate over women's roles in the church is the latest episode in a centuries-long conflict between advocates of egalitarian and hierarchical worldviews," he wrote. Egalitarians repeatedly referenced slavery as an example of an unjust hierarchy that previous generations of Christians had defended by citing a straightforward reading of the Bible. But that did not stop conservatives from sanctioning hierarchy. Although nineteenth-century Christians had mistakenly used the Bible to support slavery, they said, that did not render irrelevant scripture's endorsement of gendered hierarchy. According to conservatives, biblical defenses of slavery ignored that God had never established the "peculiar institution." They regarded slavery as a sinful system that Christians had helped to abolish.[38]

Conversely, God had established both the family and the church, and God had given instructions for how to govern those institutions: men should lead them. Conservatives argued that this in no way compromised the equality of men and women. After all, wrote conservative Stephen Kovach, "Scripture teaches the eternal subordination of Jesus to God the Father . . . [but] this does not make him inferior to the Father in essence and dignity. The same may be true for women or any other person in a different or 'subordinate' role in the church today." Kovach summed up most conservatives' view of scripture. They believed, quite simply, that the Bible endorsed certain hierarchies.[39]

In fact, conservatives who defended a gendered order argued that scripture outlined clear and distinct roles for men and women, a position they called "complementarianism." Complementarians took their name from the belief that God created men and women to fulfill complementary roles—not the same roles. In so doing they differentiated themselves from egalitarians, though complementarians took pains to avoid calling women inferior or otherwise implying belief in the unequal worth of men and women. "Yes, there is equality of personhood. Yes, we are both created in the image of God. Yes, we both come to God in the same way," said complementarian Dorothy Patterson. "But we have also a responsibility of how we relate to one another and that's submission and head-ship."[40] Complementarians defended the essential equality of men and women, even as they argued that women ought to submit to male leaders (whether husbands or pastors).

In 1987, complementarians codified their beliefs in a document called the Danvers Statement.[41] It held that "the emergence of roles for men and women in church leadership that do not conform to Biblical teaching . . . backfire[s] in the crippling of Biblically faithful witness." Moreover, signers charged that egalitarians presented a "threat to Biblical authority as the clarity of Scripture is jeopardized and the accessibility of its meaning to ordinary people is withdrawn into the restricted realm of technical ingenuity." (Note how the authors framed their position as a clear and accessible reading of scripture.) In the face of the egalitarian threat, the Danvers Statement affirmed "distinctions in masculine and feminine roles," including "the husband's loving, humble headship" and the restriction of "some governing and teaching roles" within the church to men. The Bible did not simply acknowledge differences between men and women; it stipulated that men assume leadership roles in families and churches.[42]

Complementarians further clarified their stance in the 1991 volume *Recovering Biblical Manhood and Womanhood*. Editors John Piper and Wayne Grudem billed their five-hundred-page tome as "a response to evangelical feminism." They solicited essays from seminary professors throughout the country, each dealing with a particular facet of biblical teaching concerning gender. The main contention of evangelical feminists—that men should not exercise authority over women in either home or family solely on account of their gender—met with harsh critique in *Recovering Biblical Manhood and Womanhood*. In his analysis of Genesis 1–3, Raymond Ortlund contended that the creation story established the principle of male-female equality as well as the rule of male headship. "In the partnership of two spiritually equal human beings, man and woman," wrote Ortlund, "the man bears the primary responsibility to lead the partnership in a God-glorifying direction." In a subsequent essay, George W. Knight spelled out the ramifications of this arrangement: "God has called men to serve as leaders in marriage and the church, and women to submit themselves willingly to their leadership."[43] By enlisting a star-studded lineup of evangelical intellectuals to write sustained defenses of male headship, *Recovering Biblical Manhood and Womanhood* reinforced the conclusions of the Danvers Statement, which the book reprinted in an appendix. Authors for the volume unanimously concluded that God established distinctions between men and women during creation, and that faithful biblical witness must reflect those distinctions by assigning men alone to leadership roles in churches and families.

As complementarianism coalesced into a formal movement, with official policy statements and a cadre of committed leaders, it found its strongest support in the South, specifically among Southern Baptists. Throughout the conservative resurgence, Southern Baptists had passed resolutions that declared their support for complementarian positions. Messengers to the 1980 convention affirmed a resolution that affirmed the "equal worth but not always the sameness of function of women" and opposed the Equal Rights Amendment. Four years later, messengers passed a resolution against the ordination of women. It stated, "The Scriptures attest to God's delegated order of authority (God the head of Christ, Christ the head of man, man the head of woman, man and woman dependent one upon the other to the glory of God)." Given this hierarchy, delegates resolved to "encourage the service of women in all aspects of church life and work other than pastoral functions and leadership roles entailing ordination."[44] Convention minutes uncharacteristically reported the vote tally (58 percent to 42 percent in favor of the resolution), perhaps because the close margin reflected the divisive nature of the issue. But by the mid-1980s, complementarians had gained an upper hand among convention messengers.

The 1984 resolution against women's ordination demonstrated the theological rationale for conservative Southern Baptists' establishment of the new patriarchy. According to the resolution, the Apostle Paul restricted the pulpit to men in order "to preserve a submission God requires because the man was first in creation and the woman was first in the Edenic fall."[45] This language made clear that SBC conservatives had attached a moral economy to their campaign against evangelical feminism. God had created man first, and woman had sinned first. That order of events, clearly stated in the book of Genesis, provided conservatives with the biblical imprimatur for defense of the new patriarchy. Once again, conservatives' populist reading of the Bible played into their theological reasoning. Whereas evangelical feminists read the creation narrative as a document that reflected the patriarchal culture of ancient Judaism, complementarians saw it as a simple statement of male prerogative. They felt no particular burden to adjust this interpretation of scripture in order to mollify modern sensibilities. God's word had made clear that men were to lead.

This theological justification for masculine privilege struck moderates as anachronistic and perverse, and moderate seminary professors—many of them charged with teaching biblical studies—provided some of the loudest critiques of the 1984 resolution.[46] It was no surprise, then, when complementarian teachings stood at the heart of a controversy pitting moderate seminary faculty members against conservative trustees at Southern Baptist Theological Seminary in Louisville, Kentucky, the denomination's flagship school. In 1992, SBC conservatives took control of Southern's Board of Trustees. Moderate president Roy Honeycutt retired soon thereafter. Upon Honeycutt's retirement, trustees elected conservative Al Mohler to replace him. Mohler's election stunned many observers because he was only thirty-three years old at the time, yet the trustees thought that because Mohler had served under Honeycutt and understood Southern's culture, he would be able to shepherd a smooth, gradual transition of the seminary.

The trustees underestimated Mohler's desire for change. He embarked on an aggressive plan to point Southern's faculty in a strongly conservative direction. Events came to a head early in 1995, when Mohler refused to approve a faculty hire in Southern's Carver School of Social Work because the recommended candidate approved of women's ordination. Diana Garland, the dean of the Carver School, made public Mohler's rejection of the potential hire. Mohler subsequently asked for Garland's resignation. Upset by what they perceived as a breach of precedent and procedure, faculty members passed a resolution that "deeply grieve[d]" Garland's termination. Two days later, tempers flared at a faculty meeting that participants later termed "Black Wednesday." Timothy Weber, who believed the Bible sanctioned the ordination of women, confronted Mohler publicly at that meeting. Though he had been hired by conservative trustees only three years earlier, Weber asked, "Could I be hired today?" In front of the entire faculty, Mohler told him no. Southern Seminary had drawn a line in the sand. Only those who rejected women's ordination could win a spot on the faculty.[47]

The fallout from Black Wednesday and subsequent events resulted in a widespread exodus of faculty members, but the larger message of the controversy at Southern was that SBC conservatives would provide institutional backing for the complementarian movement, which claimed support from across the nation. Complementarians decided to house the Council for Biblical Manhood and Womanhood (CBMW) on the campus of Southern and lauded the seminary in the first CBMW newsletter. A front-page article reported that "despite opposition from students and faculty, the administration and trustees of SBTS . . . recently stood firm in their decision to hire only faculty members who are opposed to the ordination of women as pastors." The *CBMW News* approvingly quoted Mohler, who declared that beliefs about gender roles "will be in the coming decade one of the crucial dividing lines separating evangelicals committed to biblical authority and inerrancy from those who are seeking to transform evangelicalism from within."[48] Southern Baptists, though late to intra-evangelical debates about gender roles and biblical authority, perceived themselves as leaders of conservative Christians committed to biblical teaching, and they cited their institutional commitment to maintaining biblical gender roles as the key evidence of their faithfulness to scripture.

Southern Baptist conservatives rooted their defense of complementarianism in a particular reading of scripture, but a tradition-bound denominational culture certainly contributed to their stance on gender issues. In the mid-1970s, only a handful of women served Southern Baptist pulpits. The increase in female pastors by the mid-1980s only masked an abiding prejudice against them, according to one of the women who tried to become a Baptist preacher. During the late 1970s, Jane Aldredge Clanton enrolled at Southwestern Baptist Seminary in Fort Worth, Texas. She described the seminary as a place of "pervasive sexism." One professor "never called on a woman to lead in prayer . . . [or] answer a question in class," said Clanton. "Fundamentalist preacher boys . . . wanted me to defend what I was doing." Certain professors supported Clanton, but by the end of her seminary experience, she was thoroughly disillusioned with Southern Baptists. After graduation, Clanton took a preaching job at a Methodist church in Waco, despite maintaining her membership in a Baptist church and her belief in Baptist principles. Clanton's story revealed that even in the late 1970s, when SBC conservatives derided denominational seminaries as bastions of liberalism, Southwestern fostered a climate of male privilege that alienated women attempting to challenge denominational tradition.[49]

Even so, when SBC conservatives won the battle for control of the denomination, they enacted policies that went against traditional Baptist polity, which ascribed ultimate authority to local congregations. The issue of homosexuality provides an instructive example. Messengers to the convention first addressed it in 1976, when they passed a resolution that "affirm[ed] our commitment to the biblical truth regarding the practice of homosexuality" and "urge[d] churches and agencies not to afford the practice of homosexuality any degree of approval through ordination, employment, or other designations." Yet, even in this unambiguous condemnation of homosexuality, messengers "acknowledge[d] the autonomy of the local church."[50] Baptist polity has historically vested final authority for all decisions on membership, ordination, and practice in local congregations. While the convention might frown on churches that endorsed homosexuality, they could not force conformity.

During the conservative resurgence, that changed. Messengers to the 1988 convention passed a strongly worded resolution that linked homosexuality to the spread of AIDS, said that it signaled "a depraved nature," and called it "an abomination in the eyes of God." The resolution included no concession to the autonomy of local churches. By 1992, the SBC's hard-line stance had filtered down to the state level. The North Carolina Baptist Convention disfellowshipped two member churches, Binkley Baptist in Chapel Hill and Pullen Baptist in Raleigh. Binkley planned to ordain a practicing homosexual, while Pullen was considering blessing a same-sex union.[51] The SBC upheld the state association's decision and even took the unprecedented step of barring any churches that formally approved of homosexuality from attending the annual meetings. These developments signaled the consolidation of conservative power and, moderates contended, violation of the principle of local church autonomy. Even moderates who disagreed with Binkley and Pullen's endorsement of homosexuality defended those congregations' right to determine their own policies.

Conservatives, however, argued that their decision to disfellowship the North Carolina congregations was both consistent with Baptist principles and imperative. "What is at stake" in the controversy, wrote Timothy George, "is the right of a community . . . whether local congregation, association, state or national convention, to define for itself, under the leadership of the Holy Spirit, the acceptable doctrinal perimeters of its own fellowship."[52] Local church autonomy, said conservatives, did not license SBC churches to follow principles antithetical to Christian belief. They viewed opposition to homosexuality as a key marker of Christian identity. The centrality of opposition to homosexuality reflected the ethos of the new patriarchy. SBC conservatives' notion of manhood imagined men as the leaders of traditional families, a view conservatives rooted in their reading of scripture. As such, churches could not afford to pander to "alternative lifestyles." God had ordained a gendered order. Conservatives saw the decision to break with Binkley and Pullen as a mandatory consequence of those churches' decision to ignore God's will.

Indeed, conservatives thought biblical teachings about gender to be so important that their revision of the Baptist Faith and Message—the first revision since 1963—included only one new section: one on the family. Passed by messengers in 1998, the section on the family asked the wife "to submit herself graciously to the servant leadership of her husband," whereas the husband was "to provide for, to protect, and to lead his family." This "submission statement" attracted considerable attention from national media. The *New York Times* published a front-page story noting that the amendment passed "overwhelmingly." The *Times* also pointed out that four years earlier, Roman Catholic bishops had drafted a statement on the family that called for "mutual submission" of wives and husbands. Southern Baptists would have deflected criticism had they simply adopted that language. But Southern Baptist conservatives rejected the language of mutual submission (and rarely followed Catholics' lead, in any case).

They believed an official endorsement of men's leadership in families honored scriptural teaching. More important, conservatives felt that holding the line on gender roles represented the foremost difference between them and their moderate opponents. CBMW president Tim Bayly said, "Christians are being tested in this matter in a way that we're being challenged on few other issues today."[53] Southern Baptists' firm stance on gender thereby distinguished them as some of the most conservative members of evangelicalism—a distinction they relished.

Southern Baptist conservatives' campaign for control of the convention introduced a new type of patriarchy. Whereas older patriarchies had relegated women to subservience through unspoken cues and social customs, the new patriarchy explicitly barred women from leadership roles through a particular reading of scripture. This new patriarchy did authorize some leadership roles for women willing to defend it. Dorothy Patterson, a theologian who has served on faculty at both Southeastern and Southwestern seminaries, became a leading spokesperson for the conservative position. Patterson prefaced talks to mixed audiences by saying, "I see there's some men here, but I've been asked to come and to share with you women."[54] This disclaimer indicated her allegiance to the conservative position that women should not instruct men in the church, even though some men might hear her talk. Patterson, to be sure, did not often address mixed-gender gatherings; she spent most of her time teaching female-only audiences. But her affirmation of conservative gender teachings, alongside her marriage to a leading architect of the conservative resurgence, enabled Patterson to carve out a prominent, if unofficial, leadership role within the SBC.

Even so, a patriarchy by definition privileged men, and the conservative resurgence formalized that bias within the SBC. The convention's endorsement of masculine prerogative bucked trends within the broader culture, which continued to endorse gender equity by prescribing equal access for women to all roles in society. Even within the community of conservative American Christians, a significant proportion advocated for feminist causes. But Southern Baptists chose a different path. Whereas feminists lamented the failure of women to achieve equality in businesses, families, and churches, conservative Southern Baptists viewed it as an acknowledgment that God had ordained different roles for men and women. To them, these different roles did not signal inequality. Rather, they marked boundaries that God has imposed on the world since creation. Progressives who fought against God's creation plan thereby undermined the divine economy. By endorsing hierarchical gender arrangements, conservative Southern Baptists embraced a countercultural ideal of sorts. Their biblical and theological defenses of the new patriarchy helped create a subculture where the outmoded view of men and women as fundamentally different creatures thrived.

NOTES

The author thanks Ellen Kuniyuki Brown and Barry Hankins at Baylor for their expert assistance, and Steve Berry, Curtis Freeman, Brantley Gasaway, Matt Harper, Sarah Johnson, and Grant Wacker for their generous criticisms.

1. Gregory Tomlin, "Patterson's Advice on Boys: A Dog, a Gun and a Dad," *Baptist Standard*, 6 October 2003, 22.

2. See, for example, Christine Leigh Heyrman, *Southern Cross: The Beginnings of the Bible Belt* (New York: Knopf, 1997), 161–205; Anne C. Loveland, *Southern Evangelicals and the Social Order, 1800–1860* (Baton Rouge: Louisiana State University Press, 1980), 198–218; Donald G. Mathews, *Religion in the Old South* (Chicago: University of Chicago Press, 1977), 81–184; Bertram Wyatt-Brown, *Southern Honor: Ethics and Behavior in the Old South* (New York: Oxford University Press, 1982).

3. Historian David Chappell has argued that white southerners found little justification for white supremacy in the Bible, and that previous historians have overestimated the church's support for racial segregation; see Chappell, *A Stone of Hope: Prophetic Religion and the Death of Jim Crow* (Chapel Hill: University of North Carolina Press, 2004), 107, 112. Also Charles Marsh, *God's Long Summer: Stories of Faith and Civil Rights* (Princeton, N.J.: Princeton University Press, 1997), 82–115.

4. In a recent study, sociologist Brad Wilcox termed contemporary male evangelicals "soft patriarchs," using this term to denote that while evangelical men publicly defend traditional, patriarchal family structures, they actually display more involvement with domestic responsibilities and child rearing than do liberal and mainline Christian men. See William Bradford Wilcox, *Soft Patriarchs, New Men: How Christianity Shapes Fathers and Husbands* (Chicago: University of Chicago Press, 2004). Like Wilcox, I use "patriarch" to indicate those who defended a social system that ascribes leadership roles to men, but I do not intend any negative or misogynistic connotations of that word.

5. Any chronicler of the Southern Baptist controversy faces a dilemma related to terminology. Conservatives referred to the 1980s as the period of "conservative resurgence," while their opponents called it the "fundamentalist takeover." Similarly, conservatives called moderates "liberals," while moderates called conservatives "fundamentalists." In the interest of fair representation, I employ the terms that partisans chose for themselves. I use "conservative" rather than "fundamentalist" and "moderate" rather than "liberal." In choosing this terminology, I have taken my cues from Barry Hankins, *Uneasy in Babylon: Southern Baptist Conservatives and American Culture* (Tuscaloosa: University of Alabama Press, 2002), 11–13.

6. Oral Memoirs of W. A. Criswell, the Texas Collection, Baylor University, Waco, Texas.

7. David T. Morgan, *The New Crusades, the New Holy Land: Conflict in the Southern Baptist Convention, 1969–1991* (Tuscaloosa: University of Alabama Press, 1996), 30.

8. The SBC has made full text of every resolution passed at the annual convention meet-

ings available online at http://www.sbc.net/resolutions/AMResSearch.asp. The "Resolution on Disavowing Overt Political Activity in Selecting Officers" is buried at the bottom of the *Resolution on Appreciation for Porter Wroe Routh,* Southern Baptist Convention, 1979, http://www.sbc.net/resolutions/amResolution.asp?ID=396 (accessed 29 March 2007).

9. Quoted in Walter B. Shurden and Randy Shepley, *Going for the Jugular: A Documentary History of the SBC Holy War* (Macon, Ga.: Mercer University Press, 1996), 56.

10. Quoted in ibid., 215.

11. For fuller accounts of the SBC controversy, see Nancy Tatom Ammerman, *Baptist Battles: Social Change and Religious Conflict in the Southern Baptist Convention* (New Brunswick, N.J.: Rutgers University Press, 1990); Hankins, *Uneasy in Babylon;* Bill Leonard, *God's Last and Only Hope: The Fragmentation of the Southern Baptist Convention* (Grand Rapids: W. B. Eerdmans, 1990); Morgan, *New Crusades.*

12. This definition of inerrancy comes from the Baptist Faith and Message Statement, which was initially drafted in 1925 and revised in 1963 and 2000. The phrase "truth without any mixture of error" appears in all three versions (*Comparison of 1925, 1963 and 2000 Baptist Faith and Message,* Southern Baptist Convention, 2000, http://www.sbc.net/bfm/bfmcomparison.asp [accessed 29 March 2007]).

13. Leonard, *God's Last and Only Hope,* 31; Barry Hankins, *God's Rascal: J. Frank Norris and the Beginnings of Southern Fundamentalism* (Lexington: University Press of Kentucky, 1996), 3; Oral Memoirs of Timothy Weber, 1998, the Texas Collection.

14. These phrases come from the titles of two influential studies: Rufus Spain's account of late nineteenth-century Baptists and Barry Hankins's book about late twentieth-century SBC conservatives. See Rufus B. Spain, *At Ease in Zion: Social History of Southern Baptists, 1865–1900* (Nashville: Vanderbilt University Press, 1967); Hankins, *Uneasy in Babylon.*

15. Hankins has argued that by developing a sense of social crisis, Southern Baptist conservatives "became" American evangelicals. That is, they joined the larger evangelical world as they adopted evangelicals' sense of cultural estrangement (Hankins, *Uneasy in Babylon,* 14–40). See also James Leo Garrett, E. Glenn Hinson, and James E. Tull, *Are Southern Baptists "Evangelicals"?* (Macon, Ga.: Mercer University Press, 1983).

16. Harold Lindsell, *The Battle for the Bible* (Grand Rapids: Zondervan, 1976), 20, 21, 24.

17. Donald W. Dayton, "Battle for the Bible: Renewing the Inerrancy Debate," *Christian Century,* 10 November 1976, 976; Harold Lindsell, *The Bible in the Balance* (Grand Rapids: Zondervan, 1979), 16, 17.

18. Dayton, "Battle for the Bible," 976; Lindsell, *Bible in the Balance,* 12.

19. Carl L. Kell and L. Raymond Camp, *In the Name of the Father: The Rhetoric of the New Southern Baptist Convention* (Carbondale: Southern Illinois University Press, 1999), 18; quote in Shurden and Shepley, *Going for the Jugular,* 27.

20. The Glorietta Statement took its name from the Glorietta Baptist Conference Center

near Santa Fe, N.Mex., where SBC seminary presidents presented the document at a Peace Committee prayer retreat in October 1986. It is quoted in full in Shurden and Shepley, *Going for the Jugular*, 210–11.

21. In fact, moderate leader Cecil Sherman resigned from the SBC Peace Committee, a group that attempted to reconcile moderates and conservatives, because the Glorietta Statement convinced him that conservatives controlled the SBC machinery entirely (Leonard, *God's Last and Only Hope*, 146–47).

22. Fisher Humphreys, "Biblical Inerrancy: A Guide for the Perplexed," in *The Unfettered Word: Southern Baptists Confront the Authority-Inerrancy Question*, ed. Robison B. James (Waco, Tex.: Word Books, 1987), 49. Humphreys' sentiments call to mind the dilemmas confronted by theologically conservative intellectuals during the fundamentalist-modernist controversy in the early twentieth century. See, for instance, Grant Wacker, *Augustus H. Strong and the Dilemma of Historical Consciousness* (Macon, Ga.: Mercer University Press, 1985), 113–23.

23. Oral Memoirs of Morris Chapman, 1998, the Texas Collection.

24. 1 Timothy 2:12, NIV; "1 Timothy 2:13—a Simple, Straightforward Verse That Egalitarians Cannot Explain," *CBMW News* 2 (1996): 13.

25. The Billy Sunday quotation can be found in Margaret Bendroth, *Fundamentalism and Gender, 1875 to the Present* (New Haven, Conn.: Yale University Press, 1993), 24. See chap. 3 of Bendroth for an extended discussion of this point.

26. Quote in Shurden and Shepley, *Going for the Jugular*, 82; Tim Bayly, "Where Have All the Fathers Gone?" *Journal of Biblical Manhood and Womanhood* 20 (1999): 7.

27. Oral Memoirs of Morris Chapman.

28. Oral Memoirs of Mark Coppenger, 1998, the Texas Collection.

29. *Resolution on Honor for Full-Time Homemakers*, Southern Baptist Convention, 1987, http://www.sbc.net/resolutions/amResolution.asp?ID=1094 (accessed 5 July 2007).

30. Oral Memoirs of Dorothy Patterson, 1999, the Texas Collection; Ephesians 5:22–28, NIV.

31. Oral Memoirs of R. Albert Mohler, 1997–1999, the Texas Collection.

32. Ibid.

33. For the history and development of this movement, see Pamela Cochran, *Evangelical Feminism: A History* (New York: New York University Press, 2005).

34. Letha Scanzoni and Nancy Hardesty, *All We're Meant to Be: A Biblical Approach to Women's Liberation* (Waco, Tex.: Word Books, 1974), 60, 205.

35. Because individual churches ordain ministers in the SBC, exact ordination statistics are hard to come by. A 1976 article claimed that before the publication of *All We're Meant to Be*, female SBC pastors numbered in the single digits. Seven years later, an article estimated that number around two hundred; Sarah Frances Anders, "Women in Ministry: The Distaff of the Church in Action," *Review and Expositor* 80 (1983): 30; C. R. Daley, "Current Trends among Southern Baptists," *Western Recorder*, 5 August 1976, 2. Both articles are cited in Hankins, *Uneasy in Babylon*, 308n13. Historian Leon McBeth estimated that approximately fifty women had been ordained in

SBC churches between 1964 and 1979 (Leon McBeth, *Women in Baptist Life* [Nashville: Broadman Press, 1979], 16).

36. Timothy Weber, "Evangelical Egalitarianism: Where We Are Now," *Journal of Biblical Equality* 1 (1989): 71, 72, 76.

37. Samuel Terrien, *Till the Heart Sings: A Biblical Theology of Manhood and Womanhood* (Philadelphia: Fortress Press, 1985), 194.

38. Scanzoni and Hardesty, *All We're Meant to Be*, 203; Weber, "Evangelical Egalitarianism," 72; *Resolution on Racial Reconciliation on the 150th Anniversary of the Southern Baptist Convention*, Southern Baptist Convention, 1995, http://www.sbc.net/resolutions/amResolution.asp?ID=899 (accessed 20 April 2007). See also Hankins, *Uneasy in Babylon*, 240–71.

39. Stephen D. Kovach, "Egalitarians Revamp Doctrine of the Trinity," *CBMW News* 2 (1996): 1, 3–5. On this point, see Paul Harvey, *Freedom's Coming: Religious Culture and the Shaping of the South from the Civil War through the Civil Rights Era* (Chapel Hill: University of North Carolina Press, 2005), 246.

40. Oral Memoirs of Dorothy Patterson.

41. The document took its name from Danvers, Mass., where conservative leaders met to draft and sign the document. The location of that meeting suggests that SBC conservatives were part of a larger movement, but their commitment to complementarianism eventually won them control of the movement's most important institutions.

42. *The Danvers Statement*, 1987, http://www.cbmw.org/about/danvers.php (accessed 10 April 2007).

43. Raymond C. Ortlund Jr., "Male Female-Equality and Male Headship: Genesis 1–3," in *Recovering Biblical Manhood and Womanhood: A Response to Evangelical Feminism*, ed. John Piper and Wayne Grudem (Wheaton, Ill.: Crossway Books, 1991), 95; George W. Knight III, "The Family and the Church: How Should Biblical Manhood and Womanhood Work out in Practice?" in *Recovering Biblical Manhood and Womanhood*, 345.

44. *Resolution on Women*, Southern Baptist Convention, 1980, http://www.sbc.net/resolutions/amResolution.asp?ID=1091 (accessed 10 April 2007); *Resolution on Ordination and the Role of Women in Ministry*, Southern Baptist Convention, 1984, http://www.sbc.net/resolutions/amResolution.asp?ID=1088 (accessed 9 April 2007).

45. *Resolution on Ordination and the Role of Women in Ministry*.

46. See, for instance, Charles H. Talbert, "Biblical Criticism's Role: The Pauline View of Women as a Case in Point," in *The Unfettered Word: Southern Baptists Confront the Authority-Inerrancy Question*, ed. Robison B. James (Waco, Tex.: Word Books, 1987), 62–71.

47. Hankins, *Uneasy in Babylon*, 76–88.

48. "Southern Seminary Stands Firm," *CBMW News* 1 (1995): 1.

49. Oral Memoirs of Jane Aldredge Clanton, 1986, the Texas Collection.

50. *Resolution on Homosexuality*, Southern Baptist Convention, 1976, http://www.sbc.net/resolutions/amResolution.asp?ID=606 (accessed 11 April 2007).

51. *Resolution on Homosexuality,* Southern Baptist Convention, 1988, http://www.sbc .net/resolutions/amResolution.asp?ID=610 (accessed 11 April 2007). At the time, moderates still exercised significant power within the North Carolina Baptist Association, and many moderates agreed with conservatives that the association could not sanction homosexuality (Morgan, *New Crusades,* 186–87).

52. Timothy George, "The Priesthood of All Believers and the Quest for Theological Integrity," *Criswell Theological Journal* 4 (1989), http://www.founders.org/FJ03/ article1_fr.html (accessed 19 April 2007).

53. *Comparison of 1925, 1963 and 2000 Baptist Faith and Message;* Gustav Niehbur, "Southern Baptists Declare Wife Should 'Submit' to Her Husband," *New York Times,* 10 June 1998; "CBMW News Interview: Executive Director, Tim Bayly," *CBMW News,* 2 (1997): 3.

54. Oral Memoirs of Dorothy Patterson.

CONTRIBUTORS

MATTHEW MACE BARBEE is an instructor of Ethnic Studies at Bowling Green State University. He is currently preparing a manuscript on race and public memory in post–World War II Richmond, Virginia.

STEVE BLANKENSHIP is an assistant professor of History at Georgia Highlands College. He is author of "Adding Hollywood to the American History Survey" (*Teaching History—A Journal of Methods*).

EDWARD J. BLUM is an assistant professor of History at San Diego State University. He is the author of *W. E. B. Du Bois, American Prophet* and *Reforging the White Republic: Race, Religion, and American Nationalism, 1865–1898*.

CHRISTOPHER BREU is an associate professor of English at Illinois State University. He is the author of *Hard-Boiled Masculinities*.

JOE CREECH is the assistant director of the Lilly Fellows Program in Humanities and the Arts and an adjunct assistant professor of History and Humanities at Christ College, the Honors College of Valparaiso University. He is the author of *Righteous Indignation: Religion and the Populist Revolution*.

SETH DOWLAND is a lecturing fellow in the Duke University Writing Program. He is working on a manuscript entitled "Defending Manhood: Gender, Social Order, and the Rise of the Christian Right in the South, 1965–1995."

KRIS DUROCHER is an assistant professor of History at Morehead State University. Her current project is entitled "Lessons in Black and White: The Racial and Gender Socialization of White Children in the Jim Crow South, 1887–1939."

CRAIG THOMPSON FRIEND is an associate professor of History at North Carolina State University. He is the author of *Along the Maysville Road: The Early*

Republic in the Trans-Appalachian West and the coeditor with Lorri Glover of *Southern Manhood: Perspectives on Masculinity in the Old South.*

JOHN HOWARD is a professor of American Studies at King's College, London. He is the author of *Concentration Camps on the Home Front: Japanese Americans in the House of Jim Crow* and *Men Like That: A Southern Queer History.*

ROSE STREMLAU is an assistant professor of History at the University of North Carolina at Pembroke. She has published on the impact of interracial sexual violence on Indian communities, and she currently is revising her manuscript on Cherokee families and resource use.

KAREN TAYLOR is an associate professor of History at the College of Wooster in Wooster, Ohio. Her current project compares patriarchy's impact on nineteenth-century men in Boston, Savannah, and Denver.

BENJAMIN E. WISE is a postdoctoral fellow at the Center for the Study of the American South at the University of North Carolina at Chapel Hill. He is completing his manuscript entitled "Cosmopolitan Southerner: The Life and World of William Alexander Percy."

LaVergne, TN USA
04 June 2010
184917LV00001B/68/P